Construction management in practice

Construction management in practice

Richard Fellows, David Langford,
Robert Newcombe and Sydney Urry

Longman
Scientific &
Technical

Longman Scientific & Technical,
Longman Group UK Limited,
Longman House, Burnt Mill, Harlow,
Essex CM20 2JE, England
and Associated Companies throughout the world.

First published 1983 by Construction Press
Reprinted by Longman Scientific & Technical 1988, 1990, 1991

British Library Cataloguing in Publication Data
Construction management in practice.
1. Construction industry—Management
I. Fellows, R. F.
624'.068   HD9715.A2
ISBN 0-582-30522-5

Library of Congress Cataloging in Publication Data
Main entry under title:
Construction management in practice.
Bibliography: p.
Includes index.
I. Construction industry–Management.
I. Fellows, Richard, 1948-
HD9715.A2C648   1983   624'068   82-8256
ISBN 0-582-30522-5

Produced by Longman Singapore Publishers Pte Ltd
Printed in Singapore

Contents

Preface

This book is concerned with the practical application of management principles and techniques in the construction industry. It is intended primarily for students in universities, polytechnics, and colleges who are following courses in building, civil engineering, quantity surveying, and architecture but it will also be of value to those who are practising in these fields. The standard is that of university and CNAA degrees and the examinations of professional institutions such as the Chartered Institute of Building and the Royal Institution of Chartered Surveyors.

We have aimed to present the concepts as succinctly as possible and to show their relevance to the day-to-day problems of the industry. To this end we have included many illustrative examples in the text and review questions at the ends of chapters. References and bibliographies are provided for those readers who may wish to study particular topics in greater depth.

Despite careful checking, some errors may remain and any criticism or correction will be gratefully acknowledged.

RFF
DAL
RN
SAU   *Uxbridge, March 1982*

Acknowledgements

A book of this kind could not appear without the help of many people, and the authors owe much to the writings of others whose names appear in the references or bibliographies.

We are particularly grateful to Colin Bassett for his advice and encouragement during the writing of the book; to Carrie Batt, Marianne Bevis, Ann Conway, and Sue Tarling for their care in preparing the typescript; and to the publishers for their efforts in the production of the finished volume.

Abbreviations used in text

Organisations

ACAS	Advisory, Conciliation and Arbitration Services
ASP&D	Amalgamated Society of Painters and Decorators
ASW	Amalgamated Society of Woodworkers
AUAW	Amalgamated Union of Asphalt Workers
AUBTW	Amalgamated Union of Building Trades Workers
AUEW	Amalgamated Union of Engineering Workers (Construction Section)
BAS	Building Advisory Service
BCIS	Building Cost Information Service (of the RICS)
BDA	British Decorating Association
BDC	Brick Development Association
BICS	Building Industry Careers Service
BRE	Building Research Establishment
CBI	Confederation of British Industry
CCA	Cement and Concrete Association
CECCB	Civil Engineering Construction Conciliation Board
CIOB	Chartered Institute of Building
CIMB	Construction Industry Manpower Board
CITB	Construction Industry Training Board
CRE	Commission for Racial Equality
DHSS	Department of Health and Social Security
DoE	Department of Employment
ECA	Electrical Contractors' Association
EEF	Engineering Employers' Federation
EIU	Economist Intelligence Unit Ltd.
EEPTTU	Electrical, Electronic, Plumbers, Telecommunications Trade Union

FCEC	Federation of Civil Engineering Contractors
FMB	Federation of Master Builders
FTATU	Furniture, Timber and Allied Trades Union
GMWU	General and Municipal Workers' Union
HSE	Health and Safety Executive
ICFC	Industrial and Commercial Finance Corporation
JCT	Joint Contracts Tribunal
MAC	Mastic Asphalt Council
MSC	Manpower Services Commission
NAS	National Association of Shopfitters
NEB	National Enterprise Board
NEDO	National Economic Development Office
NFBTE	National Federation of Building Trades Employers
NFPDE	National Federation of Plumbers and Domestic Engineers
NFRC	National Federation of Roofing Contractors
NJCBI	National Joint Council for the Building Industry
NWRA	National Working Rule Agreement
OCPCA	Oil and Chemical Plant Constructors' Association
PCA	Plant Contractors' Association
RIBA	Royal Institute of British Architects
RICS	Royal Institution of Chartered Surveyors
STAMP	Supervisory, Technical and Administrative, Management and Professional section of UCATT
TGWU	Transport and General Workers' Union
TRADA	Timber Research and Development Association
TSA	Training Services Agency
TUC	Trades Union Congress
UCATT	Union of Construction Allied Trades and Technicians
UDC	Urban Development Corporation
UDG	Urban Development Grant

Terms

ACT	Advance corporation tax
AE	Annual equivalent
APA	Amount per annum
ASF	Annual sinking fund
BQ	Bill of quantities
CCA	Current cost accounting
CPM	Critical path method
DCF	Discounted cash flow
ERI	Effective rate of interest
FIFO	First in first out
GDP	Gross domestic product
HCA	Historic cost accounting
IRR	Internal rate of return
LIFO	Last in first out
ME	Monetary expectation
NPV	Net present value
PPC	Probable profit contribution
PQS	Private quantity surveyor
PV	Present value
PW	Present worth
RI	Rate of interest
RT	Rate of tax
SF	Sinking fund
SMM	Standard Method of Measurement of Building Works, 6th edn
UMA	Union membership agreement
USM	Unlisted securities market
YP	Years purchase

Chapter 1

Construction management in practice

This book is concerned with management in the context of the construction industry, and this industry possesses a number of features that distinguish it from others. As a result, construction management practice differs from that observed in other industries. In this first chapter, therefore, the following topics will be discussed:

1.1 Characteristics of the construction industry
1.2 The nature of construction management
1.3 Managing a business
1.4 Managing people
1.5 Managing money
1.6 Management techniques.

1.1 Characteristics of the construction industry

A study of construction company profiles published in *Building* during the last decade confirms the impression, gained by reading Order XX of the Standard Industrial Classification entitled 'Construction', of an industry comprising a group of heterogeneous and fragmented firms. Not only are there large differences *between* firms in terms of size and scope of work, but *within* firms there is often a great diversity of activity. Typically, a large construction company may be engaged in activities ranging from general building and civil engineering to materials manufacturing, property development, trade specialization, and even open-cast coal-mining. In addition, there are the design consultants – architects, engineers, quantity surveyors, etc. – many of whom now practise in multidisciplinary firms. Peripheral services such as materials supply and plant hire, and the newly emerging project management firms, contribute to a complex industrial structure.

The size of the industry is impressive, both in terms of output and employment. Construction currently produces approximately 6 per cent of GDP and employs around 2 million people, 7–8 per cent of the total workforce.

The industry exhibits other characteristics which, taken individually, are shared with some other industries but which, in combination, create unique conditions calling for a unique management approach. Some of the more important characteristics of the building construction industry which influence management practice are outlined below.

(a) Size of firms

Construction is essentially a large industry of small firms. *Housing and Construction Statistics 1978* show that of the 91,520 firms recorded, 85,362 or 93 per cent employed less than 25 people and could arguably be classified as small. Conversely, only 54 firms, 0.06 per cent, employed more than 1,200 people. The small firms were responsible for 27 per cent of the work carried out in 1978 and the large firms for 16 per cent of the total. No single firm or group of firms has a monopoly. This size profile has obvious implications for construction management practice, which will be discussed in later chapters.

(b) Construction projects

The industry is a project-based industry. Firms undertake a range of discrete projects of relatively long duration, constructed outside and geographically dispersed and fixed. The majority of such projects are tailor-made to a client's requirements, designed upon prescribed fee scales and built for a price established through the competitive tendering system which operates extensively in the industry. This system creates an unusual situation in which the product, i.e. a building, is sold before it is produced – a reversal of normal manufacturing practice. Individually, such projects frequently constitute a significant proportion of a firm's workload with serious consequences if things go wrong.

(c) Workforce

The operatives are predominantly young, male, and casually employed, with a strong craft tradition. In recent years there has been a distinct increase in the practice of subcontracting in all trades in response to fluctuating demand and employment legislation; this has to a large extent frustrated unionization of labour. Building production managers and staff have traditionally come from this craft background but the trend is towards staff from technician and degree courses. The professions – architects, engineers, and quantity surveyors – have, in the last 100 years, developed quite a sophisticated system of registration and training.

(d) Ease of entry to the industry

While the design consultants have an effective form of registration and control over members, there are few constraints to setting up a building contracting business. Voluntary registration schemes have largely failed to attract membership and the long-standing problems of consumer protection remain, particularly for private clients. The system of interim payments during construction projects, coupled with extensive credit concessions for materials purchasing and highly developed plant hiring facilities, mean that firms have minimal capital requirements; this has encouraged an influx of hopeful entrepreneurs. Sadly, their demise has often been equally easy, though much more painful for their clients, creditors and staff who are left, respectively, with broken contracts, little redress, and unemployment.

2

(e) Separation of design and production

The traditional separation of design and production in the building industry, and the consequent difficulties that can arise during the construction projects, have been described in several major reports (Emmerson 1962, Banwell 1964, Wood 1975). Economic pressures in times of recession have weakened this dichotomy with design and production organizations seeking to diversify their operations by offering a wider service. The decline in public sector building, with procurement methods which largely fossilized this separation, and the relaxation of the RIBA Code of Conduct, are two important agents of change.

(f) The nature of demand

The demand for construction projects is essentially what economists call 'derived' demand. It is derived from the need for buildings in which to live, to manufacture or store goods, or in which to operate various services. Building is thus strongly related to the state of health of the general economy and to the level of interest rates and business activity in particular. The fact that buildings are capital items make them natural targets for expenditure cuts by both government and the private sector. This has led to the characteristic fluctuations in demand which are familiar to construction firms and to the more permanent downturn which occurred in the mid 1970s.

(g) The Government's role

Successive governments have generally exacerbated these demand fluctuations by using the industry as a regulator for the economy. This has been achieved by direct intervention as a major client for the industry, and indirectly through the manipulation of interest rates to control private sector building demand. In addition, there has been the increasing regulation of building standards and land-use through building regulation and planning legislation. Technical innovation (e.g. industrialised building) and procedural changes (e.g. in competitive tendering arrangements) have also been foisted onto the industry from time to time.

Each of these factors can be found in other industries but together they form a unique combination. As a result, the practice of management in the construction industry differs in many respects from that found elsewhere.

1.2 The nature of construction management

1.2.1 The components of construction

The components of every commercial transaction are a *customer* who wants a product, the *product* itself and a *firm* which designs, makes and/or sells the product. The construction industry is no exception. The principal components in any construction situation are the *client*, the *project*, and the *firm*.

The *client* may be defined as the sponsor of the construction product or service. The client may come from the private or public sector of industry, commerce or government. It may be a private individual or a large corporation. It may have a continuing building programme or build only once in its lifetime. Most clients are outside the construction industry and, therefore are not familiar with common practices in the industry.

The *project* is the design and production of the construction product. That product may, for example, be a building, or a bridge, or a motorway. The construction project is complex, discrete, and often bespoke. It is a distinctive undertaking, drawing on the skills of a variety of people operating within a well-defined financial and contractual framework.

The *firm* is the design and production unit in the construction industry. The firm is the permanent and continuing component and the base for the long-term development of resources. Only those firms *directly* involved in design and/or production will be considered. These are:

(a) firms offering a design or design-related service to the client;
(b) building contractors;
(c) firms offering a design and production service to the client (including speculative developers).

1.2.2 Component interactions

The interactions between the components are simply illustrated in Fig. 1.1. As indicated, the client initiates the project process and appoints the construction firm. The client's role is therefore critical in any construction event. That this basic fact is overlooked is evident from the bitter comment of an industrial client in a survey carried out by the National Economic Development Office (NEDO 1978): '. . . the participants in the construction process are excessively concerned with their roles *vis à vis* other participants and insufficiently responsive to the needs of the manufacturing industry'.

Any review of construction management practice should start with the client, the client's needs and the response of the firm to that need. The shift from a 'production-orientated' to a 'client-orientated' outlook by construction firms is essential for survival in a shrinking construction market; hence the need, as stressed in this book, for construction managers to think more carefully about the strategies to be adopted by their firms. The interaction of firms and the project is shown in Fig. 1.1 as a matrix relationship. The implications of this are that, in a sense, any construction firm is simply an aggregation of the projects it has at that time and any construction project is simply the collective contribution of a number of firms. Further, a highly *interdependent* project process is executed by a large number of *independent* firms. This phenomenon, and its consequences, were highlighted in two perceptive reports by the Tavistock Institute (1965 and 1966). They coined a phrase to describe this important relationship: 'interdependent autonomy'.

The increasing technological complexity of construction projects has led to a greater differentiation of specialist roles, and this in turn has led to the need for more effective integration of these specialists. Townsend and Edwards (1958)

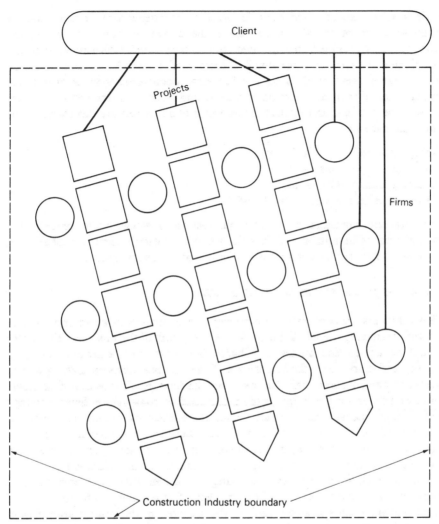

Fig. 1.1 The components of construction

pointed out that traditionally the construction industry has achieved integration by the market operating through many separate contracts between clients and firms, and between one firm and another. Clients find this system so confusing that the industry is slowly responding with radical and more realistic methods of project management which attempt to concentrate and improve integration.

1.2.3 Construction management in practice

From the preceding analysis and Fig. 1.1 it can be seen that construction management can be viewed in two dimensions – project management and business management – which are, in practice, interdependent. In this book the emphasis is on business management in the context of construction but the related aspects of project management are also considered. Other books consider complementary areas in more detail: Burgess and White (1979) concentrate on project management, while Brech (1971) is largely concerned with the operational management of both construction businesses and construction projects. Four key areas in the strategic and tactical management of a business are dealt with in the following chapters:

Managing a business (Chs 2 and 3)
Managing people (Chs 4–7)
Managing money (Chs 8–10)
Management techniques (Chs 11 and 12)

The strategic management of the business as a whole must precede the management of its human and financial resources. Management techniques are, essentially, aids to the management of a business and its resources.

1.3 *Managing a business* (Chs 2 and 3)

These chapters are concerned with managing the business as a corporate whole, not with managing the whole business, i.e. every part of the business. This latter should be left to line managers. Chapter 2 defines the meaning of business strategy and emphasizes the importance of the strategic decision-making role in providing the business with direction and leadership. This is called strategic management, and is a role that is often neglected in construction firms. Strategy and strategic management operate within the framework of the organizational structure of the business. The design of a structure that is appropriate to a firm's strategy is shown to be a critical element in the financial performance of a business. The impact of leadership on performance is also highlighted.

Chapter 3 shows how a business strategy for a construction company can be formulated and discusses some of the problems that are likely to be encountered in introducing such a strategy. Each of the activities in the strategy formulation process are discussed in detail: clarifying objectives, the appraisal of the construction business and its environment, the matching of the firm's capabilities to the opportunities in the market, and the final selection of the strategies that will be pursued. These strategic choices should be recorded in a strategic plan, and the format for such a plan is given. Brief mention is made of the follow-up action required to implement the plan.

1.4 *Managing people* (Chs 4–7)

Construction is a labour-intensive industry and is likely to remain so for the foreseeable future. The management of staff and operatives is critical to the success of any business. Chapter 4 traces the evolution of industrial relations in the industry and reviews current practices. Two systems of industrial relations are identified, the *formal* national agreements and the *informal* systems that operate at site level. Suggestions are made for improving procedures through greater consultation, decasualization, and a national wages policy.

The problem of ensuring that adequate manpower is available to cope with widely fluctuating construction demand is tackled in Chapter 5. There is increasing interest in manpower planning in the construction industry, stimulated, no doubt, by the changes in attitudes and legislation regarding employment, discussed in Chapter 4. These have made the 'hiring and firing' approach less acceptable so that manpower planning has become part of the company's strategy, reiterating the point made in Chapter 3.

The construction industry's poor safety record has been widely publicized and has led to the tightening of legislation and to its stricter implementation. The criticism has focused mainly on safety of site operations which are the most obvious expression of unsafe working, but the point is made in Chapter 6 that unsafe working practices are often the inheritance of poor design. Architects and engineers should ensure that their designs can be built safely. However comprehensive the safety legislation and however strict its implementation, enduring improvements in safety can only be achieved by a change of attitude, and not only at site level. Safety-consciousness should start with the chief executive as a key element in business strategy and philosophy, and should then permeate to all levels in the business.

The role of personnel management – the department responsible for the recruitment, induction, training and welfare of people – is discussed in Chapter 7. Traditionally, in the construction industry, this function has been decentralized and delegated to site managers or has been the part-time responsibility of one of the directors or top managers, e.g. company secretary. Construction firms have been slow to recognize the advantages of appointing a personnel manager in terms of uniformity of employment practices and the development of special personnel skills and knowledge. Many firms have been forced to create a full-time post in order to ensure compliance with employment legislation. Again, it is important that personnel policies have top management support and are framed within the context of the total business plan. Industrial relations, manpower planning and safety may all be facets of the personnel management role.

1.5 Managing money (Chs 8–10)

One of the characteristics of the construction industry, mentioned earlier, was the generally low level of capital required by construction firms. This fact has led many firms into the fatal neglect of this critical aspect of managing a business. The majority of construction firms which fail each year do not lack construction skill and knowledge, or competent people, but rather are driven into bankruptcy through poor financial control.

Chapters 8, 9, and 10 examine the process of financial management from the obtaining of finance, through its allocation within the business and to projects, to measuring the efficiency with which financial resources are used. Chapter 8 discusses the financial requirements of the various forms of business ownership found in the construction industry, identifies possible sources of capital for a construction firm and discusses how these will lead to a unique capital structure.

The allocation of the funds thus obtained to the cost and profit centres of the business through departmental and project budgets is the next logical step in the process of financial management, and is outlined in Chapter 9. The basis for such financial decisions, which may directly affect the survival of the firm, is the systematic approach to investment appraisal described in this chapter. The traditional measure of the efficiency with which a business is being managed has been the profitability and growth of that business. This is the subject of Chapter 10, where the complexities of standard financial reports are explained and those accounting ratios that are particularly relevant for construction firms are examined.

1.6 *Management techniques* (Chs 11 and 12)

Since the early 1960s a number of numerical techniques have been introduced to assist the decision-making process. They do not relieve the manager of the responsibility of taking decisions but they help to provide the information on which he can base those decisions and can show him the outcomes to be expected. They complement, but do not replace, his experience and intuition.

The strong advocacy of these techniques when they were first introduced led to their misuse in many instances. Critical path analysis, for example, was presented as a panacea for many ills in the construction industry and interest in this technique waned when it did not achieve all that was expected. Managers have now gained experience of its use, and CPA has become established as a useful tool for planning complex projects.

Several techniques that are relevant to construction management are described in Chapters 11 and 12. They require only elementary mathematics and numerical examples show how they can be applied to problems of optimization. In particular, they are concerned with achieving economies of time and cost under conditions of limited resources. These chapters give quantitative support to the chapters on business strategy and, particularly, to the chapters on financial management.

Such is the scope of this book. Each chapter starts with an overview of the content of the chapter and concludes with a summary of the main ideas together with relevant questions for consideration and suggestions for further reading.

References

Banwell Report (1964) *The Placing and Management of Building Contracts for Building and Civil Engineering Work*, HMSO

Burgess, R. and White, G. (1979) *Building Production and Project Management*, Construction Press

Brech, EFL (ed.) (1971) *Construction Management in Principle and Practice*, Longman
Emmerson Report (1962) *A Survey of Problems Before the Construction Industry*, HMSO
NEDO (1978) *Construction for Industrial Recovery*, HMSO
Tavistock Institute (1965) *Communications in the Building Industry*, Tavistock
Tavistock Institute (1966) *Interdependence and Uncertainty*, Tavistock
Townsend, H. and Edwards, R. S. (1958) *Business Enterprise*, Macmillan
Wood Report (1975) *The Public Client and the Construction Industries*, HMSO

Chapter 2

Strategic management

Every business needs direction – that is, a defined course or courses of action that the business will pursue in both the long- and short-term future. Without such direction the business is like a ship without a rudder, carried on the current of circumstances from crisis to crisis until it encounters a crisis that is too big to handle or that lasts just too long. The business then becomes another bankruptcy statistic – statistics in which construction firms predominantly and tragically feature.

The purpose of business strategy is to give direction to an enterprise; specifically to give long-term direction to the firm. This is achieved through some form of strategic planning and control of the business. Formal planning and control of construction projects is well known and widely used in the construction industry. Construction firms of all sizes and types have been using increasingly sophisticated project planning and control techniques, appreciating the contribution such techniques make to the successful completion of projects. It is surprising, therefore, to discover that at the business level formal planning is little used or esteemed by construction firms and that even some of the largest contractors have been slow to adopt systematic planning procedures – this in spite of the evidence of the last two decades that the implementation of a clearly formulated business strategy enables a firm to reap real benefits, not the least of which is the improved chance of survival in the face of shrinking or fluctuating markets.

The responsibility for directing the business lies with the strategic management component of the enterprise, which may be an individual or a group. Traditionally this role has been the prerogative of top management in the firm, but the current trend is towards a much wider participation in strategic decision-making.

Strategy and strategic management do not occur in a vacuum; they occur within a specific business which has a unique organization structure. This organization structure is the facilitating framework through which business strategy is implemented, and will therefore influence strategic decisions and be affected by those decisions.

Current practice and trends in the strategic management and organization of construction firms will be discussed in this chapter under the following headings:

2.1 The nature of business strategy
2.2 The necessity for business strategy
2.3 Strategic management
2.4 Business strategy and organization structure

For the purposes of this chapter the terms 'business strategy', 'corporate strategy', and 'corporate planning' are assumed to be synonymous.

2.1 The nature of business strategy

Business strategy is the result of strategic decisions. The study of business strategy is, therefore, to a large extent the study of strategic decision-making.

The explicit statement of business strategy is the strategic plan for the enterprise. The implicit statement of business strategy is present and previous strategic actions by the firm.

It is important, therefore, to distinguish between those business decisions which are *strategic* and those which are *tactical*.

2.1.1 Strategic and tactical decisions

Strategic decisions are the few broad long-term decisions which affect the future of the whole business. They are occasioned by the need of the firm to anticipate and respond to changes inside and outside the business. They attempt to answer the following questions that a firm may face:

(a) What are we trying to achieve? What are our objectives?
(b) What opportunities are open to us?
(c) What threatens the future of the business?
(d) What are we good at doing? What are our strengths?
(e) What are our weaknesses?
(f) What are our current strategies?
(g) What strategic choices do we have? What should we do?

Strategic decisions are basically 'what shall we do?' decisions.

Tactical decisions are, by contrast, 'how shall we do it?' decisions. They are operational decisions made for parts of the business; estimating, buying, and accounting decisions are of this type. Construction project decisions are generally tactical unless the project represents such a large proportion of the company's total workload that the consequences of a wrong decision would be disastrous for the whole firm. Such decisions assume strategic significance.

This chapter will focus on strategic decisions. Subsequent chapters will deal with some of the tactical decisions a business will have to make.

2.1.2. Business strategy

It was stated in the previous section that the strategic plan was the expression of business strategy. A process of *formulation* precedes the preparation of this plan and a process of *implementation* must follow the *publication* of the plan. This total process of *formulation–publication–implementation* is the essence of business strategy. The main steps involved in the process are shown in Fig. 2.1.

(a) Formulation
This is the reflection or thinking stage of the process and contains two steps:

Step 1: Clarify objectives. Objectives are the desired future conditions that the business strives to achieve and as such are the critical first step in the formulation of a business strategy. Any firm must know *where* it is going (the destination) before deciding *how* to get there (the route to be adopted). Objectives are concerned with 'ends'. It is important to clarify and state explicitly the objectives of the firm so that everyone in the firm is clear about where the firm is going and can tailor their contribution accordingly. In addition to giving a sense of direction, objectives form the basis for measuring performance and exercising control over business operations.

Step 2: Decide strategy. Strategy is the formulation of courses of action which the business will adopt in the pursuit of objectives. Strategy is concerned with 'means' or the route to be followed. Decisions are necessary because there will invariably be a range of options open to the business and a choice of strategy will have to be made. This strategy should attempt to match the opportunities available to the firm with the capability of the firm to exploit those opportunities.

(b) Publication

Step 3: Strategic plan. The culmination of the formulation phase will be the preparation and publication of a *strategic plan* for the business. This plan lies at the 'isthmus' of formulation and implementation, and is the vital link between reflection and action. It should contain a synthesis of the objectives and strategies that the firm will pursue in a stated period of time and will form the basis and impetus for action.

(c) Implementation
This is the action stage of business strategy and consists of two steps:

Step 4: Give directions. However well formulated the strategic plan, unless action is taken to implement it, the plan will remain a useless piece of paper. In the 'one-man' business the responsibility for action will rest with the person who formulated the plan. In the majority of businesses the responsibility for action

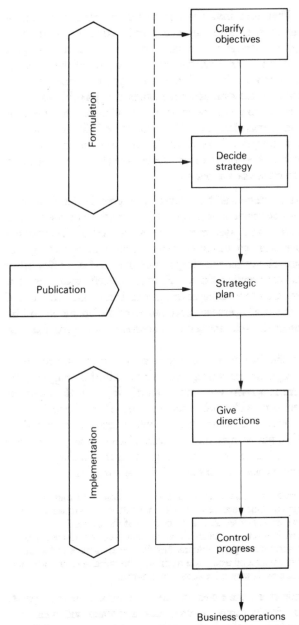

Fig. 2.1 Outline of the business strategy process (after Argenti, 1974)

and results will lie with subordinates and others in the firm, and thus the giving of directions to the various parts of the organization is an important step in the process. It is essentially the dividing up of the total strategic task of the enterprise between the divisions or functions of the business.

Step 5: Control progress. This step involves comparing planned with actual results for the firm, noting unacceptable variances, and taking any corrective action necessary. In a perfect situation it would only be necessary to give directions, but in practice control is an essential continuing part of the process. As shown by the feedback arrow in Fig. 2.1 the main point of reference for assessing business performance is the strategic plan (when it is possible to adjust performance). On occasions it may not be possible to achieve the levels of performance given in the strategic plan, in which case it will be necessary to review the objectives and strategies of the formulation stage, as indicated in Fig. 2.1 by the broken arrows. This control loop creates a cycle of decisions and actions which is essential to business strategy.

This process of business strategy will be discussed in greater detail later in Chapter 3, but mention must be made at this point of the method of conducting the process. The terms 'formal' and 'systematic' are often used in the business literature to describe business strategy and may imply a greater degree of rigidity and sophistication than is actually employed. In practice the need is for flexibility and simplicity, particularly for smaller firms. 'Formal' merely indicates that formal approval has been given by top management of the firm to the inclusion of the process just outlined in the total operating procedures of the business, and by implication that top management will instigate, encourage, and participate in such a process.

'Systematic' means that the business will adopt a systematic approach to formulating and implementing business strategy as described in this chapter. The assumption here is that there is a right way and a wrong way to make business decisions and 'that better decisions will be obtained with less effort if certain steps in the decision-making process are completed in this sequence rather than that ...' (Argenti 1974). An equally important benefit of a systematic approach is that it should ensure that sufficient time is given by the firm's management to the consideration of strategic issues. As Argenti (1974) again points out:

> ... it is the pressure for short-term results that is mainly responsible for a company's failure to give enough thought to long-term results. The most effective counter to this phenomenon is for senior executives to set aside a proportion of their time for discussing matters of strategic importance. Even if their discussions are unstructured, even if they merely identify what strategic problems they face, even if their skills and knowledge of techniques of corporate planning are minimal, the mere setting aside of a period for thought on a routine basis would be better than nothing.

While the need for a system is clear, the extent of the system must be appropriate to the size and type of firm. For example, a systematic approach will mean one thing to a multinational construction corporation and something entirely different to a small local builder or professional practice.

2.1.3 Misconceptions about business strategy

Having defined business strategy, it is equally important to dispel some fundamental misconceptions about the subject as many firms are deterred from attempting to introduce a sensible business strategy because of these misconceptions.

(a) A fundamental fallacy is that business strategy means planning every aspect of the business in great detail, over long periods of time. This is obviously ludicrous and impossible. Business strategy is concerned with planning for the business as a whole, as a corporate entity, not planning the whole business (i.e. not with planning the operation of every department in great detail). This latter belongs to the realm of tactical decision-making, and should be left to the line executives.

(b) Business strategy is not planning in great detail. Business strategy is essentially long term and, therefore, given the associated uncertainty, cannot be detailed. The preparation of huge thick strategy documents is patently a waste of time, as the future cannot be planned to that degree of detail. The strategy-makers will only have sufficient information to make broad decisions, to answer the few significant questions which will vitally affect the long-term future of the business. This requires only a short document of a few pages, as will be discussed later.

(c) Another argument is that because of the uncertainty just mentioned any form of long-term thinking is not worth the effort. In practice the rationale for having a business strategy is this very uncertainty, for if there were no uncertainties then yesterday's solutions and strategies would also be applicable tomorrow.

(d) It is often said by small firms that business strategy is all right for large firms who have the resources to conduct the exercise but is not really appropriate for the smaller firm. This arises because of a misunderstanding of the nature of business strategy as pointed out in (b). There is a level of strategy making sophistication appropriate to every size of firm, but the essential feature in all cases is simplicity not complexity.

(e) A corollary to the previous statement is that answering these few broad questions does not entail the use of sophisticated techniques requiring computers and model building. As Argenti (1980) points out: 'If you are faced with a situation that is so complex that you have to used advanced techniques, you are simply not standing far enough away from your company ... If you have to use such techniques, you are not doing corporate planning; you are far too involved with detail.'

(f) The need for a business strategy is often associated with an aggresive programme of acquisitions and mergers and if a firm is not undertaking such a programme, then the formulation of a clear strategy is probably not important. This is nonsense, for the non-diversified firm may be more vulnerable to changes in the environment and therefore may require to think through its strategy more rigorously.

(g) Business strategy has often been seen in the past as a strategy for growth and expansion. Many construction firms are today facing the problem of maintaining their existing business size or even, in some cases, enforced shrinkage. Maintenance and shrinkage strategies are legitimate strategies in certain circumstances, and can be important components in a firm's long-term survival.

(h) Having a distinct business strategy is not an automatic guarantee of increased profitability for this is also dependent upon other factors, such as operational efficiency. However, a firm which is being run *effectively* – i.e. is doing the right things – is more likely to be successful than a more *efficient* firm which is merely doing things right. In many firms the business strategy is seen as a defensive approach to running the firm; as preventing losses rather than improving profitability. Besides, profitability is only one aspect of a firm's total strategic thinking, as will be discussed later under 'objectives'.

(i) There is often confusion between business strategy, marketing and budgeting. The difference lies in the scope of each. Marketing is concerned with products and services that the firm will offer and budgeting is essentially exercising financial control over the business. Marketing and budgeting are therefore both a part and a result of business strategy which is concerned with much wider issues than these.

(j) Lastly, business strategy is *not* the consolidation of the various plans submitted by departments in the firm. These plans will be parochial and tactical in nature, and while they may form the basis of strategic thinking they should never be a substitute for it. A classic example of this approach in the construction industry is that adopted by a geographically dispersed housing development company which holds a regular annual meeting at which area managers are expected to present their 'build' and 'sales' plans for the coming year. These are then summated into a strategy for the whole business for the next year. This is not strategic planning; it is merely large-scale tactical planning.

Many businesses resort to thinking about business strategy when the firm is facing a crisis, often a crisis of survival. This is entirely the wrong time to think about the long-term future of the enterprise; it is better to concentrate on measures that will ensure short-term survival – that is, tactical measures. Conversely, the formulation of business strategy may trigger survival action, as will be shown.

2.2 The necessity for business strategy

To define business strategy is not to prove that it is necessary. To point to the failure of firms without a clear business strategy does not prove that those firms would have fared any better with a clearer concept of their business. Although, as defined, business strategy gives a comprehensive view of the business, it is only one view. Many firms with a sound business strategy have foundered because of operational errors (particularly in construction where, owing to project size, the cost of operational errors is very high) or as a result of the personality traits of top management. However, there is evidence to suggest that provided a business is being conducted in an efficient manner by competent management, a clear business strategy will enhance the effectiveness of the enterprise and improve its resilience in the face of a hostile environment (Lansley 1981). Surprises need not be disasters.

2.2.1 Strategy versus flexibility

One of the main objections to the introduction of business strategy to a firm is that it will limit the freedom of action open to the firm's executives. Strategy is seen as the antithesis of flexibility. It is argued that the sheer randomness of opportunities demand that a business be infinitely flexible in its response. There is little doubt that a strategy restricts the opportunities a firm can exploit, but very few companies are able to capitalize on these 'instant' and unforeseen chances. These are more than offset by the 'predictable' opportunities which emerge from a systematic approach to strategy. In any case, a firm which has pursued a policy of balanced development of the total resources of the business in line with a sound strategy is likely to have a greater capacity for flexibility than a less well-developed company.

It is often said that any form of forward planning is impossible because of the nature of the construction industry; that the problems of fragmentation, intensity of competition, and fluctuation of demand require a totally flexible response. Lansley (1981) has shown that those firms which adopted a sophisticated approach to planning during the volatile decade of the 1970s were more successful in riding the storm and even developing their businesses than those construction companies whose planning effort was 'underdeveloped'.

The antagonism towards formal business planning in the construction industry arises from a less obvious source – the personality traits of the businessmen. A large number of the men in charge of the fortunes of construction firms are of the 'buccaneering' breed who actually enjoy and thrive on being in a state of continual crisis. It is not that they cannot plan but rather that they do not wish to! Nor is this attitude confined to the top executives in construction; Mintzberg (1980), in a study of the role of the chief executive, has shown that this action orientated anti-planning view prevails among such men. Lumsden (1971) identifies

> ... two ways in which businesses are run: management sit back and wait for opportunities to occur in the hope that the demand will coincide with what the company has to offer; or management look ahead and systematically develop their company so that by anticipation it is always organized to exploit opportunities for profit and growth as the pattern of demand changes.

Many construction businesses which claim to adopt the latter method actually employ the former 'reactor' approach.

2.2.2 The advantages of not having a business strategy

Ansoff (1968) gives three advantages which a firm will derive from *not* having a business strategy:

(a) The company will save executive time, cost, and talent by not engaging in formal planning activities.

17

(b) The opportunities of the firm will not be restricted to those included in the strategic plan.

(c) The business will gain the advantages of the delay in decision-making; fuller information, for example.

Against these must be set the advantages of having a business strategy.

2.2.3 The advantages of having a business strategy

The advantages of having a business strategy are:

(a) The firm's management will take time to consider the *important* strategic issues rather than just react to the *urgent* tactical matters which often *seem* more important.

(b) The process of formulating a business strategy will force the firm to identify its strengths and weaknesses and build up a business 'capability profile'.

(c) Opportunities in the market place will be identified before they arise, allowing the firm time to prepare to exploit a market leadership position.

(d) This analysis of market opportunities will also highlight the risks involved in pursuing particular strategies and thus provide a basis for ranking those opportunities.

(e) The credentials of competitors will be subject to a much more searching analysis than previously conducted, which will enable the business to take advantage of any foibles thus revealed.

(f) The firm will better be able to anticipate changes in markets and prepare offensive or defensive action to cope with these changes.

(g) A corollary of this last point is that such sophisticated market intelligence will also reveal trends which are occurring in the firm's environment; trends which are often obscured until it is too late for the company to react.

(h) Continual 'crisis management' will also be avoided, although as previously stated the firm's executives may actually enjoy this situation.

(i) Necessary changes in the structure and operating procedures of the business in response to strategic changes can be introduced over a much longer time-scale with less disruption to existing operations. This is particularly important to large corporations and even medium-sized firms with long established infrastructures which make it difficult for them to change quickly. Smaller firms are of a more organic nature and are able to adapt more readily.

(j) A well-defined business strategy will focus the efforts of all those involved in the enterprise and thus enhance corporate harmony.

(k) The systematic development of all the resources of the business, both physical and human, will result from the formulation of a strategy for the whole business and the subsequent tactical plans. The sense of security which this engenders in staff should improve motivation.

(l) Last, but not least, will be the effect on the strategic decision-makers themselves, first, in presenting them with the opportunity to review strategic matters and to make genuine strategic decisions, and, second, in creating a climate of strategic thinking in which managers can exercise their judgement on the broader organizational aspects of the business. It has been argued that regardless of the value of the strategic plan which is produced, the process of strategy formulation is beneficial in itself in stimulating executive thought.

Ansoff (1968) concludes: 'It would seem that for most firms the advantages of strategy will outweigh those of total flexibility.' This is the main thrust of this chapter.

2.2.4 A contingency view of business strategy

It was stated in 2.1.2 that it was important for a firm to adopt an approach to strategy formulation that was appropriate to the characteristics of the business. The most crucial of these characteristics is the *size* of the enterprise, given the fact that similar types of firm are being considered, i.e. construction firms. Small businesses will need a simple system of strategic decision-making that can be operated by a single individual or a small group on a part-time basis. The larger corporation can afford to appoint full-time executives and corporate planners to concentrate solely on the strategic elements of the business. The five-step process outlined in 2.1.2 should be followed by all businesses regardless of size, but the depth of effort at each step will obviously depend on the extent to which the resources of the firm are allocated to the process. The larger enterprise is able to employ specialist personnel and advanced computer-aided techniques, and this is probably necessary because of the far-reaching nature of the decisions that have to be made. This, however must be qualified by the point made in 2.1.3(d) that these techniques should be aids to decision-making and not an end in themselves. The smaller business operates on a relatively shorter time-scale and in a narrower sphere of strategy and, therefore, requires a less sophisticated system.

A related characteristic is the *diversity* of the operations of the firm. This is usually a function of size although some small firms are more diversified than some large firms. The point is that the degree of diversity will determine the extent of environmental surveillance required to sustain the variety of market coverage which the firm must maintain. It will need to develop a more comprehensive business strategy of greater complexity than the single product/service business.

A third characteristic is the *structural form* of the firm. A fully integrated organization will require a fully developed business strategy, whereas a company which has a holding company form and comprises independent and unrelated businesses will utilize a partially developed strategy with a strong financial component of control.

The *management style* of the firm's leaders will also determine its strategic style. An entrepreneurial business leader will rely to a large extent on intuition in making strategic decisions and thus operate within a very 'loose' business strategy framework. Conversely, a professional manager will be much more conservative in his decision-making mode and prefer to have a precise business strategy to implement.

These and other factors will determine a uniquely appropriate business strategy for every firm at a certain stage in its evolution. There is only one strategy that is absolutely right for a particular business in a specific situation; finding that strategy is the fundamental purpose of the formulation stage of business strategy, which is described in the next chapter.

2.2.5 Business strategy and performance

Hussey (1974) states in Chapter 2 of *Corporate Planning: Theory and Practice*, 'There can only be one justification for the introduction of a system of corporate planning into a company – a belief that it can lead to improved results, which for the businessman means increased profits.' He then proceeds to review a number of studies of British and American planning practice and concludes, 'Evidence so far available suggests, as we have seen, that planning leads to better perform-ance.'

Taylor and Sparkes (1977) also raise the question,

'How does the performance of companies using corporate planning compare with those which do not? Studies in the USA (Thune and House 1970, Ansoff 1969) indicate that companies that use corporate planning significantly outperform companies that use informal methods. One finding was that companies with corporate planning performed around 30– 40 per cent better in terms of earnings per share, earnings on common equity, and earnings on total capital employed. This better performance was not, of course, proof of the benefits of corporate planning, so the study examined the extent to which performance had improved after corporate planning had been introduced. The improvements were impressive: sales grew by 38 per cent, earnings per share grew by 64 per cent and the share prices increased by 56 per cent. The evidence, therefore, strongly suggests that corporate planning can lead to significant improvements in performance.'

These studies indicate a clear correlation between business strategy and performance for firms in general, but what of construction firms in particular? Lansley (1981) says,

. . . our recent research shows that the level of sophistication of a firm's corporate planning is one of the surest indicators of a firm's ability to perform well in the future. Of 26 (construction) firms studied during the mid-1970s recession, eight had adopted sophisticated methods of planning, relative to firms of a similar size and type of business, and eight had adopted fairly unsophisticated planning methods. All the firms entered the recession in a good state of health, but those with relatively unsophisticated methods fared very badly indeed. All suffered substantial reductions in their business – and several went into liquidation. Of the relatively sophisticated firms, five fared extremely well, growing and developing substantially throughout the recession – only one performed poorly.

It is evident from the above that construction firms can also benefit from the introduction of an explicit form of business strategy.

2.3 Strategic management

Business strategy has been defined as a five-step process of clarifying objectives, deciding strategy, preparing a strategic plan, giving directions, and controlling progress.

Strategic management is the management role or function which initiates, activates, and operates this process of business strategy. In other words, strategic management is the dynamic element in business strategy. The definition of strategic management as a *role* or *function* has two important implications. First, this role is not necessarily automatically associated with a particular level in the hierarchy of the organization. Traditionally it has been seen as the prerogative of the top level or levels of management in the business to perform this task, but the current trend is towards greater participation at all levels in the firm, including shared strategic decision-making. Anyone in the company who has the requisite skill, knowledge, and authority can perform this role. Second, it is implied that while the role is prescribed, the interpretation of that role will depend on the personality of the 'actor' who performs it. There is scope for a range of highly individual approaches to strategic management.

2.3.1 The necessity for strategic management

The necessity for strategic management stems from the need for business strategy; but in addition to conducting business strategy, strategic management fulfils three other critical functions:

(a) It provides direction to the whole enterprise – in a business with purposeful strategic leadership people feel the firm is going somewhere and are thus better motivated to contribute to the objectives that have been set.
(b) The elusive corporate harmony mentioned earlier is more likely to be achieved in a firm which has strong direction from the strategic managers. The result will be greater unity between the independent parts or departments of the business.
(c) Strategic management is specifically entrusted with deciding what the firm's response will be to changes inside and, especially, outside the business. No one else has the breadth of knowledge to appreciate the significance of these changes and to decide the action that should be initiated to cope with the changes. In one sense strategic management is the management of change.

The reason strategic management is weak in some firms is that management become too enmeshed in the operational aspects of the business and neglect strategic matters; this particularly the case where managers in key positions in the company have a strong technical background, as in the construction industry. The temptation to become involved in familiar and interesting project problems is often greater than ex-site executives can resist. This problem can only be overcome in two ways:

(a) There should be a specific allocation of *time* to the consideration of the business strategy. All firms of whatever size can do this.
(b) Larger corporations can create a corps of executives to deal exclusively with strategy issues, as described by Chandler (1966).

This study of large American corporations traced the historical development of the organization structure of these companies as they grew and adopted new strategies. A significant feature was the creation of a so-called 'general office' at the top the organization whose members were encouraged to withdraw from operational commitments to concentrate on strategic decisions. The operations of the business were then undertaken by semi-autonomous product or geographical divisions whose executives made operational decisions within the strategic framework established by the general office. Subsequent studies by Channon (1973, 1978) have shown that British manufacturing and service sector companies have followed a similar pattern in their structural evolution. The service sector study included a number of large construction companies.

2.3.2 Strategic management modes

There are a number of ways of practising strategic management in a business. The mode adopted depends upon the following factors:

(a) The *size* of the firm will obviously influence the executive time and talent that can be devoted to thinking about strategy, as previously discussed. The small enterprise must be content with part-time strategic management, whereas the larger organization can indulge in the luxury of a full-time mode.
(b) The form of corporate *leadership* is another important aspect. Four pure types of business leadership may be discerned:
    1. *Entrepreneurial.* This is where the business is led by a single individual, often the founder of the firm, who is responsible for all the critical strategic decisions.
    2. *Family.* Firms where the top management job of chairman and/or chief executive is held by a member of the controlling family group who are often direct descendants of the company's founder or founders.
    3. *Professional.* Firms where the top management positions have passed to professional managers who have no lineal descendancy to the company's founder.
    4. *Partnership.* A form of owner-management adopted by a large number of smaller construction firms, particularly professional practices, who do not wish to form a limited liability company for personal or ethical reasons.
    In types 1, 2, and 4 above the strategic management role is frequently restricted to those with a financial interest in the business whereas in 3 there is often a much wider distribution of strategic influence.
(c) The *style* of management which characterizes the organization will determine the extent of participation in strategic management. An *autocratic* approach to

managing the business will result in the centralization of strategic decision-making, with an individual or a small group retaining the power in the firm. A *democratic* style of management will encourage a company-wide involvement in the formulation of strategy.

The choice of strategic management method ultimately focuses on *external* or *internal* modes.

(a) *External*. This entails importing the necessary expertise from outside the company in the form of full- or part-time consultants or by appointing a non-executive director. The advantages of using this method – a detached and unbiased look at the business by individuals wth wide experience – have to be offset against the disadvantages of higher costs and limited commitment to the firm, together with a less penetrating insight into the internal workings and personalities of the business.

(b) *Internal*. This involves appointing an individual or a team of people from within the organization. Many companies have created the position of corporate planner specifically to fill the strategic management role. This approach has met with varying degrees of success depending upon the level at which the post is established, the attitude of other executives, and the personality of the planner. The setting up of a strategic management team comprising the chief executive and other key managers seems to be the ideal solution for many modern businesses. As Argenti (1980) points out,

> This style has two enormous advantages. First, it overcomes the problem that defeats so many autocrats, namely, that the business world today is so multifaceted that no one man can comprehend the implications of everything happening around him. Secondly, it is participative. Not only do more people have a chance to make a contribution to the running of their company, but also, when the plan is agreed, it is their plan; they have agreed it and will work hard to bring it to a satisfactory conclusion.

For many firms these advantages will outweigh the disadvantages of a longer decision-making period and the possibility of compromise strategies which may seem dull and unimaginative compared to those of the entrepreneur.

The strategic management mode finally selected will, to an extent, depend on the factors discussed earlier – the size of the firm, its form of leadership, and its management style. It will certainly affect the quality of the business strategy which evolves and, consequently, the long-term future of the business.

2.4 Business strategy and organization structure

2.4.1 Strategy, structure, and performance

If business strategy is the process of formulating and implementing a strategic plan and strategic management is the dynamic element which steers and motivates business action, then the organization structure of the firm is the framework within which both strategy and strategic management occur. Business strategy and strategic management are both meaningless outside the context of a business organization; it follows, therefore, that strategy and structure must be interrelated. This link between strategy and structure, well known by astute businessmen, has recently been verified by an extensive research programme conducted under the auspices of Harvard University (Dyas 1972, Thanheiser 1972, Paven 1972, Rumelt 1974, Channon 1973) and Manchester Business School (Channon 1978). The impetus for this programme came from an earlier theory which was derived by Chandler (1966) from his study of the growth of four American corporations – Du Pont, General Motors, Standard Oil Company, and Sears Roebuck. The essence of his theory was that 'structure follows strategy' or 'that a company's strategy in time determines its structure'. This positive relationship found to exist between strategy and structure was then empirically tested and refined by Chandler using data from the seventy largest US corporations in nine industries.

The study by Channon (1978) of the strategic, structural, and financial histories of the largest 100 service industry companies for the period 1950–74 is particularly relevant to construction firms as it includes seven construction corporations – Richard Costain, Taylor Woodrow, John Laing, George Wimpey, Trafalgar House Investments, Wood Hall Trust, and London & Northern Securities. *Strategy* was defined as the extent of diversification and international activity together with the acquisition policy adopted. *Structure* was classified in terms of the formal organization structure (i.e. functional, holding company, multidivisional, critical function) and the corporate leadership mode (i.e. entrepreneurial, family, and professional management). *Financial performance* was measured using conventional accounting ratios for growth and profitability. The findings of the research confirmed Chandler's thesis that structure follows strategy, for as the companies had diversified from offering a single product or service to offering a range of related or unrelated services or products so the pressure for organizational change proved irresistible if efficiency was to be maintained, with functional forms giving way to the more appropriate holding company and multidivisional structures. Significant relationships were also found to exist between the strategic and structural variables and financial performance. The strategy of related diversification, extending the original business by the addition of related business activities, gave superior financial performance to either limited or unrelated diversification. As might be expected, an aggressive acquisition policy proved to be a very effective vehicle for achieving rapid business growth but resulted in inferior profitability performance. Increased international activity did not, in general, lead to better financial performance, but in the case of the construction companies did give greater stability of workload by offsetting the effects of fluctuating demand at home. The influence of formal organization structure on financial performance was less definite with higher growth being associated with multidivisional structures and greater profitability with functional and critical function structures. There were, however, significant increases in all aspects of financial performance when companies switched from the holding company to the multidivisional form. The most interesting structural implication was the impact of the corporate leadership style on financial performance. Entrepreneurially led businesses considerably outperformed both family led and professionally managed businesses on all the performance measures. In turn, family firms achieved better financial results than those firms run by professional managers. This would seem to emphasize the importance of an equity stake in the business; the shareholdings of professional managers were generally low. It is interesting that many of the construction corporations were dominated by entrepreneurs or their descendants. There was a marked contrast between the strategies adopted by the long-established construction companies – Costain, Taylor Woodrow, Laing, and Wimpey – and those of the newer conglomerates. The older companies had grown rapidly between 1918 and 1939 as house builders, and during World War II had become involved in civil engineering projects for the war effort. The post-war domestic rebuilding programme provided the opportunity to further develop major contracting expertise and the possibility of pursuing a strategy of related diversification through backward integration into the manufacture of construction materials and forward integration into property development, particularly during the property boom of the 1960s and early 1970s. In contrast the newer companies had been created since 1945 by individual entrepreneurs and were much more diversified than the major contractors, with interests in property, investment, contracting, engineering, house building, shipping, hotels, newspapers, and so on. These firms had reached the top 100 service industries group very quickly through a strategy of aggresive acquisition as opposed to the slower and largely internal expansion of the older construction companies.

2.4.2 Strategy and structure of the smaller construction firm

A subsequent study by Newcombe (1976) further extended this exploration of the link between strategy and structure to small and medium-sized construction firms. It became obvious early in the research that the definitions adopted by Channon for a multi-industry study would have to be adapted in order to differentiate the strategies and structures of these smaller firms operating within a single industry.

(a) Strategy
This was defined in terms of *market diversification* and *geographical expansion*.

1. Market diversification was chosen in recognition of the distinct nature of the different markets which exist within the overall building market. General contracting, civil engineering, speculative house building, property development, building products, plant hire, etc., are all within the construction market but each requires a different set of resources, skills, and management expertise. A successful general contractor may fail miserably in speculative house building (as many have), or in civil engineering. Conversely, a civil engineering contractor may undertake a building contract at his peril. On a specialization/diversification continuum, a firm operating in a single market could be termed a specialist firm, while at the other extreme a firm operating in many markets may be called diversified. Four market diversification strategies were identified:

- *Single market:* Firms which grew by expansion within one market.
- *Dominant market:* Firms which grew by expansion within one main market but in addition had entered secondary markets.
- *Related market:* Firms which grew by expansion by means of entry into related markets, by offering related services or products, by use of related technology, by related vertical activities, or some combination of these.
- *Unrelated market:* Firms which grew by expansion into new markets, offering new services and products and using new technologies unrelated to the original market scope.

2. Geographical expansion – that is, geographic centralization or decentralization – was seen as a critical element in the analysis of construction firms, whose task, by the very nature of the building industry, is geographically dispersed. The importance of geographical expansion as a definite strategy for construction firms has been highlighted by several studies of the industry and this was selected as a second dimension of strategy. Four degrees of geographic expansion were identified: local, regional, national, and international.

(b) Structure
This was defined as the formal organization structure of the firm, as may be shown on an organization chart. Channon (1973) identified three stages of structural development – functional, holding company, and multidivisional – which coincided with increasing diversification. Being concerned in his research with the largest UK corporations he did not include a structural classification for the smaller company which may not have reached the functional stage. Therefore, an earlier stage of organizational development, called 'integrated', was added to the three stages given by Channon. Thus, the four forms of organization structure adopted were:

- *Integrated:* In this form there was no division of the total task of the business into specialized functions, but many unrelated activities were grouped under a single individual or, in extreme cases, were executed by a single person.
- *Functional:* In this form the business was subdivided into a series of specialized functions, culminating in the office of the chief executive who performed the role of co-ordinator and general manager of all the individual functions.
- *Holding company:* This consisted of a system of semi-autonomous subsidiaries or companies, held together only as a corporate legal entity.
- *Multidivisional:* This was typically composed of a general office, usually divorced from operations, which serviced and monitored the operating divisions. The divisions were based on product, service, geography, or some combination of these.

(c) The strategy/structure model
Using the definitions of strategy and structure previously outlined, it was possible
to construct a strategy/structure model with which to observe the evolution and
structure of construction firms. The model is two-dimensional with market
diversification on the horizontal axis and geographical expansion on the vertical
axis as shown in Fig. 2.2. The model has four zones to which firms may be
allocated and through which they pass during strategic and structural evolution.
A firm will be placed in a particular zone depending upon the extent of
diversification and geographic decentralization adopted. If structure follows
strategy it is anticipated that firms will adopt organization structures appropriate
to the strategic zone in which they are currently situated. The strategic and
structural characteristics of construction firms in each zone were then predicted
as follows:

Zone 1: Specialization/centralization.   Firms in this zone will adopt a strategy of
specialization, operating in a single market (e.g. a small works contractor) or a
dominant market (e.g. a general contractor with a small estate development
section). The firms will be small or medium sized with an integrated or functional
organization structure and will seek work in a limited local or regional area. Given
the structure of the industry with a predominance of small and medium-sized
firms, it is expected that this will be the most densely populated zone.

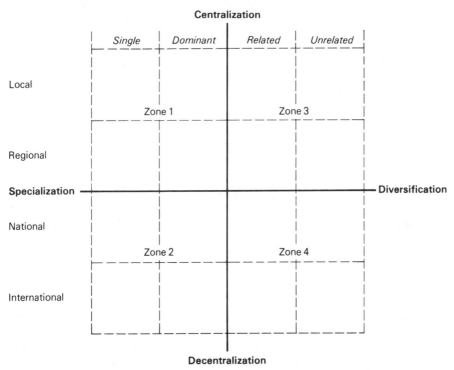

Fig. 2.2 The strategy/structure model

Zone 2: Specialization/decentralization. Firms in this zone will remain specialists as they operate in a single or dominant market situation, but they will have spread geographically to give national or even international coverage for their specific service. An example of this type of firm would be a speculative housing company or a holding company with subsidiaries offering similar services. This geographical expansion will not only rapidly increase the size of the firm but will also radically alter its organization structure. The structure will typically consist of a number of autonomous or semi-autonomous regional offices offering the same product or service with a central office providing group services, and planning and controlling operations. Typical central office services in a speculative housing development company would be house design and land purchase.

Zone 3: Diversification/centralization. Firms in this zone will have diversified into two or more related markets (e.g. general contracting and estate development) or unrelated markets (e.g. general building and civil engineering or building products), but none of these markets will dominate the firm's operations. Although diversified by market these businesses will still operate within strict geographical boundaries; indeed, the decision to remain regional may have initiated diversification to avoid workload fluctuations in a limited market. A multidivisional structure with market divisions and a general office providing central services and planning and controlling the operating divisions would be expected. It is probable that companies operating in related markets will be exploiting the synergistic advantages within their central services. The reason for regional restraint may be simply managerial discretion, particularly in entrepreneurially or family controlled firms.

Zone 4: Diversification/decentralization. Companies in this zone will operate in two or more distinct markets through a network of regional offices. The multidivisional structure will be further subdivided on a geographical basis to enable large companies to compete effectively in local or regional markets. In some companies this may be extended to overseas markets controlled by an international division or company. Central services incorporating planning, finance, and personnel may be expected but divisions and regions will enjoy considerable autonomy. Most of the large UK contractors would be in this zone. Another type of structure to be observed may be the holding company with subsidiaries offering diverse services in different geographical locations.

These zonal characteristics are illustrated in Fig. 2.3, and the evolution of firms *within* zones and *between* zones may now be examined.

(d) Evolution within zones

Strategic and structural changes within zones are expected to be relatively smooth. For example, the transition from an integrated to a functional structure in zone 1 is natural and logical and will occur gradually as particular responsibilities are delegated by the founder or his descendants. Again, in zones 2 and 3 the opening of another regional office or the addition of another market division,

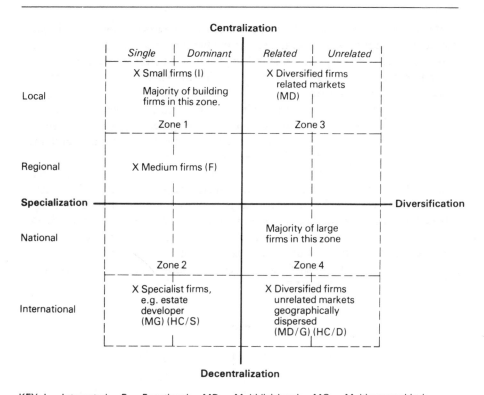

KEY: I = Integrated;   F = Functional;   MD = Multidivisional;   MG = Multigeographical;
MD/G = Multidivisional/geographical;   HC/S = Holding company/single market;
HC/D = Holding company/multiple markets

Fig. 2.3 The strategy/structure model showing zonal characteristics

although important, are extensions of an existing strategic and structural configuration. By the time firms reach zone 4 they have usually acquired a sound market base and the extension of their activities into other markets or areas of operation represent a relatively minor commitment of total resources. This is why large firms can make mistakes that would ruin smaller firms, and survive with little obvious or long-term effects.

(e) Transition between zones
Both the *nature* and *direction* of the transition between zones need to be considered.

The *nature* of the transition between zones, in contrast to the relatively smooth evolution within zones, is expected to be marked by severe internal turbulence and organizational change. The realization in a functional zone 1 company that further expansion requires the delegation of long-held authority to divisional managers coupled with dramatic organizational redesign is no doubt a traumatic experience. The decision to expand geographically is again a watershed in the firm's evolution. Small wonder that some firms choose to remain in a particular zone; transition is the result of deliberate strategic choice knowing that structural change must follow. Indeed, many firms have sought the aid of outside consultants in clarifying the structural implications of strategic decisions, which extend beyond a new organization chart to a new system of controls and probably a new style of management.

The *direction* of transition is determined by the strategy adopted by a firm. The zonal model is at odds with other corporate development theories in suggesting that various paths of evolution are possible. These multiple paths and their underlying strategy may usefully be examined using the zonal model.

It is assumed that all evolution starts in zone 1 and proceeds in the direction of zone 4. The evolution within zone 1 has already been described and it is likely that *all* firms will develop a functional structure of some sort because it is an extremely efficient structure if the firm is operating within a narrow market scope. Numerous studies and company histories show this to be a common development for all types of firms. This is shown in Fig. 2.4. It is when the limits of zone 1 are reached that evolution patterns become more complex and varied. Three paths may be pursued.

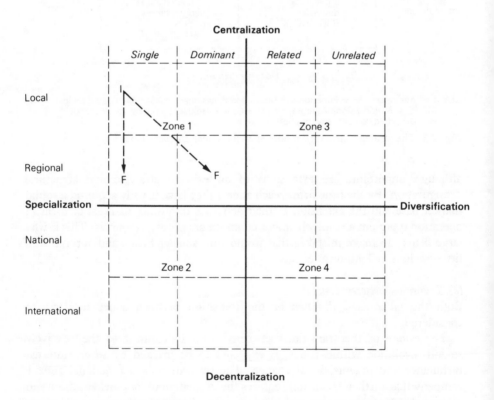

KEY: I = Integrated;   F = Functional

Fig. 2.4 The strategy/structure model showing evolution in zone 1

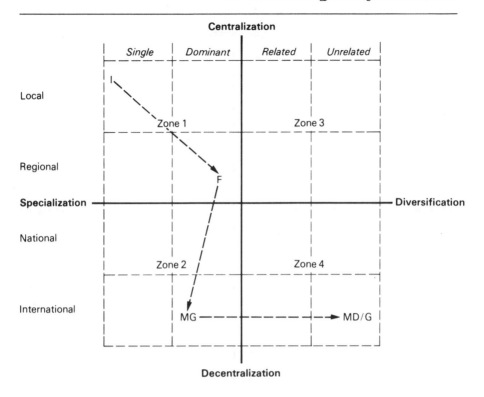

KEY: I = Integrated;   F = Functional;   MG = Multigeographical;
MD/G = Multidivisional/geographical

Fig. 2.5 The strategy/structure model showing evolution through zones 1–2–4

One path is shown in Fig. 2.5. The sequence is: zone 1–2–4. This path will be pursued by a firm which adopts a strategy initially of specialization in a single or dominant market and chooses to grow by expanding geographically, having fully exploited its local and regional area. The firm may stop in zone 2 and perhaps pursue its policy of specialization to an international level. Once a strong geographical base is established it may decide to seek a wider market base through diversification, in which case a transition to zone 4 will be made.

Another path is shown in Fig. 2.6, where the sequence is: zone 1–3–4. Following this path the firm would diversify within its original operating area to achieve greater market coverage and thus move to zone 3. Again, a firm may choose to stay in this zone or it may seek geographical expansion in some, or all, of its selected markets and move to zone 4.

A third path is a direct move from zone 1 to zone 4, as in Fig. 2.7. This move is, however, unlikely because it represents such an enormous change in both strategy and structure simultaneously. It could be adopted by a firm seeking rapid market and geographical growth through the acquisition of diverse and scattered businesses, or by a company changing from a functional to a holding company structure.

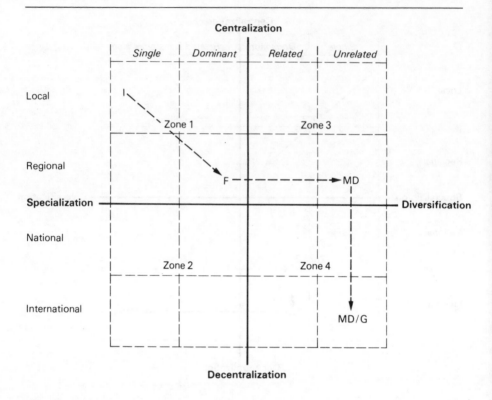

KEY: I = Integrated; F = Functional; MD = Multidivisional;
     MD/G = Multidivisional/geographical

Fig. 2.6 The strategy/structure model showing evolution through zones 1–3–4

While these zonal evolution patterns are seen to be the most logical for growing firms, a reversal or modification of strategy is not ruled out. Having moved from zone 1 to zone 2 a company facing declining profits may decide to return to zone 1 by closing down its regional offices. A modification of strategy may lead a firm to adopt the sequence: zone 1–2–3. This would follow a decision to curtail geographical expansion in favour of regional diversification. A number of other routes are obviously possible.

(f) Strategy, structure, and evolution of construction firms
The model described above was then tested against the strategic and structural configurations and case histories of a number of construction companies of various sizes and types, with turnovers in 1976 ranging from £1.3 million to £348 million and from 80 to 18,000 employees. The sample included a small local builder with a single market strategy, a number of regional contractors with single, related, and unrelated strategies, a national speculative house building company, and an international construction firm with distinctly unrelated market

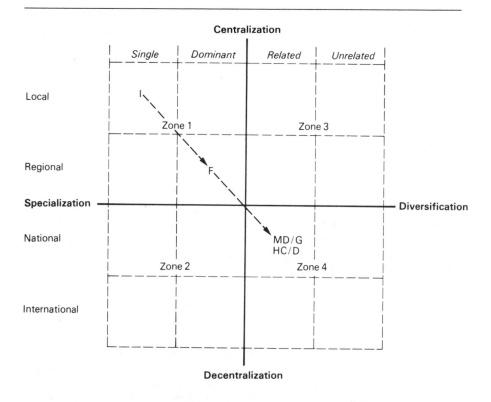

KEY: I = Integrated;   F = Functional;   MD/G Multidivisional/geographical;
HC/D = Holding company/multiple markets

Fig. 2.7 The strategy/structure model showing evolution from zones 1–4

strategy. All but one of the firms had a structure appropriate to its strategy as predicted by the model; it is worth noting that the firm with an inappropriate organization structure has subsequently ceased trading. The link between strategy and structure for these generally smaller firms was thus confirmed. Although financial performance was not specifically investigated, it became apparent during discussions with the executives in the firms that zones 2 and 3 were high-performance zones. Specifically, the multi-geographical house builder and the regional contractor with the related strategy had both achieved remarkable rates of growth in turnover and profitability.

A study of the case histories of the firms revealed that they had all started as small, local, single market companies and that evolution of both strategy and structure had followed the typical patterns suggested by the zonal model. The firms had adjusted their organization structures in order to pursue particular strategies or, more often, had been forced to redesign the structure of the company because a mismatch with strategy had resulted in declining profits. Further, the strategic and structural histories of the firms tended to confirm the nature of evolution of the construction firms. The evolution within the strategic zones had been gradual and relatively smooth, almost incidental. In contrast, the transition between zones was characterized by rapid and revolutionary change and the result of deliberate strategic decisions by the top management of the firm.

Summary

Three key elements in any successful business are its strategy, its strategic management mode, and an appropriate organization structure. Attention to these elements is a matter of strategic choice by the firm's ruling managers; they may be deliberately or accidentally neglected. Unsuccessful businesses frequently neglect these elements. A business may even operate efficiently in the short term without a clear strategy or a planned organization structure, but long-term success stems from effective strategic decisions.

Strategic decisions are the 'what shall we do?' decisions in contrast to the more pressing and numerous tactical 'how shall we do it?' decisions. The neglect of strategic decisions is often the result of the conquest of the urgent over the important.

Business strategy is the result of strategic decisions. This decision-making is exercised through a process of formulation and implementation of a strategic plan. Formulation consists of clarifying the objectives of the business and deciding the strategies to be pursued. This stage culminates in the production of a strategic plan for the business. Unless it is converted into effective action the plan is useless, however carefully prepared. Implementation of the plan entails giving directions to the people responsible for its implementation and establishing some form of monitoring system to ensure progress towards the targets that have been set.

Some of the myths and the mystique associated with business strategy have been shown to be nonsense. There are definite advantages for construction firms of all sizes and types in having and enacting a clear business strategy; not least of these advantages are the possibility of better performance and a greater chance of survival.

The responsibility for formulating and implementing business strategy rests with the strategic management of the enterprise. The strategic management role must be filled by someone, or by a group of people, either on a full-time basis as in the larger firm or on a part-time basis in the smaller business. The trend towards a wider participation in strategic decision-making is likely to continue and should result in greater satisfaction and increased motivation within firms.

There is little doubt that structure must follow strategy. The evolution of a firm's strategy will necessitate the redesign of its organization structure for effective implementation of that strategy. A strategy of diversification is best handled through a divisional structure, and geographical expansion will lead to a decentralized structure.

The implications of these elements – strategy, strategic management, and structure – for the performance of construction firms has been the underlying theme of this chapter.

Questions

1. Distinguish between 'strategic' and 'tactical' decisions giving examples from the construction industry.
2. Why is a 'systematic' approach to formulating and implementing business strategy so important? What are the steps involved in this approach?
3. Strategy is seen as the antithesis of flexibility. Discuss.
4. Why is strategic management neglected in some businesses? What are the probable consequences of such neglect? What steps can the managers of firms take to ensure that adequate attention is given to strategic matters?
5. Discuss the advantages and disadvantages of external and internal strategic management modes.
6. 'Structure follows strategy.' Discuss the implications of this statement for managers of construction firms.
7. Recent research has found significant differences in the financial performance of firms led by entrepreneurs, family management, and professional managers. What other characteristics would you expect to find in construction firms with these three different leadership styles?
8. What strategies are likely to lead to high financial performance for construction firms? Why?

References

Ansoff, H. I. (1968) *Corporate Strategy*, Penguin

Ansoff, H. I. (1969) Does planning pay? *Long Range Planning*, Mar.

Argenti, J. (1974) *Systematic Corporate Planning*, Nelson

Argenti, J. (1980) *Practical Corporate Planning*, George Allen & Unwin

Chandler, A. D. (1966) *Strategy and Structure*, Anchor Books: New York

Channon, D. F. (1973) *The Strategy and Structure of British Enterprise*, Macmillan

Channon, D. F. (1978) *The Service Industries – Strategy, Structure and Financial Performance*, Macmillan

Dyas, G. P. (1972) 'The Strategy and Structure of French Industrial Enterprise.' Unpublished doctoral dissertation, Harvard Graduate School of Business

Hussey, D. E. (1974) *Corporate Planning: Theory and Practice*, Pergamon Press

Lansley, P. (1981) Corporate planning for the small builder, *Building Technology and Management*, Dec., pp. 7–9, 12

Lumsden, P. (1971) Business planning in construction, *Building*, Feb./Mar.

Mintzberg, H. (1980) *The Nature of Managerial Work* (2nd edn), Prentice Hall: Englewood Cliffs, NJ

Newcombe, R. (1976) 'The Evolution and Structure of the Construction Firm.' Unpublished MSc thesis, University College, London

Paven, R. J. (1972) 'The Strategy and Structure of Italian Enterprise.' Unpublished doctoral dissertation, Harvard Graduate School of Business

Rumelt, R. P. (1974) *Strategy, Structure and Economic Performance*, Harvard Graduate School of Business

Taylor, B. and Sparkes, J. R. (1977) *Corporate Strategy and Planning*, Heinemann

Thanheiser, H. T. (1972) 'Strategy and Structure of German Industrial Enterprise.' Unpublished doctoral dissertation, Harvard Graduate School of Business

Thune, S. S. and House, R. J. (1970) Where long-range planning pays off, *Business Horizons*, Aug.

Chapter 3

Construction business strategy

In 2.1.2 business strategy was defined as a process consisting of three stages (formulation, the strategic plan, and implementation) and five steps, as illustrated in Fig. 2.1. This chapter will focus on the first three steps (clarify objectives, decide strategy, and prepare the strategic plan) as it is felt that these steps will be least familiar to practising construction managers. The implementation steps are well known and practised by managers at the operational and project levels, and simply need to be applied at a higher strategic level. The manager with a participative style of management will allow responsible subordinates maximum discretion in implementing directions by the way in which those directions are framed, and the time span of control allowed. There should be no exception with strategic directions and control. This process of formulating and preparing a strategic plan will now be explored in greater detail using Fig. 3.1 as a framework.

The sequence shown in the flow chart in Fig. 3.1 is widely recognized in practice as being a systematic and logical approach to business strategy. All three stages – formulation, strategic plan, and implementation – are indicated, as is the short-term survival strategy stemming from the company analysis. The activities involved in the first two of these stages as given in the boxes of the flow chart, and the problems of introducing business strategy to a firm will now be considered under the following headings:

3.1. Clarify objectives
3.2. Decide strategy
3.3. The strategic plan
3.4. Introducing business strategy to the firm

As stated in 2.1.2, formulation is the reflection or thinking stage of the business strategy process, the stage at which a systematic search for a strategy is conducted. This is uncharted territory for many construction managers and the rationale of this chapter.

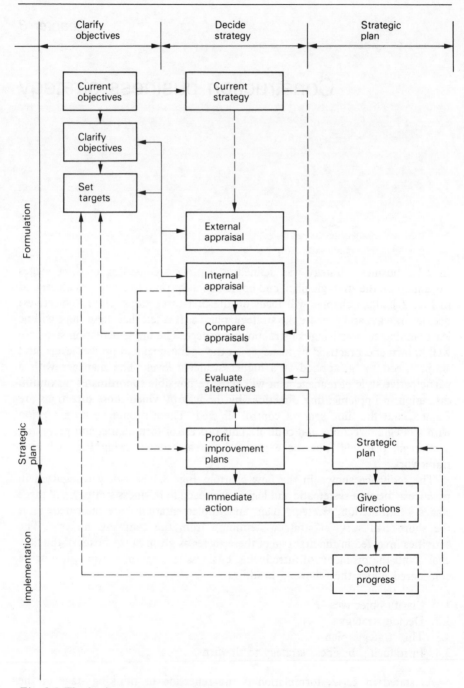

Fig. 3.1 The business strategy process

3.1 Clarify objectives

Every business is a purposeful organization directed towards the achievement of objectives. These objectives may be explicitly stated or implicitly derived from a study of the behaviour of the firm and its managers.

As previously defined, objectives are the desired future conditions that the business strives to achieve and constitute the critical first step in the formulation of a business strategy.

The clarification of objectives entails the review of current objectives to assess their validity, the proposal of new additional or replacement objectives, and the quantification of these objectives where possible in the form of targets.

Two classes of objectives for business organizations have been widely recognised: *economic* and *non-economic*. In addition, firms accept certain *constraints* and *responsibilities* which may influence their objectives.

3.1.1 Economic objectives

The focus of the classical microeconomic theory of the firm was on economic objectives – specifically that the firm could be represented by a single entrepreneur whose sole objective was to maximize profits. That this was a simplistic view which fitted conveniently into early economic thinking has long been realized, but profit maximization has remained a central tenet of business ideology. This view of economic objectives has, however, been increasingly challenged.

With the evolution of the joint stock company and the subsequent separation of ownership from control, a new concept of the economic objective of the firm has emerged. The distribution of ownership among a large number of shareholders has shifted control to a small group of professional managers who have little equity stake in the company and therefore little incentive to maximize profits. It is argued that these managers benefit more directly from maximizing the growth of the firm while maintaining a minimum acceptable level of profit for the shareholders.

A further challenge to profit maximization came from Drucker (1958) who proposed *survival* as the central purpose of the firm. Drucker's thesis is that to ensure long-term survival a firm may have to accept short-term objectives that conflict with profit maximization.

It is instructive to relate these three theories to the construction industry.

The ease with which an individual may enter the construction industry, coupled with the prospect of high rewards for hard work, have encouraged the formation of a large number of entrepreneurially led firms. The majority of these firms have remained small but, according to Channon's 1976 study, many of the largest construction firms were dominated by enterpreneurs or by their descendants. It might, therefore, be expected that profit maximization would be a prime objective of construction firms if classical economic theory is correct, but in practice this is seldom true. There is evidence that, for the most part, construction firms do not seek to maximize profits but rather, pursue other objectives. Above a certain level of profit the entrepreneur may value his leisure or partaking in civic duties more highly than profit and 'there is considerable support in the contracting industry for the idea that contracting is a "way of life" and that many contractors would not wish to cease business even if they could obtain a higher return on their capital and labour by using it in some other way' (Hillebrandt 1974). The spectacular growth of the largest UK construction corporations between 1919 and 1939, and especially since 1945 has often been accompanied by modest profit performance which seems to point to a preference for growth rather than profitability.

A similar effect has been noted where the separation of ownership and control has occured in construction firms which supports the second theory.

There is little doubt that Drucker's survival motive is dominant in construction firms of all sizes. In times of recession in the industry there is a well-known tendency for contractors to 'buy' work by submitting tenders for building projects at cost or less to maintain their workload and ensure survival.

Typical economic objectives for a contracting firm given by Barnard (1981) are:

> growth of turnover, earnings, market share in existing markets and number of markets in which the firm operates (types of construction clients, localities, etc.); stability of annual gross turnover, gross profit, return on investments (ratio of gross profit to total assets, fixed assets or shareholders equity) and in utilization of scarce physical or human resources held by the firm.

These objectives can be expressed in terms of specific targets to be achieved during a specified period of time.

3.1.2 Non-economic objectives

Non-economic objectives are less tangible and are often a reflection of the basic philosophy of the firm's founders or owners. They represent principles of business conduct which cannot be quantified but which exercise considerable influence on strategic thinking.

In addition, there are the objectives of other participants in the firm. These result from a more complex and realistic view of the firm than that of traditional economic theory. The firm is seen as a collection of divergent interests – managers, workers, shareholders, suppliers, clients, etc. – each with their own objectives. The reconciliation of these interests is a major part of the strategic management role.

These objectives will act as a modifying influence on the primary economic objectives. This modification may be the outcome of direct management action in recognition of the participant's wishes or be arrived at by negotiation between a 'coalition' of the firm's members, as envisaged by Cyert and March (1963).

Typical non-economic objectives for a contracting firm, put forward by Barnard (1981), are:

> ... internal political, e.g. retention of control by the existing owners or board; external political, e.g. to avoid intervention by central, local or other government bodies; to meet reasonable aspirations of employees and to develop them to their full potential; to serve clients and the general community well; to maintain a good reputation within the industry.

3.1.3 Constraints

Anything which limits the firm's freedom of action is a constraint. Broadly, constraints may be *external* (e.g. public reaction) or *internal* (e.g. company policy).

3.1.4 Responsibilities

These are obligations which a firm undertakes and which have no direct bearing on its economic objectives. Sponsorship is one example which many companies are assuming.

3.2 Decide strategy

Having clarified the objectives of the business, together with any constraints and responsibilities that will be assumed, the next step is to determine the courses of action that will be taken in pursuit of those objectives. The courses of action open to the firm will depend on the capabilities of the company and the opportunities in the market which the firm is able to exploit. Key activities to be undertaken, as shown in Fig. 3.1, are an *internal appraisal* of the company's performance and capabilities, an *external appraisal* of the opportunities and threats in the firm's market environment, a *comparison of the results* of the internal and external appraisals to identify the options available to the business, and finally the *evaluation of alternative courses of action*.

3.2.1 Internal appraisal

The purpose of the internal appraisal is to identify the strengths and weaknesses of the business in order to build up a 'capability profile' of the firm, i.e. to find out what the firm does well and what it does badly. The firm's managers may feel that they know this already, but they are often surprised at the results of this review. The internal appraisal entails the analysis of key aspects of the business, some of which are now discussed.

(a) Corporate trading performance
This is a review of the financial performance of the whole business and the comparative performance of the various parts of the business during its recent

past, say the last five years. Standard financial measures of profitability and growth, discussed in Chapter 10, will be used to compare the performance of the business with that of other firms of a similar size and character and to conduct an internal comparison of the cost and profit centres of the business. The basis for this analysis can be the raw financial data obtained from the firm's balance sheets and profit and loss accounts, or the use of ratio analysis through membership of such organizations as Interfirm Comparison, which is particularly helpful in conducting comparisons with other businesses. The results of this survey will show how well or how badly the firm has performed in the recent past, and the relative success of the departments and divisions of the business.

(b) Current services and products

The services and products offered by construction firms usually require the co-ordinated efforts of several departments or divisions in the firms and it is therefore useful to trace the costs and profits of each service or product. In view of the strong building project base of most construction firms, it is vital to study the contract trading analysis. This involves studying recent and current contracts to see if there is any significant difference in profitability between different types and sizes of contract and whether there are any discernable trends, i.e. increasing or declining returns. The results of this analysis should point to those types of project which the firm is able to complete successfully with high profit margins. A further comparison of the contribution of each type of contract to turnover and profits is often very revealing.

(c) Organizational analysis

The organization structure of the firm should be examined and its design carefully charted. This is essential because most structures are the result of piecemeal decisions taken as the firm grew and the business will almost certainly need reorganizing to meet the demands of current and new strategies. An inventory of the background, training, and expertise of working principals and key personnel should be built up from personnel records. The total expertise of the firm will restrict its choice of strategies, unless it is prepared to import those skills from outside the business. The identification of areas of skill in which the firm is deficient is a by-product of this analysis. The firm's record of manpower planning, industrial relations, and safety should also be reviewed at this stage. The method of conducting such a review is described in Chapters 4, 5, and 6.

(d) Management succession

From the inventory of principals and key personnel it should be possible to draw up a management succession plan to meet the firm's short- and long-term management requirements. The preparation of this plan frequently reveals a distinct lack of competent middle managers capable of filling the top jobs without considerable further training and development.

(e) Employee attitude
The aspirations of employees and their attitude to changes which the firm may wish to introduce must be ascertained by direct questioning or by the administration of a questionnaire. Resistance to change is often encountered in construction firms although, equally frequently, changes are viewed as career opportunities and anticipated with enthusiasm. The trend towards greater participation by all employees in strategic decision-making means that firms must give increasing weight to consultations of this kind.

(f) Company position in markets
Tendering success ratios should be calculated by contractors for each type of work and compared with local and national competitors. A related calculation will give the keenness of mark-up on tenders and the influence of adjustments in that mark-up on the success ratios. It is often salutary to realize that a significant increase in mark-up could be made, adding considerably to profitability, without any marked effect on the success rate of tendering.

(g) Control systems
The opportunity should be taken at the time of this general review of the company to examine the control systems the business operates. The systems employed by construction firms are sometimes antiquated and have not kept pace with the increasingly sophisticated information needs of the business, both at head office and site levels. The relative cheapness of today's microcomputer systems means that almost any size of business can afford an appropriate installation. Precise control of labour, materials, and plant is now possible.

(h) Fixed assets
The physical facilities which a firm has are often underutilized – a valuable head office site, a plant yard, a joinery shop, and so on. Although the working capital requirements of construction firms are generally lower than other types of firm it is grossly inefficient to have money unnecessarily tied up in fixed assets.

(i) Company policy
An important, and frequently overlooked, contribution to the strengths and weaknesses of a business is the policy of the decision-makers in the firm. Policy will preclude certain options from consideration and will thus limit the strategies the firm can pursue. For example, the directors of some contracting firms have a policy which states that they will not work for certain types of client or undertake some types of work, e.g. speculative housing.

The end result of the internal appraisal will be a list of the firm's strengths and weaknesses, which is effectively a current capability profile of the business. This list will be used to screen opportunities which are identified during the external appraisal and also serve as a starting point for the development of the business.

The results may be so damning that they trigger immediate action to ensure survival, as shown in Fig. 3.1.

3.2.2 External appraisal

The purpose of the external appraisal is to forecast the pattern of demand and competition in the forward planning period – it is forward looking in contrast to the largely backward-looking internal appraisal. It will entail market research to find present and potential opportunities and to enable the firm to assess the strength of the threats in its environment.

This appraisal should preferably be conducted in parallel with the internal appraisal, and on no account should decisions be taken before the results of both appraisals are available.

As well as being forward looking, this analysis is, by definition, outward looking to events and trends occurring outside the firm and also probably outside the firm's control. The volume of information currently available about these events and trends requires a firm to limit its search to the few aspects which will vitally affect its business. In narrowing its search the firm may have to call on the services of outside experts, for example, consultants and forecasting bodies.

In conducting the external appraisal the business can concentrate on five broad areas: *competitive* trends, *political* trends, and *economic, social,* and *technological* trends. The first four areas can be further analysed by adding a geographical dimension, considering the effect of these trends at the *local, national,* and *international* levels.

Before examining each of these areas, the problem of uncertainty must be recognized. Any appraisal which focuses on future events in a rapidly changing environment must be subject to considerable uncertainty, and the results obtained regarded with a degree of scepticism. Uncertainty can be reduced to an extent by obtaining better and more reliable information from specialist organizations, but, as previously pointed out, the use of sophisticated techniques is no guarantee of accuracy and in some cases may even be counter-productive. The firm can further contain uncertainty by restricting its attention to a small number of major opportunities and threats, as suggested earlier, and by the device of specifying a range of probable results with a minimum and maximum accepted level – for example, if one forecast is for a 5 per cent growth in industrial building demand and another is for a 3 per cent growth, these can be taken as maximum and minimum targets for the firm and the consequences of each being achieved for the firm's future prospects can be calculated. This will give a range of results acceptable to the company and, because of the wider focus, greater certainty of a successful outcome.

(a) Competitive trends

This is the study of the present and possible future actions of competitors, and of competitive changes in the markets in which the firm is interested – for example the entry of new competitors, mergers and failures of competitors, new forms of competition, and so on. An understanding of competitive trends is of particular importance in an industry such as construction, where competition is fierce. Competition on price alone through a system of competitive tendering is currently giving way to selection based on wider criteria and contractors are responding by offering design-and-build, management contracting, and other novel services to clients. In the wake of recent changes in their code of conduct, architects are also becoming more competitive and extending their services through forward and backward integration into pre-design activities and production management respectively. Local patterns of competition are quite different between regions – there is a marked contrast, for example, between the South West and the London area. Nationally in the UK fewer large projects are being undertaken than in the 1960s and early 1970s, and this has created greater competition among the larger contractors and professional practices who have the capability to compete for this type of work. This has led these larger firms to seek expansion in international markets, where initially British companies were very successful, particularly in the Gulf states and former British colonies, but recently there has been increasing international competition from Japan, Korea, and America. Relevant competitive trends need to be carefully monitored by the systematic and continuous collection of data. Sources of information about competitive trends are published data (company reports, press cutttings, etc.) and from personal contacts, i.e. institutional meetings, conferences, suppliers representatives, etc.

(b) Political trends

While, as stated previously, a legitimate objective of a firm might be 'to avoid intervention by central, local, and other government bodies', no business today can be immune from political pressure in its various forms. At local level, protracted delays in obtaining planning permission, and the curtailment of local public sector building programmes, have drastically affected many contracting and professional firms. Besides being an important client to the construction industry, the national government can act indirectly through legislation on safety, tax, noise, employment, etc., and through the regulation of the economy, to affect construction companies. Construction firms operating overseas frequently encounter the problems of political instability and the fact that construction projects often assume political importance as evidence of economic prosperity.

(c) Economic trends

It is difficult to distinguish between economic and political trends because of their interdependence. Economists refer to construction demand as 'derived' demand that arises indirectly as a result of the need for buildings and facilites to house and service the production and distribution of goods and services. Construction demand is, therefore, closely related to the health of the economy at local, national, and international levels. In particular, the business climate and the level of investment are critical factors which any construction firm would be wise to study. Economic trends in regional development, the treatment of urban decay, the regulation of the economy, the manipulation of interest rates, and national economic growth and decline are important indicators for construction firms.

(d) Social trends

These include demographic movements, as building generally follows population concentrations, and changes in education, working hours, housing, leisure, retirement, sports provision, and holiday patterns. For example, time-sharing of holiday accommodation offers opportunities to develop previously uneconomic sites which many developers and construction firms have seized. Pressure groups, particularly those concerned with conservation, may pose a threat to proposed construction projects. The scope and significance of social change in any strategic planning period is so enormous that some professional help in interpreting the signs is almost essential.

(e) Technological trends

Construction firms are likely to be affected by technological changes in two areas: business systems and site systems. Microelectronics revolutionized business systems with cheap, reliable, and sophisticated equipment to perform a wide variety of data handling and processing activities. This offers construction firms the facilities for project monitoring not available before. At site level a gradual change in materials, methods, and equipment will continue. Instances of technological innovations on site are the use of plastics (especially in plumbing), trussed rafters, timber-framed housing systems, and materials handling equipment. The popularity of timber-framed houses reflects an underlying social change of attitude by purchasers and building societies.

The conclusion of the external appraisal will be the compilation of a list of opportunities currently and potentially open to the business, counter-balanced by a list of threats that the firm faces in the strategic planning period. These opportunities and threats should then be ranked in terms of, first, the impact the occurrence of such events would have on the firm and, second the likelihood of their occurrence. This ranking will act as a screening device, leaving only those opportunities and threats of strategic significance for further strategic debate.

3.2.3 Comparison of the results of the internal and external appraisal

This is the point in the formulation process at which realistic options for the business are established. As indicated previously, the internal and external appraisals will probably be prepared concurrently and thus independently. This is, therefore, the first occasion on which the strengths and weaknesses of the business can be compared with the opportunities and threats in the firm's environment – and a salutary experience it often is!

Certain opportunities can be eliminated immediately as being inappropriate for the firm, and some threats discounted as being irrelevant. The remaining opportunities should be ranked as probables – those that match the firm's strengths – and possibles – those that the firm might be able to exploit if it is prepared to introduce changes into its organization to strengthen specific areas of the business. The conversion of these probable and possible opportunities into concrete courses of action is the last activity in deciding strategy.

3.2.4 Evaluate alternative courses of action

Any firm is faced with four possible courses of action: *existing* strategies, *expansion* strategies, *diversification* strategies, and *shrinkage* strategies. These are illustrated in Fig. 3.2.

(a) Existing strategies
This is basically continuing to offer existing services to existing markets. Provided that this is a conscious strategic decision and not the result of abdicated responsibility, it is a sound strategy for most firms. Choosing this course of action should not be thought to imply 'no change' however, for the business could seek a greater market share from existing clients, or better profits from existing products or services through increased efficiency.

(b) Expansion strategies
Various expansion strategies are shown in Fig 3.2 but the common feature is that one of the dimensions of strategy – either services/products or clients/ geographical area – is held constant, while the other dimension is progressively changed, preferably in the directions indicated by the arrows. Vertical expansion on the matrix is called market development; examples are a contractor undertaking the construction of standard factory units for an existing client in a

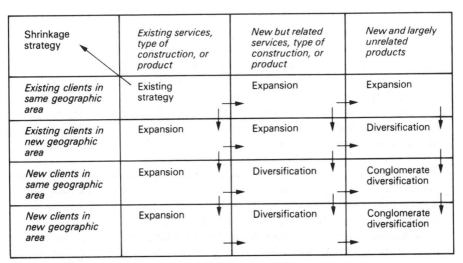

Shrinkage strategy	Existing services, type of construction, or product	New but related services, type of construction, or product	New and largely unrelated products
Existing clients in same geographic area	Existing strategy	Expansion	Expansion
Existing clients in new geographic area	Expansion	Expansion	Diversification
New clients in same geographic area	Expansion	Diversification	Conglomerate diversification
New clients in new geographic area	Expansion	Diversification	Conglomerate diversification

Fig. 3.2 Alternative growth strategies (after Grinyer, 1972)

new region of the country, or a speculative housing developer offering the same house types to new purchasers in a new geographic area. Horizontal expansion in Fig. 3.2 is called product service development; typical examples are an architectural practice offering pre-design site selection services to clients through backward integration, or a contractor moving into property development, as many contractors have done, through forward integration.

(c) Diversification strategies

Two forms of this strategy are shown in Fig. 3.2 – diversification and conglomerate diversification – but these are simply a matter of degree. The significant feature is that change is occurring on both dimensions of strategy at the same time; the firm is introducing new and largely unrelated products or services to new clients and possibly in a new geographic area. Construction examples would be a London – based building contractor establishing a chain of Do-It-Yourself shops in the north-east of England, or a quantity surveying practice operating in the UK offering project management services to clients in the Middle East.

(d) Shrinkage strategies

The management literature only recognizes the foregoing three strategies; it is assumed that, if a business changes, it will expand or diversify. There seems to be almost a 'growth ethic' in any discussions on business strategy. Construction firms have always prided themselves on their flexibility – the ability to expand and contract as demand fluctuates – which is seen as an essential prerequisite for any business in the construction industry. Devices, such as subcontracting, are used to facilitate this flexibility. The acknowledgement of shrinkage as a legitimate strategy for construction firms is made by Lansley *et al.* (1979), who identify two types: *retrievable* shrinkage and *irretrievable* shrinkage. Retrievable shrinkage is defined as 'shrinkage while retaining the character of the business so that it may be easily reversed; for example, reduction in staffing and overhead costs'. Irretrievable shrinkage is 'shrinkage which alters the character of the business and which cannot readily be reversed; for example, closures of sub-offices or sister firms and not maintaining contact with the work'. A third form mentioned by Lansley *et al.* is *considerable* shrinkage which is a 'major reduction in activities, cessation of trading'. This is presumably involuntary and therefore not a strategy at all. The two previous strategies may be forced on the firm by circumstances, but if a deliberate decision is taken to reduce business activities then that is a tenable strategy.

Two important considerations will influence a firm's choice of strategy; namely, *risk* and *synergy*. Continuing existing strategies involves the least risk as the firm is offering familiar services to well-known markets and clients. Both expansion and shrinkage strategies involve a greater degree of risk the further the business moves from its existing strategy into semi-familiar territory; there is the danger with expansion that the firm may overreach itself and in pursuing a shrinkage strategy it may sink to an 'irretrievable' level. The greatest risk, however, lies in diversification strategies where the firm is offering unfamiliar services to little known or unknown markets and clients. Only if objectives cannot be achieved with existing strategies should expansion or shrinkage strategies be considered, and only when these strategies have been exhausted should diversification be entertained. A business owes it to its members not to take unnecessary risks.

Synergy is an important concept in business strategy. It is often described as the '2 + 2 = 5' effect to denote the fact that the business seeks a strategy with a combined performance that is greater than the sum of its parts. Synergy is a measure of joint effects which accrue from the economies of scale of a combined operation, economies which may occur in any area of the business – marketing, production, investment, plant, research, management, or any other sector. For example, a speculative house builder may find synergistic opportunities in local authority house building because of production and financial control synergy. A contractor with a strong joinery division could seek synergy in the manufacture of timber-framed housing components to obtain economies in marketing, administration, and production. By definition, synergy is greater in expansion than in diversification , which is another good reason for following the strategy sequence described under 'risk'.

The evaluation of the risk and the synergy potential of an opportunity is a critical part of the role of strategic management in the business. Further evaluation of specific strategies would include the resources required (human, physical, and financial) to support the strategy, the practical steps required to convert the strategy into action, and a final reconciliation of each strategy with the objectives, strengths, and weaknesses of the business, particularly whether it will enable the firm to meet its financial targets. This final screening should leave the few useful strategies which are appropriate for a particular business.

(e) Strategic mode

One further decision must be made concerning the *strategic mode*; that is, the way in which the selected strategies will be implemented. To decide strategy is rather more than just deciding strategies; consideration must also be given to the means to be adopted by the business in operating these strategies. Again the firm has four choices: *acquisition* or *merger*, *joint ventures*, *licences* or *agencies*, and *service/product development*.

1. Acquisition or merger. One method of achieving rapid expansion or diversification is to acquire or initiate a merger with a complementary firm. This mode is often associated with aggresive entrepreneurially led firms, but in fact is a conservative policy. Taking over a firm with a fund of expertise in a particular area, whether that is a service/product area or a geographical area, avoids the problems of starting from scratch and the danger of costly mistakes. This is called *start-up synergy,* for considerable cost and time savings can be made by acquiring a going concern. Many of the largest construction corporations in the UK have adopted this strategic mode to achieve phenomenal rates of growth in the last twenty years (Channon 1978). Other less ambitious contractors and professional practices have also found this an attractive way to grow and diversify.

2. Joint ventures. The main advantages in undertaking a joint venture with another firm are the pooling of experience and the sharing of risks. This mode has been found to be particularly advantageous to contracting and professional firms when undertaking large and complex overseas construction projects, but has also been successfully used by construction firms in the UK. This method allows a business to participate in projects that would otherwise be outside the scope of their experience and finances: for example, a joint venture between a joinery firm and a house builder to promote timber-framed housing. Another well-established method in the construction industry is a joint venture between a client and a construction company – e.g. a landowner and a private house builder – who agree to share the profits of their joint enterprise; or an agreement to co-operate between a local authority which possesses land but has no money to develop it and a developer who has expertise and finance but no land. The problems are those of any marriage of convenience – namely, work-sharing and profit-sharing disagreements.

3. Licences or agencies. This is a useful means of avoiding the costs of research and development and of gaining a well-tried and successful product or system without incurring a substantial investment. Many construction firms have obtained licences to manufacture, market, and erect prefabricated building systems in precast concrete, steel, and timber. During the government sponsored industrialized building era of the 1960s some large contractors obtained permission to manufacture precast concrete flat systems developed by European companies and invested in the building of precasting yards which, in the event, proved to be loss-makers and were ultimately closed. Similar experiences were encountered a decade later with North Sea oil platforms. An agency is a popular method where a service is involved; e.g. cavity wall insulation, drain clearance, etc.

4. Service/product development. This strategic mode is distinct from the previous methods in entailing entirely internal growth. This home-grown approach has been a feature of the strategy of the largest UK construction companies and professional firms since World War II (Channon 1978) and a popular method with construction firms of all sizes. The disadvantages of high investment and slow development are considered to be more than offset by the enhanced career opportunities for loyal staff and the higher degree of control that the firm retains over operations. With the elimination of sharing and licensing costs, profits can ultimately be higher.

If one or a combination of the first three methods is chosen by the strategic managers in the business, then the firm faces a lengthy and painstaking period of negotiation. It may only be possible at this stage in the planning process to specify the strategies to be pursued and initiate investigations into various strategic modes, but decisions should be made about both elements of strategy. As already indicated, certain strategies and strategic modes are naturally complementary – for example, expansion into related services and the services/product development mode, or diversification and acquisition – but each combination should be carefully studied before any long-term commitments are made.

The formulation of strategy is now complete. The business has systematically set its objectives and targets, identified its strengths and weaknesses, assessed the opportunities and threats in the market, sifted through a plethora of possible strategies and strategic modes, and selected those few major strategies that will guide the business through the coming planning period. The next step is to compile these decisions into a concise document that can be published to members of the firm, thus forming the framework within which tactical decisions can be taken.

3.3 The strategic plan

The strategic plan is the explicit statement of business strategy. It should contain a synthesis of the findings and decisions made during the formulation stage. It is the means of communicating the findings and decisions to those people responsible for converting the strategies into operational plans. It will also be the yardstick against which the performance of the whole business and the efficiency of the departments and divisions of the business will be judged.

3.3.1 Presentation

It follows from what has been said that the strategic plan is a written document, but this does not mean it is a complete and final statement of business strategy. While some strategies within the control of the firm can be implemented immediately, with a reasonable degree of confidence in their success, others will have to be investigated and their viability tested. It would be inappropriate, therefore, to present the plan in a printed leather bound form which would give a false impression of finality – it is essentially a working document to be amended as circumstances change and strategies are confirmed or rejected. It is a starting point for strategic and tactical action.

3.3.2 Style

There is no right way or wrong way of writing the plan; it may be in narrative, tabular, or diagrammatic form, or more likely a combination of all three. The overriding consideration is clarity, and the style of presentation should be suited to the element of the plan under consideration, the personality of the drafter, and the time and resources which the firm can devote to it. To produce a concise document the main elements of the plan can be given in broad, summarized form with supporting detailed data contained in appendices.

3.3.3 Length

There can be no prescribed length for the plan but, as with all business reports, it should be as short as possible; Argenti (1980) suggests that ten to fifteen typed pages should be sufficient for most firms. The danger of becoming involved in too much detail will increase with the number of words. Details of all the debates that took place before decisions were made need not be included; nor *every* strategy that was considered and rejected. Certain features of the firm will influence the length:

(a) A complex firm pursuing a highly diversified, multinational strategy will probably require a longer plan than a single service/product type business operating within the UK.
(b) As a general rule, a large corporation will need a thicker document than a smaller firm, but this is not necessarily so and depends on the other factors mentioned.
(c) A business which is facing a crisis should, in addition to instigating immediate tactical action as suggested earlier, formulate a long-term strategy for the business as a matter of urgency to hopefully avoid a repetition of present circumstances. Such a plan is likely to be longer than the plan of a similar but more stable business.
(d) An ambitious and thrusting strategic management will be operating a wider range of strategies than a less ambitious business.
(e) A firm with a centralized and autocratic style of leadership that is limited to those strategies which appeal to the top management will probably produce a shorter document than that produced by a more participative company.

3.3.4 Content

There is little concensus in theory or practice about what a strategic plan should contain; nor should there be. It has been stressed previously that every business will adopt a unique strategy related to internal and environmental situations, and will thus require a unique strategic plan. However, there are some guidelines which provide a framework within which a firm can develop its individual plan.

(a) Introduction
This section should define the scope of the plan, the period it covers, the deliberately prescribed limitations, and the relationship of this plan to other previous and present plans, if any. Some idea of the broad philosophical underpinning of the plan might also be given.

(b) Assumptions
The assumptions that are important for an understanding of the plan should be stated. This would include statements about the extent of government interven-

tion (e.g. registration, nationalization, mandatory fee scales, etc.), markets, clients continuing to patronize the firm, successful completion of current ventures and projects, key personnel remaining with the firm, and so on. The risk, if any, if these assumptions are not realized should be assessed and stated here or later in the plan.

(c) Economic objectives and targets

The broad financial expectations from pursuing the strategies stated in the plan should be given here with detailed supporting data relegated to the appendix and cross-referenced to this section. A statement of the annual economic expectations for the period covered in the plan would be given in terms of:

- *Profitability:* the expected increase in pre-tax profits on assets employed in each year of the plan. This should be given in actual figures and percentage terms, highlighting the differences between the first and last year of the plan.
- *Profits:* the improvement in gross and net profits on value of work done in the period of the plan.
- *Value of work done:* the increase in value of work undertaken by the firm in each year of the plan given in figures adjusted for inflation.
- *Dividends:* the percentage of profits after corporation tax to be distributed to ordinary shareholders, the balance to be retained in the company.

These and other objectives could also be given in the form of ratios, as discussed earlier. Cash flow projections would be shown in this part of the plan, as would a review of the recent performance of the firm compared to the objectives of the last plan or related to similar businesses.

The device of using minimum and maximum targets to give a wider spread of acceptable results as a bulwark against uncertainty could usefully be employed here.

(d) Non-economic objectives, constraints, and responsibilites

The basic philosophy of the business mentioned in (a) would be extended in this section to indicate how the objectives and aspirations of owners, employees, clients, etc., are to be met. Constraints which have a bearing on the strategies selected, whether from sources inside or outside the business, should be stated here, as should the responsibilities the firm will assume. This section of the plan will often form the basis of a policy statement published by top management as a permanent part of company documentation and literature.

(e) Current strengths and weaknesses

A list of the current strengths and weaknesses of the business gleaned from the internal appraisal and possibly presented under the headings suggested in 3.2.1 would constitute this part of the plan. They should be cross-referenced to those strategies which will exploit the firm's strengths and to those strategies designed to correct or compensate for the weaknesses identified. Some weaknesses will not be resolved in the planning period and should be stated as such.

(f) Opportunities and threats
This section should contain only those opportunities and threats for which specific strategies have been devised and should be cross-referenced accordingly. Again, a useful structure for this section would be that given in 3.2.2.

(g) Strategies
This section is the nub of the plan. There could be an introductory schedule of those strategies considered but rejected which would be 'first reserves' if the selected strategies proved untenable. The proposed courses of action to be adopted during the plan's life, in terms of strategies and strategic modes, can be classified in any way which is appropriate for the business – by present operations, by division, by departments, by business centres, by geographical regions, by country, etc.

When the plan has been drafted and agreed by all concerned it can be published and copies of the whole plan or parts of it given to those executives who will be responsible for its implementation.

3.4 Introducing business strategy to the firm

The problem of introducing business strategy to a firm is the problem of changing the attitudes of the managers in that firm. As stressed in 2.3, it is not a technique but rather a style of management which must be adopted by the firm's strategic decision makers. Although, as described in this chapter, a seemingly mechanistic process is followed, the adoption of this process is symptomatic of a fundametal change of attitude by the firm's strategic mangers. It is the cultivation of a 'whole business' view among the firm's top management and, in particular, by the chief executive or chief partner. Unless the firm's leaders are convinced of the necessity for a business strategy, and *show* that they believe in its importance by their positive attitude and actions, then the whole exercise is doomed to failure.

To change attitudes takes longer than that required to introduce a technique. To run through the formulation process (described in this chapter) for the first time will take a year or more. There must be a continuing commitment to the control of the progress of the plan for its life-span, the making of modifications to the plan if and as required, and the preparation of a new plan when the old plan is exhausted. It is through this long-term cycle of activities that the attitudes and habits of people are gradually reshaped and reinforced by the success or failure of the business strategy process.

It is because of this extended time-scale for introducing business strategy to a firm that it may be necessary to take certain urgent steps to ensure the survival of the firm as mentioned in 3.2.1, but management must beware that this approach does not become a style of management – often called 'crisis management', which is endemic in many construction firms. The only successful long-term antidote to such a style of management is the adoption of a formal and systematic approach to formulating and implementing business strategy.

To change attitudes will require education as well as time. The education of management can be achieved through a series of practical steps which will be described later, but first the way in which business strategy evolves within a firm will be considered.

3.4.1 The evolution of business strategy systems

Five major types of strategic decision-making systems adopted by construction firms were identified by Woolven (1978):

(a) *Ad hoc*
(b) Extended budgeting
(c) Partially formalized
(d) Formalized
(e) Strategic management

The five systems represent stages in the evolution of business strategy, and were defined by Woolven as:

(a) Ad hoc
The first planning system is characterized by low sophistication. The planning effort is slight and is irregular and informal. Planning only occurs when there is a crisis, and is not therefore a continuous process. Firms using this system are 'reactors', waiting for opportunities and problems to arise before paying them any attention. They seek only one 'acceptable' course of action to achieve objectives, often the first one considered. There is a lack of overall direction or strategy and, as a result, decisions are disjointed and managers 'muddle-through', i.e. they have no clear goals, they only act when forced to, they consider only a few convenient alternatives, and they attempt to take the easiest course of action. This system is typical of that used by small-sized construction firms.

(b) Extended budgeting
The next recognizable system is 'extended budgeting'. There is now a recognition of the need to undertake planning. Although the planning effort is still informal it is now relatively regular (i.e. annual), but the method adopted is still naïve. Top management's concern is still on operational matters rather than strategy; as a result, planning tends to be little more than half-year financial budgeting exercises. The annual financial budgets (referring mainly to costs) are used as the basis for operating plans. There is little consideration of strategic matters and planning consists of an unquestioned extension of what the firm is already doing, and in the same markets. As the planning is not explicit it is not recognized by managers throughout the organization as company policy. This system is used by many medium-sized construction firms.

(c) Partially formalized

The next system is partially formalized and marks the stage at which organizations begin to attempt to act strategically. There is now a positive formalized planning effort with top management devoting time, money, and energy to planning activities. At about this stage it is possible that a specialist corporate planner will be introduced into the organization. Although the planning is now formal it may still remain irregular, reacting to trigger signals, i.e. to solve *one* particular problem or to investigate *one* particular opportunity. It is not yet a continuous process; nor is it fully comprehensive or rational and there is no overall integration of the planning effort. Firms with this type of planning are likely to be medium-sized to large construction firms.

(d) Formalized

This is the system described in this chapter. Planning is not only formal, it is also regular. Large construction firms are likely to adopt such a planning system.

(e) Strategic management

Beyond this fourth planning system three further possible developments are likely to occur. First, the traditional resistance towards planning may overcome the planning effort. Typically this occurs when the initial enthusiasm of the chief executive towards planning wanes. This may come about because of the failure of planning to fulfil what was expected of it, or because of the use of a system which is too inflexible or bureaucratic to cope with a rapidly changing environment. When this does occur the planning system reverts to a partially formalized system.

Second, when a firm achieves a very large size, or when it manages to obtain a major share of a market, it becomes a dominant firm. Owing to its size, and the resultant reputation for ability, the dominant firm is constantly being presented with opportunities. It does not, therefore, require an aggressive planning system to search out opportunities and may revert to a partially formalized system.

Third, it is becoming apparent that even a fully formalized planning system has its limitations unless it is accompanied by a fundamental and permanent change of attitude by the management of an enterprise. This stage is reached when strategic thinking not only becomes engrained in top management but pervades the whole organization whereby all managers think and act strategically. The basic philosophy of strategic management is that strategic thinking should transcend the whole organization; it should not be confined horizontally across the organization (i.e. top management) but should penetrate vertically through it to all levels of management. This approach was discussed earlier in 2.3.1.

In his survey, Woolven was unable to identify any construction firms which fitted into this last category. What did emerge from a comparison of all the firms was a clear picture of the evolution of the business strategy system as a firm grew and diversified. This is further confirmation of the complementary changes which accompany the evolution of a firm's strategy and organization structure, as discussed in 2.4.

3.4.2 Introducing business strategy: practical steps

There appears to be a widely accepted sequence of steps to follow when introducing business strategy to a firm.

(a) Convince the chief executive

This is particularly important, and most difficult, in the entrepreneurially led firm; but in firms of all leadership modes a genuine business strategy can never be developed unless the chief executive believes in a systematic approach to business strategy and initiates, supports, and maintains the necessary action to bring it to fruition.

(b) Generate enthusiasm in top management

Not only the chief executive but his whole team must be harnessed to the considerable task of overcoming resistance and even hostility to the changes which will follow the introduction of business strategy by setting an example of enthusiasm and a willingness to accept these changes.

(c) Choose the strategic management mode

It was suggested in 2.3.2 that an internal or an external mode for managing business strategy activities could be adopted. The choice must now be made between appointing external consultants or non-executive directors and the appointment of a corporate planner or the creation of a business strategy team. A combination of these options is often adopted in practice when, say, a team of top executives is assembled, assisted by either a corporate planner, a consultant, or a non-executive director acting as secretary and adviser to the group. As stated in 2.3.2, the method currently favoured is the creation of a team of managers from within the firm to obtain commitment to the strategies agreed, and further, to encourage wider participation in strategic decision-making at all levels. The following steps assume that this policy will be adopted by the chief executive.

(d) Form a business strategy team

The composition and constitution of this team is critical to the success of any business strategy effort. The chairmanship should automatically fall to the chief executive to stress the importance attached to this exercise, and to ensure a balance is achieved between the vested interests of the various top managers in the team and the parts of the company they represent. It will also give the team authority to obtain information that may be vital but confidential, and to make and implement strategic decisions. The position of secretary has already been discussed in (c) above and involves the normal duties of recording decisions, offering advice, progressing action between meetings, etc. The remaining members of the team must be selected carefully to obtain the balance of opinion and expertise mentioned earlier, within the context of a particular company. The problem is seldom who to bring into the team, but who to leave out. Some members will be automatically seconded to the team because of their powerful positions in the company, but others will be selected according to the specific strategies being considered – for example, the chief estimator if new types of work are to be sought, and according to the firm's views on the extent of participation, contracts managers, site managers, or job architects might be invited to join the team.

(e) Train the team
It will almost certainly be necessary to conduct a training programme about business strategy for the members of the team when a formal system is first introduced to the firm. This may take the form of:

1. individual discussions with each member of the team by an experienced corporate planner or consultant;
2. the publication and use of a corporate planning manual as described in Hussey (1974), Chapter 20;
3. running an in-company seminar with the help of inside or outside experts (which has the advantage of being tailored to the firm's unique needs);
4. attendance at an external corporate planning conference or course (where all or only part of the subject matter may be relevant to the firm).

Frequently a combination of these methods is adopted.

(f) Communications in the firm
At this point in the process it would be advisable to call a meeting of all the staff, or at least key individuals, to inform them of the pending introduction of a systematic approach to business strategy and to canvass opinions and attitudes to this new way of running the business. If top management really values participation then the opportunity might be taken at this meeting to form syndicates under the leadership of a member of the planning team to discuss specific strategic issues. In addition to giving a greater sense of involvement and engendering enhanced commitment by all concerned, a wider basis for strategic decisions will result from tapping this reservoir of company experience.

(g) Strategy formulation meetings
A series of meetings of the business strategy team at approximately monthly intervals will then be needed to enact the process described in this chapter:

1. *Clarify objectives* (3–4 meetings taking approximately 3 months). The economic and non-economic objectives of the firm must be clarified together with the responsibilities and constraints to be assumed by the firm; these objectives should be quantified as far as possible in the form of targets.
2. *Decide strategy* (9–12 meetings taking approximately 9 months). This is the data collecting and sifting stage of the process so that meetings will review information as and when it becomes available as a result of the internal and external appraisals. The analysis of opportunities and threats and the conversion of these into specific strategies will dominate the latter meetings of this stage.

3. *Prepare strategic plan* (1–3 meetings taking approximately 1–3 months). The preparation and presentation of the plan may be completed quickly, or may take longer if it is to be published when wording may be critical.

Thus the formulation phase can typically take 12–18 months to complete.

(h) Implementation meetings
These will consist of regular meetings between executive team members and their subordinates to give directions and agree action plans, programmes, and budgets.

The whole business strategy team should meet every three months to monitor performance and control progress towards the objectives set in the plan. As discussed earlier, it may be necessary to modify the plan in the light of new circumstances.

3.4.3 Why business strategy sometimes fails

The introduction of business strategy to a firm is not an easy option; it is much easier to muddle through making ad hoc decisions as the need arises. Unless this in-built inertia can be overcome the failure of business strategy can be expected. Some typical causes of failure are:

(a) The chief executive does not believe in using a system for deciding strategy and does not support, or only half-heartedly supports, the planning effort.
(b) Even if the chief executive is enthusiastic, his key personnel may resist the introduction of business strategy for personal or parochial reasons, or just to maintain the status quo.
(c) All key personnel must be involved. If some managers are allowed to opt out of the process annd pursue their own individual strategies, then disillusionment with the planning effort will quickly spread to other members of the team.
(d) The sanctity of certain current activities of the firm may frustrate the introduction of a rational set of strategies and thus invalidate the process. All current strategies, however long-standing, should be rigorously reviewed during the internal appraisal, their compatibility with new strategies considered, and the decision to retain or reject them for the future taken as a result of rational analysis.
(e) A low level of participation by members of the business is often a cause of failure; lack of involvement breeds lack of commitment or even a desire to see the plan fail.
(f) As stated in 2.1.2, no strategic plan can succeed unless and until it is implemented. A failure to give adequate direction or to control progress will inevitably lead to failure.
(g) The attempt to handle too much detail or to make decisions that should be strictly operational will destroy any strategic planning effort.
(h) A similar effect will occur where over-sophisticated techniques and procedures swamp the goodwill and enthusiasm of everyone concerned. The excessive use of forms and computer print-outs is symptomatic of this effect.

These and other causes of failure can be avoided, as many firms enjoying the long-term benefits of a systematic approach to business strategy will testify.

Summary

Formulation of business strategy is the stage which is most easily, and often most readily, neglected by construction managers because of the pressure of recurring operational problems which are often urgent and sometimes important. The uncertain and unpredictable nature of building project operations demand a constant stream of tactical decisions which can all too easily squeeze out strategic thinking. Hence the need, particularly in construction firms, for a formal and systematic allocation of executive time and talent and other resources to the process of business strategy formulation.

Clarifying objectives, both current and proposed, is seen as an essential prerequisite to business strategy to give direction to the whole exercise. These objectives are of two types: economic and non-economic. In the construction industry economic objectives are considerably tempered by other business and individual motives and by non-economic objectives, constraints, and responsibilities.

The search for a unique strategy or set of strategies begins, when objectives have been established, with an internal appraisal of the business to determine its strengths and weaknesses together with an external appraisal of the firm's environment to identify the opportunities and threats which may be present.

Following these analyses, a synthesis of the agreed objectives and the findings of both internal and external appraisals must be produced.

The options thus identified are then subjected to progressive screening through the evaluation of possible courses of action and their consequences for the long-term future of the business. This is where a manager's judgement and intuition will be a vital foil to overconfidence in the accuracy of the results of the analysis and sythesis stages.

Ultimately strategic managers must make strategic decisions and commit these decisions to paper in the form of a strategic plan. This is an important formal communications exercise as well as the basis for the implementation of selected strategies.

While it is thought important, for the reasons given, that a firm adopt a systematic approach to business strategy as described in this chapter, it is recognized that other less sophisticated methods of strategy formulation exist in the construction industry. These less sophisticated systems are seen as stages in the evolution of the business strategy process within a firm and, although in practice these other systems are related to the size and type of construction firm, many more businesses than at present could profitably adopt a formal and systematic business strategy.

Not that the introduction of a business strategy system is likely to be easily or quickly accomplished; the success of this introduction will depend to a large extent on the commitment of the chief executive and the top management team, and the pace at which attitudes can be changed. A series of practical steps, starting with the gaining of this commitment, have been outlined; but following these steps is by no means a guarantee of success. Possible reasons for failure have been given as a guide to what should be avoided.

The long-term success of business strategy for any construction firm depends upon its becoming a style of management rather than just a process.

Questions

1. 'Organizations do not have objectives, only people have objectives.' Discuss this statement in the context of setting strategic objectives for a construction firm.
2. Why is profit maximization seldom a practical objective for construction firms despite the dominance of owner-managers in the industry?
3. Describe the steps involved in conducting an internal appraisal of a construction business to determine its strengths and weaknesses.
4. Discuss the relative importance of factors which may present opportunities or pose threats to a construction firm.
5. 'Synergy is greater in expansion than in diversification.' Discuss.
6. In formulating business strategy, is the sequence of activities important? Why or why not?
7. Distinguish between strategies and strategic modes and outline the strategic choices open to a construction firm.
8. Write a report to the managing director of a medium-sized construction firm describing the procedure for introducing a formal system of business strategy formulation to the company. Strategic decisions are currently made in an *ad hoc* way. Stress the problems likely to be encountered by the chief executive and suggest how these problems may be overcome.

References

Argenti, J. (1980) *Practical Corporate Planning*, George Allen & Unwin

Barnard, R. H. (1981) A strategic appraisal system for small firms, *Building Technology and Management*, Sept., pp. 21–4

Channon, D. F. (1978) *The Service Industries – Strategy, Structure and Financial Performance*, Macmillan

Cyert, R. M. and March, J. G. (1963) *A Behavioral Theory of the Firm*, Prentice Hall: Englewood Cliffs, NJ

Drucker, P. F. (1958) Business objectives and survival needs: notes on a discipline of business enterprise, *The Journal of Business*, **31**, no. 2 (Apr.), pp. 81–90

Grinyer, P. H. (1972) Systematic strategic planning for construction firms, *Building Technology and Management*, Feb. p. 8

Hillebrandt, P. M. (1974) *Economic Theory and the Construction Industry*, Macmillan
Hussey, D. E. (1974) *Corporate Planning Theory and Practice*, Pergamon Press
Lansley P. R., Quince, T. A. and Lea, F. E. (1979) *Flexibility and Efficiency in Construction Management*, Ashridge Management College
Woolven, D. R. (1978) 'A Comparative Study of Theoretical and Empirical Investigations into Strategic Decision-Making in Construction Firms,' Unpublished MSc thesis, University College, London

Chapter 4

Industrial relations

In most developed countries, the topic of industrial relations is at the forefront of managers' minds when attempting to run industrial organizations. The focus of the debate has often been the manufacturing industry, but periodically the building industry has seen sharp struggles between management and labour.

The post-war period in the British building industry has been characterized by an uneasy alliance between the parties to the industrial relations machinery. In a sense this is due to the well-established pattern of bargaining within the industry and the relative numerical weakness of the allied trade unions.

This review of the industrial relations system in construction is broken down into six sections:

4.1 The history and development of industrial relations
4.2 The role of the employers' associations in building
4.3 The role of the trade unions
4.4 The industrial relations machinery
4.5 Special industrial relations problems of large sites
4.6 Management responsibilities with industrial relations

4.1 The history and development of industrial relations

Although relationships between employers and employees can be traced back to the mediaeval guilds, the modern period of industrial relations commenced at the beginning of the nineteenth century, when the building industry underwent a profound change.

Prior to the Industrial Revolution, the client undertook to organize the building project, with master craftsmen of each principal trade being asked to undertake specific aspects of the work. With the nature and magnitude of the type of buildings required to provide the infrastructure for an emerging capitalist nation, the role of the master builder was enhanced because he now tendered for the complete building.

This change had its implications for established rules governing the conduct of industrial relations; tradesmen resented the development of the master builder because it impinged upon their opportunities to become master craftsmen themselves. As Cole (1953) observed: 'The general contractor was apt to be intolerant of the traditional rules and customs of the various trades.'

In the main, bargaining concerning wages was localized, and with the development of the piecework system of payment, was often individually rather than collectively bargained. The new master builders employed workers at the rate of wages pertaining to a town or locality and expected them to work under the customary conditions; hence, 'custom' has become a basic component of understanding between employees and employers. The piecework aspect to wages was also widely adopted for building labour – then, as now, the unions saw this as a challenge to their ability to organize effectively. Marx (1867) summed up the new system of payment when he described the piecework system as 'the form of wages most suited to the capitalist method of production.'

Despite the legal barriers imposed by the Combination Acts of 1799 and 1800, building workers and building employers formed organizations. In the first instance workers formed combinations under the guise of friendly societies and employers took advantage of the jurisdiction of friendly local magistrates to collect together to discuss common problems.

The Combination Acts allowed sentences on any working man of three months in jail or two months' hard labour if he was found guilty of combining with others for the object of increasing wages or decreasing hours. Sentence was by two magistrates, not a judge. Appeal against sentence was not allowed unless £20 surety was given; this represented approximately twenty weeks' wages for a bricklayer at that time. A fine of £10 was levied upon anyone helping with the expenses for anyone convicted under the Acts. The Acts also forbade employers' combinations, but there is little evidence of enforcement against employers.

The friendly societies of building workers existed until repeal of the Combination Acts in 1824, after which unions of building workers developed rapidly; they had a strong base from which to work. Hilton (1968) accurately suggested that '... Certainly the building unions which made themselves effective in the immediate post repeal [of the Combination Acts] period, did not act as if they were newly formed, naïve and inexperienced organizations. Instead they bore that quality of militancy and independence against which all the statutes over the last 500 years had complained.'

The trade unions in building grew rapidly, and as soon as eight years after the repeal the first national union was formed, which attempted to weld together the multitude of local associations. In 1832 the Operative Builders Union was formed, whose aim was to 'advance and equalize the price of labour in every craft' (Postgate 1923). In 1833 its membership was 49,000. However, employers' associations retaliated with the 'Document' which attempted to gain pledges from employees that they would not join the Operative Builders Union. The 'Document' asked employees to sign the following statement (Postgate 1923): 'We the undersigned do hereby declare that we are in no way connected with the General

Union of Building Trades and we do not and will not contribute to the support of such members of this said union, as we are or may be out of work in consequence of belonging to such unions.' Clearly, to seek such a pledge would embitter industrial relations and several localized strikes ensued.

As the Industrial Revolution intensified, the massive civil engineering projects generated large contracting organizations, which further strengthened the employers at the expense of the trade unions. The 1850s found trade union organization weak and divided, while employers were forming a successful national organization – the Central Master Builders Association – which, in 1859, organized a 'lock-out' of 24,000 London-based builders after a union had called for a nine-hour working day. This lock-out demonstrated that trade unions also required national organization, to co-ordinate recruitment and policy. However, while there was general agreement to move towards a central trade union authority, there were disagreements over the nature and structure of such a body. Two views could be detected: the *traditionalists* and the *amalgamationists*. The traditionalists saw the builders' union based upon local democracy with a decentralized administration and decisions concerning strike action to be taken at the work face. The amalgamationists saw the union movement best served by caution, restraint, conciliation, with a centralized administration who would vet any strike action considered by workers.

The amalgamationists' argument succeeded for two reasons. First, the employers were seeking to establish standardized working rules and the amalgamationists' preference for negotiation as opposed to industrial action matched this initiative. Second, the government favoured the more moderate policy of this group and had influenced the climate of opinion which favoured their rise to supremacy.

By the late 1870s the case for national institutes for the conduct of industrial relations had been established and the master builders widened their organization to form the National Association of Master Builders of Great Britain, with sixty-four employers and nineteen local associations. By 1892 it had grown to 1,300 members (NFBTE 1978) and in 1899 it formally became the National Federation of Building Trades Employers (NFBTE).

Despite these national organizations, industrial relations still retained its local character, with a plethora of district rules and conventions. It was not until 1904 that a nationwide basis for industry-wide bargaining was established. Yet the scope of such bargaining was limited until 1920 when the National Wages and Conditions Council was formed with a view to negotiating a national working rule agreement for the building industry. This agreement 'covered rates of wages, extra payments, overtime, payment for night gangs and travelling and lodging allowances to be fixed nationally with provision for regional and local variations. This progress marked the birth of the NJCBI' (NFBTE 1978).

The National Wages and Conditions Council was superseded by the National Joint Council for the Building Industry (NJCBI) in 1926. The unions proposed to this body that wage rates be stabilized, with a five-day, forty-hour week and the principles of tool money and a guaranteed working week established. Most of these demands were not established as working conditions until after World War II, when the unions' strength was enhanced by a shortage in the supply of tradesmen. The buoyant economic conditions of the 1950s had allowed employees to make steady gains in wages and conditions. Throughout the 1960s union membership began to decline, despite the reduction of the working week from $46\frac{1}{2}$ hours to 44 hours in 1960, a further fall to 42 hours in 1961 and, by 1965, stabilized at 40 hours per week. It fell to 39 hours in 1982.

Union membership in construction continued to fall and it has been mentioned that the relative weakness has been one reason for the relatively stable industrial relations in building. Burgess (1975) identifies other reasons for this pattern. He suggests that the pattern of relationships 'lacks well-defined phases', which is partly due to the structure of the industry, in particular the relative absence of technological change and its complex relationship with cyclical fluctuations in the economy. The comparative industrial peace in the building industry has, no doubt, been partly due to the effectiveness of the negotiating machinery that has evolved, but generally it has been due to the weakness of the trade unions and 'the continuing craft sectionalism if not exclusiveness which divided workers among themselves' (Burgess 1975).

The accuracy of this statement is evidenced by the multitude of parties attached to the negotiating machinery in construction, and at this point it would be useful to examine their roles and responsibilities more fully.

4.2 The role of employers' associations in building

In general, employers' associations have six principal roles to perform, namely, representing their member firms on the following issues:

4.2.1 Economic questions

Employers have long recognized that by combining they were more able to withstand demands for better wages and conditions from trade unions. It has been a long-established trade union negotiation tactic to 'leapfrog' in terms of wages and conditions, isolating one employer at a time. The employers' associations represent the employers' interests in a collective manner by undertaking negotiation with trade unions on a national basis over the questions of wages and conditions of employment. But this general role is supplemented by giving advice and assistance to individual member firms when dealing with their particular labour problems.

4.2.2 Advisory

Employers' associations provide members with an information service which is related to companies' trade or commercial functions. Areas included in this service would be the impact of legislation upon the building industry, a wages monitoring service, research and development progress reports. In a sense, this particular service reflects the federal structure of the building employers' association, where much of the lubrication for industrial relations is provided by local associations with the central body acting as a co-ordinator.

4.2.3 Regulatory

Employers' associations regulate and administer agreements they have reached on behalf of their members and generally provide facilities for the settlement of disputes between unions and individual managements. In this respect, the employers' associations attempt to stabilize relationships between the parties to the industrial relations machinery.

4.2.4 Representation

Employers' associations, in common with trade unions, seek to have their point of view made known to the decision-makers. In particular, it will make representations to government, especially when seeking to amend specific legislation, but at a more general level, employers' associations will attempt to become party to economic planning in respect of the building industry.

4.2.5 Technical and commercial service

The structure of the construction industry, with the largest number of firms being concentrated into the small to medium-sized organizations (see Fig. 4.1), means that an employers' association will often be asked to provide a technical and commercial advisory service. Issues which are likely to be foremost here are assistance in negotiating contractual conditions, legal advice, cost and estimating advice along with miscellaneous commercial advice for matters on which a small to medium-sized contractor would not have in-house expertise.

4.2.6 Political influence

Traditionally, the building employers' associations have supported the Conservative Party, as expressed by donations to party funds. In 1979 the 150 leading publicly quoted companies concerned with the construction industry donated £166,792 to the Conservative party, which represents 10 per cent of the total donations received. Obviously, donations from private companies will add to this figure (Labour Research Department, 1980).

The reasoning behind such support is not difficult to detect. The Conservatives have an ideology for the support of private industry and enterprise and clearly, this will be to the taste of the employers.

In parallel to the trade unions there are several employers' associations allied to the building industry. The largest of these is the NFBTE, which has over 11,000 members and represents 13 per cent of the 84,000 firms identified as being within

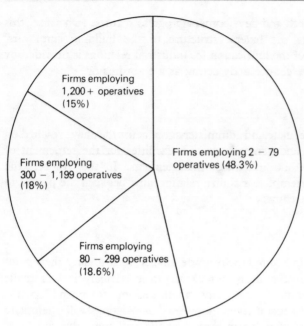

Fig. 4.1 Employment of operatives by size of firm 1978

the field of the construction industry. The NFBTE has ten regional federations covering 185 local associations. This structure gives the NFBTE a very decentralized nature, with head office acting as an advisory service and negotiations force in the NJCBI (see Fig. 4.2).

A rival body to the NFBTE is the Federation of Master Builders (FMB), which claimed a membership of 18,850 in January 1979. The bulk of this membership is derived from the small building firms and the self-employed, and the object of the FMB is to look after the interests of the small or medium builder on a national basis. While the FBM have a larger membership then the NFBTE, its influence upon the industry is smaller – this is due in part to the structure of the industry with the largest number of firms having few employees. Thus the small jobbing builder is likely to be independent and so more organizationally disparate than larger firms making their influence weaker. This is reflected in the FMB's small representation on the NJCBI.

The third major employers' association is the Federation of Civil Engineering Contractors (FCEC) which, in 1979, had a membership of 541. It has a highly centralized administration reflected in the disputes procedures operated by the Civil Engineering Construction Conciliation Board (CECCB), which has a national authority. This compares with the more localized situation in building. The FCEC does not have a series of local associations and its members communicate directly with head office. Other employers' associations peripherally involved in the building industry are the Electrical Contractors' Association (ECA), which organizes electrical contractors, the Engineering Employers' Federation (EEF)

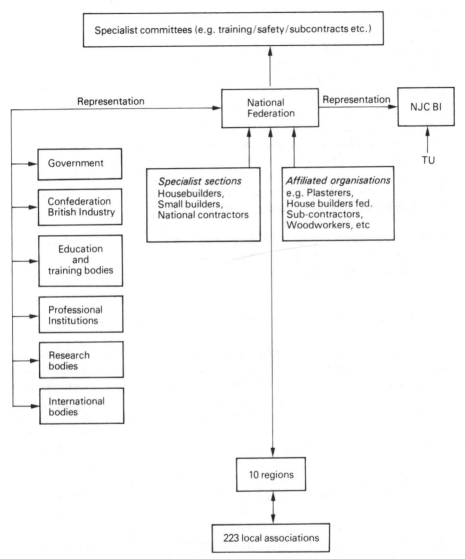

Fig. 4.2 The structure of the NFBTE

which deals with steel erectors and, perhaps, the most powerful of all, the Oil and Chemical Plant Constructors' Association (OCPCA) which, in spite of having only fifty-five members, plays a central role in the conduct of industrial relations on large industrial sites.

The diversity of employers' associations does little to harmonize industrial relations in construction, but it must be said that this very diversity matches the industrial relations practice of the industry. The employers' federations (other than the ECA) do not seek strict control over the activities of their members.

Even at the wages negotiation table, the employers seek to establish a 'basic wage' below which building workers should not fall and individual employers and trade unions are free to negotiate supplements to these basic terms and conditions agreed at national level. The local autonomy has been a response to the growing size of companies who have had the authority and confidence to negotiate separately with the trade unions. The growing professionalism of managements and the ability to provide internally the advisory service which previously the employers' associations provided. Economic conditions have also weakened the employers' associations. During the 1960s labour was scarce and individual companies had to compete for the available skilled labour. This undermined the authority of the employers. Additionally, incomes policies which attempted statutory control of wages has meant that employers have sought to deal directly with employees, offering in-lieu payments outside of the incomes policy and nationally agreed rates of pay.

Despite this decentralization of bargaining, the employers' associations allied to the building industry have played an invaluable role in determining the character of the industrial relations system in construction.

4.3 The role of the trade unions

The role of the trade unions within Britain has become almost as popular and perennial a topic of conversation as the weather. Politicians, media pundits, *et al.*, have all advanced views of what the role of trade unions within a capitalist state should be. Popular among these are that trade unions have too much power, trade union leaders cannot control their membership, most workers (especially trade union members) do not work hard enough, etc. Occasionally the view is put forward that management must share some responsibility for the situation, but, in the main, the focus for debate has been on the trade unions. Many managers in the building industry, because of their position, will express the former view, but will often find themselves in a dilemma. The construction manager may have established a rapport with trade union officials and is likely to oppose any measures which may be seen to upset these relationships. Painful surgery is good for the other fellow! Within the current debate about industrial relations, many managers will favour tough legal sanctions against the trade unions. After previous experience with draconian legal sanctions – the Industrial Relations Act – remained largely a dead letter, managers often prefer to deal with industrial relations in a pragmatic rather than a legalistic manner. This conciliatory view is, however, not wholly shared by managers within construction. At the 1979 CBI conference, a certain construction company moved a resolution which pressed for the outlawing of the closed shop – a resolution which was narrowly carried against the desires of many leading industrialists who had day-to-day experience in dealing with trade unions.

Yet there is a paradox – while the forms of the debate about industrial relations has often been detrimental to trade unions, more and more of the working population have joined them (see Fig. 4.3) and this growth has been reflected within the major building trades union UCATT (see Fig. 4.4). Despite this, the absolute numbers of trade unionists in the building industry are small in comparison to the labour force as a whole. The reasons for this are manifold. The craft sectionalism still apparent has already been mentioned, but other reasons can also be identified. The downturn in trading within the building industry is certainly prominent; with 350,000 building workers unemployed in April 1980, the unions are not well placed to recruit new members. Second, the concentration of union members within direct labour organizations has meant that as the importance of these organizations has declined, the unions have had to recruit more extensively from the private sector, and this is a difficult operation. Third, some employers have actively involved themselves in 'blacklisting' union activists, which isolates their workforce from the effects of trade union activity at site level. Finally, the industry is dependent upon casual labour which, by its nature, is unlikely to have developed a trade union consciousness.

Notwithstanding these problems, the trade unions in construction have a presence, albeit that officials often worry about the numerical strength of unionism within such an important industry. *House's Guide to the Construction Industry* (Lansdell 1981) identifies the unions involved in construction with their

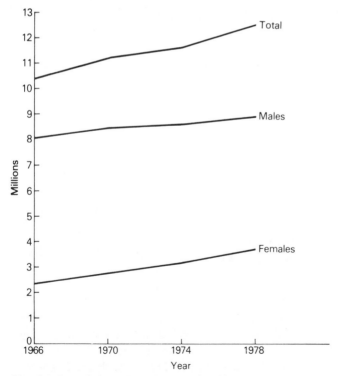

Fig. 4.3 Growth in trade union membership

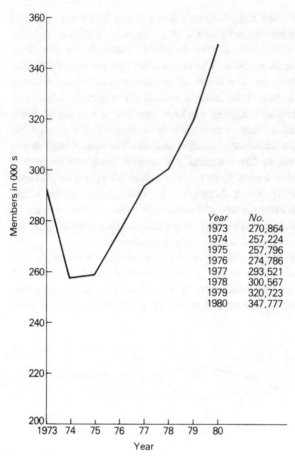

Year	No.
1973	270,864
1974	257,224
1975	257,796
1976	274,786
1977	293,521
1978	300,567
1979	320,723
1980	347,777

Fig. 4.4 The growth of UCATT

numerical strength:

UCATT – 320,723
STAMP (Supervisory, Technical and Administrative, Management and Professional section of UCATT) – 4,522
TGWU   – 100,000 (estimated figure)
AUEW   (Construction section) – 25,000
GMWU   – 50,000
AUAW   (Amalgamated Union of Asphalt Workers) – 3,012

UCATT is the foremost of the building trade unions and is a product of the union amalgamations of 1972. At this time several of the old craft unions came together to form UCATT. The need for trade union mergers had been set out some four years earlier in the *Royal Commission on Trade Unions and Employers'*

Associations 1965–1968 (Donovan 1968). The report pointed out

> ... that there is scope for many more mergers between unions. In particular, it seems to us that problems caused by a multiplicity of unions organizing in individual factories would be considerably eased in a number of important industries if certain groups of craft unions could be encouraged to amalgamate. This is particularly true of engineering and construction.

Furthermore, George Woodcock, TUC General Secretary from 1960 to 1970, had encouraged the union movement to seek mergers wherever a common interest bound them together. Given the background of declining membership of the traditional trade crafts, amalgamation became an expedient necessity rather than ideological commitment. In 1972 agreement was reached between three principal building unions of the day, namely, the Amalgamated Society of Woodworkers (ASW), the Amalgamated Society of Painters and Decorators (ASP&D), and the Amalgamated Union of Building Trades Workers (AUBTW).

As with most trade unions, the local branch is the basic unit of the organization. UCATT has approximately 1,600 branches with the size of the branch varying according to location. Branches of UCATT meet on a monthly or fortnightly basis. Traditionally, branches are composed of tradesmen of one craft, although the craft sectionalism of the union is being broken down by branch mergers and the establishment of branches containing all trades. The structure of UCATT is shown in Fig. 4.5 (Wood 1979).

The other major force within the construction industry is the Transport and General Workers Union (TGWU). This union, because of its general nature, is organized by trade groups with building and civil engineering having its own trade group organization. This consists of national officers and regional organizers who are elected by members in branches allied to the construction industry. The structure is illustrated in Fig. 4.6. As can be seen, the grass-roots membership is organized into regional sections and, in a general union such as the TGWU, workers in a particular industry are organized into industry-based branches such that a region will have building trade branches organized around a geographical area or a particular site. These branches elect one delegate to serve on the Regional Trade Group, which meets on a quarterly basis and has a full-tme official to service it. However, quarterly meetings will not be able to cope with emergency matters and, consequently, an Emergency Trade Group is drawn from the Regional Trade Group. The Emergency Trade Group consists of three delegates from the Regional Trade Group plus a chairman and full-time official. Within the TGWU there are eleven different trade groups, each of which elects a delegate to serve on the Regional Committee which overviews the work of the region. At the time, the Building Trade Group will elect delegates to the National Committee of Building Trade Groups. This body holds meetings on a quarterly basis and its prime function is to review National Joint Council business. The National Committee of Building Trade Groups also elects one delegate to serve on the Executive Council of the union. The Executive Council is served by the

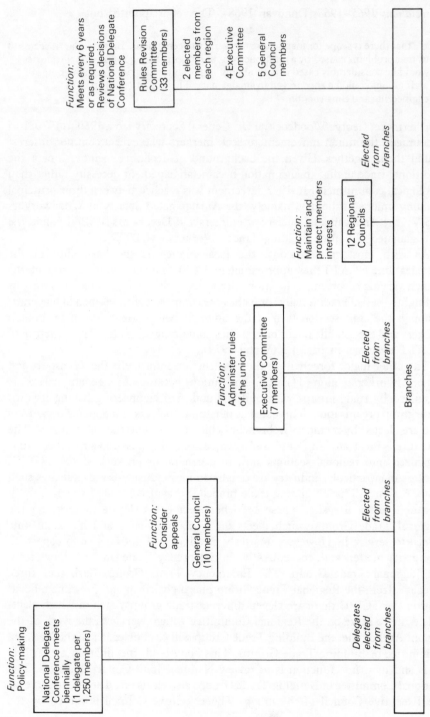

Fig. 4.5 The structure of UCATT

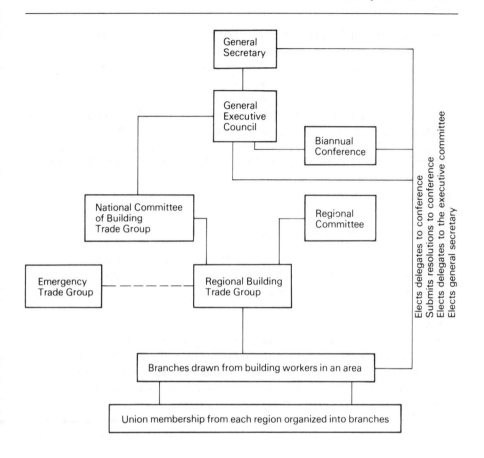

Functions of each committee:

Building Trade Group	– Each region is broken down into areas and one delegate is elected from each area to serve on the Regional Trade Group. Each Regional Trade Group has a full-time secretary. Meets quarterly.
Emergency Trade Group	– Three persons drawn from trade group + chairman + secretary. Discuss emergency matters.
Regional Committee	– All eleven trade groups elect delegates to serve on the regional committee. Administers the region.
National Committee of Trade Groups	– Quarterly meetings, discusses NJC matters. Delegates elected from regional trade groups.
Union Executive Committee	– One member elected from each national trade group. Delegates elected directly from the regional membership.
Biannual Conference	– The sovereign body of the union. Delegates elected from the region on a trade group basis. Monitors the work of the General Executive Council.
General Secretary	– The chief officer of the union — elected by ballot of the whole membership of the union.

Fig. 4.6 Structure of TGWU

General Secretary of the union, who acts as its chief officer. This person is elected by secret ballot by the whole membership of the union.

The union holds a biannual conference to which delegates are elected from regions on a trade group basis. At these conferences policy is established and the work of the Executive Council is monitored.

The competing nature of trade unions for members often means that trade unionism within construction is poorly organized. However, the relatively small number of full-time officials means that much of the day-to-day negotiation is conducted by shop stewards at site level. This group of people has become increasingly important in the last few years and merit special consideration of their role.

4.3.1 The role of the shop stewards

This group of lay officials for the trade union movement have been the focus of much public debate over the last ten years. Often their role has been presented in a negative manner, being typecast as surly, self-interested, and mindlessly militant, but research carried out at the workface has constantly denied this popular image. Clack (1967) wrote 'the convenors and shop stewards did not appear [to be a] driving force behind labour unrest, but could be more validly regarded as the shock absorbers in the industrial relations machinery'. In another study by Marsh *et al.* (1971), the overwhelming proportion (80 per cent) of managers thought that stewards were 'helpful', 9 per cent felt that they were obstructive, and 11 per cent had no views to express. However, this survey was carried out in the engineering industry where a more formalized and well-established system of industrial relations exists. Construction, with its lower union density, may present a different picture, with managers reluctant to talk to stewards or negotiate with the labour force. Despite this reluctance, more and more negotiations are taking place at site level, with particular emphasis upon bonus earnings, and in the context of decentralized bargaining the steward will have an important role to play. UCATT's *Shop Stewards' Handbook* (UCATT 1979) sums up the two features of the role of the stewards: 'Firstly: within the framework of the agreements covering the job, the steward is there to protect the work interests of the members who elect him and whom he represents. Secondly: the steward is there to see that all workers eligible on the job to join the union are UCATT members and remain members.'

However, the steward is often in a dilemma; on the one hand the industry has national agreements and on the other, site agreements negotiated by management and stewards which may seem counter to the national ones. The wages drift between nationally agreed rates and take home pay has reinforced the gap between national agreements and site settlements. These disparities have emphasised the role of the steward in local negotiations. As the TGWU *Shop Stewards' Handbook* (TGWU 1974) states: 'Our plans for high wages based upon the maximum extensions of plant and local bargaining depend upon workshop representatives who are able to take the initiative and play a positive part in negotiations with management.' This decentralizing of bargaining followed the recommendations of the Donovan Commission (1968) in respect of plant bargaining and it has had its impact upon the autonomy of the steward. This autonomy is often resented by management, but the experience of several firms who undertake to meet their stewards regularly have found that they have been less troubled by sporadic visits of stewards who lack knowledge of the issues involved. Long-serving stewards will know what can be achieved, the strength of their membership, and the limits of management action. Therefore, the encouragement of meeting with stewards can be of mutual benefit to stewards and management.

However, in many cases the role of the shop steward will be determined by management attitudes. Management can assist the relationships by providing facilities for the steward, in particularly by instituting a 'check-off' system by which management deducts trade union subscriptions from the wages or salaries of employees and pays the money directly to the union. This does much to stabilize trade union membership. As the Donovan Commission pointed out: 'On the whole we think the check-off is a useful arrangement.' Other facilities provided by management will obviously vary from site to site, but in certain circumstances could include facilities for interviewing new employees, accommodation for meetings, access to a telephone and even office equipment. Additionally, employers are legally required to allow stewards time off for trade union duties without loss of pay, the cost of such provisions could be more then outweighed by the advantages of a healthy industrial relations climate.

More often than not managers use shop stewards as quasi-management, acting as a go-between in communicating management decisions. This is a misunderstanding of the role of the steward. Management must use its own line management to inform the workforce of its decisions; however, such decisions are more likely to find acceptance by the stewards if the stewards have been involved during some stage of the decision-making process.

4.4 The industrial relations machinery

It has been stressed earlier that there is a diversity between the national agreements and local conditions pertaining on site. This diversity is a reflection of the formal and informal systems of industrial relations, which are held to co-exist within industry as a whole. In building, the formal system of industrial relations is characterized by the existence of the National Working Rule Agreement with its assumption that its influence is industry-wide and is capable of imposing common standards upon a diverse industry. Central to this acceptance of the formal system is the understanding that most, if not all, matters can be covered by collective agreements, with pay being determined by industry-wide settlements. Disputes arising from the formal system are derived from differences in interpretation of the national agreements.

In contrast, there is the informal system, which depends upon the wide autonomy of construction managers and trade unions to determine appropriate industrial relations standards. This autonomy recognizes that collective bargaining at the site level is just as important as bargains at the national level. At the local level, the issues which can be considered are extremely wide and will incorporate such issues as discipline, redundancy, work practices, etc. and will have a strong basis of 'arrangements' and 'understandings' acting to police the system.

It can be seen that the informal system can undermine the regulative effect of the National Working Rule Agreement, but many have argued that it is more important than the formal system. However, it must be stressed that total dependence upon the informal system is courting danger, since it is likely to lead to very diverse conditions between company sites and an overreliance upon expedient methods of dealing with immediate industrial relations policy.

Hence, collective bargaining is carried out at national and site level and while local agreements have a long history, industry-wide bargaining has been in evidence since the formulation of the NJCBI in 1926. Since this time the organization has become the most important consultative body existing within the industry. The NJCBI is a joint management/union body, with council existing at the national, regional, and local levels, and in each case it is composed of equal numbers of employers' federation and trade union representatives. Figure 4.7 illustrates the structure of the NJCBI. Within this structure the most important committees are the ten committees at regional level, where thirty members sit – fifteen from employers, fifteen from the trade unions. It is these councils which may initiate amendments to vary the national working rules to suit the particular circumstances of the regions for which they are responsible. The regional council also has the right to determine whether or not area councils should be appointed and, if it decides to set one up, has the power to define its composition and functions. At the national level, the National Working Rule Agreement is drawn up. This is a substantive agreement which attempts to set down minimum standards for the industry as a whole. Areas which the NWRA covers include the following:

- wages
- working hours and overtime premiums
- holiday entitlement
- incentive schemes
- termination of employment
- sick pay
- safety, welfare provisions
- tool allowances
- lodging and travelling allowances
- special rates for less than normal jobs
- pension schemes
- apprentice rates of pay
- trade union recognition procedures
- disputes procedures

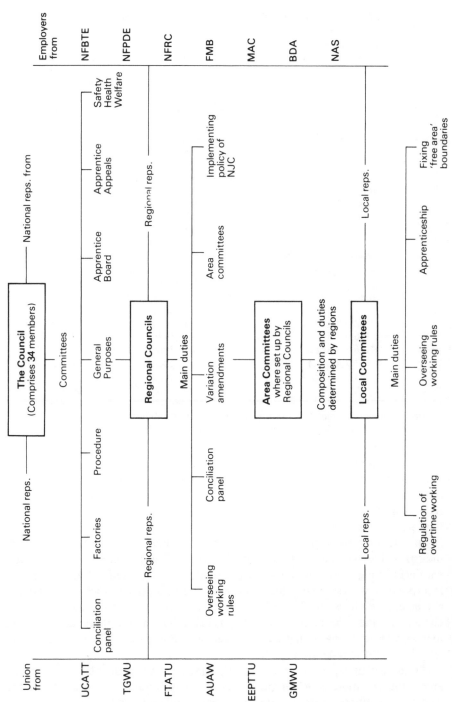

Fig. 4.7 National Joint Council for the Building Industry

Table 4.1: Wage drift of craftsmen and labourers, aged 21 and over, 1971–79

Year	Craftsmen: skilled Average gross hourly earnings excl. effect of overtime* (pence)	Class 1 areas Building and Civil Engineering NWRA hourly rates† (pence)	Wage drift. Difference between average gross hourly earnings and NWRA hourly rates (pence)
1971	59.9 (Apr.)	50.0 (June)	+ 9.9
1972	66.1 (Apr.)	65.0 (Sept.)	+ 1.1
1973	88.3 (Apr.)	67.5 (June)	+20.8
1974	101.2 (Apr.)	72.5 (June)	+28.7
1975	127.6 (Apr.)	85.2 (Feb.)	+42.6 Increase
1976	148.8 (Apr.)	92.5 (June)	+56.3
1977	162.2 (Oct.)	92.5 (June)	+69.7
1978	180.6 (Apr.)	110.0 (June)	+70.6
1979	205.2 (Oct.)	129.9 (June)	+76.0
	Labourers: unskilled		*Wage drift*
1971	52.8 (Apr.)	42.5 (June)	+10.3
1972	57.8 (Apr.)	55.5 (Sept.)	+ 2.3
1973	71.4 (Apr.)	57.5 (June)	+13.9
1974	82.8 (Apr.)	61.5 (June)	+21.3 Increase
1975	106.3 (Apr.)	72.5 (Feb.)	+33.8
1976	126.9 (Apr.)	78.5 (June)	+48.4
1977	141.2 (Oct.)	78.5 (June)	+62.7
1978	154.3 (Apr.)	94.0 (June)	+60.3
1979	170.9 (Oct.)	110.0 (June)	+60.9

Source: * *Annual Abstract of Statistics* (Dept of the Environment)
  † *Handbook 1978–79* (Federation of Civil Engineering Contractors)

In addition to this national agreement, locally made procedural agreements are strongly in evidence. These are site- or company-based deals which can be used to settle disputes and grievances, but they may be extended to cover dismissals, redundancies, recruitment, trade union representation, and other matters. In reinforcing extensive procedural agreement, the Donovan Report pointed out: 'Over the last 30 years there has been a decline in the extent to which industry-wide agreements determine actual pay.' This reflection has application within building, since there has been a tendency for procedural agreements to incorporate a wages and conditions element – the proper province of substantive agreements such as the NWRA. In the main, this has concerned the bonus element of the take-home pay but, as Table 4.1 shows, there has been an increasing wages drift – that is, the difference between the NWRA hourly rate and the actual take-home pay.

An important aspect of procedural agreements is the principle of 'status quo ante' (the situation which applied before). This means that changes in the working conditions, rates for the job, bonus schemes, manning levels, etc., should not be made without prior consultation with the trade unions. It is now TUC policy to insist upon a 'status quo ante' clause in all new procedural agreements.

With national firms, there is a tendency for procedure and substantive agreements to be made between national officers of the union and the employers, and where such arrangements are made there is a tendency to write in details of working arrangements and site conditions. By doing this, areas of possible differences are removed and as people employed know what has been agreed, there is less likelihood of a dispute when the contract has commenced.

However, the question of disputes should not be overstated. While the building industry has the conditions for unrest – dangerous working conditions, low basic pay supplemented by fragmented bonus arrangements and the fundamental unease in relationships between the employed and the employer – strikes have not been a dominant feature of the industry. Table 4.2 illustrates this point.

Table 4.2: Comparison of number of working days lost per thousand workers in construction to that for all industries and services 1956–77

Year	Working days lost per thousand workers	
	All industries and services	Construction
1956	0.088	0.049
1957	0.353	0.054
1958	0.146	0.099
1959	0.244	0.100
1960	0.137	0.077
1961	0.136	0.192
1962	0.257	0.147
1963	0.075	0.231
1964	0.099	0.077
1965	0.125	0.081
1966	0.101	0.088
1967	0.119	0.129
1968	0.211	0.153
1969	0.309	0.190
1970	0.499	0.181
1971	0.626	0.202
1972	1.104	3.224
1973	0.324	0.127
1974	0.661	0.189
1975	0.271	0.188
1976	0.149	0.413
1977	0.457	0.234
1978	0.414	0.327

4.4.1 Disputes procedure

In the main, the absence of disputes can be partially explained by the comprehensive disputes procedure laid out in the NWRA and operated by the NJCBI. The NWRA disputes procedure identifies two types of potential grievance: the individual case and the collective case. With respect to the former, the NWRA advises that the individual should speak to his or her immediate supervisor and attempt to resolve the issue at the workface. Failing settlement at this level, the individual may take up the matter with the site manager and at this meeting the individual may be accompanied by the union steward.

In the collective cases it is the responsibility of the steward or union convenor (where more than one union is involved) to take the matter to site management. If a satisfactory resolution cannot be found, then the facts are reported to the trade union full-time official. If management and full-time official cannot agree, then the disputes procedure of the NJCBI can be invoked. This consists of two separate procedures: the normal procedure and the emergency procedure. The building industry is unique in recognizing two disputes procedures, with one to deal with emergencies.

4.4.2 The normal procedure

This processes a dispute when a stoppage of work is not imminent and the issue concerns events or practices on a particular site. The dispute is referred to a local or area joint industrial council of the NJCBI, which is composed of trade union and employer representatives. In the event of a failure to agree at the local level, the question is referred to the regional level and, again, if no resolution is found, a national consultative panel is convened.

4.4.3 The emergency procedure

This unique procedure is invoked when a stoppage of work is imminent and the issue is one which has implications for the building industry as a whole. In this route, a regional conciliation panel is convened within seven days. This body makes a decision, but either union or employer can appeal against the decision to the National Conciliation Panel.

4.4.4 Civil engineering

In civil engineering the disputes procedure reflects the centralized nature of its employers' association – the FCEC. Here, there is only one arbitration panel – the CECCB, which is a national body without local agencies.

Notwithstanding these procedures, key responsibilities for the avoidance of lengthy stoppages lies with site management and site union representatives. The fact that the vast majority of grievances are resolved without recourse to the formal disputes procedure is due, in many cases, to the fact that many site supervisors have been craft trained and are therefore sensitive to the desires expressed by the operatives. The onset of technically educated supervisors may change this situation; if the present conditions are to continue, attention must be paid to adequate training in manpower management.

As the structure of industrial relations machinery grows more complex, there is an increasing need for adequate training for the labour representatives on sites, i.e. the shop stewards. The need for more formal training of shop stewards in the dispute procedure has been stressed in many reports and the needs of the building industry are, perhaps, greater in this respect, due to the diverse nature and types of work conditions and the transitory nature of the employment.

4.5 Special industrial relations problems of large sites

Serious industrial relations problems are often experienced on large industrial sites. Frequently, national Press coverage has been given to stoppages and long disputes on projects of national importance. The complexity and nature of the industrial relations on such sites are such that they merit special consideration.

The essential feature of large sites is that they assume a great importance to a regional and national economy and this fact focuses attention upon the necessity for early completion. Both management and operatives recognize this fact and, as such, management are prone to deal with trade union demands without regard to the wider industrial relations environment. Each site is considered unique and therefore a dispute requires expediting at the earliest stage, irrespective of the labour costs. An additional problem is the nature of large sites themselves; often it will be a multi-union site, each competing for membership and authority. Permanent and casual workers are fused together, often not harmoniously. Invariably, jobs will have a multi-contractor basis and each will follow separate industrial relations policies. Finally, supervisors are often casual and do not get to know the operatives.

The above conditions are a prescription for poor industrial relations, but the situation is compounded by anarchy in the wages policy on large industrial sites. A variety of national agreements will pertain on an industrial site; for instance, the following agreements may cover different elements of the workforce:

National Working Rule Agreement
Civil Engineering Working Rule Agreement
Electrical Contracting Agreement
Mechanical Contracting Agreement
Oil and Petrochemical Constructors' Association Agreement
National Agreement for the Engineering Construction Industry

Each of these can be negotiated without reference to any other, and the accumulative problem is that all of the agreements (with the exception of the ECA) establish a basic pay and allow site negotiations to supplement this, mainly for bonus arrangements. This has led to the situation where there are a variety of earnings by operatives of the same trade, employed by different contractors on the same site. The report of the National Economic Development Office on large industrial sites (NEDO 1970) found that for one particular trade, earnings varied as much as 71 per cent on top of the lowest paid in that trade.

On some sites independent agreements have been made which unify earnings between trades, and this tends to stabilize the situation, but clients and employers have often been concerned that this process unification has led to high wages being attained by the unions. However, it would seem from the NEDO research that pay dominates the causes for stoppages on large industrial sites. They have analysed the recorded stoppages as follows:

Cause of stoppage		% occurrence
1. Wages:	Bonus	24
	Other	17
2. Dismissal		19
3. Site conditions		8
4. Working practices		7
5. Sympathy		7
6. Demarcation		5
7. Redundancy		3
8. Other		10

These figures record the known stoppages and do not account for go-slows, restrictive practices, etc. What is noticeable in the above figures is the high proportion of disputes arising from bonus difficulties. It has long been argued that a national agreement along the lines of the NWRA for the building industry should be instituted for large sites. The EEF launched such a document in 1982 in conjunction with the AUEW and other engineering unions. It was expected that this agreement would give greater consistency of wage rates, earnings, site conditions and benefits, thus reducing chain reactions of claims and disputes. A more ordered industrial relations could result in workers and supervisors recognizing the requirements of the large site agreement and, hence, movement between sites could be more ordered, with a consequent decasualizing of the labour force. Some have argued that the strengthened agreement for large sites would enhance the authority of the official trade union leadership at the expense of site-based shop stewards.

Perhaps the most pertinent advantage of the special national agreement for large sites is that it could involve contractors and subcontractors who are currently tied to agreements which may be inconsistent. But the claim for a consolidated rate is not really a realistic proposal when bonus payments – always a subject for site negotiation – will always erode the principle of equal payment. It is accepted that site agreements have advantages, namely:

(a) negotiation at the start of a job can be anticipated in order to reduce questions of demarcation and productivity;
(b) overtime can be controlled;
(c) the amount of shiftwork can be determined;
(d) the facilities to be available for shop stewards can be decided;
(e) a policy can be formulated on the selection for redundancy.

It is clear that the industrial relations situation on large sites needs improving and the investigations carried out by NEDO identified real problems of industrial relations on unique sites, the agreement sponsored by the EEF is the fruit of such observations. However, in common with the Donovan Commission, the NEDO report recognized the necessity for locally based agreements to be the basis for secure industrial relations on construction sites.

4.6 Management responsibilities with industrial relations

The construction industry has often been criticized for its lack of a coherent industrial relations policy. A strategy to improve industrial relations could be broken down into the following areas:

4.6.1 Extending full-time industrial relations officers
4.6.2 Training in industrial relations
4.6.3 Extending joint consultation
4.6.4 Decasualizing the industry
4.6.5 A coherent wages policy.

4.6.1 Extending full-time industrial relations officers

The Cameron (1967) report on the Barbican and Horseferry Road disputes found that failure of effective communication and consultation between management and operatives was one of the major reasons for the ultimate stoppages of work. Hilton (1968) further suggested that much of the £700,000 additional wages bill on the Horseferry Road contract could have been avoided if the management had appointed a person with specific responsibility for industrial relations. The lack of specific industrial relations expertise was highlighted by a report on the training and development of field managers in engineering construction (NEDO 1971), where it was found that of 98 construction managers with 22 companies, 73 per cent of the managers felt that they would benefit from additional training in industrial relations procedures. What the survey also found was that none of the companies employed a full-time industrial relations officer on site.

The suggestion that construction companies add to their overheads by employing additional expertise in industrial relations will not command universal acceptance, but, as has been shown, the price of failure in this area can be high.

4.6.2 Training in industrial relations

The necessity for training in industrial relations has often been highlighted. A report by the Commission for Industrial Relations (1972) showed that industrial relations training was inadequate, and it identified six ways in which the industrial relations scene could be improved:

(a) The aim for every company should be to develop regular training schemes for those newly appointed or elected.

(b) Each company should provide basic industrial relations training to existing managers and shop stewards.
(c) Each company should consider the contribution of training towards solving problems and improving industrial relations.
(d) Employers should provide each employee with a guide to the grievances, disputes, and disciplinary procedures, i.e. furnish workers with copies of the Regional Working Rule Agreement.
(e) Trade unions should provide shop stewards with a basic training in their functions, powers, and responsibilities within six months of their taking office.
(f) Training and education committees should be established within a company.

Progressive management recognizes the need for such training, but unions also have a responsibility to provide training for their officials and stewards on site. This training can assist the communication aspect and lead to an appreciation of the opposite point of view. The Employment Protection (Consolidation) Act, 1978 provides that reasonable, paid, time off for training shall be allowed to trade union officers with duties concerned with industrial relations. However, the training has to be relevant to the officers' duties and has to be approved by the TUC or the officers' union. The philosophy has been incorporated in the NWRA for the building industry. Provision for the training of union stewards has been made in Rule 7.11, which states: 'Accredited union stewards should be encouraged to attend a training course in industrial relations and should be granted release from work by the employer for that purpose.'

The question of 'time off' can create problems. There must be a distinction between the time off work for training courses and duties concerned with management–union industrial relations, which is legally permissible, and the time off for trade union activities as a representative of a steward's union, which does not qualify for pay. Advisory, Conciliation and Arbitration Services code of practice *Time off for Trade Union Duties and Activites* (ACAS 1977) does not specify the amount of time that a trade union offical should be allowed to take, other than it should be *reasonable*. It is in the interpretation of what is 'reasonable' that management–union relations become difficult. Management may be well placed if they seek to define the percentage of time that a steward can have for trade union duties within a procedural agreement. Clearly this will vary from site to site, but recognition of the steward's rights can only assist in sound industrial relations.

4.6.3 Extending joint consultation

Earlier, evidence was presented to suggest that managers were willing to co-operate with trade unions, but unfortunately the building industry does not necessarily conform to this general pattern. Increased industrial relations training and familiarity of management with the role and work of trade unions will assist in creating stability in management–union relations. But the machinery for such stability is important – in many ways the work of the NJCBI has done much to foster industrial peace, but this is merely the formal national system and it requires to be reinforced by more widespread use of joint consultative committees. Presently, consultative committees are not common within the building industry and their use has mainly been confined to very large sites and direct labour organizations. Yet the benefits of joint consultation are very real. It can become part of a company's communication system, seeking to exchange views, aspirations, and information between management and employees. If successful consultation is to occur, the following principles should be adhered to:

(a) Top management must have a sincere belief in the system.
(b) It must be recognized that consultation is different from negotiation. (Consultation implies that advice is sought from either side; negotiation is based on bargaining when union and management seek agreement on specific issues.)
(c) The necessity of a set of aims which consultation seeks to achieve. Consultation can begin with very limited aims and gradually be extended, but at some stage the aims must be clearly identified.
(d) Consultative committees must seek to draw representatives from all sections of the firm. This will include site managers if joint consultation is undertaken at company level and first line supervisors if the arrangement is based on site.
(e) There must be careful selection of the topics which are the proper province of a consultative committee.

In addition to joint consultation, the involvement of union representatives on working parties at head office or site level, with a free exchange of information, along with adherence to the ACAS code of practice on the disclosure of information for collective bargaining, can do much to ensure a harmonious working relationship between trade unions and management.

4.6.4 Decasualizing the industry

Langford (1974) reviewed the effect of labour-only subcontractors upon the construction industry, and in a survey of workers directly employed by contractors he found that 76 per cent of the sample felt that labour-only adversely affected the bargaining power of trade unions at site level. This fact may not, superficially, be disturbing to management and may even be regarded as a positive feature, but viewed in the longer term, the dependence upon labour-only subcontracting and upon a casual labour force, could, as a consequence, lead to non-observance of national agreements, with a commensurate decline in the influence of the accepted machinery of industrial relations in building.

The NJCBI has attempted to regularize the use of labour-only within the framework of the NRWA (Rule 10). However, this clause is largely a dead letter and many contractors wilfully ignore this particular clause. The unions' response has been to take the issue to individual sites, and many stoppages have been caused by the desire of companies to use a casual labour force. Labour-only subcontracting is seen by the unions as a threat to their capability to organize within the industry, and Bayley (1973) points out:

> As long as employers are reluctant to tackle the problem they will be subjected to industrial action.
>
> Sound industrial relations require, among other things, an acceptance of a responsibility for seeing that the agreements are observed. The absence of sanctions against defaulting employees can only emphasise the importance of the bodies concerned and this, in turn, does not make for a healthy climate for industrial relations.

Of equal concern in this area is the volume of labour turnover within the building industry. Phelps-Brown (1968) estimated that the average labour turnover of employees in the construction industry was 79 per cent – approximately double the national average. Some ten years later, the annual turnover was considered to be 59 per cent (EIU 1978). More recently, the Office of Population and Census Surveys (1980) reviewed the situation and found that the labour turnover was high, with 40 per cent of the 20–35 age group having had four or more jobs within the previous five years. This picture of a casualized labour force has its implications for industrial relations. Workers continually moving here to familiarize themselves with different management styles, varying bonus targets, working practices, and site agreements. As has been seen, such problems exacerbate the difficulties that employers face in managing industrial relations.

Many proposals have been made to decasualize the industry, including a compulsory register of employers and employees. However, despite promptings from the Construction Manpower Board and the trade unions, employers have resisted compulsory registration, but have acceded to the principle of a voluntary register of employers. Movement towards a more thorough registration of building labour can only assist in decasualization and its consequent positive impact upon industrial relations in construction.

4.6.5 A coherent wages policy

It has been pointed out that the wages structure within the building industry is chaotic. In many cases, the situation is due to historical factors, but the multiplicity of elements in a wage packet do little to aid clarity. At worst, the wage packet can be made up of seven different elements, namely:

- the basic wage
- overtime earnings
- guaranteed minimum bonus
- bonus earnings
- travelling time
- tool money
- other allowances, e.g. height money, machine use, boot money, etc.

The now defunct National Board for Prices and Incomes (1968) recognized that the wage structure in the building industry desperately required a job evaluation scheme. The present system of expediently manipulating basic rates, overtime and bonuses to make a composite living wage is clearly unsatisfactory, with unskilled or semi-skilled workers in a locality earning more than craftsmen in another area. Additionally, contractors will offer plus rates for merit and this practice will vary from job to job, region to region, and firm to firm. A job evaluation scheme could assess jobs in terms of skill, responsibility, effort required, and working conditions experienced. Once relativities have been established, this would enable similar grades of workers to be paid a universal rate which would not vary from site to site or region to region. The present payments system does not reflect the different skills required in building and fails to consider the rapid technological advances which will have a potent impact upon traditional trades, while leaving others untouched.

The FMB and the NFBTE have long realized that there is a wide gap between the basic wage and actual earnings, but the NFBTE are reluctant to consolidate the many items of the wage into the basic rate because it would increase bonus and overtime earnings for workers. Yet the industry must move away from the illusory position of low basic wages enhanced by such devices as overtime and incentives as a means of producing a living wage; the basic rate must stand as an acceptable wage in its own right. The major problem would be the transition from the current situation, with its historical base, to a new wages system, and this could involve 'buying out' the old system before gaining recognition for the new one. A high-wage policy may create difficulties when labour is scarce and when firms who are in strong competition for labour offer plus rates to attract or their workforce. Regional and economic planning of the industry's workload could, however, alleviate this problem to some extent.

A move towards a new standard rate of pay would nevertheless need to be accompanied by a high degree of discipline from employers and unions. This is not impossible (as has shown, for example, by the electrical contracting industry). To some extent the parties currently excluded from the NJCBI, the FMB, and the TGWU have attempted to move towards the consolidation of pay rates through a new joint industrial council – the Building and Allied Trades Joint Industrial Council. Both these parties have recognized that for much of the building industry, dependence upon bonus rates is not appropriate since the small firms undertake work which cannot be directly measured and is not sufficiently repetitive to merit the setting of bonus targets. Time will tell if this new industrial council will extend its influence into the long-established NJCBI.

Summary

It has been observed that there are two systems of industrial relations in construction: the formal and the informal. The formal system is determined by the NWRA and the informal system depends upon understandings and agreements reached at the site level. Although the systems are often seen to be incompatible, there is widespread recognition that they must co-exist. The informal system is important to the conduct of industrial relations in construction, since it will encourage democratic participation in industrial relations by managers and workers at the site level. However, universal dependence upon the informal system would not be conducive to a harmonized policy of industrial relations, nor would the unions be willing to accept a reduction in pay or conditions of workers in areas that are not strongly unionized. But the informal system is a useful adjunct to the formal system, where basic pay and conditions can be established, and the two systems need to complement each other in an industry which is diverse and decentralized. However, improvements in the industrial relations procedure needs to be considered, particularly in the areas of consultation, the use of casual labour, and the wages policy of the industry. Attention to these issues can establish the framework for a successful industrial relations policy for the building industry.

Questions

1. In comparison with many other industries, construction has a good record in industrial relations. Discuss the factors which give rise to this situation.
2. Explain the paradox of supposed public hostility to trade unionism and the rapid numerical growth of trade unions in the post-war period. Why has this level of growth not been reflected in the construction industry?
3. Evaluate the role of the employers' associations in the construction industry. How is this role changing?
4. A dispute breaks out on a large site over revised bonus targets. A period of intense activity follows, whereby the men down tools to attend mass meetings. The management have not been informed of the intended meetings. This occurs several times.

   In negotiations, the site convenor claims that his members have to work harder to earn the same bonus. The management argues that if the men give standard performance, they can earn 33 per cent bonus. They have done work study to prove it. The convenor states that he did not know a work-study exercise was taking place. Moreover, he does not have the facilities to check incentive schemes.

   Several meetings are held between the parties but they do not resolve the matter. The convenor has registered several 'failure to agree' forms with the full-time official.

   After two weeks, agreement has not been reached and the men threaten strike action if their demands are not met within five days.

   (a) Outline the steps, through the negotiation machinery, that are necessary for a resolution of the dispute.
   (b) Discuss the action necessary to generate a better climate of industrial relations.

5. Large industrial sites are often the flash-point for industrial relations in construction. Explain why this is often the case and how the situation could be improved.
6. Clients have a responsibility to improve industrial relations in construction. Discuss how the client can have a positive impact upon site industrial relations.
7. Explain the reasons for the absence of a well-developed shop stewards' movement in the construction industry. What can the unions do to stimulate the growth of such a movement and what should the employers' response be to any such developments?
8. Are trade unions in construction governed democratically? Argue your case with reference to the structure and organization of the trade unions.
9. The authority of the National Joint Council for the Building Industry is under threat from rival industrial councils. What impact upon the negotiating machinery of the industry will this development have?
10. You have been appointed as the industrial relations manager of a large construction company. Your first task is to introduce yourself to the senior site staff and to explain the role you expect to fulfil. Prepare a paper, to be sent to senior site staff, which identifies your role and its relationship to the work of sites.

References

ACAS (1977) *Code of Practice 3 – Time Off for Trade Union Duties and Activites*, HMSO
Bayley, L. G. (1973) *Building: Teamwork Or Conflict?*, George Godwin
Burgess, K. (1975) *The Origins of British Industrial Relations*, Croom-Helm
Clack, G. (1967) 'Industrial Relations in a British Car Factory,' Department of Applied Economics, University of Cambridge
Cole, G. D. H. (1953) *Attempts at General Union*, Macmillan
Commission for Industrial Relations (1972) *Industrial Relations Training*, Report No. 33, HMSO
Donovan, T. N. (1968) *Royal Commission on Trade Unions and Employers' Associations 1965–1968*, HMSO
EIU (1978) *Public Ownership of the Construction Industries*, Economist Intelligence Unit
Hilton, W. S. (1968) *Industrial Relations in Construction*, Pergamon
Labour Research Department (1980) Political donations in 1979, *Labour Research*, Aug. pp. 170–2
Langford, D. A. 'The Effect of Labour-Only Subcontractors upon the Construction Industry.' Unpublished MSc thesis, University of Aston, Birmingham
Lansdell, D. A. E. (ed) (1981) *House's Guide to the Construction Industry*, House Information Services
Marsh, A., Evans, E. O. and Garcia, P. (1971) *Workplace Industrial Relations in Engineering*, Federation Research Paper Series No. 4, Engineering Employers Federation
Marx, K. (1867) *Capital*, Vol. 1 (1970 edn), International Publishers: New York

Cameron Report (1967) *Report of a Court of Inquiry Into Trade Disputes at the Barbican and Horseferry Road Construction Sites*, HMSO

National Board for Prices and Incomes (1968) *Report No. 92 – Pay and Conditions in the Building Industry*, HMSO

NEDO (1970) *Large Industrial Sites*, HMSO

NEDO (1971) *The Training and Development of Field Managers in Engineering Construction*, HMSO

NFBTE (1978) *An Outline History of the NFBTE 1878–1978* National Federation of Building Trades Employers

Office of Population and Census Surveys (1980) *Labour Stability in Construction*, HMSO

Phelps-Brown, E. H. *Certain Matters Concerning Labour in Building and Civil Engineering*, HMSO

Postgate, R. (1923) *The Builders History*, Labour Publishing Co.

TGWU (1974) *Shop Stewards' Handbook* Transport and General Workers Union

UCATT (1979) *Shop Stewards' Handbook*, Union of Construction Allied Trades and Technicians

Wood, L. W. *A Union to Build – the story of UCATT* Lawrence and Wishart

Chapter 5

Health and safety in construction

The necessity for construction firms to adopt sound safety policies has seldom been questioned, but the manner in which the industry is to pursue its general adherence to safe working conditions has often been hotly disputed. Trade unions in building have always called for statutory control, while employers have preferred to deal with the situation without the external pressure which the law can apply. Notwithstanding this fundamental divide, there is universal recognition that there is a moral and economic necessity to maintain safe working practices on the construction site. Unfortunately, the construction industry has become stereotyped as an accident prone industry, in fact only the mining and fishing industries have higher fatalities per 1,000 workers employed. Depressingly, the accident rates experienced closely correlate to the level of activity within the industry, indicating that when workload is high, safety tends to receive less attention. In this section, the legal, economic, and moral aspects of safety in construction will be discussed, and for the sake of convenience the chapter has been subdivided into six sections, namely:

5.1 Health and safety in construction: the magnitude of the problem
5.2 The development of safety legislation
5.3 Health and safety legislation
5.4 The costs of safety
5.5 The role of the safety officer
5.6 Safety policies, organization, and arrangements

5.1 Health and safety in construction: the magnitude of the problem

Over 1,880 people have been killed in the construction industry over the period 1968–78. In addition, every year, approximately 35,000 workers are injured seriously enough to keep them away from work for three or more days. Construction accidents mostly happen to men going about their daily work and, consequently, those involved with site safety must not only concern themselves with large, technically complex, sites but also with the more routine problems of

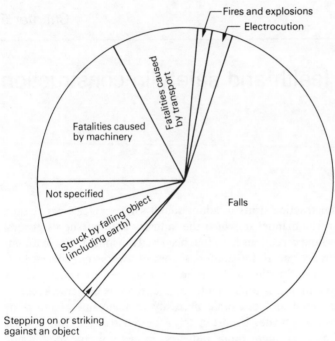

Fig. 5.1 Pie chart of causes of fatalities in construction

fragile roofs, site transport, scaffolds, etc. The Health and Safety Executive's figures for the sources of fatal accidents confirm that the commonplace operation is the most hazardous. The pie chart in Fig. 5.1 indicates the sources of fatalities in 1977 and Fig. 5.2 shows the same for notified injuries. As can be seen, by far the greatest risk arises from falls and, perhaps more surprisingly, the vast majority of accidents occur to experienced tradesmen and building workers engaged in simple traditional activities. Part of the problem arises from the nature of the work, but attitudes towards safety should compensate for this. A site worker has a greater autonomy in carrying out work than, say, a factory worker, and therefore there must be a corresponding degree of responsibility for his own safety and the safety of others. However, the trends in accident performance give some encouragement in the absolute numbers involved. Figure 5.3 demonstrates that there has been a decline in fatalities and notifiable injuries, but it must be pointed out that the annual returns fluctuate considerably. What is less encouraging is that over the ten years up to 1977, the fatalities have averaged at around 16 per 100,000 people at risk, which is five times greater than that for the manufacturing industry. With respect to disabling injuries, the chances of such an event are almost twice that for the rest of industry. Many explanations have been sought for this. The demands for higher productivity which is being met by new building methods and mechanization, coupled with the casual nature of employment within the industry, have been put forward as the main explanations. The Swedish equivalent of the Building Research Establishment (BRE) has

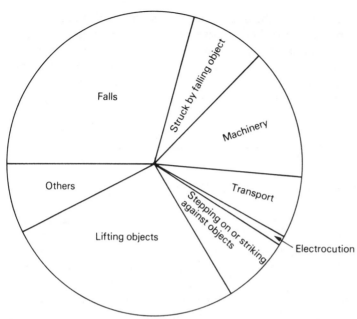

Fig. 5.2 Pie chart of causes of notifiable injuries (Source: *Health and Safety Executive*)

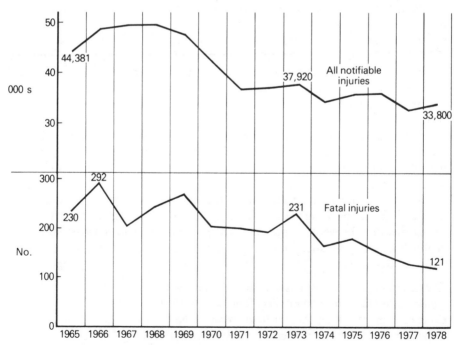

Fig. 5.3 Notifiable injuries to Health and Safety Executive in the construction industry
(Source: *Health and Safety Executive*)

identified stress as a major contributor to accidents, the stress being caused by the accelerated tempo of work carried out on sites with construction times being too short and the trades working tightly behind one another, creating stressful, and consequently more hazardous, working conditions. This progressive attitude of the Swedes towards accidents is reflected in their good record in construction safety, having an accident rate less than half that occurring in the UK. Except for Sweden, Britain's accident prevention work is probably more effective than its European neighbours and it is developing even further as the Health and Safety at Work etc. Act 1974 and its associated regulations become better understood.

5.2 The development of safety legislation

The problem of occupational safety is not a new one. Factories Acts have been in existence since 1833, with the passing of the first Factory Act. This piece of legislation was primarily directed towards the control of safety in textile mills, but despite such a limited scope, the early statutes had one important aspect – they established the factory inspectorate, the policing agent of the legislation, and initiated the concept of a body of experts who were able to enforce the legislation. The existence of the inspectorate has been an enduring feature of the health and safety legislation which, in the main, has developed in a piecemeal fashion, with various industries and processes being covered by specific legislation at particular points in time. Periodically, the piecemeal nature of safety legislation is recognized and attempts are made to consolidate legislation. The Factories Act (Consolidation) of 1937 sought to rationalize matters and this Act applied to 'factories belonging to, or in the occupation of, the Crown and to building operations and works of engineering construction undertaken by, or on behalf of, the Crown' (1937). This consolidated Act gave the construction industry rudimentary guidelines on subjects such as the covering of excavations, the security of ladders and fencing, etc. Additionally, the factory inspectorate were to be informed about the commencement of new construction works. Further Factories Acts followed in 1948 and 1959 which amended the 1937 legislation, with the most recent being passed through Parliament in 1961 – this still being a statute today.

The construction industry falls within the scope of the Factories Act despite its nature of operations being widely different to those pertaining in a factory. It was recognized that the whole of the 1961 Act could not apply to construction, but it enabled specific regulations for construction to be incorporated: i.e. the Construction Regulations of 1961 and 1966. They included the following regulations:

Construction (General Provisions) Regulation 1961
Construction (Lifting Operations) Regulations 1961
Construction (Working Places) Regulations 1966
Construction (Health and Welfare)   Regulations 1966
The Asbestos Regulations were added in 1969 and the Abrasive Wheel Regulations in 1970.

Despite periodic attempts to consolidate safety legislation, there still remained a mass of laws and statutory instruments which governed industrial health and safety. By 1970 it was estimated that approximately two-thirds of the country's workforce were protected by more than 30 statutes and 500 statutory instruments. Changes in the law reflected the attitudes of various governments towards safety and, as a result, developments were expedient rather than principled. By 1970 it was widely recognized that health and safety legislation required overhauling and Lord Robens chaired a government committee entitled 'Committee of Enquiry on Safety and Health At Work'. This committee had extremely wide terms of reference and its brief related to the whole field of occupational risk and the protection of the public from hazards connected with industrial and commercial work. The final report of the committee was released in 1972 with radical proposals for the future of health and safety legislation. In particular, it identified several key difficulties with existing legislation:

(a) There had been an empirical approach to the problem of health and safety, whereas the area was one which required systematic analysis. To remedy this situation a single statute of general application would be required to replace the mass of existing legislation.
(b) The existing law was of a complex nature and should be replaced by a simple statute which held within it simply assimilated concepts of general application.
(c) The enforcement procedures lacked reality. The solution proposed was that prosecution should not be a matter of first resort, but new procedures should be introduced which would encourage compliance with the law.
(d) The emphasis of past legislation had been upon the workplace environment and this should be widened to include the protection of visitors and the general public.
(e) Previously, emphasis had been placed upon technical safety standards resulting in the negligence of the working system used; a greater emphasis on management responsibilites for providing and maintaining a safe system of working was deemed necessary.
(f) There had been a failure to involve the workforce in safety matters and this should be corrected by active involvement of trade unions at shop floor and national level.
(g) There was a multiplicity of agencies who were responsible for enforcement, i.e. local authorities, factory inspectorate, fire brigades, police, etc.

The report also conceded that progress in the safety field was often limited by the negative approach to regulation of health and safety. In many ways, the Robens Committee report moved towards accepting the Swedish system of occupational health and safety, with its emphasis upon the positive benefits of good welfare and safety rather than the punitive aspects associated with the British system.

The report suggested that a greater emphasis upon personal responsibility and voluntary effort within a legal system would produce a substantial increase in awareness and consciousness of safety problems at work. The statute was to be enforced by a stronger and more powerful inspectorate with greater responsibilities for managers and employees.

The Robens Committee report was almost immediately accepted by government and opposition and the essential aspects of the committee's work became law under the aegis of the Health and Safety At Work Act in 1974.

5.3 Health and safety legislation

The Health and Safety at Work etc. Act 1974 supplemented the old legislation such as the Factories Acts and the Offices, Shops and Railway Premises Act. The Health and Safety at Work etc. Act 1974 was initiated with the intention of creating a single legal and administrative structure under which all workers and the public at large were to be protected. It is an enabling statute imposing a general care on all people associated with work activities and so it is a change from previous health and safety legislation which were more concerned with physical harm.

Generally, the Act consists of new, or at least more specific, obligations on managers, supervisors, and worker representatives and has four particular aims:

(a) to secure the health and safety and welfare of persons at work;
(b) to protect persons other than persons at work against risks to health and safety arising out of, or in connection with, the activities of persons at work;
(c) to control the keeping and use of explosive or highly flammable or otherwise dangerous substances and generally prevent the unlawful acquisition, possession and use of such substances;
(d) to control the emission into the atmosphere of noxious or offensive substances.

One of the principal objectives is to involve everybody at the workplace – management and workpeople – to create an awareness of the importance of achieving high standards of health and safety, and the primary responsibility for doing what is necessary to avoid accidents and occupational ill-health lies with those who create the risks. With the Act came specific duties that employers should perform. In particular, Section 2 of the Health and Safety at Work etc. Act 1974 specifies that employers are to ensure the health, safety and welfare of all employees. From the generalized duty, employers have detailed responsibilities:

● to develop systems of work which are practicable, safe, and have no risk to health;
● to provide plant to facilitate this duty, and this general requirement is to cover all plant used at the workplace;
● to provide training in the matter of health and safety; employers must provide the instruction, training, and supervision necessary to ensure a safe working environment;

- to provide a working environment which is conducive to health and safety;
- to prepare a written statement of safety policy and to establish an organizational framework for carrying out the policy; the policy must be brought directly to the attention of all employees.

However, employees also have specific duties namely:

- to take care of their health and safety and that of other persons who would be affected by acts or an omission at the workplace;
- to co-operate with the employer to enable everyone to comply with the statutory provisions.

Obviously, these general duties imposed upon employers and employees have to be backed up with an effective inspectorate. The structure of the inspectorate is shown in Fig. 5.4.

Clearly, the inspectors are the persons who will be directly involved in checking the safety of particular sites. As such, they are granted the power to enter sites, at any reasonable time, for the purposes of inspection. The inspection procedure may include the taking of photographs, samples, etc., and the inspector may request site managers to provide documents or any other information he may require in carrying out his duties. The inspector has a duty to inform the workforce on a site of any matters which are likely to be deleterious to the workers' health and safety, but the inspector is also obliged to give the same information to the employer. If the inspector finds that a site is in breach of the requirements of the Act, then three possible remedies exist:

- the issue of improvement notices;
- the issue of prohibition notices;
- the issue of 'seize and destroy' instructions.

The *improvement* notice means that if a site is in contravention of a statutory provision, an inspector may serve an improvement notice, stating his opinion concerning the breach of regulation, the particulars of the breach, and the demand that the contractor rectify the situation within a given period. The *prohibition* notice arises when the inspector is of the opinion that construction activities being carried out involve the risk of serious personal injury. The inspector must state why, in his opinion, a prohibition notice is necessary. The prohibition notice will instruct a person not to carry on with an operation until the necessary steps have been taken to improve safety. These notices may be immediate or deferred. With *seize and destroy* notices, the inspector may seize and destroy any article or substance which causes an imminent danger to persons.

While these penalties have statutory authority, many observers have suggested that fines imposed have been too low and have often been inconsistent. In *An Employer's Guide to Health and Safety Management*, Arscott (1977) presented a series of case studies on accidents in construction. Some of the cases presented are quoted below.

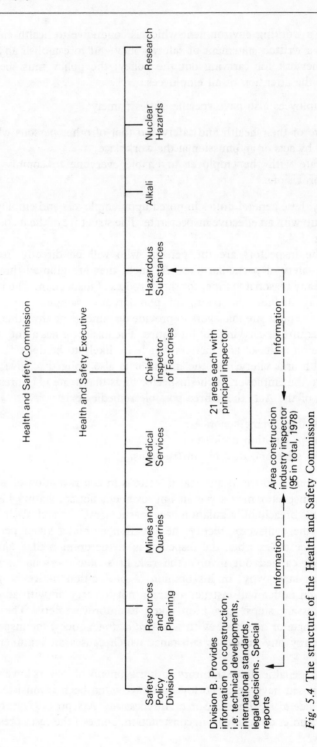

Fig. 5.4 The structure of the Health and Safety Commission

Case 1. A carpenter fell from a roof when trying to avoid a pile of roof slabs dislodged by a sling suspended from a crane.
Fine: £150.
Case 2. A soffit for a concrete slab not properly supported with metal props out of line, raking not properly braced, etc.
Fine £200.
Case 3. A crane overturned, killing a youth. The crane was overloaded, its safe warning device was defective and weekly inspections were not carried out.
Fine: £210.
Case 4. Two 11kV cables fell after being hit by a lorry. Workers received shocks and burns.
Fine: £75.

However, the cases quoted may be unrepresentative and recent penalties would seem to be reflecting more concern over safety. Furthermore, the Health and Safety at Work Act set out to move the balance of safety control towards positive prevention of accidents rather than punitive action after the event.

The machinery for the detailed prevention of accidents is embodied by codes of practice. Under Section 16 of the Health and Safety at Work Act 1974 the Health and Safety Commission has the power to draw up or approve codes of practice for specific working procedures. Observance of codes of practice are admissable as evidence in any criminal proceedings for an offence under the Health and Safety at Work etc. Act 1974. Firms may draw up their own codes of practice, but it is important that these are approved by the Health and Safety Commission.

Allied to the Health and Safety at Work etc. Act 1974 are Regulations, and those which have a bearing upon construction are summarized in Appendix A on page 310.

5.4 The costs of safety

The moral responsibility for safety has been stated and, as we have seen, there is a legal requirement for the provision of safe working environments. But added to these is an economic incentive to ensure safety. To many managers who have been brought up on the importance of controlling costs and time, the economic argument is the most forceful. In construction the costs of accidents can be immense – in 1979 the Health and Safety Executive estimated that total losses amounted to £30 million in 1975. However, this figure is merely an estimate and there is still the question: 'Can a meaningful cost be applied to accidents?' For material losses in which no injury occurs the accounting of loss can be easily assessed; but where human loss is concerned, the costing becomes more difficult – life or a physical facility cannot crudely be financially evaluated, yet it has been widely recognized that monetary compensation to either the injured party or relatives (in the event of a fatality) has to be paid. While the courts, the insurers, and the DHSS have produced a large number of precedents, the amounts of compensation paid are very variable. Those who process their claims through the courts generally do better than those who take out-of-court settlements.

Most compensation payments are paid by contractors' insurers, but this fact should not detract from an incentive to improve safety. Insurance companies will base premiums upon historical evidence, and a poor safety record will inevitably be reflected in premiums. However, doubt has been raised as to whether the premium loading is adequate, since many insurance companies will spread the risk rather than sharply discriminate between good and bad risk organizations. This has often proved frustrating for companies with progressive accident prevention policies, who feel that their attitude to the problem is not being recognized by the insurers. One approach to this problem is to treat the direct costs of accidents and the costs of preventative measures taken to avoid them as the total accident cost and then seek to minimize this cost. In construction the costs of accidents will fall as safety measures increase; this is presented graphically in Fig. 5.5. If this relationship is accepted, then we have two components: accident cost and prevention cost. As we reduce risk, the accident cost will also be reduced, but in order to reduce risks we must spend money on accident prevention. Therefore, we have an intersection of graph lines in Fig. 5.6. Now, by adding together the accident cost and the prevention cost, we shall develop a dish shape (Fig. 5.6) and the lowest part on this curve will indicate the optimum expenditure on safety prevention.

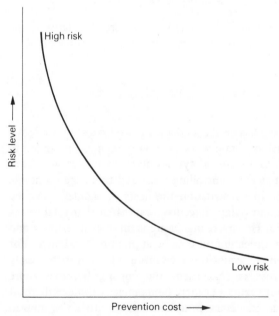

Fig. 5.5 The relationship of costs to safety measures

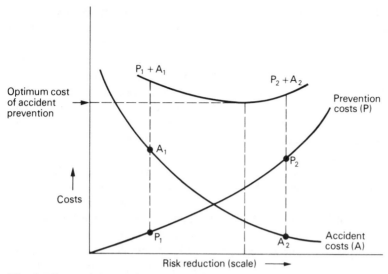

Fig. 5.6 Determining optimum costs of accident prevention

The difficulty with this approach is that it does not take into account the subjective nature of many accident costs Sinclair (1972) has attempted to quantify accident costs by breaking accidents down into three parts: fatalities, serious injuries (over four weeks off work), and other injuries. The cost of accidents can then be expressed as:

$$C_A = R_D \times (A_{sD} + A_{oD}) + R_S(A_{sS} + A_{oS}) + R_O(A_{sO} + A_{oO})$$

where
C_A = annual accident cost per worker

R_D = annual risk of death per worker

R_S = annual risk of serious injury per worker

R_O = annual risk of other injury per worker

and average A_s = subjective element of cost

A_o = objective element of cost

With subscripts D, S, or O for death, serious injury, or other injury, as above.

Sinclair has applied this method to large groups of workers, and with industry-wide figures the cost of each accident has some relevance when compared against the cost of prevention.

The cost of prevention can be based upon more objective data. Companies can abstract from records the costs of safety in terms of the provision of safety administration, protective clothing and equipment, insurance, extra manning for safety reasons, estimated loss of production due to unavoidable hazards on sites, etc. The value of the costs of prevention per worker can be compared against the

103

costs of accidents per worker. Sinclair has argued that when the preventative costs of accidents equal the costs of accidents, the optimum cost of prevention has been reached. This approach has its critics, since there will be a time lag between the institution of preventative measures and their effect, but it can be used as a mental yardstick by which accident prevention programmes can be evaluated.

A simpler, and probably more practical, approach was put forward by Capp (1977) who analysed the actual cost of accidents in industry. The cost assessments are based solely on the working days lost by injury which are reported to the Health and Safety Inspectorate. The study was carried out in 1970 when approximately 23 million days were lost through accidents or industrial disease, with the average accident/incident ratio of 34/1,000. However, these figures are based upon reported accidents which resulted in more than three days off work but, as many surveys have pointed out, considerable numbers of firms in construction do not report all accidents. One such survey was carried out in April 1964, when the number of claims for industrial injury benefit relating to people injured in construction work was compared with the number of injuries actually notified by employers to HM Factory Inspectorate during the same period. The study revealed that some 58 per cent of legally notifiable cases were not being reported. The results are summarized below and there is no reason to believe that under-reporting has changed since that time.

Industry	No. of injuries reported	No. notifiable but not reported	Total	% failure to report
Construction	2,485	3,432	5,917	58
Manufacturing	13,986	6,336	20,322	31

Hence, the real cost of accidents may be far greater than that revealed by calculations based on official statistics. Nonetheless, it is useful to evaluate the available data. Several assumptions are made:

(a) The loss to a company is the total return for an employee's labour at an average daily rate of £20, with companies involved in accidents having to pay 200 per cent of this figure; 20 days average absence.
(b) Two hours has been assumed as the time lost for treatment and incidental disruption and assistance to injured persons.
(c) The average cost of repair or replacement resulting for each incident of property damage is £100.
(d) Insurance premiums are increased by 20p per £100 of wages.
(e) There is an accident/incident rate of 33 accidents per 1,000 workers (1977 figures).
(f) Each year, 240 working days are available.

From the above assumptions, the calculated cost of £138.32 per employee to a company with 1,000 employees is presented in Table 5.1.

Table 5.1

Predicted accident rates	Category	Actual number	Loss	Value
1	Reported accident. Loss to company: 200% of wage rate	33	33 × 20 days = 660 days lost per 1,000 workers at 200% = 1,320 days at £20 per day	£26,400
10	Minor accidents	330	330 × 2 hours = 660 hours lost per 1,000 workers = 73 days at 200% = 146 days at £20 per day	£2,920
30	Property damage	990	990 × £100	£99,000
	Insurance costs		20p per £100 wages for 1,000 workers $\left(\dfrac{0.2 \times 5,000}{100}\right) \times 1,000$	£10,000
Total cost per 1,000 employees				£138,320
Cost per employee				£138.32

To the figure of £138.32 wasted per employee is to be added the consequential costs such as delay and lost production and, therefore, the figure is, by nature, conservative, and estimates of the rates of direct loss to consequential loss have been made from 100 to 300 per cent. Hence, expenditure upon safety may be an economic as well as a legal and moral necessity.

However, it is important to stress that the economic aspects of safety should not be seen as the prime motivator for construction safety. The central issue is the intangible elements of a whole and healthy workforce for construction. Cost considerations and calculations of cost optimization can only be seen as a guide to determining priorities and improvement of health and safety in construction.

5.5 The role of the safety officer

Contractors should give careful thought to the role of the full-time safety officer. Two basic concepts exist about this role:

(a) safety officers should be advisers to site management; and
(b) the safety officer undertakes the safety responsibilities on behalf of sites.

It has been argued that site management must have a prime concern for safety upon their sites and, therefore, it would seem consistent with this view that the role of the safety officer should be to advise line management on the specific aspects of health and safety matters. From this the safety officer must have sufficient status to carry out his duties *vis-à-vis* all levels of company management.

Obviously, the role of safety officer will vary from firm to firm, depending upon the size of the organization and the type of construction work undertaken, but, in general, it will consist of the following duties:

(a) formulating the company's safety policy;
(b) advising management on legislation and safety matters;
(c) assisting in the drafting of safe working procedures and codes of practice;
(d) reporting and investigating accidents with the preparation and analysis of safety records;
(e) safety training;
(f) safety propaganda;
(g) safety assessments of site management;
(h) carrying out inspections of sites;
(i) monitoring the work of the safety committees.

In carrying out these duties the safety officer must, at all times, work in close harmony with management and the trade unions to ensure that no aspect of safety is neglected. Clearly, the qualifications of a safety officer will vary, but as with most occupations in construction, energy, intelligence and personality are, perhaps, the most important personal characteristics. In order that the safety officer can talk authoritatively to site managers, a technical background is often desirable, but this must be complemented by a strong commitment to safety, with an ability to convey this attitude to others.

The ability to transmit enthusiasm for safety is central to the safety officer's role, since it implies that the safety officer must motivate site managers to have a concern for safety. The authoritarian approach seldom works in construction, and it has been observed that good safety officers favour a policy of gradually influencing site managers and taking every opportunity to give advice when it is sought. It is easy to see this course of action as weakness, but many will identify the persuasive rather than authoritarian approach as the best way forward if line managers are to become more directly involved in safety. The safety officer who sees himself or herself as an internal factory inspector will certainly make problems by stirring up resentment, such that site managers have no incentive for improvement. However, the soft approach does have its disadvantages. Site managers who regularly fail to be influenced by the safety officer in their day-to-day decisions are not identified for reprimand by senior management. If safety officers only progress by influencing those managers who invite their influence, the uninterested man remains unconvinced that changes are necessary. Although it is unpalatable, the safety officer must clearly identify poor safety performers so that internal measures can be taken.

The company safety officer will also have to co-operate with other functional specialists within the firm. Contacts will need to include the training officer to ensure that internal company courses have an adequate safety content, and the safety officer will also have to work closely with any medical officer the company may employ, since the work of the safety officer and those responsible for occupational health are closely interlinked.

In larger companies the safety officer must be able to carry out executive duties within a department. This function may include the supervision of assistant safety officers, safety inspectors, clerical staff, statisticians, etc. This responsibility will extend to presenting the board of directors with essential information on safety matters. Such a role would necessitate an ability to quantitively evaluate statistical data and present these data in a clear, concise, form.

5.6 Safety policies, organization, and arrangements

As has been seen, the Health and Safety at Work Act radically departs from the previous safety laws in that there is a strong element of self-regulation of safety, with a view to firms having an efficient organization for health and safety. This approach of self-regulation has obviously created problems for firms operating in the construction industry. Management has to contend with a variety of problems which will vary from site to site during the progress of the job. Climate, regional differences in the labour force, time of year, type of contract, method of payment, type of employment practices, and labour mobility all mean that construction management will have a difficult job to control safety on the site. Additionally, as employers have expected a building to be completed on time and within the estimated cost, safety has often been regarded as an imposition upon the drive to satisfy these primary objectives.

Successful firms within the industry have solved their difficulties without affecting productivity and have effectively integrated the safety and health of the workforce into the mainstream of their organizational operations. Progressive management will argue that the safety and health of workers must be as equally well organized as the commercial aspects of their company.

However, there is a wide diversity in attitudes to safety within the industry. It is noticeable that of the fatalities recorded in 1977, only 21 per cent of the total occurred in large companies, and this fact needs to be balanced against the large proportion of the industry's workforce employed by the larger contractor. Perhaps it is not surprising that the larger organizations have a better safety record than the more casual operators within the industry, since it is widely recognized that a company's safety policy lives or dies by the support it receives from top management. This commitment to safety from the top is important and it must be emphasized that a safety policy developed by management must be more that a statement of good intent, but senior management must show a commitment to safe and healthy working conditions throughout the company. The Health and Safety Commission have identified a reasonable test of sincerity:

they suggest that top management should be seen to support site management when decisions are taken which relegate profit below a concern for safety.

In general, the safety policy must be backed up by organization and arrangements which will secure the maximum effect. A typical organization structure for the control of safety is shown in Fig. 5.7. It is not intended to describe the detailed arrangements for the organization for safety, because each company will have its own style and manner of operations and the intention behind the self-regulation principle is that safety policies should reflect a compatibility of safety procedures and general organization. However, some general rules can be developed:

(a) the delegation of responsibility for safety down to the workface;
(b) the identification of key personnel to direct the safety effort in specific areas of work (e.g. plant maintenance, keeping of records, etc);
(c) the development of job descriptions which emphasize that site managers are accountable for safety on site:
(d) the monitoring of safety by the safety officer of a company and the submission of reports to senior management in such a manner that they have a picture of what is happening on site in terms of health and safety;
(e) placing a strong emphasis on the development of safe systems of work;
(f) the importance of good communications between sites and head office over safety matters.

The last point, concerning communications, needs close attention. In particular, firms may need to ensure that safe systems manuals are transmitted to sites where they will be needed. Additionally, information will need to flow between sites and head office which will make senior management aware of the site conditions and will alert sites to the senior management's attitude toward safety. Finally, a good communication system can assist in the circulation of information concerning new hazards within the company and the industry in general. The transmission of information concerning safety has been one of the traditional roles of the employers' associations, and the NFBTE and the FCEC have played an important part in providing information on matters of health and safety to their members. Other organizations involved in the provision of data are the Building Advisory Service (BAS) and the Building Research Establishment (BRE), as well as trade unions allied to the construction industry.

5.6.1 Training

Many of the larger contractors have a well-developed programme of safety training, but as yet there is no systematic or comprehesive training provision within the industry. Much of the training carried out is done in-house and is occasionally supplemented by the Construction Industry Training Board (CITB).

Safety training should begin with the new employee and continue throughout the time he or she is with the company. The type of training, frequency, material presented, and by whom the material is presented, will obviously vary with the

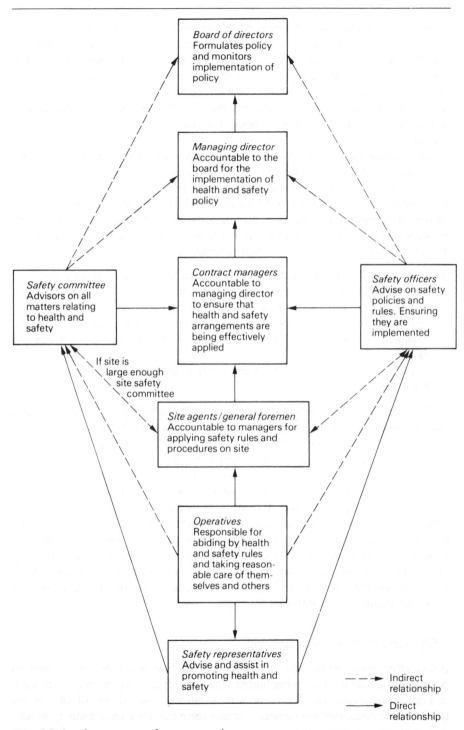

Fig. 5.7 A safety structure for a contracting company

type of employment and trade involved. However, safety training should be given to all employees regardless of previous experience. The focus of this in-house training should, of course, be the company's safety policy, but specific information may need to be imparted verbally with a discussion of the company's attitude to safety. Such items as the necessity of wearing protective clothing for particular tasks, the location of the first-aid equipment, and the person(s) qualified to administer first aid are pieces of basic information which can be transmitted verbally.

Even experienced workers can benefit from additional on-the-job safety training. One of the most effective means is the use of periodic safety meetings with the use of visual aids to dramatize the effects of poor adherence to safe procedures. However, such meetings should only be long enough to present the desired information, and are often best undertaken in an informal setting where workers can contribute observations concerning safety on site. Some of the matters that can be discussed at such meetings could include:

(a) information on accidents that have happened elsewhere on similar sites (the company safety officer should keep site managers informed about such accidents and any conclusions that have been drawn from them);
(b) indicating precautionary measures necessary on any new section of the work;
(c) reviewing first-aid procedures (see review of Health and Welfare Regulations);
(d) pointing out (preferably without mentioning names) any unsafe practices that have been noticed.

To supplement such general training, an in-depth training for specific trades may be necessary. In this respect a number of encouraging developments have taken place, perhaps most significantly in the training of scaffolders. In 1974 a report from the Joint Advisory Committee on Safety and Health in the Construction Industry (1974) recommended that scaffolders who were to erect temporary structures over 5 m high should hold a certificate of competence, which would have been gained from a recognized course. Clearly, further certification will necessitate an expansion of training facilities and this may only be the first step in having a more systematic approach to safety training. The Health and Safety Executive have established a working party with representatives from the Training Services Agency, with a view to identifying areas of work or classes of workmen in the construction industry on whom scarce training resources might be concentrated.

5.6.2 Accident prevention planning

It has often been argued that safety in construction is a function of external conditions, accident levels being higher when money is tight, interest rates high, and inflation advancing. Yet these very conditions should not of themselves inhibit safety consciousness on site. It would seem that for a safer industry several requirements are demanded.

(a) *Changing attitudes to safety*

It is widely accepted that management and workers jointly contribute to the inherent risks associated with construction work. Both accept the high injury rates as a 'fact of life' with the annual accident figures at company and industry level acting as a catalyst for action or inaction. If accident figures for a particular year are better than the previous year, complacency sets in; if they are worse, then safety becomes more central to the concern of the company and the industry. There may also be a normalizing process associated with accident rates. Firms who have achieved low returns on accident rates over several years are considered as having untypical returns, along with firms who have high accident rates. To stay within the boundaries of the previous year's returns is often seen as an acceptable philosophy. Inevitably, counting the number of accidents will continue, but a more positive approach may be possible by counting the number of lives 'saved'. For instance, it has been estimated that between ten and twenty lives have been saved on the construction of the Forth Bridge project by instigating specific safety measures. With this approach in mind, the Construction Central Operations Unit of the Factory Inspectorate encouraged the measurement of safety performance beyond the comparison against the previous year's statistics. Such an approach would systematically classify a hazard for its significance and principle cause, with the result of identifying whether an accident arose through the failure of site supervision or from inadequate training or information.

A more quantitative analysis can be determined by the use of 'critical incidence techniques', whereby information is collected on hazards, near misses and unsafe conditions and practices from experienced personnel. The technique involves interviewing workers regarding involvement in accidents or near accidents. Tarrents (1977) has noted that people are more willing to talk about 'close calls' than about serious accidents in which they were personally involved, the implication being that if no loss ensued, no blame for the accident would be forthcoming. In effect, the critical incidence technique accomplishes the same as an accident investigation, by identifying the type of hazards that could result in injury or damage. It has been estimated that for every mishap there are 400 near misses and, consequently, by sampling all persons in a firm, a large sample size can be built up from which causes of possible accidents can be derived. It is common for similarities to appear in reports of hazards and near misses and these may be used as indications of areas in which improvements are necessary. However, such a scheme could produce more paperwork in a situation where managers are gradually being overloaded by increasing workloads, but a firm with a strong commitment to safety will expect managers to take care of this matter, by careful husbandry of time or the appointment of site safety specialists.

This approach is one of many which attempts to measure site safety performance. In 1976 the Construction Control Operations Unit of the Factory Inspectorate attempted to encourage firms to use their available data to review safety performance over the preceding twelve months. Central to this approach was the systematic classification of every hazard, with indications of its significance and principal cause. In this way it is possible to note whether the hazard arises from a failure in site supervision, senior management, or through inadequacies in training, instruction, or information. However, this approach should not be seen in a wholly negative manner, with positive aspects of site safety being recorded as well as the misdemeanours. But the identification of responsibility for an accident has its drawbacks in that a safety officer requires co-operation from line management if his or her job is to be done effectively. By allocating responsibility, the safety officer may destroy a good relationship and, hence, the motivation of line management to improve safety on site. Assessment schemes can be unpopular with line management, because they are seen as threats to their self-esteem, with the reaction that line management can become obstructive in order to cope with threats. In particular, line management may start to question the measurement criteria, with the consequence that the importance of safety inspection is demoted. Also, the source of the assessment – the safety officer – becomes another source of external pressure, rather than a co-operative colleague. These difficulties can be overcome by using the assessment as a measure of positive values and not negative ones, with each hazard being assessed systematically for its liability to cause accidents and the extent of the risk it poses. If a numerical scale is used, then this should be adjusted where satisfactory protective features are noted on site. This aspect is important, since site managers are being assessed in what they have achieved in terms of safety and health. It emphasizes that safety can be managed in the same way that other aspects of the resources imputted in a construction site. Care should obviously be taken to ensure that an assessment discussion is not carried out in an authoritarian way, with the company safety officer sitting in judgement on the site management team. Equally important is the correct structuring of assessments so that site managers feel that they are receiving fair treatment. Of particular importance in this respect is the alerting of site management as to when assessments will be taking place, information on the criteria of assessment, pointing out the health and safety issues that are of prime concern. Finally, the assessment should begin by giving site management the opportunity to discuss the difficulties they have experienced in attaining high standards of health and safety. Naturally this process of co-operation is not meant to obscure the facts – if a site is poor, then this must be said – but the basic principle is to encourage positive attitudes rather than hostility and resentment.

The Health and Safety Executive have attempted to allocate responsibility on an industry-wide basis and their research reveals that considerable improvement is possible. Figure 5.8 shows those responsible for controlling the precautionary measures thought necessary for the prevention of fatal accidents. It can be seen from the histogram that only 12 per cent of the total fatalities were due to unforeseeable events.

Other approaches are available for the planning and management of safety. If accident prevention is to be a reality, concern for safety must commence at the planning stage of construction work. Many contractors will use CPM (critical path methods) as a planning tool and there seems no reason why the safety aspect should not be integrated into this programme. Each element of the network can

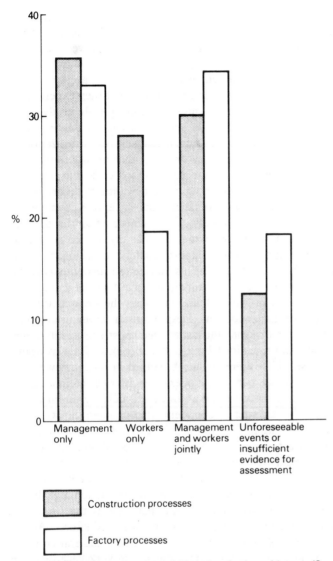

Fig. 5.8 Allocation of responsibility for fatal accidents. (Source: *Health and Safety Executive*)

be assessed for safety requirements necessary for the work. For instance, in-house manuals can direct management by highlighting safety on a whole series of operations. However, design also has a role to play and, clearly, the architects and engineers must develop designs which can safely be constructed. Construction technology is rapidly changing and concern for safety needs to be reviewed when innovative designs are being considered. Indeed, many educationalists have argued that designing for safe construction should feature more prominently in undergraduate courses for architects and structural engineers.

(b) Safety and incentives

Working hours and incentives also have a bearing upon accidents and management may wish to review policy on these issues in order to improve health and safety. It has long been accepted that efficiency falls when excessive overtime is worked, but accompanying the fall in efficiency is a rise in accident rates (experiments with women working a 12-hour day showed that they experienced two-and-a-half times the accident rates of those working a 10-hour day). In construction, the use of overtime is widespread, and the reasons for this are clear: workers like the additional income and management can gain better utilization of existing manpower. However, the moral to be drawn is that managers who are concerned with safety and accident prevention need to look closely at overtime working, and it may be necessary to limit actual working hours to 50 per week.

Construction workers are also highly dependent upon incentive payments to supplement the basic pay. Piecework is widely used in construction through the labour-only subcontracting system of employment. It has often been suggested that labour-only subcontracting does little to improve safety consciousness or to encourage safe working methods at site level. This may be the effect of haste, the lack of stability within the labour-only workforce, and the financial gains to be reaped from an early finish, all of which tends to lessen the importance that should be attached to safe working conditions. Despite this, a survey undertaken by the Phelps-Brown Committee (1968) illustrated that most site agents interviewed considered that accident rates for labour-only subcontractors were about the same level as for those directly employed. Langford (1974) reviewed the situation in 1974 and found that 78 per cent of operatives interviewed in a survey felt that labour-only subcontractors were not as aware of safety requirements as directly employed workers. Management respondents corroborated this with a 75 per cent assent to the same question. The primary incentive scheme for directly employed workers is a production bonus scheme. This type of incentive would appear to do less harm. Various reasons have been put forward for this. Many people have often argued that incentives do little to directly motivate but benefits arise from the intangible effects of better organization or production and this in itself will create a safer working environment. Another view is that incentive bonuses are so often a lottery and have little to do with workers' efforts. As the authors of *2000 Accidents* (Powell *et al.* 1971) observe: 'In the general accident situation bonus pay is unlikely to correlate with accidents at work because there are few cases where it properly reflects the human work content of the task.' However, abandoning bonus payments in the construction industry would be universally condemned when it constitutes an important element of the take-home pay. Nonetheless, management must be aware of the additional hazards which may be created by the use of bonus schemes and to evaluate how far incentives to safer performance can be incorporated into their operation. But incentives are not limited to finance. There can be competitions between sites to encourage better safety performances. Such schemes have the benefit of encouraging safety awareness on site and fostering a spirit of co-operation between management and workers about safety matters. Competitions do, however, have their detractors, who argue that they encourage non-reporting and non-recording of accidents. As one union official dryly commented when his firm had won a safety award: 'It's all walking wounded. That's what we call it.'

The general conclusion is that while incentives to greater output and greater safety should not be discouraged, they should be carefully examined to ensure that they do not contain features which militate against genuine safety and accident prevention.

Summary

It has been argued that contractors have a moral, economic, and legal commitment to ensure that working conditions on site are healthy and safe. But the responsibility for safety must commence upstream of the construction phase of a project; architects and engineers must have the technical knowledge to design buildings which can be safely constructed, as well as a commitment to safe working conditions for site workers.

To generate safety consciousness within construction organizations, a firm lead must be taken by top management. It is recognized that finance and lost production are convenient measurements of accidents, but accidents should generate an emotional response, and if this emotion is genuine it will carry conviction. A firm's safety policy which is founded upon compassion will more often succeed, since it will be impervious to shifts and changes in fashion and production schedules and, consequently, will be less easily diluted. Senior management can do much to implement the policy by adhering to the requirements of the Health and Safety at Work Act and its associated regulations. In particular, the encouragement of safety committees which can monitor progress in respect of safe working methods, but more importantly, to act upon recommendations and reports from the safety committee (s) and to discipline any person in breach of relevant safety laws and codes of practice. Obviously, adequate tools, tackle, plant, and protective clothing must be provided and these items can be framed within a budget for the development of health and safety.

Finally, management should not see safety merely as a hindrance to productivity, but as a component of an efficient mechanism of production.

Questions

1. Outline the principal features of a safety policy for a construction company.
2. Discuss the potential sources of conflict between a company safety officer and a site agent. How best are such differences resolved?
3. Assess the impact of the Health and Safety at Work Act upon the construction industry. Are such legislative interventions necessary for the improvement of health and safety in construction?

4. It has been suggested that accident prevention costs can be optimized. What are the advantages and disadvantages of this approach to construction site safety?
5. Explain how a safety audit can be carried out on construction sites and identify potential problems in carrying out such a task.
6. Are safety committees useful agencies for monitoring safety on construction sites? Amplify your answer with reference to the work of safety committees.
7. Can concern for safety be integrated with project planning? If so, explain how. If not, explain why.
8. Can the 'critical incident technique' be usefully employed on construction sites? Draw up a method statement of how this could be carried out.

References

Arscott, P. (1977) *An Employer's Guide to Health and Safety Management*, Kogan-Page

Capp, R. H. (1977) *Engineer's Management Guide to the Elements of Industrial Safety*, Institution of Production Engineers

Health and Safety Executive (1974) *Report of Advisory Committee on Safety and Health in the Construction Industry*, HMSO

HM Government (1937) *The Factories Act*, HMSO

Langford, D. A. (1974) 'The Effect of Labour-Only Subcontractors upon the Construction Industry.' Unpublished MSc thesis, University of Aston, Birmingham

Phelps-Brown, E. H. (1968) *Certain Matters Concerning Labour in Building and Civil Engineering*, HMSO

Powell, P., Hale, P., Martin, J. and Simon, M. (1971) *2000 Accidents*, National Institute of Industrial Psychology

Sinclair, T. C. (1972) *A Cost Effectiveness Approach to Industrial Safety*, HMSO

Tarrents, W. E. (1977) *Utilizing the Critical Incident Technique as a Method of Identifying Potential Accident Causes*, Washington, DC: US Department of Labor

Chapter 6

Manpower planning

It has been widely recognized that human resources are vital for construction organizations. Yet the industry has a momentous task in forecasting and planning its manpower requirements which enables the full utilization of this resource. To many within the industry an attempt to plan manpower is a fruitless task as there are too many variables for the goal to be realized. A more progressive view is that it is wasteful and uneconomic not to have a manpower plan with specific objectives. This purview often led government to seek predictions of manpower through the (now defunct) Construction Industry Manpower Board whose objectives were to carry out macro manpower planning for the industry. Many of its manpower predictions were based upon aggregates of manpower plans developed at the operating level within the individual firms which comprise the industry.

It must be recognized that any manpower plan for the industry or for individual firms must be flexible since the construction industry is often used as an economic regulator and shifts in government policy for the construction industry will obviously have repercussions upon the manpower needs of firms and of the industry in general. But even guidelines are preferable to the stop/go recruitment and training programmes undertaken with little foresight regarding the future needs and demands of the industry. This chapter reviews the material on manpower planning for the industry and the firm, and is broken down into the following sections:

6.1 Objectives
6.2 Procedures
6.3 Labour stability
6.4 Recruitment to the industry.

6.1 Objectives

For many years the construction industry has relied upon crisis management to solve its manpower problems – as sites opened up, labour was engaged to staff it; when the job came to an end, the operatives were laid off. This traditional approach obviously has its limitations in that it projects an image of an uncertain

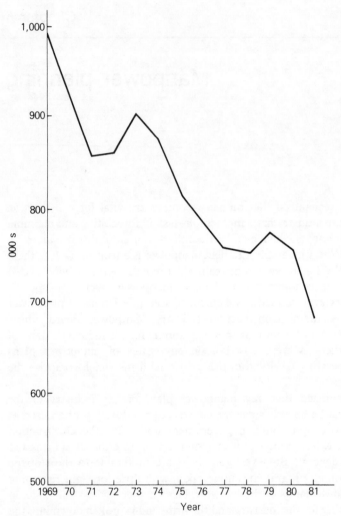

Fig. 6.1 Trends in operative employment

and unstable industry, with the numbers of operatives employed by the industry varying directly with demand for construction services. The trends in operative employment indicate this cyclical fluctuation (see Fig. 6.1). These figures merely record direct employment and if labour-only subcontracting could be included, the graph would be much more volatile. The high level of insolvencies associated with construction exacerbates this situation, and Fig. 6.2 demonstrates this fact.

Cynics may argue that these figures demonstrate the futility of attempting manpower planning for the industry, but equally it may be suggested that the instability of the labour force is a reflection of the industry's failure to undertake long-term forecasting of manpower needs. Clearly, capital-intensive industries are better placed to forecast accurately their manpower requirements, and in

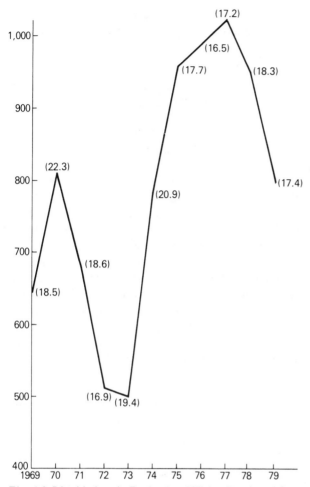

Fig. 6.2 Liquidations in England and Wales (Bracketed figures represent percentage of all liquidations)

construction the margin for error is likely to be large but a pragmatic managerial approach would suggest that a 'guesstimate' is better than none, and by doing such exercises we can reduce as far as possible the area of uncertainty in overall business planning. Therefore, to the industry and the firm, manpower planning has several advantages. A manpower plan can:

(a) reduce personnel costs because of management's ability to anticipate short-ages and surpluses of manpower and make appropriate corrections;
(b) serve as a basis for making use of employees' abilities and, consequently, the industry and firms can optimize their labour utilization;
(c) be used to establish the best cost balance between plant and labour utilization;
(d) determine recruitment levels within specific trades or site/head office staff;

(e) anticipate redundancies and avoid unnecessary dismissals;
(f) determine optimum education and training levels and management development programmes; and
(g) act as a tool to evaluate the effects of alternative policies.

It is important that the manpower plan be integrated into the overall business and economic planning process and, as such, it is a component of a business and macro-economic strategy.

Despite these advantages, many companies will be reluctant to commit resources to manpower planning because of the uncertainty of workload and any development of a manpower plan must commence with an analysis of the workload carried out in previous years to see if an underlying trend can be observed. For instance, the success rate of bids submitted may be valuable information along with the profile of contracts attained. Are they in the public or private sector, building or civil engineering, traditional or industrialized building? From this analysis one can move towards an assessment of labour demand, with identification of the skills required to conduct anticipated workloads and whether forecasts should be made for the whole of the organization or merely sections of it. Also, the degree of accuracy required and the period over which forecasts are to be made will be essential. Demand forecasting has become far more reliable in the last two decades and has developed a recognized body of knowledge. In *Statistical Techniques for Manpower Planning*, Bartholomew and Forbes (1979) offer a good review of the techniques available.

6.2 Procedures

If manpower planning within a firm is to be successful, a set of procedures must be followed. These can be identified as:

6.2.1 Analysis of current labour resources
6.2.2 Analysis of changes in the labour force
6.2.3 Analysis of labour turnover
6.2.4 Effects of changes in the conditions of work
6.2.5 Analysis of external factors influencing the labour supply
6.2.6 Integrating manpower plans into company organization.

6.2.1 Analysis of current labour resources

Here it is useful to retain records to show the profile of the existing workforce. Items worthy of recording would be the sex, age, education, promotability, salary, length of service, etc., of all employees. From these data, profiles of the labour structure of the firm can be attained. Histograms are a useful tool to demonstrate problem areas; for example, management may be concerned that the labour force is growing old together and therefore a histogram can graphically show the age distribution of employees (see Fig. 6.3).

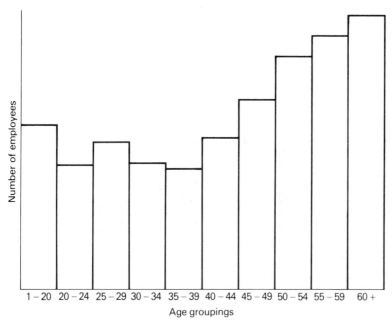

Fig. 6.3 Graphical methods of showing the age of distribution of a firm's employees

Similar histograms can be drawn for segments of the organization's employees; for example, what is the proportion of site agents with degrees or professional qualifications against those from a trade background? These analyses can throw into sharp focus impending difficulties for the future of the organization – for example, a skewed age distribution may mean that a succession policy is not being paid enough attention, or a preponderance of graduate site agents may suggest that promotion prospects for craft based persons are inadvertently being limited; alternatively, if there are few graduate/professionally qualified agents, is the firm precluding access to jobs which require a knowledge of sophisticated management techniques?

6.2.2. Analysis of changes in the labour force

It is sometimes useful to assess changes in the composition of the labour force from time to time. Again, this can be best demonstrated by using histograms (see Fig. 6.4). Such data can demonstrate the possibilities of growing imbalances within the labour force, perhaps the numbers of administrative and management staff are growing at a faster rate than the operative level employees; or perhaps the ratio of craftsmen to apprentices is decaying, indicating that the firm is not optimizing its training programme. Of course, the changes in the structure of the labour force may have been planned and may be a response to technological factors or to the type of work the company is carrying out, but more often than not certain categories of labour will drift without a labour budget or target. It may be

121

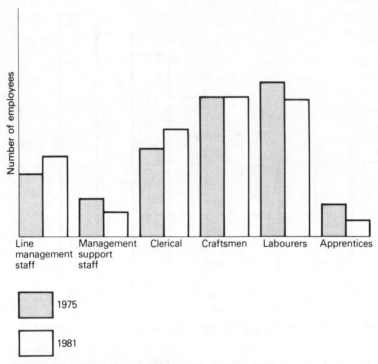

Fig. 6.4 Changes in the composition of the labour force

necessary to establish departmental structures which can be used to control the number of employees. Information such as this can assist in clarifying a staffing policy by focusing attention upon career paths for individuals – e.g. can some of the management support staff be transferred to line management if necessary?; what are the qualifications for advancement from operative to management level?

6.2.3 Analysis of labour turnover

It is common for managers in construction to be concerned about labour turnover within a firm and there are several ways of measuring this turnover. A simple manner of evaluating matters is to apply the following equation:

$$\text{Labour turnover} = \frac{\text{No. of leavers in one year}}{\text{Average no. employed in the same year}} \times 100$$

But this approach gives a fairly crude evaluation since, in such an industry as construction, ingress and egress to and from the industry is common-place. A more refined analysis may be determined by the 'cohort theory', whereby the pattern of leaving can be determined. This can be presented graphically, as in Fig.6.5. The early peak in turnover can be explained by those persons who leave early because they seldom stay long in any job. This will be followed by those who

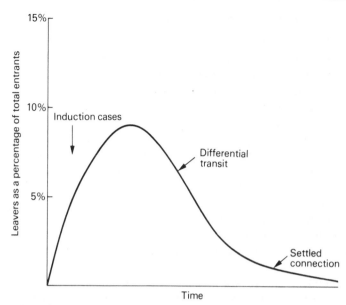

Fig. 6.5 The cohort theory of labour turnover

leave after finding out about the organization, and have found that they do not like it. After these two groups have departed, then there will be a settled connection between the individual and the firm. If the persons who have established a settled connection begin to leave in numbers, then it may suggest that something is awry within the organization. Obviously, turnover rates may vary from site to site and high turnover on particular sites may be an expression of concern over bonus earnings or the style of management on the site.

It is advisable for a supervisor to interview those persons leaving the firm to determine their reason for leaving, for often the stated reason may hide real or imagined grievances. Discussion may help to rectify any dissatisfaction. Many building firms may not feel that it is necessary to maintain tight records of starters and leavers, but it is essential if a firm is to have a good manpower policy. Should labour turnover be excessive, then records will show the extent of the problem and corrective action can be taken if required.

However, it would be dangerous to assume that a high labour turnover indicates internal problems. Hyman (1976) in a study of labour turnover in two engineering plants suggested that economic conditions were central to the level of labour turnover. Factors within the firm determine a worker's willingness to seek new employment, but external factors influence his ability to find it. Additionally, wages are not a prime determinant in labour turnover; if it were and workers were assumed to act in accordance with economic rationality (i.e. seek out high wages at all times), then the movement of workers would flow in one direction. Security of employment can be far more influential, particularly for workers with family commitments.

6.2.4 Effects of changes in the conditions of work

Here the manpower plan of a company will be influenced by changes in corporate objectives and evironmental changes. The corporate objectives of a building firm will have been formulated by the perceived opportunities over a period of time. The choice of these objectives will be influenced by the availability of work, finance, machinery, and human resources. With respect to environmental changes, it may be clear after analysis that there are alternative opportunities to which the resources of the company can be applied. For example, during the 1970s many firms operating exclusively in the civil engineering market moved into general building work in order to sustain turnover and keep their resources employed. It is, therefore, necessary for a firm to monitor market and business changes. Such data can be used as a guide to the type of manpower changes they are likely to face. At the elementary level, this may mean reductions in the traditional trades and increases in multi-trade operatives to a more sophisticated manpower forecast necessary if a firm is considering opening up a precast concrete yard.

However, more mundane factors will influence matters; for instance, if the NWRA reduces the normal weekly hours of work, if the retirement age is changed by government, if the overtime rates are re-negotiated, etc. All these factors will have an influence upon the manpower requirement of a construction firm.

6.2.5 Analysis of external factors influencing the labour supply

So far, we have concentrated upon the internal supply of labour that needs to be available to meet expected demand conditions within the firm. By matching future requirements against existing resources of manpower, the manpower planner will be able to judge the type of recruitment programmes required. But, as has been seen, to make such judgements in isolation from the economic and social environment would be rash. There is little point in planning business expansion if the labour to service new workloads is not going to be available. Similarly, construction programmes need to take into account the likely labour supply to particular contracts. A vital part of a manager's job is therefore directed towards analysing the factors which will have a bearing upon the supply of labour of the firm in general and individual contracts in particular. Some of the factors which will have a bearing upon labour supply are:

(a) population density in the area of a contract;
(b) local unemployment levels in the principal building trades;
(c) current competition from other contractors in the area and the likely future competition;
(d) local transport facilities;
(e) availability of short-term housing within the area;
(f) the impact of local government training centres and the work of the CITB;

(g) the impact of legislation, e.g. early retirement, Youth Opportunities Pro-
    grammes, etc.;
(h) subcontracting arrangements.

It will clearly not be possible for managers to measure precisely the effect of
local and national supply factors upon a firm since employment practices within
firms will vary, and the best a company can do is to carry out an intelligent
appraisal of the direction of the way the external labour market is working.
Specialist advice is always available from the Department of Employment.

6.2.6 Integrating manpower plans into company organization

The whole of the manpower planning procedure can be expressed diagrammati-
cally as in Fig. 6.6, from which we can see that manpower in construction is a key
economic resource and, therefore, should claim equal attention to that given to
production and profits. This fact has given rise to increased attempts by
construction companies to plan their manpower requirements. Those companies
which have undertaken an element of manpower planning have often recognized
the benefits in terms of higher efficiency and productivity as a result of better
utilization of its manpower resources and the elimination of waste in recruitment
and training.

However, in such a labour-intensive industry, the best results for this exercise
are gained from integrating a company's manpower plan with overall company
objectives; therefore, the manpower planner in construction will need to forecast
the total available market and a company's anticipated market share in order to
translate these business predictions into manpower requirements. Second, the
manpower planner will need to point out to top management the constraints that
manpower will place upon company objectives. Such forecasts can be based upon
five-year intervals, with monitoring at stages between such dates. Even so, the
unpredictability of the construction market means that a large margin for error
should be built into the plan. Nonetheless, guidelines, albeit loose ones, are
better than none at all.

The Department of Employment (1974) have devised a list of key points for
successful manpower planning, and it would be useful to restate them:

(a) Manpower planning must be recognized as an integral part of overall business
    planning. The manpower planner needs to know the company's objectives in
    terms of sales, markets and growth.
(b) Top management backing for manpower planning is essential.
(c) Manpower planning responsibilities should be centralized in order to co-
    ordinate consultation between management levels.
(d) Manpower plans should be developed in consultation with employees and
    their representatives.
(e) The forecast period should be long enough to allow remedial action to be
    taken.

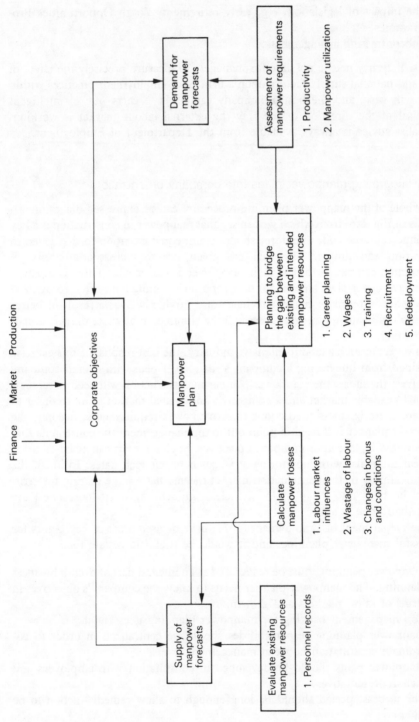

Fig. 6.6 Manpower planning within corporate objectives

(f) Personnel and other statistical records must be complete, up to date and readily accessible.
(g) The forecasting technique selected should be that best suited to the data available and the degree of accuracy required.
(h) Forecasts should be prepared by skill levels rather than by aggregates of workers of different skill levels.
(i) The forecasting techniques, and also the forecasts, need to be constantly revised and improved in the light of experience.

6.3 Labour stability

Despite the advantages of manpower planning to individual firms, the process is intrinsically difficult in an industry in which labour instability is endemic. A major component of the labour force in previous years has been labour-only subcontractors. However, due to the decline in workload, this practice has been on the wane since the mid-1970s. Notwithstanding this, the stability of labour in construction is still cause for concern. CIMB report (1980) observed that the incidence of lump labour had declined and the residual instability of labour was mainly created by instability of demand, arising from government policy. However, it must be recognized that government (of whatever hue) has always used the construction industry as an economic regulator and that it is necessary to stabilize the labour force, despite the difficulties arising from this constraint. One of the mechanisms proposed has been a series of registers covering employers and employees in the industry. The CIMB suggested that the NJCBI establish a voluntary register for those firms primarily involved in the building segment of the construction industry and the CECCB be empowered to establish a voluntary register for those in civil engineering. In order to qualify for registration, a firm would have to agree to the following conditions:

(a) abide by the NWRA;
(b) abide by codes of practice, safety codes, and employment legislation;
(c) pay employers' liability insurance (up to £250,000 cover);
(d) pay a registration fee.

To many this may seem a revolutionary concept, but the principle of voluntary registers concerning the use of labour-only subcontracting had been accepted within the NWRA. Furthermore, trades allied to the building industry, such as electrical and plumbing work (with their own joint industrial board) have already accepted the necessity for employer registration. In line with this, the NJCBI have accepted the principle of registers but there are practical difficulties, foremost amongst which is: 'Who shall be eligible to enter such registers?' In such a wide-ranging industry it would be important to identify those in scope for a register, and here the CITB definition of those falling 'within scope' could be useful.

Additionally, the CIMB recommended that operatives should be accorded certificates which would record their training achievements and skills held. Such

127

certification could do much to improve the status of the construction industry, as well as provide hard data to assist in manpower planning. Such a move could also assist in improving the qualitative nature of the labour force, in that certificates could be documentary proof of training carried out in a systematic way with a rigorous form of assessment. This criterion would distinguish it from certificates of attendance and certificates of competence. The latter, of course, relate to the way in which skill is exercised at work, not the standard of performance attained in training.

Such a move would also have other benefits. For instance, a certificated labour force for construction could assist in determining training priorities, and here the CIMB have identified an order of priorities: first, safety training; second, the provision of training where no formal schemes exist; and, finally, on-the-job training. The construction industry has made a start in this respect, with the introduction of the Scaffolders Record Scheme which applies to all scaffolders, and it stipulates that anyone who has not reached a set level of competence must not be employed on work over 5 m high without adequate supervision. The categories of scaffolders have been agreed – trainee, basic, and advanced – with requirement for training, experience, and pay for each level. Plans are being formulated by the NFBTE, FCEC, and the Plant Contractors' Association (PCA) to extend such schemes to cover plant operators.

The services industry has also adopted a graded structure, and the various grades are shown in Fig. 6.7. The gradings of individual workers are determined by the relevant joint industrial board, based upon information supplied by the employer, and from this, grade cards are issued.

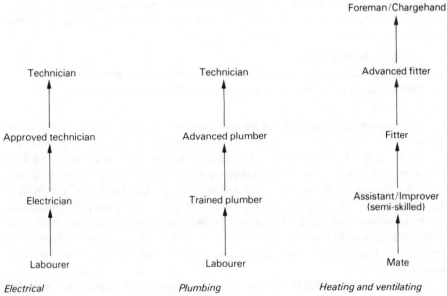

Fig. 6.7 Services industry labour grades

Yet the demands for registration and the subsequent decasualization of the industry have not appeared from a vacuum. Research by the Office of Population and Census Surveys (1979) revealed some remarkable figures regarding the nature of the construction labour force. For example, 41 per cent of the sample surveyed had experienced an average of six months unemployment within the last five years; 40 per cent of the sample had to leave a job because of redundancy; and about 50 per cent of jobs were left involuntarily, with few men receiving redundancy payments. This can be backed up with the mobility results, where 40 per cent had remained with their current employers for the last five years or more; 18 per cent had experienced one change of firm; 13 per cent had experience two changes of firm; 11 per cent had experienced three changes of firm; 7 per cent had experienced four changes of firm, and 11 per cent had had five to thirteen changes. Of those persons moving firms, 51 per cent had moved voluntarily and 38 per cent had moved because of redundancy or dismissal; 18 per cent of the sample and been made redundant more often than they had left firms voluntarily. It is interesting to note that the greater number of jobs, the greater the sense of dissatisfaction with security. Dissatisfaction is particularly strong if the person is made redundant or is sacked. To many men in construction, this level of mobility is an inevitable condition of employment and most seem to attempt to make the best of the situation. Nonetheless, a sense of dissatisfaction is felt about the low level of job security. This point is particularly pertinent when balanced against the widespread desire for continuity of their current employment. (Job security is important to 90 per cent of the men.)

Construction employers are, of course, cognisant of the problem and many of the larger firms accept that labour stability is difficult to attain, but list it high on the company objectives. Firm rejecting the policy have higher labour turnover rates. Several points have emerged from recent research carried out by the Building Economics Research Unit at University College, London (1980). In particular, those firms whose production strategies were based upon measurable bonus schemes experience a high turnover, whereas plus-rates and relaxed supervision render lower turnover. This is reinforced by Paterson and Blain (1981) who also found that operatives preferred stability with a decent basic wage to potentially high bonus earnings. Those firms providing better welfare facilities than the statutory minimum had significantly lower turnover rates. Surprisingly, high labour turnover rates were associated with high usage of labour-only subcontractors. This may be contrary to expectations where a small and stable core staff would be used, supplemented by a pool of highly mobile subcontractors.

From the above it can be seen that company and management attitudes are clearly important influences upon labour turnover. Those firms who felt that recent employment legislation had influenced matters experienced high turnover, whereas those firms who had a 'commitment' which was impervious to legislative processes had low turnovers of labour. Indeed, the available evidence suggests that employment legislation introduced during the period 1965–80 has had little effect upon labour turnover. The Phelps-Brown Committee also studied labour turnover in 1965 and reported almost the same level of turnover as that found in the 1980 survey. Reductions in turnover can also be attained by close attention to a formal policy towards manpower, particularly a formal recruitment policy, with initial interviews and a structured induction period.

Hard as a firm may try, it will not, of course, be possible under the current economic organization of the industry to ensure total stability – the fragmented structure of the industry prevents this even if it were desirable. But instability has unsatisfactory implications for the workforce in terms of redundancy payments, for while two years in the statutory minimum qualification for redundancy pay, few construction workers qualify for it or receive it. With fluctuating workloads and short duration contracts, construction workers are clearly disadvantaged in respect to these statutory rights. One solution mooted is that at the end of a job a person is laid off by the industry; the worker would then qualify for redundancy pay. In a sense, the person is made redundant by the industry rather than by an individual firm within it. Clearly there would need to be a qualifying time period before a worker would be declared redundant by the industry. Additionally, in order to keep skilled men within the industry, a system of fall-back pay to top-up unemployment benefit has been suggested. Obviously, the funding of such systems would be necessary. Levies have been suggested as a method of providing this fund, along with unclaimed money from the holidays-with-pay scheme. Naturally the NFBTE have resisted this move, claiming that the industry could not afford such schemes and this view has been endorsed by the Government. In contrast, the FMB have agreed in principle to the fall-back pay idea.

6.4 Recruitment to the industry

It has already been pointed out that the balance of supply and demand for construction labour is difficult. In 1981 unemployment in construction topped 350,000, yet in some parts of the UK contractors have difficulty in recruiting certain skills. The reasons for this are that unemployment if often regional in nature and people cannot move owing to the shortage of housing in the areas where jobs are available. Recruitment to the industry should not be a problem with so many unemployed, but to many in the industry it is a matter of concern, particularly the quality of recruits. Contractors are not necessarily getting the pick of school-leavers and graduates. Perhaps there are reasons for this – the picture of the industry presented to recruits is that of an unattractive, dirty and dangerous industry and, consequently, it is not surprising that it does not get the pick of bright school-leavers. In a recent survey conducted by *Building* (Murphy 1980) 86 per cent of fifth and sixth formers said that they had never thought of entering the construction industry and of the 14 per cent who had considered it, half of them had rejected the idea. Typical quotes were 'I would like to spend my life in a more fruitful and interesting form of employment', 'I have much higher aims in life than the building industry'. In a sense, these reactions are responses to the image of the building industry. Such illusory images obviously have a direct effect upon recruitment and the quality of recruitment will affect the industries' capacity to operate efficiently, as well as to accommodate and stimulate change. So there is a necessity to market the industry so that school-leavers are attracted to it. Superficially the industry sells itself with glossy photographs of large jobs, but school-leavers and careers officers may be cynical about the likelihood of working on such jobs. To counter these attitudes the NFBTE and the Chartered Institute of Building (CIOB) set up the Building Industry Careers Service (BICS) in 1979, and in its first fifteen months it has distributed half a million leaflets and has contributed to several careers conferences.

Such an industry-wide approach supplements those efforts of large firms who have their own literature, training department, and firm ideas of the type of person they want to recruit. Also, medium-sized firms operating within a specific geographical area often have a good record in recruitment and training, and this is valuable in establishing the idea of permanence in the industry.

Summary

Manpower planning has become an important managerial function over the last two decades and this has sponsored the Manpower Services Commission (MSC) and the Training Services Agency (TSA) to state their belief in the principle of the approach. It is widely recognized that it will be difficult to undertake manpower planning, in an industry as uncertain as construction, but the industry in general and firms in particular need some kind of manpower plan, however crude, to enable them to plan the utilization of labour resource to the maximum benefit of the industry, firms, and individual employees.

Without manpower plans the industry lurches between having insufficient skilled operatives and management to cope with the demand, with all the implications on quality and completion times, and having labour surfeits and sometimes painful task of laying off employees. But it must be made clear that such an imbalance is mainly the result of stop/go policies for the construction industry.

However uncertain manpower planning may be for construction it is nevertheless important, and a central feature of a company's manpower plan is that it is integrated into overall company operations – it is part and parcel of business planning, not separate from it. Specifically, manpower plans can be used to monitor the effectiveness of the use of labour with audits of the current manpower position, and can act as a foundation for any necessary recruitment and training plans. At the other end of the employment spectrum, manpower planning can assist in anticipating redundancies and avoid unnecessary dismissals. Much of the foregoing naturally depends upon forecasting the demand conditions and the technological changes that will have an impact upon manpower demands. It is the accuracy of this forecasting which presents most problems to the construction industry.

Usually manpower plans are prepared on a five-year rolling programme with intermediate short-term plans to satisfy tangible workload and production conditions.

Questions

1. In such an economically volatile industry as construction, there is no purpose in a firm undertaking manpower planning. Discuss.
2. Analyse the reasons for the high level of labour turnover in the construction industry. Outline steps which could be taken to improve matters.
3. The profile of the construction industry workload is changing, with far more resources being allocated to maintenance work. What impact will such changes have upon the structure of the labour force and how can such changes be accommodated by the industry?
4. In periods of full employment, the construction industry often had difficulty in recruiting and holding high-calibre personnel. What are the reasons for this?
5. Registration of building employees has been suggested as one means whereby the industry could become stabilized. Discuss the benefits and drawbacks of this suggestion.
6. Many contractors have argued that extensive employment legislation has had the effect of destabilizing labour within the industry. Do you think that this assumption is correct? If so, argue the reason for your assent. If not, state your objections.
7. Account for the decline in the use of labour-only subcontractors. How have such groups influenced manpower planning in the industry?
8. What prospects are there in adopting a grading structure for construction labour along similar lines to the building services industry? What practical problems can you foresee if such an approach were to come to fruition?

References

Bartholomew, D. and Forbes, F. (1979) *Statistical Techniques for Manpower Planning*, John Wiley and Son

Building Economics Research Unit (1980) *A Study of Labour Mobility in the Construction Industry*, University College, London

CIMB (1980) *Report to Secretary of State for the Environment*, HMSO

Department of Employment (1974) *Company Manpower Planning*, HMSO

Hyman, R. (1976) Economic motivation and labour stability, *Manpower Planning* (edited by D. Bartholomew), Penguin

Murphy, N. (1980) Image of the industry, *Building*, 9 May, p. 31

Office of Population and Census Surveys (1980) *Labour Stability in Construction*, HMSO

Paterson, J. and Blain, B. (1981) It isn't just the money, *Building*, 3 July, pp. 29–30

Chapter 7

Personnel management

For many years there has been concern that the construction industry is not making full use of personnel officers. As early as 1944 the Simon Committee on the Placing and Management of Building Contracts (1944) observed: 'The selection and education of personnel managers is one of the aspects of the building industry in which there is most room for improvement.' Some twenty years later the Phelps-Brown Report (1968) found that the situation had not changed very much. This committee found that 'In this industry which employs one in every ten working males there appears to be very few trained and qualified personnel specialists.' To many people this reluctance to place much emphasis upon personnel is symptomatic of an industry which has been used to a casual approach to employment. Yet, as the Phelps-Brown Report (1968) pointed out:

> There is a fundamental need in the industry for positive employment policies. The growing technical sophistication of the industry has not been matched by any parallel development in the handling of personnel relations. We believe that many firms in the industry do not pay enough attention to the task of developing and making the best use of their manpower from operative level upwards.

No doubt there are many reasons for this reluctance to employ full-time personnel specialists; certainly the fragmented structure of the industry is a contributory factor, but perhaps more relevant is the decentralized nature of firms within the industry, with site managers often having a great deal of autonomy to handle some aspects of personnel. Another feature of the construction industry is the preponderance of small firms who see little benefit in employing such a specialist. In such organizations there will often be a direct relationship between the principal and the operative, which will mean that any grievances can be speedily and amicably settled. Furthermore, building work has traditionally more variety associated with it and this in itself can eliminate many of the frustrations with which a personnel manager has to deal.

Nonetheless, overdependence upon the personal approach may be limiting for such methods can be based upon unthinking tradition. Tradition, although important, has shortcomings as a means of retaining goodwill and has been a declining force in industry, advancing education and alternative employment opportunities have challenged the assumptions of tradition. A traditional approach can also inhibit change in employee–employer relations. Often, relationships in the industry are based upon paternalism: 'I know what's best for the workers on my site' is not an uncommon expression, but better education, the development of trade unions, and a greater ability to think for oneself has rendered paternalism a redundant method of dealing with personnel matters.

Additionally, if a company has no formal personnel policy it will often mean that there is not a strategic approach and, consequently, a strong emphasis is placed upon expediency. This naturally leads to variability in decisions and resulting senses of grievances. The empirical, piecemeal approach to personnel management is clearly inadequate.

If the foregoing is accepted, then it is necessary for firms to develop a coherent approach to personnel management and this section expands upon the demand for policy and the mechanics of the operation.

What is personnel management?

Personnel management is part of the management process concerned with human factors within the organization. Such human factors will be ever present and the process of dealing with them is the principal function of personnel management. Many firms will undertake this task in a formal way, whereas others will deal with it covertly. However the function is managed, it will have several objectives.

(a) Its focus is a concern for people, either individually or in groups.
(b) It attempts to optimize human resources with appropriate manning and effective working.
(c) It considers the relationship between the individual and the group.
(d) It attempts to provide job satisfaction to employees.

Obviously these broad definitions will need to be backed up by a policy which underpins the effective running of a personnel function. Such a policy needs to be broad but it should have common principles, and these are elaborated upon below:

(a) A personnel department needs to be a specialist agency within the firm, with a brief to assist top management in developing policy and line management to implement this policy. As such it is an advisory service which should not usurp the function of management but should remain as a functional specialist department.
(b) In order to operate effectively there is a necessity to plan operations and the objectives of the personnel department need to be defined within the context of overall company objectives. Such objectives need to be based upon respect for and equity between individuals, with decisions considered in the light of the effect they will have upon workers. A participative approach is considered by many to render most benefits.
(c) The personnel policy must be well known by the employees. This could entail the recording of the grievance procedures, disciplinary codes, etc.
(d) The personnel policy should be related to the organization and structure of the company. The elements of personnel management – e.g. employment,

training, pay and conditions, negotiations, communications, etc. – should be seen as complementary to good company organization. Moreover, the policy is in itself a reflection of how employees see the firm. Anecdotal expressions such as 'a good firm to work for' are suggestions that the personnel policy is right. Such expressions can be registered at the formal and informal levels; formally by the wages and working conditions, etc., and informally in terms of management styles, the manner in which instructions are given and the authority afforded to employee suggestions.

Within the framework of this policy, the personnel manager will have to supply specific functions, such as:

7.1 Recruitment and selection
7.2 Induction to the company
7.3 Statistics on labour turnover, labour stability, and absenteeism
7.4 Development and administration of redundancy schemes
7.5 Education and training schemes
7.6 Communications.

These functions will be in addition to those previously discussed, i.e. industrial relations, health, safety and welfare, and manpower planning.

7.1 Recruitment and selection

Often, the responsiveness of line management to the personnel manager will depend upon his/her ability to provide the right person for a particular job, for this function is essential to the build-up of an effective labour force. But due to the peculiar operating characteristics of construction – autonomous production units each requiring labour and management – it has been shown that many building firms recruit labour at site level without reference to overall company needs. For example, bricklayers may be desperately required on one site while another is turning bricklayers away. This all too common problem would suggest that centralization of recruitment is the more effective solution since overall labour needs can be evaluated at head office level and common standards for entry can be applied. But, having said this, the responsibility for final engagement must lie with site management, since they are responsible for the management and control of the labour they are sent. Also, the *laissez-faire* approach to recruitment often taken at site level means that recruitment is often done in a hurry, with the consequence of a less than optimum use of labour arising from this type of selection. This point is confirmed by Tatton (1972) who observed

considering that building is a major industry comparatively few organizations within it have a full-time personnel manager with the authority to devise the required (recruitment and training) programmes. . . . even quite large organizations a surprising number of people to whom applicants should write have little to do with the personnel

135

function at all. . . . . In a situation where recruitment is regarded very much as a part time activity handled by say, individual line managers as and when a requirement arises, results must be indifferent.

To many, an excessive level of formality will be an unnecessary burden upon overworked site managers, especially when there is widespread recognition of what a particular operative will be required to do; but the advent of extensive legislation concerning employment has meant that employment procedures need to be vigorously controlled if a company is to avoid appearing constantly before industrial tribunals. Such legislation has meant that there will be a standardization of employment conditions, with far less autonomy for individual companies. The establishment of minimum employment standards by the State has done much to stabilize labour within the industry. Furthermore, such standardization has prevented companies vying with each other in the provision of employment conditions. Additionally, if labour stability is to be sought within the organization, level of formality can be useful. In particular, the site mangement could provide the personnel manager with details of the job to be filled and the specific operating conditions pertaining to the job. Such a request may be based upon a simple proforma which could contain the following information:

- job title
- list of duties
- pay, conditions and hours of work (usually determined by conditions of the NWRA)
- the physical environment of the job
- the person to whom the employee will be responsible.

Such information can help the personnel manager to identify the job and can be used to prepare any necessary advertisements. The central personnel office can supplement this by providing details of the company, social facilities, training opportunities and future prospects. It may be possible to fill the vacancy from within the company, but if not, the details prepared by site management should direct the personnel manager to specific sources for likely applicants, be they the careers office, job centre, employment agency or advertisement in local, national, or trade Press.

If recruitment of new employees is necessary then it is important to adhere to selection procedures. Naturally, the practice and vigour of selection will vary according to the level to which the appointment is made. Notwithstanding this, many firms prefer all applicants to fill in an application form which can standardize basic information. Obviously the level of detail required will vary according to job classification, with more sophisticated forms being necessary for managerial appointments. Some firms have also experimented with selection tests. In the main, these have attempted to correlate intelligence tests for recruits with their subsequent success. The correlations tend to be obscure and, if anything, are inversely related (this fact may merit further investigation, but one hypothesis is that the highly intelligent person is more likely to question managerial assumptions and, consequently, be regarded as 'troublesome' or 'rebellious' by existing management). The intelligence tests were eventually reduced to providing a bench mark but, when this had been established, other factors such as drive, energy, commitment, social skills, etc., came into sharper focus as criteria for success.

Following the receipt of an application form the personnel manager may wish to interview applicants. This interview is important and sufficient time should be dedicated to it. A systematic approach to interviewing pays dividends, with questions directed with a view to revealing attitudes and skills which closely match the job requirements. Interviewing applicants is a skilled task and many companies have sought to improve this facet of their personnel management by providing specialist courses for those involved.

7.2 Induction to the company

As has been seen (p. 123), there is a tendency for a high separation rate at the early stages of employment. Difficulties may be experienced in settling down to a new job within a new organization. Within the construction industry, accommodating a change of job may be less unsettling due to the relatively high incidence of job changes, but if labour stability is to be sought, then an early development of a 'sense of belonging' should encouraged. In this matter, information about the organization can help. Many construction companies find it beneficial to supplement verbally transmitted information with company handbooks and printed company rules and disciplinary procedures. Such information can be prepared as a package for the new starter and within it the statutory obligation to provide a copy of the safety policy can be included. At no later than thirteen weeks after commencement, the new employee must be given a written contract of employment. The details of such a contract are summarized in Appendix B on page 316.

However, the formal induction procedures need to be reinforced by attitudes which welcome the new recruit. It is important that the new employee is well received by the workforce and, if necessary, follow-up interviews should be conducted to monitor the employee's adaptation to the work and organization.

7.3 Statistics on labour turnover, labour stability, and absenteeism

Essentially, this function is one of record-keeping. The basic problems of labour turnover have been discussed elsewhere in this book, but a vital index for the personnel manager will be labour stability. This may be calculated by the following formula:

$$\text{Labour stability} = \frac{\text{No. of employees with at least 1 year's service}}{\text{No. currently employed}} \times 100$$

The figures attained from such a calculation will show the rate at which the labour force is being diluted by workers with little experience of the company. In the manufacturing industry, a labour stability index of less than 70 per cent indicates that the company is operating with a significant proportion of inexperienced workers, which will inevitably lower performance and quality standards. In construction this ratio will probably need to be reduced due to the inherent instability of labour and the high level of subcontracting.

Those leaving the firm voluntarily should ideally be interviewed by their immediate supervisor to determine the reason for leaving. Recording the stated reason can assist in identifying employment dissatisfaction which the company may be able to rectify.

In the case of a dismissal, the reasons for the dismissal must be recorded and the company must satisfy itself that the provisions laid down by the Employment Protection Act have been followed (see Appendix B, p. 316). In order that justice is seen to be done, internal appeals may be necessary. Given the necessity for tight control, the administration of dismissals is probably best done from the central personnel department. Of equal concern is the problem of absenteeism. In many areas of the country, site management has become sufficiently concerned to institute attendance bonus, whereby a bonus payment is made if the employee attends work for the whole week and loses this if there is a period of absence during the week. Again, simple records should be maintained which can show the extent of the problem. Different sites will have different rates of absenteeism and there are a multitude of factors which will influence matters, including earnings, location of the site, the nature of the labour force, the nature of the work itself, the regional unemployment level, etc. For whatever reason, monitoring of the situation is vital and one approach to the problem has been to remove an employee's clock card and substitute a temporary card. When the employee returns to work, he/she collects the permanent card from a supervisor and explains his/her absence. This approach is seen as giving management the opportunity to encourage consistency in attendance at work. However, to many operatives such a move could quite reasonably be interpreted as undue pressure, and their view may be that if they are to be laid off when management no longer requires labour, why should they oblige management when labour is in demand. This atmosphere of suspicion and mistrust can permeate industrial life in an industry which is casual in its approach to the utilization of labour.

7.4 Development and administration of redundancy schemes

Construction firms have often argued that the uncertain nature of the business, changing technology, and greater mechanization mean that redundancy will be inevitable. Sharp recessions and government legislation since the mid-1960s have ushered in a necessity to undertake a level of redundancy planning. The legislation concerning redundancy in the Employment Protection (Consolidation)

Act 1978 (see Appendix B) has also demanded a tightening of the administration for redundancy.

This particular piece of legislation has mitigated some of the effects of redundancy upon an individual in terms of financial security, but the social and psychological effects of redundancy can be devastating to an individual. This factor demands that a company pre-plans any redundancy; if it does not, then good relationships with trade unions, employees, and the public at large may suffer. Moreover, pre-planning is required in order to retain the balance of necessary skills for completion of existing projects. The fear of redundancy may also have a debilitating effect upon morale and productivity. If redundancy is in the offing, good workers who do not have many years' service may leave of their own volition with a consequent impact upon the balance of the labour force. The forward planning of manpower requirements can assist in defusing potentially dangerous situations and reveal if excesses of manpower are likely to occur. If such a position arises, then a construction company can adopt a variety of strategies, among which could be:

- policy of no recruitment other than for 'essential' vacancies
- transferring people from one region to another
- retraining of the existing labour force to match requirements
- the phasing of any redundancies over a period of time
- the use of voluntary redundancy
- considering whether redundancy counselling services should be employed

Such strategies can be part of a redundancy policy which will be a component of long-term planning. Such plans may never be used, but it is better to be prepared for such contingencies as they will avoid any snap decisions. The costs of making people redundant should not be ignored, particularly where the statutory minimum payments are often exceeded by internal negotiations; and although the Redundancy Payments Act 1965 allows companies to recoup some of these payments, companies will inevitably be committed to extensive expenditure. Furthermore, if redundancies are to be made it is vital that the Department of Employment be notified in advance.

At the moment, the industry is seldom troubled by having to make large numbers redundant because of the casual nature of the industry and the legal requirement of two years' service for qualification for redundancy payments, the strategy being to retain long-service employees and release those with shorter service. But this approach may need to be changed if proposals put forward by the CIMB – that a person is redundant to the 'industry' rather than a firm operating within it – reach fruition (see p. 130).

7.5 Education and training schemes

The trend over the last few years has been for the industry to accommodate lower levels of activity, and this is likely to continue in the foreseeable future. Such a state of affairs has obvious implications for the labour structure of the industry and one view is that the future construction industry will not require more but better educated and trained staff and operatives. The personnel manager will have a responsibility to identify the education and training needs of the company and make recommendations on the policy to be followed, so that individual firms have the necessary expertise to carry out their business efficiently. Within this context the personnel manager will need to set and administer training courses for operatives and management staff.

In many ways the establishment of the CITB, brought about the Industrial Training Act 1964, has played a leading role in stimulating firms to undertake training for the industry. At whatever level training is undertaken, it should by systematic and be based upon prepared programmes to meet specific objectives. Naturally, these objectives will vary according to the level.

7.5.1 Training

Training can be discussed under two broad headings:

(a) Apprentice training
(b) Technician and management training

(a) Apprentice training

By the large, this type of training is well understood within the industry and is characterized by indentures for a four-year period. Three broad types of training system exist:

(a) *Standard scheme* – where twenty-eight weeks are spent at college during the first year, followed by block or day release in the second and third years.

(b) *Block release* – where blocks of training are undertaken at a local technical college throughout the indentured period of training.

(c) *Day release* – where apprentices are given one day each week to study during the first three years of their apprenticeship.

Whichever scheme is adopted, the apprentice should be registered with the National Joint Training Scheme for Skilled Building Occupations. This is administered by a standing committee of the National Joint Council and the operating principle is that anyone being trained for a building trade enter into a Training Service Agreement which insists that an apprentice shall attend classes. Plumbers and electricians are not party to this scheme, but come under their own Joint Industrial Board.

Of these three options, the standard scheme has proved most popular since the apprentices have some skill to offer when they start on site after their twenty-eight week training period in a technical college. Whatever approach is adopted, close monitoring of training is essential; without proper supervision apprentices can lose interest, particularly if the training they are receiving is perceived to lack purpose. The personnel officer responsible for training must ensure that the apprentice has been inducted to the firm in a proper manner and it is wise to insist upon a probationary period before full indentures are signed. Reports from site and college can assist in monitoring progress and, if necessary, the apprentice should have interviews to discuss the progress of his or her training. In order to maintain morale and enthusiasm, an 'activity' based training programme, with the emphasis on 'doing' rather than 'watching', is advisable. The traditional approach to training of 'sit by Nellie and watch her do the job' is almost defunct and it has been widely recognized that this is not the most effective manner of carrying out programmes. Not least among the problems of this approach is that 'Nellie' may not wish to impart her skills. Also, the person being watched is probably not trained to give instruction; poor working methods may be transmitted and the person being watched may fear a fall in bonus earnings if too much time is spent instructing the apprentice. For the apprentice, boredom may set in by just watching.

The wages of apprentices are tightly controlled by the NWRA which lays down proportions of the basic wage which the apprentice should receive, (see Table 7.1).

Table 7.1

| Age on entry | % of basic wage | | |
	1st year	2nd year	3rd year*
16	50	70	90
17	60	80	90
18	80	85	90
19+	85	90	95

* After three years of training, apprentices are eligible to earn bonus.

Recurrent concern is expressed that the industry does not put enough effort into training, and an examination of the trends regarding the intake of operative trainees entering the industry reveals in an erratic picture in which training patterns are seen as being more responsive to trading conditions in the industry than an intrinsic desire to train young people. One response to criticism about the magnitude of training is that a future construction industry will not need the current level of craft specialists (see Fig. 7.1) and that the industry should be training multicraft operatives. As yet, the unions have not responded positively to this overture, fearing a dilution of traditional skills, but with maintenance work absorbing more of the demand for construction work with its concomitant demand for 'Jacks of all trades', this prospect cannot be ruled out.

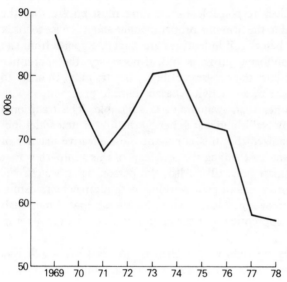

Fig. 7.1. Operative trainees in construction. (Source: *Housing and Construction Statistics*)

(b) Technician and management training

While the construction industry has experienced a decline in the overall numbers employed in the last ten years, the proportion of the industry's workforce employed in administrative, professional, and managerial work has increased (see Fig. 7.2). The reasons for this are manifold: increasing technical sophistication of buildings, tighter construction budgets and package dealing, together with a reluctance to dismiss key staff. In general, this increased technical and managerial complement is likely to want to develop their skills over a period of years and this desire must be matched by a company's willingness to provide technical and managerial training. Undoubtedly there has been a great improvement in the quality of such training, and this has been in response to the demand. It is the role of the personnel manager to analyse the training needs of supervisors, technical, and management staff.

While the main focus of the CITB has been upon operative training, they also have a role in management training and have successfully developed courses for foremen in management and planning techniques at their training centre in Bircham Newton, Norfolk. Trade associations such as the Cement and Concrete Association (CCA), the Brick Development Association (BDA), and the Timber Research and Development Association (TRADA) also run specialist courses for those in construction. In contracting, these have been supplemented internally by course which have discussed specific aspects of company policy, be they technology, sales and marketing, planning, quality control, work study, industrial relations, or safety. But doubt still exists as to whether sufficient management training is being carried out. Certainly, the level and frequency of in-service training is much less than that carried out in the European or American

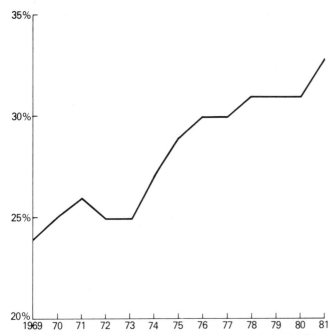

Fig. 7.2 APT staff as a proportion of operative staff. (APTC staff are Administrative, Professional, Technical and Clerical grades.) (Source: *Housing and Construction Statistics*)

construction industries. As the Finniston Report (1979), *Engineering Our Future*, observed: 'The technical and professional development of an engineer does not cease once he is qualified – indeed this is just the beginning.' This comment could equally be applied to construction management personnel. Certainly the CIOB has pioneered the study of construction management through its professional examinations and the Site Management Training Scheme (where site foremen are given block release or day release courses in management), but the provision of education and training beyond this level is patchy. Several universities have set up postgraduate courses in construction management, but very few of these can be undertaken on a part-time basis. Furthermore, the CITB have to approve courses before companies are eligible for grant aid and this restricts companies and individuals in their selection of courses. Up-to-date information can be obtained on management courses from an organization called the National Training Index, which provides companies with comprehensive data on external management courses, in-company training schemes, a classification of courses under subject headings and, perhaps most importantly, assessments of courses in terms of their quality – these being based upon reports sent in by participants.

Success on such courses can provide the basis of selection for promotion since it is vital for companies to ensure that staff and operatives develop their potential. Such a process can be placed in the context of succession planning, whereby individuals are groomed for particular jobs within the organization. It is

143

important that the criteria for promotion are widely known; each firm will need to develop such criteria in the light of their own operations. Factors such as qualifications, age, experience, past performance, energy, ambition, and social skills will come into the equation and it is incumbent upon the personnel manager to evaluate such criteria and communicate them to employees.

The latest development in construction management is the increasing demand for project managers – persons who can manage complex projects but are separated from the traditional roles of the building team. This in turn has generated demand for specialist education programmes to supply the industry with qualified personnel. Two programmes have been mooted: the first by the CIOB, who looked for initiatives from educational establishments who would launch project management courses which would be open to all of the building professions; the second comes from the Royal Institute of Chartered Surveyors (RICS) who, in conjunction with the College of Estate Management, intend to set up a two-year, part-time postgraduate course, but entry will be restricted to RICS members. In a sense, this restriction is regressive, since education and training for new project managers needs to be multidisciplinary, with the various professions sharing knowledge and expertise to produce a broadly educated person. We will have to wait to see the development of these initiatives.

Sophisticated management training programmes may, however, be limited to the larger firms within the industry, but, smaller firms can obtain the benefits of size by collaborating and forming training groups. Such organizations can be funded by subscription from smaller, local contractors, with the employment of a full-time training officer who can co-ordinate training for group members. Such a scheme offers the benefits of training advice, monitoring, and in-house courses to the smaller firm. The CITB encourage the formation of such training groups and will often advise on their initiation.

7.6 Communications

In the construction industry it has often been assumed that the close personal contacts which exist between operatives and management make formal communication systems unnecessary. Yet this very informality can lead to the extensive use of rumours and hearsay to transmit information – methods that can give rise to frequent misunderstandings. Employees who have little knowledge of the way their job fits into the overall pattern of company organizations are at the mercy of rumours, particularly about events on other sites. From this it is important that the personnel manager stimulates a desire for good communications – keeping employees informed about matters which affect them. Items which should be communicated could include the following:

- changes in the conditions of employment, e.g. pay, overtime, bonus, shift-working, etc.
- contracts that the company have won

- vacancies within the firm
- promotions
- retirements
- pension schemes
- profiles of individuals within the company (at operative and management level)
- plant and manpower use
- reports from particular contracts
- news of social and sporting events.

Such information can be passed on in a number of ways, with the most basic being a notice board, but the available evidence is that notice boards are only read by a small proportion of the employees. Company magazines or news-sheets have more impact, particularly if they are professionally produced. Such communication systems, overseen by the personnel manager, will do much to engender a feeling of belonging to the firm, particularly if they are run in conjunction with the consultation procedures discussed in Chapter 4.

A full-time personnel officer?
Despite the necessity of carrying out the above functions, many construction firms consider the employment of a full-time personnel officer, in what is intrinsically a casual industry, to be wasteful. With so many small firms in the industry, it is easy to see why many firms do not feel that they have reached the critical point where specialization of this management function is required. This is confirmed by Downham (1974) when he surveyed the personnel function in eighty-eight firms and found, as could be expected, that company size was a key factor in whether a firm had a personnel department. But size will only be one criteria which needs to be considered. The severity of personnel problems and the barriers to increased productivity and company growth, along with the success of a decentralized personnel function, will all be determinants. The incidence of personnel problems may also be useful as a 'guide'; for example, if the firm is experiencing employment problems in terms of labour scarcity, a higher than average labour turnover, widespread absenteeism and problems of transferring labour this may point to a greater need for specialization in personnel matters. Expansion of the company in terms of its activities or turnover may create personnel problems. Growth of companies tends to sever informal relationships between operatives and management and this may happen without management realizing it until problems arise. With the traditional emphasis upon the completion of the task in hand, people can often be forgotten in periods of company growth.

Associated with growth is that management styles or structural changes of the firm take place. At certain points management may wish to move from a personal to a more structured management style (e.g. moving from a private to a public company) and a personnel manager may be appointed as a part of this change. The personality of senior management may also dictate the necessity for full-time personnel manager – senior management may wish to focus their attention upon production problems, bidding strategy, etc., and leave the overseeing of the human aspects to a full-time personnel manager.

Naturally, decisions of whether a full-time personnel manager will be required cannot be divorced from cost. The use of such a specialist can be justified upon social grounds, but this is not likely to be an acceptable reason to an industry operating within small profit margins. It is difficult to evaluate the cost, because figures are difficult to obtain and some of the essential costs incurred by personnel matters or by a personnel department are submerged into the general costs of management and administration. The Industrial Welfare Society (1962) estimated the costs of a personnel department at about 1 per cent of the wage bill. Such a cost may seem difficult to bear, but the impact of employment legislation and demands for a more secure industry for workers have necessitated a more systematic handling of personnel matters, with a consequent improvement in the effectiveness of labour employed.

Summary

Despite its slow start, the construction industry is recognizing that there is an increasing need for personnel managers to act as a functional specialist service to line management. Too often has total reliance been placed upon site managers to manage personnel matters in an expedient manner. To many site managers this is the natural order of things; since he or she has responsibility for the site, this should be matched by authority to hire or fire whom they like, establish bonus targets, and set the tone of discipline on the site. Personnel management conducted at the operational level obviously has benefits for individual sites, and this will mean that personnel requirements are linked with production. But equally, such a decentralized approach does little to afford security of employment or ensure that personnel matters are given the appropriate level of priority. Such decentralization may lead to anarchic and disparate policies being formed at site level and it is often seen as advantageous to centralize the personnel function so that special skills can be brought to work and ensure uniformity of personnel practice.

This uniformity of personnel practice cannot be developed out of the context of overall business organization and, as such, a personnel policy is a vital component of the company's organization. A personnel policy should receive considerable attention from top management, as it will live or die by the support it receives at this level. Such a policy should be directed towards ensuring that the company has a labour force which is of the right size and has the correct balance of skills and experience. Yet this mechanical operation will not render benefits unless the workforce has the confidence in the personnel manager to ensure that action can be implemented.

This has put the focus upon the two principal elements of the personnel manager's job within construction. The first will be assistance in policy formation with respect to personnel – this broad policy should be based upon a concern for people at their work, but obviously, more detailed policy will be required in respect of training programmes, recruitment and redundancy schemes, pay structures, etc. The second element will be the day-to-day administration of personnel in terms of employment, welfare, transfers, records, etc. It is this integration of policy definition, working up such policies into detailed application, and the implementation of policy which are the essentials of personnel management in construction.

Finally, there is a need for personnel management specialists in building to alleviate the haphazard recruitment, the anarchic wage structure of many firms and the *ad hoc* manner in which many personnel matters are dealt with. To carry such a responsibility, the personnel manager in construction must have the personal qualities and the necessary technical background to convince a still sceptical industry.

Questions

1. Identify the benefits of a structured personnel policy for a construction company. Amplify how such a policy can be used to improve morale and productivity at site level.
2. Discuss the advantages and disadvantages of hiring all operative labour at site level. If labour is hired at site, how can the potential friction between site and personnel office be reduced?
3. Prepare a paper for submission to a company's site agents which gives them a basic grasp of the aspects of employment law which have the most bearing upon the construction industry.
4. Discuss the utility and limitations of formal selection tests (e.g. aptitude, attainment and personality tests) as part of the recruitment process for site management staff.
5. In the near future it may be necessary to train multicraft operatives. Would this strategy be beneficial to the industry and the individual?
6. Assess the importance of maintaining personnel records in a construction company. How can such records be useful in sustaining a personnel policy?
7. What factors would need to be taken into account if a board of directors of a construction company were considering appointing a personnel officer?
8. Develop a working paper which lays down the criteria for promotion from site agent to contracts manager. How are the criteria you feel important to be measured?

References

Downham, M. J. (1974) Personnel Management, *Occasional Paper No. 6, Chartered Institute of Building*, Ascot

Finniston, M. (1979) *Engineering Our Future*, HMSO

Industrial Welfare Society (1962) *The £.s.d of Welfare in Industry*, Industrial Welfare Society

Ministry of Public Buildings and Works (1944) *The Placing and Management of Building Contracts*, HMSO

Phelps-Brown, E. H. (1968) *Certain Matters Concerning Labour in Building and Civil Engineering*, HMSO

Tatton, M. (1972) Building a better image in the job market place, *Building Technology and Management*, 10 Dec., pp. 5–6

Chapter 8

Financing business units

One of the major problems facing any business enterprise is that of obtaining finance. This is a problem not merely of quantity but also of type. The situation is further compounded by legislation and by the dynamism of the economy, but perhaps more fundamentally by the requirement to minimize costs.

Before a discussion of how various types of business may be financed and how a suitable financial structure can be selected, certain basic concepts must be appreciated and some assumptions made. Economies are dynamic, but for the purpose of analysis the situation is frozen so that the effects of changing one variable may be evaluated. Economic man, whether an individual or a firm, is assumed to act rationally to maximize utility, usually considered to be the maximizing of satisfaction for an individual consumer or the maximizing of profit for a firm.

Profit is a term for which there are several definitions. Those concerning accountancy (gross profit and net profit) will be considered later (Ch. 9). In economics, total profit is usually considered to comprise two elements: normal profit and super-normal profit. Normal profit is that level of surplus of income over expenditure which accrues to the entrepreneur over the long period and is the minimum return required by him to retain his investment in that use. (The long period is that length of time in which all the firm's costs of production may be charged – the fixed, variable, and semi-variable costs.) Thus, in the long period normal profit may be regarded as a quasi-cost, for if the firm does not achieve (at least) its normal profit, it should cease trading.

Super-normal (also called abnormal, monopoly or excess) profit is profit earned in excess of normal profit and may be a short-period or long-period situation depending upon the type of competition prevailing.

The margin is a very useful and important concept in economic analysis. It is a concept of increments, the marginal unit being the last unit produced or consumed (or the production or consumption of one additional unit).

The average is a broader concept, usually considering an entire spectrum of activity. An average is usually an arithmetic form of calculation; for example, average total cost is the total cost of the operation divided by the number of units of output produced. Averages naturally tend to follow the trend set by margins.

(Averages and margins are most commonly encountered in connection with costs and revenues of firms and industries, often in the context of equilibrium analysis.)

8.1 Types of business unit

The construction industry comprises a wide variety of firms from the single-person enterprise to the large, multinational public company. Each firm will have its own financial structure and requirements but it remains meaningful to consider categories of firm as the differences are rarely fundamental within each category.

8.1.1 Single-person enterprises

This is the simplest form of business unit. As the title implies, the owner of the firm is the firm, at least from the legal viewpoint. The owner has unlimited liability which means that he is personally liable for the debts of the firm, so that if the firm has insufficient assets to meet its liabilities, the assets of the owner may be realized (sold to obtain money) to meet the outstanding liabilities.

Single-person enterprises operate primarily on capital supplied by the owner, especially in the early stages of trading. The capital will have been obtained by saving or borrowing from individuals or a bank, any such loans being secured often against the owner's personal assets (e.g. a mortgage on the owner's house). Naturally, if the firm develops successfully, it may be possible to secure a loan against the assets of the firm.

It is not surprising that single-person enterprises constitute the small firms of an industry, and construction is no exception. That is not to say that single-person enterprises have no employees; they frequently do, but not very many per firm. Further limitations, such as the managerial and organizational ability of the owner, lack of technical expertise, and often contentment with being the owner of a small firm (sometimes coupled with a 'fear' of expansion) tend to keep the size of these enterprises small. The work they undertake is also at the lower levels of the size scale, being jobbing work, small extensions (usually to houses), occasionally small-scale new work (again usually housing), and specialist trades (such as plumbing, roofing, and electrics) direct to domestic clients or local contractors.

8.1.2 Partnerships

Partnerships occur in various forms but under the Partnership Act 1890 a partnership is defined as 'the relation which subsists between persons carrying on a business in common with a view of profit'. Thus a partnership may be implied by conduct by sharing the profits of a business with another person. However, it is more usual, and indeed more reasonable, for a partnership to be under a formal partnership agreement. The agreement will normally specify such important aspects as the capital contributed by the partners, their roles in the firm, any interest payments in respect of the partners' capital investments, the method of sharing any profits, and so on. Unless the partnership agreement specifies to the contrary, a partner may dissolve the partnership by giving notice to the other partner(s); also the death or bankruptcy of a partner dissolves the partnership. A partner is further precluded from selling his share in the firm to anyone else without the consent of the other partner(s).

The number of partners in any firm is usually limited to between two and twenty. Certain partnerships are exempt from this restriction; e.g. solicitors, architects.

Partners are normally subject to unlimited liability in respect of the debts of the firm but under the Limited Partnerships Act 1907 a limited partnership may be created. A limited partner enjoys limited liability; i.e. the partner is liable for the debts of the firm up to the amount which he has invested only. However, a limited partner has no right to participate in the management of the firm and all partnerships must have at least one general partner (who has unlimited liability).

Normally the name of the firm will not contain the names of all the partners. Until recently, all the partners had to register their names and nationalities with the Registrar of Business Names (Registration of Business Names Act 1916), but this requirement was repealed by the Companies Act 1981.

Partnerships do not pay corporation tax. The partners are assessed for income tax under the Schedule D provisions which, although an individual requirement for each partner, in practice is usually achieved by the firm providing details of the income of each partner from the partnership.

The legal parameters relating to partnerships tend to limit the size of this type of firm. The feature of most partners being subject to unlimited liability is a major constraint; hence it is most unusual for building firms to be partnerships. It is in the professions where partnerships are common. Most professional institutions in fact prescribe that their members may not form incorporated associations and so the single-person enterprise or the partnership are the only types of firm which such persons may form. Thus, most architectural, surveying, engineering, quantity surveying, and similar professional organizations are partnerships, but although a few partnerships are very large, employing many hundreds of people, the usual size of firm is small, say three to eight partners with ten to thirty employees.

8.1.3 Companies

Several types of firm may include the word 'Company' in their name; a partnership may be known as 'X and Co', but a company is more usually regarded as an incorporated association which has a legal identity distinct from its owners and those who participate in its activities. Incorporated associations are registered under the Companies Acts and their owners, in the vast majority of instances, enjoy limited liability. A limited company will, therefore, have the word

151

'Limited' in the last part of its name and an unlimited company will have the word 'unlimited' as the final word of its name (Companies Act 1981).

A company (an incorporated association in this text) obtains a separate legal identity upon registration with the Registrar of Companies who issues to the company a Certificate of Incorporation.

In order to obtain a Certificate of Incorporation, the promoters of the company (those people who wish to form the company) must deliver the Memorandum of Association and (usually) the Articles of Association to the Registrar of Companies together with a statement of the company's nominal capital and a list of the people who have agreed to become directors. The Certificate of Incorporation signifies that the company is a body corporate and has perpetual existence, independent of its members. (A company may, of course, be dissolved under prescribed conditions.)

The Memorandum of Association sets out the objects of the company and the type of business to be undertaken. It is a statement of the fundamental principles which govern the company. The Memorandum must state the following:

(a) The name of the company. If the company is limited by shares or guarantee, the last part of the company's name must contain the word 'Limited'. Undesirable names will be refused registration, e.g. where the name of the new company is so similar to that of an existing company that the two could be easily confused.

(b) The address of the company's registered office. This need not be the company's head office and is quite commonly the office of the company's accountants or solicitors.

(c) The objects of the company; the purposes for which the company has been created. This clause will be consulted by those considering trading with the company or by those considering investing in the company. The members of the company may, by obtaining an injunction, restrain the company from undertaking activities outside its stated objects (ultra vires). It is due to the fundamental nature of this clause that it is very difficult to alter, and so it is common for the objects clause to be as widely scoped as possible.

(d) A statement that the liability of members of the company is limited (for companies limited by shares or by guarantee).

(e) A statement of the share capital and its division (for companies limited by shares).

(f) A statement of the guaranteed capital (for companies limited by guarantee).

The Articles of Association set out the internal organization of the company and its rules for management. It is optional for a company limited by shares but is obligatory for a company limited by guarantee or an unlimited company to deliver the Articles of Association to the Registrar of Companies.

The Articles of a company limited by guarantee must state the number of members with which the company proposes to be registered. For an unlimited company the Articles must state the number of members and, if applicable, the share capital with which the company proposes to be registered. In either type of company the Registrar must be promptly informed of any increase in the number of members of the company.

The signatories of the Memorandum of Association are the original members of the company. It is usual for the membership of a company to be increased by further people taking up shares and having their names entered in the company's register of members.

If a company limited by shares does not deliver Articles of Association to the Registrar, the model articles contained in the Companies Acts will apply. The model articles will apply even if the company does deliver Articles in so far as the delivered Articles do not exclude or modify them. (The model articles are the regulations contained in Table A of the Companies Act 1948.)

As the provisions of the Articles of Association are of less fundamental significance than those of the Memorandum; it is easier for the Articles to be changed. However, one area of importance is the permitted scope of action of the directors, particularly in binding the company contractually.

Every company must hold an annual general meeting which all its members are entitled to attend. At this meeting the affairs of the company over the preceding trading year are reviewed in the light of the accounts for that period and the directors' report. This meeting is of great importance where significant issues are often debated and decided, those most commonly arising being the distribution of any profit, the election or re-election of directors and the appointment of auditors. A company may also hold extraordinary meetings.

The directors of a company are responsible for overall control of the operations and the general management. Their duties are quite strictly controlled by the provisions of the Companies Acts. Notably, they have a fiduciary duty to the company to avoid a conflict of their personal interests with the interests of the company, a duty not to take advantage of their position to achieve personal gain and, of course, a duty of care in the exercise of their functions.

As a company is itself a legal personage and is thus distinguished from its members, it has a separate and continuous existence. The life of a company may, however, be brought to an end (the company is dissolved) by the process of winding-up. Compulsory winding-up will occur upon the happening of certain events, the most common of which is that the company is unable to pay its debts and an unpaid creditor has successfully presented a petition to the court to have the affairs of the company wound up. The court will place the affairs of the company in the hands of the official receiver prior to the appointment of a liquidator.

The winding-up may be voluntary. Here a resolution for winding-up will be passed by the members of the company who will then appoint a liquidator. This is usually done for restructuring purposes.

The third possibility is for the winding-up to be under supervision. This is where a resolution for winding-up has been passed by the company but is subject to a court order for the winding-up to be under supervision. The liquidator is, therefore, under some supervision by the court.

Private companies

The Companies Act 1980 defines a private company as '. . . a company that is not a public company'.

The majority of private companies are limited, thus their members have a liability to contribute to the debts of the company on its being dissolved, up to a maximum of the amount unpaid on their shares (if any) or the amount they have guaranteed. There are, however, strict limits appertaining to the shares of private companies: the number of shareholders must be a minimum of two but a usual maximum of fifty; there can be no invitation to the public to take up shares; and the rights of shareholders to transfer shares are restricted.

There are many reasons why a private company may be considered to be a preferable type of firm to a partnership. These will usually include the limiting of the liability of the members (a limited partner is precluded from participation in the management of the partnership), the tax incentives (company car, etc.), and the easier raising of capital as more people may become members of the firm.

Within the construction industry private companies are a very common form of business enterprise. For obvious reasons they will comprise the smaller companies ranging from the two-person contractor (often subcontractor) upwards, their size being restricted by constraints such as capital requirements. Thus the current upper size limit for a private company would be that of a local contracting firm.

Public companies

A public company is defined in the Companies Act 1980 as

> . . . a company limited by shares or limited by guarantee and having a share capital, being a company –
>
> (a) the Memorandum of which states that the company is to be a public company; and
> (b) in relation to which the provisions of the Companies Acts as to the registration or re-registration of a company as a public company have been complied with on or after the appointed day . . . .

Under this Act the minimum number of shareholders in a public company was reduced from seven to two. Also the Memorandum must now state the name of the public company to conclude with the words 'Public Limited Company'.

A public company must deliver the written consent of the directors to act as such to the Registrar of Companies and their agreement to take and pay for the shares which qualify them to be directors. Even after the Registrar's certificate has been issued, a public company may not begin trading until the directors have actually taken up and paid for their qualifying shares.

In order to raise capital from the public by inviting people to subscribe for shares or debentures, a public company must first issue a prospectus. The prospectus must comprise information relevant to the invited investment including the identities of the directors, the profits which have been made or which are anticipated, the amount of capital required by the subscription, the company's financial record, the company's existing obligations in respect of existing contracts, details of any voting rights, and the dividend rights of each class of shares. It may well be of benefit for the company to include a statement of an expert in the prospectus to assist in promoting the subscription (e.g. an accountant), but this may not be done without the written permission of that expert.

As public companies may offer their shares for public subscription, they are subject to greater control and scrutiny by the authorities than other forms of business enterprise. To 'go public' a firm must not only satisfy the statutory requirement but also the Stock Exchange. There are many advantages for the public company form of enterprise but there are also significant disadvantages. The major advantages enjoyed by a public company are:

- limited liability of its members;
- ease of raising large amounts of capital through public subscription;
- shares on sale to the public and not subject to transfer restrictions;
- usually more security due to the firm's having a large capital base;
- finance may be obtained from a wide variety of sources and, due to the reputation of the firm and the greater security offered, may be relatively cheap;
- as these firms tend to be large, they usually enjoy economies of scale in their activities;
- large firms usually have sufficient funds, security, and ambitions to undertake R & D work, innovations, and training schemes.

The major disadvantages, however, are:

- ownership and management may be divorced;
- very large organizations tend to become 'bureaucratic' and of reduced efficiency;
- quite a small shareholding may give one person effective control;
- individual members with a small shareholding usually have no effective say in the firm's operations;
- large firms sometimes become fragmented with departments reducing co-operation with each other and with head office, often pursuing their own independent goals.

It is apparent that the advantages outweigh the disadvantages resulting in a tendency for firms to grow to become large public companies, commonly achieved by takeovers and amalgamations resulting in groups of companies rather than several completely individual companies.

Thus, in the construction industry, the largest firms are public companies often of a group structure. It is common for the group to include not only building companies and civil engineering (often coupled with overseas) companies but also companies for plant hire, services work, specialist work (such as ground engineering), component manufacture, and materials manufacture. Often, in the largest building companies, the structure of the firm is regionalized with each regional division operating as a separate organization. Naturally, these firms tend to concentrate on large projects, the size of firm varying from the large local building firm upwards. Housing has usually been a separate division in a group, as has rehabilitation and refurbishment work, but recently due *inter alia* to the prevailing economic climate and government policies, many large building companies have become increasingly involved with rehabilitation and refurbishment projects.

8.1.4 Co-operatives

In the construction industry, as in most industries in the UK, co-operatives are rather rare. Those which do exist are small-scale enterprises and have very varied structures. Co-operatives commonly experience problems such as obtaining tax exemption certificates as well as scepticism from potential clients due to the unusual nature of the organization in what is generally acknowledged to be a conservative industry. Also, many are unable to give trust and credence to an enterprise in which the profit 'motive' is absent and which operates on an apparently idealistic basis of fulfilling a need and sharing the proceeds of work equally. Co-operatives often subsidise the work they do for less affluent clients from the proceeds of work undertaken for clients in a better financial position, the reasoning being that should the situation be left to the free market, the poor could not afford to have necessary building work done which would result in further deprivation through a depletion of the building stock.

Jo Grimmond, MP, Chairman of Job Ownership (a group promoting Mondragon type co-operatives) wrote (Grimmond 1980): '... The worker who has no share in the ownership has usually little to gain from the profit motive. Self-respect, the well-being consequent upon belonging to a community, and opportunities for individual enterprise, are most likely to flourish when workers come together in a business they own and control themselves ...'

Finance and capital are seen as a considerable problem for co-operatives, the sources being the members and loans from banks (usually reluctant) or other institutions and individuals. The formal establishment of a co-operative is valuable in that it gives the members limited liability, a registered co-operative being a legally recognized body in its own right.

8.2 Sources of capital

The sources of capital available to any firm are quite numerous but, as has already been noted, public companies have the greatest variety of sources available for their use and the single-person enterprise, the least variety. It is also important to seek capital not only from a legally permitted source but from a source appropriate to the type of capital required. The type of capital is dictated by the time period for which it is needed by the firm and the degree of risk involved, the former denoting the possible sources and the latter determining the most economic solution.

156

For convenience, capital is classified into three types by time period of the requirement; short, medium, and long. The short period is considered to be that length of time during which only the variable costs of the enterprise may change (usually up to one year). The long period is that length of time during which all the costs of the enterprise (variable costs, fixed costs, and semi variable costs) may change. The medium term lies between the two extremes and is that length of time during which only the fixed costs cannot be changed (usually one year to about seven years). The time period for which the capital is required is thus a very important parameter which affects not only the sources available to the firm but also the cost of the capital, due to time preference.

8.2.1 Long-term capital

Long-term finance is required to form or expand the long-term capital of the firm. It will be used to purchase fixed assets such as buildings, plant, and equipment – the durable (fixed) assets of the firm. Initially only external sources of capital – such as shares, debentures, and mortgages – are available to a firm but as profitable trading progresses, internal sources such as retained earnings, reserves, and depreciation provisions may be used. The internal sources of capital are of obvious importance as no payments must be made by the firm for the use of those funds; however, the opportunity cost of any internal funds must be considered.

Shares
Shares confer a stake in the ownership of the company upon the shareholders (the owner of the shares). Shares have a par or face value which represents the ownership contribution of each share. Shares may be fully paid up or only partly paid up, in which instance the shareholder may be required to contribute up to the unpaid amount of his shareholding should the company be dissolved. It is important to note that although such outstanding liabilities do affect share prices, the Stock Exchange share price is no evidence of whether a share is fully paid up – the share certificate and other documents appertaining to the relevant share issue should be consulted for this information.

Shares may be of several types, each with different rights. Ordinary shares, or equities, represent the major ownership and risk-bearing element of entrepreneurship. Holders of ordinary shares are entitled to a share in the profits of the company (a dividend) only after all other liabilities have been met. Ordinary shares usually entitle the holders to voting rights, the votes being in direct proportion to the shareholding (non-voting ordinary shares are often called 'A' shares). Thus ordinary shareholders, in theory at least, have control of the company but also are the main risk-bearers, having only a residual claim on profits.

Preference shares are also common, entitling the holders to a dividend up to a prescribed level prior to any distributions being made to holders of ordinary shares. Preference shares are thus a safer form of investment than ordinary shares, and so the return on investment, in the long period, tends to be lower.

157

Cumulative preference shares are rather less common and carry a right for any dividend unpaid to be carried forward for payment out of the profits of future trading periods. Participating preference shares entitle the shareholder to not only a preference dividend but also a further dividend from the company's profits of the trading period, should those profits exceed a stipulated amount (such amount being set to permit a reasonable return to ordinary shareholders prior to the participation of these preference shareholders in any further distribution).

Issues of shares are of three types: a new issue for sale, a rights issue, and a scrip issue. A new issue for sale may be made in a variety of ways and may involve various intermediaries between the company and the purchasers. Shares may be issued directly by the company by means of subscriptions or tender from prospective purchasers. More usually, however, the company will issue the shares through a specialist intermediary, most commonly an issuing house (probably a merchant bank; issuing brokers are sometimes used). The issuing house executes the majority of the administration work associated with a new share issue, will offer advice on the form and timing of the issue and, in return for a commission, may underwrite the issue in part or in total thereby guaranteeing the company a minimum amount of finance from the issue.

A rights issue is where a company offers its existing shareholders the option of purchasing new shares in proportion to the existing shareholding, usually at a low price relative to the prevailing market price of the company's shares. Any shares not taken up in this way will be sold via the Stock Exchange. Thus a rights issue is a rather cheap way for a quoted company to raise capital as any underwriting, advertising, and similar costs associated with a new issue for sale are avoided. The existing shareholders who do not wish to take up their rights may sell those rights.

A scrip (or bonus) issue does not raise any new capital for the company. It is an issue made to existing shareholders in proportion to their shareholding and is free of charge. It is an adjustment to the capital structure of the company.

It must be noted that only issues of shares and calls on any amounts unpaid on shares raise capital for the company. Sales and purchases of shares (or debentures) which occur subsequent to the issue are merely changes in the owners of the company even though the shareholders may make or lose vast sums in such transactions.

Debentures

Debentures are fixed interest securities which are issued by a company in return for a long-term loan. Usually debentures are redeemable after a specified period (commonly of around twenty years). Debentures may be unsecured but are more often secured against the assets of the company as either mortgage debentures, which are secured against specific assets, or floating debentures, which are secured against the assets generally.

As debentures represent a loan to the company they carry a fixed rate of interest. Debenture holders are creditors of the company, not owners, and as such may seek dissolution of the firm should the interest payments not be made.

Debenture interest is a cost to the firm and therefore is a deduction to be made from gross profit in determining taxable profit. The rate of interest carried by debentures depends partly on prevailing long-term interest rates as well as upon the type of debenture and, hence, the degree of risk involved. As the risk carried by debentures is usually small, the rate of interest will also tend to be quite low (for instance, when compared to the return on preference shares).

Thus, debentures are best suited to financing companies which have quite stable levels of profit and a large amount of fixed assets (e.g. property companies).

Retained earnings

Retained earnings is profit retained within the firm instead of being distributed to the owners. Therefore, retained earnings is a certain and relatively cheap source of long-term capital and indeed is the major source for many firms. Retaining earnings does, however, represent an increased stake in the firm by the owners (the ordinary shareholders in the case of a public company) and so largely accounts for the prices of shares being in excess of their par value in dealings on the stock exchange.

Depreciation

Depreciation is a bookkeeping and costing exercise by which the initial cost of an asset is written off over its useful life, i.e. the value of the asset is reduced by a predetermined amount each year. Depreciation is allowed prior to the calculation of profit. It is a means by which the costs of the amounts of the various fixed assets used in production are charged and hence recovered as part of the sale price.

For internal purposes a firm will usually provide for depreciation of an asset on a straight-line basis (the depreciation provision per year equals the cost of the asset on acquisition minus any residual or scrap value at the end of the asset's life – all divided by the estimated useful life in years) or on a reducing balance basis (a percentage of the written down value of the asset, the depreciated value of the asset shown in the company's books at the start of a year, is provided for depreciation each year such that the value of the asset is shown at either nil or its scrap value at the end of its predicted useful life). The reducing balance method of depreciating assets is generally a more accurate statement of the asset's consumption, or value reduction, pattern. For purposes of corporation tax, however, the method to be used for depreciating any asset is prescribed in the tax regulations and so it may be necessary to produce two accounts, one for internal purposes and the other for taxation purposes.

Depreciation may also be regarded as a source of capital. If no depreciation were charged on, say, machinery, a greater amount of profit would be available (after tax, of course) for distribution to the owners. Thus, reserves created by the process of depreciating fixed assets represent a stake in the firm by the owners, in a similar manner to retained earnings. However, an actual distribution to the owners of the depreciation provisions would be a depletion of the capital of the firm.

Depreciation is a relatively cheap and popular source of capital for firms and is essential for capital maintenance. Like retained earnings, depreciation provisions contribute to the market value of a company's shares being in excess of their par value.

Further sources

Several organizations provide firms with finance for long-term capital, among the most widely known being the National Enterprise Board (NEB) and the Industrial and Commercial Finance Corporation (ICFC).

Under the provisions of the Industry Act 1975 and the National Enterprise Board (Guidelines) Direction 1980, the NEB is required to pursue a *catalytic investment role*. In particular, the NEB must be satisfied that the requirements of the company concerned cannot be appropriately met by other sources of finance prior to the NEB's making loans or acquiring securities. Further, the NEB may make investments only if an *adequate* rate of return within a *reasonable* time is envisaged. The NEB's primary areas of investment must be in companies engaged in the development or exploitation of new technologies or in companies undertaking activities wholly or mainly in the assisted areas in UK. The NEB's main objectives are, thus, the promotion of private sector technological advancement and the re-generation of depressed areas.

The ICFC was formed in 1945 by various financial institutions, including the Bank of England. The ICFC provides long-term finance for an applicant firm's fixed capital requirement. Usually the firm will require the finance to enable it to expand by constructing a new factory or purchasing plant and equipment. The firms assisted are small to medium-sized companies and the finance is usually provided as a long-term, fixed interest loan (of seven to twenty years' duration and interest being payable on the outstanding balance only), as preference shares or as ordinary shares or as a combination. In 1981, the ICFC publicized the amounts of finance it would consider providing to an applicant company as being '... £5,000 up to £2m or more ...' . The total amount invested by the ICFC was £338m (March 1980) in 2,962 companies, over half of the companies receiving less than £50,000 each. Of the £338m, construction received £23.2m making that industry fourth in the league table of ICFC investments. The ICFC is also prepared to assist new companies, including start-ups and to provide further services to applicant companies (such as financial advice).

8.2.2 Medium-term capital

Medium-term capital is the most indeterminate of the three categories being regarded by some as akin to short-term and by others as akin to long-term capital. From the concept of the medium-term stated above, the sources of medium-term capital are short-life debentures, longer life bank loans and other loans of a life between two and seven years. Retained earnings may also be used to provide medium-term capital.

Bank loans

The prime considerations of the banking system – security of deposits, the required liquidity ratio, and the necessity of obtaining a reasonable return for investors – naturally tend to dictate the lending and investment policies followed. The majority of bank deposits are liable to instant or very short notice withdrawal which acts to limit the extent of all but short-term investment activities by the banks. The security requirements also act to the detriment of the provision of risk capital, the risks faced by banks being of two categories: the risk of total default by the borrower and the risk of inability of the borrower to repay a loan upon the request of the bank. A further limitation applies through the imposed reserve asset ratio which a bank must maintain. (Other restrictions are also imposed upon the banks from time to time but these tend to be of a rather transient nature.)

Thus, although a business might be sound, it is quite difficult to obtain finance from the commercial banks. Should a firm be able to satisfy the bank, by demonstrating that the purpose of the loan is commercially sound and that the loan is secure (this will involve the presentation of accounts to the bank of the firm's trading record and a commercial appraisal of the scheme for which the loan is sought), the loan will usually be made for an agreed period of between two and five years. The loan must be repaid at the end of the period and interest will be charged at a commercial rate (a rate above the bank's base rate dependent upon period, risk, etc.). Alternatively, the loan may be repaid by instalments (yearly, half-yearly, or quarterly) and interest charged on the outstanding balance only. It should be noted, however, that banks prefer to make loans for the provision of working capital (such as stocks, which will be processed and sold) which may be considered as self-liquidating (the sale of the finished product providing the funds for the repayment of the loan) and so should perhaps be more accurately considered as short- to medium-term financing.

Debentures

Debentures have been considered above in the context of long-term capital provision.

Small firms provisions

In recent years much attention has been devoted to the financial problems of small firms. In March 1981, the NEB established Oakwood Loan Finance Limited to offer loans of up to £50,000 to small firms for a period of five years. The interest applicable to any loan is set annually at about bank base rate plus 2 per cent and must be paid quarterly. Capital repayments commence at the beginning of the fourth year of the loan and are quarterly repayments. Oakwood requires similar information from the company to that required by a bank for evaluation of a loan application. It is normal for Oakwood to purchase a warrant from a company to which it is making a loan entitling Oakwood to subscribe for equity in the company at a future date. The equity warrant is purchased at the current market value and entitles Oakwood to subscribe for up to a maximum of 20 per cent of the company's equity. This will occur usually where the company expands its equity capital subsequent to obtaining a loan from Oakwood. Two facets of such an arrangement are of importance: it will aid the company's equity capital expansion and will provide Oakwood with continuing interest in the venture. Any such arrangement may also be cancelled at the company's option (prior to the equity take-up) by a predetermined payment made by the company. (This investment scheme is rather similar to those operated by certain institutional investors in connection with their financing of property companies.)

8.2.3 Short-term capital

Short-term capital provision and management is vital to the success of the firm. It is this type of capital which is required for the day-to-day activities. The sources of short-term capital are both internal and external; the main internal sources being accrued expenses and tax provisions and the main external sources being trade creditors, bank overdrafts, and short-term loans. It is the short-term finance which provides the circulating capital for the firm and assists with overcoming potential cash flow problems due to market fluctuations. Notably, the most important source for construction firms is that of the bank overdraft.

Bank overdrafts

A bank overdraft is a process whereby a customer of a commercial bank is permitted to overdraw on that account (to draw in excess of any positive balance) up to an agreed limit for a prescribed period. This is rather similar to a bank loan except that interest is payable on the amount overdrawn only for the period it remains overdrawn and the account is usually repayable on demand or upon the termination of the overdraft period. Overdraft facilities are, however, commonly renewable and so, in practice, may constitute a continual source of short-term capital or liquidity 'insurance' facility.

An overdraft is a relatively cheap form of finance due to its being a short-term facility and with interest payable only on the loan actually taken up. Overdrafts are thus very suitable for firms with a fluctuating financial requirement, such as building contractors. It is a widely held belief that almost all building firms operate on an overdraft.

Trade creditors

Initially, it is important to distinguish between trade credit and discount. Discount is a reduction in the price to be paid for a commodity, usually applicable if payment is made by the purchaser within a prescribed period (from date of invoice or date of delivery). Credit is the granting of ownership of commodities prior to payment for them. In construction, it is usual for discount and credit facilities to go hand-in-hand, notably in respect of suppliers and nominated subcontractors. Domestic and labour-only subcontractors usually offer the contractor, and the contractor usually affords the client, credit alone.

The basic concept of trade credit is to bridge the time gap which exists between the purchase of materials and the sale of a finished product (consider the provisions appertaining to nominated suppliers under the JCT Standard Form of Building Contract, 1980). Wherever payment is not made immediately upon the transfer of ownership (particularly when coupled with a use facility) credit is offered. Naturally, the credit facilities vary considerably between firms and types of firm.

Control of credit facilities, both those offered by and to the firm, is important, and bears directly upon the capital requirements. Ideally, a greater credit facility should be enjoyed by the firm than that which the firm offers to its own customers, considering not only the periods involved but the sums as well (discounts may be an added complication to this calculation).

Short-term loans

Short-term loans are available from individuals, banks, and other financial institutions. They are required for the provision of working capital, carry a prescribed rate of interest upon the entire sum, and cannot be recalled prior to the due date. Usually, short-term loans are obtained from commercial banks.

Tax provisions

A company's corporation tax liability becomes due for payment to the Inland Revenue in the year following that in which the profit, giving rise to the tax liability, was earned. The finance is thus available for use by the company for approximately one year. However, at a conference organized by CES Limited in May 1981, Frank Dobson, MP, asserted that the corporate sector's tax payments to the Inland Revenue in the financial year 1980/81, including bank windfall tax and petroleum tax, constituted approximately 8.7 per cent of the Inland Revenue's income for that year. This indicates that the prevailing rate of corporation tax (52 per cent) was not such a burden to companies as it might at first have appeared. Nevertheless, payment of corporation tax one year in arrears constitutes an important source of short-term capital.

Value Added Tax (VAT) is levied by Customs and Excise; the standard rate of VAT is set periodically and has reached 15 per cent. Any item sold by a firm is subject to VAT regulations in one of three ways: standard rate, zero rate, or exempt. Thus the purchaser pays no VAT on items which are either zero rated or exempt but the vendor's position is rather different. If an item sold is exempt from VAT, the vendor cannot recover his input tax (the VAT he has paid to suppliers in respect of that item sold); however, if the sale is zero or standard rated, the input tax is recoverable from the Customs and Excise (by way of set-off against the VAT which the firm is liable to pay to Customs and Excise from its standard rated sales).

Any firm with an annual turnover exceeding a prescribed amount (£15,000 in 1981) must be registered for VAT. Only registered firms may recover input tax. The tax balancing (payment liability and input tax recovery set-off) occurs at either the usual three-monthly or monthly intervals for VAT returns. Naturally, if a firm produces largely zero-rated commodities it should seek monthly returns to facilitate a cash flow from the Customs and Excise. Conversely, if a firm produces standard-rate commodities, its cash flow will be advantaged by having three-monthly VAT returns.

Most new construction work and alterations are currently zero rated for VAT. Repair and maintenance work is, however, currently standard rated. Thus, unless the majority of a construction firm's work (by value) is classed as repair and maintenance, it should seek monthly VAT returns. It should be noted that the cost of making the additional eight VAT returns per year should be considered prior to electing which period is to apply.

For a firm undertaking a majority of repair and maintenance work, VAT may provide a useful source of short-term capital.

Accrued expenses

Accrued expenses are a type of credit. Such expenses comprise wages, salaries, employees' expenses claims, and similar internal credit facilities.

It is evident from the nature of this facility that the amounts and periods of credit will vary, the periods being a matter of days or weeks and the individual sums small. However, especially in times of high interest rates, the overall credit facility will be of significance.

8.2.4 Stock Exchange

The Stock Exchange is primarily a market where various securities (e.g. government stocks, shares, debentures) are bought and sold. The Stock Exchange has strict rules governing transactions which are executed 'on the floor' by members of the Stock Exchange only. Brokers act as agents for members of the public or institutions, and jobbers deal in securities between brokers. The Stock Exchange is widely recognized as not only a highly organized but also a near perfect market.

Apart from acting as a securities market, the Stock Exchange performs several other important functions in connection with the sale and purchase of securities. The Stock Exchange vets any company wishing to go public (to become a public company) and prescribes certain conditions which must be fulfilled, e.g. a public company must offer at least 25 per cent of its capital for public subscription. Only companies with an equity share capital which is valued at more than £500,000 are able to obtain a Stock Exchange full listing (the placing of the price of the security on the official list – privilege granted to public companies which have satisfied the Stock Exchange Council) in order that the company's securities are tradeable on the Stock Exchange. The Stock Exchange Council is rigorous in its examination of all applications for a listing due to its role of safeguarding the investing public.

In December 1980 an alternative to the full listing (which is an expensive exercise for any company and proportionally more so for a small firm requiring to raise a relatively small amount of capital – the cost of a small issue may be approximately 5 per cent of the proceeds of the issue), the Unlisted Securities Market (USM), was introduced specifically to encourage small companies to raise capital through the Stock Exchange. Any company seeking a USM listing must be registered as a public limited company and have a suitable three-year trading record. Normally only 10 per cent of the company's authorized capital need be sold to the public. The costs to the firm of obtaining a USM listing are also lower (such as the mandatory advertising prescribed by the Stock Exchange) and so smaller companies are encouraged to raise capital through this means.

Only the initial sale of securities raises capital for the issuing company (or government). The majority of Stock Exchange transactions are subsequent to such sales and represent a change only in the ownership of the securities, changes which occur at the prevailing market price. Thus in evaluating an investment in securities, an investor will consider:

(a) any amount not paid up (thus representing a possible future liability to pay);
(b) the market price of the security;
(c) the return on the security (divided or interest);
(d) the risks involved and status of the company (government securities are generally regarded as almost risk-free),
(e) the economic climate and trends.

In a basic economic evaluation the yield of an investment is important, the yield being the return (average over a period or at a particular time) on the investment compared with its purchase price. Discounted cash flow techniques should be employed in the calculations.

8.2.5 Sale and lease-back

Sale and lease-back arrangements have been common for some time in the property development industry. The specific arrangements are, of course, peculiar to each individual dealing but may be summarized in general as when a property company which owns a development site sells the freehold to a financial institution (usually a pension fund or insurance company) in return for:

(a) a loan to finance a development (usually commercial) upon the land, the interest payable on the loan being deferred until completion of the development, and
(b) an agreement to lease the completed building back to the property company.

Upon completion of the development, the property company pays rent to the financial institution, thereby providing it with its normal rate of return on such an investment, and itself sub-lets the building to an occupier (usually a commercial enterprise) thus providing itself with an adequate return.

This process permits the financial institution to invest in specific developments while relieving commercial enterprises of the necessity to tie up large amounts of capital in the construction and ownership of their office premises.

It is noteworthy that the process of leasing plant and equipment which is employed by many organizations (e.g. computer facilities, company cars, construction plant, although this is more usually hired than leased) is carried out to avoid the necessity of long-term capital investment by the firm in these items. The capital of the firm is thus kept available for investment in the firm's specialist activities, those in which it should earn the greatest return.

8.3 Capital structures

The capital structure of a firm is governed by many variables: the field of operations; the finance available and the sources of finance; the perceptions and views of managers and investors; and (perhaps of most obvious importance) the costs of capital from the available sources.

Assuming comparable managerial expertise among firms of any certain type in a particular field of operation, the predominant factor determining the actual capital structure of a particular firm is the cost of capital. In the construction industry capital structures will vary: a property company will have a very large proportion of fixed assets; a precast concrete manufacturer will have considerable fixed assets but also a considerable stock of materials and work-in-progress; a main contractor will have fixed assets of a head office, yard, some plant but a large amount of work-in-progress; while a jobbing builder may have almost no fixed assets, a negligible stock of materials but a reasonable amount of work-in-progress (often including a significant amount of completed work for which no payment has been received due to inadequate credit control). Thus, each type of firm will need a different capital structure to suit its operational requirements.

Having already considered the common sources of capital and their applicability to the various types of firm, the cost of capital is now considered as a primary determinant of capital structure.

8.3.1 Cost of capital

Some major influences
The cost of capital to a firm cannot be divorced from the cost of capital to the investors, which can be viewed in an opportunity cost manner as the return, net of tax, which investors could earn in the next best investment (or in alternative investments) after making due allowance for any variations in the risks involved. It is thus reasonable to conclude that risk is an important element in the consideration of the cost of capital.

It therefore follows to determine what factors are of importance to a potential investor's decision. Many of the major factors have already been mentioned but may be summarized as purchase price, return, inflation, taxation, liquidity, and security or risk. It will be seen that it is possible to combine these factors in order that yield is the prime consideration.

Yield considers the return in relation to the purchase price. However, the return which should be considered is not simply the monetary interest or dividend but should include the appropriate allowances for tax, inflation, and risk. In fact, any rate of interest has three components: inflation, risk, and time-preference.

Inflation

Inflation (the opposite of deflation) is a raising of the price level in an economy relative to money incomes. If money incomes are held constant their purchasing power is progressively eroded, i.e. real incomes are reduced. Inflation has been a common feature of all developed economies in recent years.

Inflation represents a major problem for building firms; not only must they consider how to deal with the effects of inflation in the valuations of fixed assets, work-in-progress, stocks, etc. for their accounts (and accountants are not completely certain as to how to deal with inflation) but must allow for inflation in any fixed price tenders. Incorrect predictions of inflation may mean the firm makes a loss instead of a profit.

Taxation

Taxation is influential upon the cost of capital by two means: first, through the system of corporation tax and, second, through income tax levied on individuals in respect of both earned and, more importantly in this context, unearned income. In outline, corporation tax is levied on the profits of companies after the deduction of interest payments by those companies but before any profits are available for distribution.

Investment allowances in respect of capital expenditures are available for set-off against a company's corporation tax liability. The allowances vary, depending upon the type of capital expenditure (e.g. plant, for which a 100 per cent first year allowance is available; industrial buildings, initial allowance of half the cost of the new building, excluding land, is deductible in the first year of purchase and the remainder may be written off at 4 per cent per year). One further factor complicating the allowances is the location of the capital expenditure: if it is within a type of development area, the allowances will be more generous, e.g. in an enterprise zone the cost of purchasing any new industrial or commercial building may be offset in full in the first year of purchase.

Risk

Risk may be viewed as being the opposite of security, higher risks being less secure. In this context risk also embodies uncertainty (see Ch. 10). Naturally, as the security of any investment proposition is reduced, the financial incentive necessary to procure investors increases; thus, the cost of capital is inversely proportional to the security offered. Hence, investment is government securities carries a relatively low return as such an investment is generally regarded as being almost risk-free. As has already been noted, a bank will consider two forms of risk when evaluating a possible loan: the risk of total default and the risk of inability to repay the loan as the bank requires.

167

Comparison: risk and time-preference

It is now reasonable to postulate that for any group of possible investments of a similar nature (as inflation may have differential effects) over a given time period, the factor which dictates the return the investments must earn to appear equally attractive to a potential investor (i.e. the investor is indifferent between the alternatives) is risk. Likewise, for a spectrum of investments of equal risk, the factor dictating the return the investments must provide to render the potential investor indifferent between them is the period of the investments (due to time-preference). Although a time-preference rate is very difficult to determine, the social time-preference rate (the time-preference rate of society) has been estimated to be possibly as low as 2 per cent (Seeley 1972). Thus, even allowing for a considerable increase in the time-preference rate and assuming that inflation affects all parts of the economy in a uniform manner (it is unlikely that actual inflation influences would produce a significant divergence from the results obtained by using this assumption), it is risk which is the prime distinguishing factor between a spectrum of possible investments.

Gearing

Gearing is the ratio of (fixed interest) debt finance to equity finance (owners stake in the firm). Thus, gearing indicates the security of a fixed interest investment: the higher the gearing, the lower the security offered and so the higher the necessary recompense required by the debt investors. High gearing also increases the risk of the ordinary shareholders, as greater profits must be earned by the company to enable them to receive a dividend. Comparing two companies, one with high gearing and the other with low gearing, which earn the same return on their total capital, the company with high gearing will be able to pay higher dividends per share, provided the return earned is in excess of the return payable on its loan capital.

Normally, the cost to the firm of the various forms of capital will encourage it to raise debt finance, especially due to the advantageous tax position of the interest payments being offset against the firm's tax liability. However, as the amount of debt finance increases (the firm becomes more highly geared) so does the amount of risk and, hence, the cost of capital also rises, thereby effectively limiting the proportion and amount of debt finance which the firm may obtain.

8.3.2 Cost of individual types of capital

It has been demonstrated that, to a significant extent, the capital structure of a firm is dictated by the type of firm and the nature of its activities. However, there is still scope within these parameters for variation in capital structures, a major determinant of the capital structure adopted being the cost of capital.

If a firm behaves as a rational economic individual it will seek to minimize its cost of capital. In doing so it will select capital from various sources. Hence, it is of value to consider the costs of individual forms of capital and, then, how the aggregate cost of capital may be minimized.

Equity capital: New Issues

In evaluating any new issue of shares a company must consider the yield on existing shares, the expenses associated with the new issue, and the discount it must offer on the new issue to make it sufficiently attractive for takeup. The company must also ensure that the existing shareholders are not disadvantaged due to the new issue. Some existing shareholders will purchase new issue shares and the remainder of the new issue will therefore be purchased by new shareholders. Thus,

the cost of capital $= y_1 c + y_2 k + e$

where $y_1 =$ existing yield on the company's shares

$\quad\quad y_2 =$ projected yield after new issue

$\quad\quad c =$ proportion of new issue taken up by existing shareholders

$\quad\quad k =$ proportion of new issue taken up by new shareholders

and $e =$ issue expenses

(derived from Merrett and Sykes 1973).

The firm must pay dividends sufficient to provide the shareholders with their required yield on the investment, so from the firm's viewpoint the yield is the ratio of the dividend to the capital provided by the shares.

Equity capital: rights issues

$$\text{Cost of capital} = y_2 \frac{k_n}{K} + y_1 \left(\frac{k_o - s}{K} \right) + e$$

where e, y_1 and y_2 are as previous example

$\quad\quad k_n =$ capital from new shareholders

$\quad\quad k_o =$ capital from existing shareholders

$\quad\quad s =$ proceeds from sale of rights

and $K =$ total new capital

(derived from Merrett and Sykes 1973).

Retained earnings

On the face of things, retained earnings have no cost to the firm. However, they do constitute an increased stake in the firm by the shareholders as they represent profits which have not been distributed as dividends. Thus, retained earnings have an opportunity cost. Merrett and Sykes (1973) argue that a firm employing retained earnings to finance its activities is able to accept a return on its investments which is lower than the return on shareholders' alternative investments by the difference between the tax deducted at source on distribution (ACT) and the rate of personal taxation of the shareholders. (This presumes that the shareholders are taxed on their income at an average rate in excess of standard rate. This analysis also ignores any capital gains tax payable on the increased market value of shares arising from the retained earnings.)

Depreciation
Depreciation provisions may be considered in a similar manner to retained earnings – they have an opportunity cost and represent an increased stake in the firm by its shareholders. However, a distribution of depreciation provisions would produce a capital reduction, probably requiring outstanding debts to be repaid due to the depletion of the capital base, the security against which the debt was obtained. This indicates a proportional combination between the cost of debt repaid and the cost of retained earnings to calculate the cost of capital in the form of depreciation provisions.

Debentures
Debentures are normally issued at a discount. They are subject to a prescribed rate of interest per year until they reach maturity, upon which the loan is repaid by the company.

Hay and Morris (1979) consider the cost of debenture finance to the company to be i in the equation:

$$B_o = \sum_{t=1}^{t=n} \frac{bB_N}{(1 + i)^t} + \frac{B_N}{(1 + i)^n}$$

where B_o = issue price

B_N = terminal value

b = nominal interest rate on the debenture

n = life of the debenture.

t = time elapsed from issue.

It must be noted that interest paid on debentures is allowed as a cost of the firm's operations prior to the computation of any corporation tax liability. This effectively reduces the cost of this source of capital.

Trade creditors
Merrett and Sykes (1973) argue that only discounts allowed or foregone should be used to compute the cost of capital from trade creditors. They consider it preferable to treat payment delays, the true credit element, as adjustments to cash flow and their reasoning has been followed in this analysis.

Discounts for prompt payment are very common in construction in respect of almost all types of subcontractors' and suppliers' accounts. However, due to the ravages of inflation there has been a marked tendency for domestic suppliers particularly to tighten their credit control, thus domestic suppliers and subcontractors should each be considered on an individual basis (possibly leading to a weighted average calculation for practical uses). It is usual for only the discount to be forfeited by late payment and not for interest to be charged on the outstanding account. The cost of foregoing discount is obtained from

$$\left[1 + \frac{d}{100 - d}\right]^{(52/n)} - 1 = R \text{ per cent p.a.}$$

where d = per cent discount offered

n = period for payment in weeks

R = rate of interest per annum as cost of foregoing the discount.

The annual equivalent rate of interest obtained must be reduced by a factor of $(1 - T)$, where T is the rate of tax which the firm pays as loss of discount adds to the firm's costs which are, of course, tax deductable.

8.3.3 Marginal cost of capital

The marginal cost of capital is of use to a firm in deciding whether or not to undertake a project or to expand. It considers the cost of the requisite capital from the possible sources and is obviously likely to produce a cost in excess of the firms average cost of capital due *inter alia* to the additional risks likely to be involved.

8.3.4 Weighted average cost of capital

The weighted average cost of capital for a firm is of use in two major areas: in consideration of the firm's position and in evaluation of proposed changes necessitating a change in the firm's capital. Thus a weighted average technique may be used in a quasi-marginal way to evaluate a proposed investment project, such as the construction of a new building.

The weighted average cost of capital is obtained by multiplying the net of tax cost of capital (usually expressed as a percentage per annum) for each source of capital by the proportion of total capital (for the firm or project) from that source and summing these products to obtain a single percentage.

8.3.5 Optimum capital structure

The optimum capital structure is that which provides the greatest benefit to the firm. This may be considered to be providing the greatest possible return to the owner's investments in the firm. Naturally this is a somewhat complex goal; the requirements and views of the owners will vary (especially for a public company), short-term and long-term objectives and possibilities may conflict and so, given these and other problems of optimizing, it is likely, in fact, that, satisficing, will be employed to determine the capital structure of a firm.*

---

* A 'satisficing' situation is one of compromise; it is acceptable in respect of each individual criterion, but is suboptimal. See page 188 in Chapter 9.

The optimum capital structure would be such that, within the physical parameters, the marginal cost of capital employed by the firm will be equal from all available sources. This minimizes the cost of capital to the firm and so, in consequence, should maximize the owners' returns.

Satisficing, in the context of the long-period minimum return which must be earned on the owners' investment (normal profit), should permit greater flexibility in the selection of the capital structure.

Summary

The construction industry contains a large number of firms, varying in size from single-person enterprises to multinational public companies. Contracting comprises all forms of business enterprise but the construction professions are usually single-person enterprises or, more commmonly, partnerships. The co-operative movement is evident in the industry but is still in its infancy and on a rather small scale.

Numerous sources of capital are available, both internal and external to the firms. Limitations on the sources exist due to the form of business enterprise and are especially evident in respect of long-term capital provision. Recently special provisions have been introduced to assist the small firms and the evidence available indicates that the construction industry benefits directly from these provisions as well as indirectly via the general stimulation of fixed capital investment which such schemes promote. Short-term capital provision is particularly important to contractors. The Stock Exchange provides not only a market-place for trading in securities but also acts as a scrutineer to safeguard the investing public. Sale and lease-back arrangements are important in property development due to their influence on developers' capital structures and their facilitation of investment in specialist activities.

The capital structure of any firm is related to the form of the enterprise, its objectives, and the cost of capital. The cost of capital is subject to and governed by many variables which often operate independently of each other. The firm must consider these influences and their effects on the cost of the individual types of capital to determine the most suitable capital structure. The marginal cost of capital and the weighted average cost of capital will provide an indication of the optimum capital structure from the cost of capital view. The optimum capital structure is unlikely to be achieved, the concept of satisficing being more commonly employed due to the many, divergent considerations and the common requirement for a degree of flexibility.

Questions

1. What forms of business unit are to be found in the UK construction industry? Describe and discuss the activities and rules of each.

2. Why is it rare for a contracting firm to be in the form of a partnership?
3. With what requirements must a firm comply to become a company? Why may such compliance be considered essential?
4. Describe the categories into which the capital of a firm is usually classified and discuss the role of time in the classification.
5. Discuss the reasons why companies are in an advantageous position over other types of business unit for the raising of capital.
6. Discuss the role of the commercial banks in the provision of capital for the construction industry.
7. Discuss the factors which determine the cost of capital for a firm.
8. How may a firm determine the most suitable capital structure to adopt?

References and bibliography

Becham, A. and Cunningham, N. J. (1970) *Economics of Industrial Organisation*, Pitman
Bromwich, M. (1976) *The Economics of Capital Budgeting*, Penguin
HMSO *Companies Act 1948–1980*
Grimmond, J. (1980) Co-ops offer a third way, *The Guardian*, 13 Oct.
Hay, D. A. and Morris, D. J. (1979) *Industrial Economics – Theory and Evidence*, Oxford U.P.
James, P. S. (1979) *Introduction to English Law* (10th edn), Butterworths
Kay, J. A. and King, M. A. (1980) *The British Tax System* (2nd edn), Oxford U.P.
Lipsey, R. G. (1979) *An Introduction to Positive Economics* (5th edn), Weidenfeld and Nicolson
Merrett, A. J. and Sykes, A. (1973) *The Finance and Analysis of Capital Projects* (2nd edn), Longman
Midgley, K. and Burns, R. G. (1972) *Business Finance and the Capital Market*, Macmillan
Morris, D. J. (ed.) (1979) *The Economic System in the UK* (2nd edn), Oxford U.P.
Rayner, M. (1978) *National and Local Taxation*, Macmillan
Seeley, I. H. (1972) *Building Economics*, Macmillan
Sizer, J. (1979) *An Insight into Management Accounting* (2nd edn), Penguin

Chapter 9

Budgeting

Budgeting is concerned with two quite distinct areas: costs and revenues. These two aspects are drawn together by often quite sophisticated systems of performance monitoring and control, systems without which budgets are of little value. A budget is an estimate of the costs and incomes to be generated if a proposed project is undertaken. Budgets are predictions and are thus subject to accuracy constraints in respect of the techniques employed, information available, expertise of personnel, and so on. As no budget is completely accurate, it is important that the inherent error is acknowledged when monitoring and implementing control. Error should, of course, be minimized but it may be uneconomic to increase the sophistication of the budgeting system significantly (and hence its cost) once an acceptable level of accuracy has been achieved.

Fitness for purpose is a concept which should be applied as equally to budgeting as it should be to building design. The budget should provide the requisite information at an acceptable level of accuracy and for a reasonable cost to enable management to make a decision and/or monitor and control the project.

Budgeting, coupled with monitoring and control, is important to everyone concerned with construction projects; the client requires a prediction of the total cost of the project and the associated fees and charges; designers may bid for their aspects of the work or ensure that their expenditures are maintained within a prescribed professional fee; contractors will (probably) tender for the construction work and monitor their activities for profitability control. It is important to realize that such budgets are not merely predictions of a total cost or price but are time related and will indicated the pattern of accruals. It is in this time relationship which much of the importance of budgeting lies.

Updating of budgets is an important function. Budgets are usually based upon limited information and so require updating and amending as more information becomes available and as circumstances affecting the budgets change. An up-to-date budget is essential for effective monitoring and control.

Survival

In order for any business unit to survive, economic theory dictates that, in the long period, it must earn at least normal profit. How can a firm be certain of achieving this minimum profitability? Why do some firms dissolve during slump periods while others appear to prosper?

There are very many questions regarding the survival and prosperity of firms. This chapter discussess some general principles and techniques to aid success in the construction industry.

9.1 Costs

In the construction industry almost all budgeting techniques are based upon cost. However, in any sale three basic concepts are present: cost, price, and value. The cost to the purchaser is the seller's price, with value acting as arbiter between the parties. Cost is what must be given (or foregone) to obtained something. Price is what is received in return for giving up something. Value is a measure of the utility of the item(s). Thus, the price the seller asks for the commodity is the cost of that commodity to the purchaser (usually expressed as a sum of money). The value of the commodity is subjective but will be related to the exchange price such that it may be concluded that the value to the purchaser of the commodity at least equals the sum of money given up (the opposite applies to the seller).

Commonly the terms 'cost' and 'price' are used interchangeably, which sometimes results in ambiguity. In this text the above definition of the terms apply.

Several classifications of costs are in common usage. Fixed, variable, and semi-variable is a basic economics classification but in the context of the construction industry the classification of costs as direct costs and indirect costs is more widely used and understood. (Indeed, it is upon such a classification that most tenders are prepared by contractors and subcontractors.) The addition of direct costs to indirect costs gives the total costs.

Direct costs are those which vary proportionally with output, whereas indirect costs are independent of the level of output (at least, in the short period). Broadly, the definitions of the prime costs of labour, materials and goods, and plant contained in the *Definition of Prime Cost of Daywork carried out under a Building Contract* (RICS) 1975, are descriptions of elements of direct cost, and definition of incidental costs, overheads and profit describing indirect costs. (Care should be taken not to apply the definitions, so given, absolutely, as certain items defined as incidentals – e.g. tool allowances – are more correctly direct costs.)

9.1.1 Contractors' costs

A contracting organization will incur a great variety of costs which may be broadly classified as shown in Table 9.1.

Site operative labour
The cost of site operative labour is considerably in excess of the wage rates

Table 9.1 Classification of contractors' costs

Key: V, variable; SV, semi-variable; F, fixed; D, direct; I, indirect.

Cost centre	Cost classification	
Site operative labour	V	D
Materials	V	D
Subcontractors	V	D
Plant:		
Hired	V	D
Owned:		
Depreciation, obsolescence	F	I
Wear, maintenance, etc.	V	D
Line management:		
Walking gangers, etc.	V	D
Forepersons	SV	I
Site agent, etc.	SV–F	I
Head office services to site (QS engineering, buying, etc.)	F	I
Supplementary departments (estimating, marketing, accounts, etc.)	F	I
Equipment:		
Leased	SV	I
Purchased:		
Depreciation, etc.	F	I
Maintenance, etc.	V	D
Head office and other premises	F	I
Capital provision:		
Operating capital charges	V	D
Other charges (some postponable)	F	I

specified in the NWRA due to several factors, those of major cost significance being:

- the bonus system – the level of bonus often being significantly related to prevailing supply and demand conditions;
- plus rates – tool allowance, travel allowances, lodging allowances, etc.;
- employer's statutory contributions – National Insurance, etc.;
- severence payments – related to period of employment;
- non-recoverable overtime payments;
- non-productive time payments;
- sick pay;
- holiday pay;
- clothing and safety provision – donkey jacket, hard hat, etc.

Generally, the cost of site operative labour will be significantly higher in some areas than in others due to such factors as construction workload, alternative employment and conditions offered by those alternatives, labour supply, un-ionization, and construction wage expectations. Thus, such areas as London and Liverpool experience high labour costs while labour is cheaper in such areas as Devon.

However, it is not merely cost of labour which is important but its productivity. In this context such aspects as a good bonus scheme and conducive and safe conditions of work will promote labour productivity and, hence, be cost-reducing.

On a typical building project using labour employed by the contractor, the labour content will approximate to 30 per cent of the project cost. There has recently been an increasing tendency, however, for main contractors to sublet the vast majority of site operations, thereby reducing the significance of this cost category.

Materials

Materials usually account for between one-third and one-half of the cost of a building project. Smaller firms, whose size precludes the use of bulk, centralized purchasing, will have a proportionally higher cost of materials as they cannot obtain the discounts and credit facilities enjoyed by larger firms.

The second important aspect of materials cost is concerned with measurement and estimating. If a traditional standard method of measurement (SMM) based bill of quantitites (BQ) is used, materials are measured net. Thus, allowances for laps (and other unmeasured requirements) must be added (the amounts of laps being stated in the preambles section of the BQ) and priced accordingly in the tendering process.

Third, waste of materials is a significant source of unrecovered cost (and hence loss). Estimators have, traditionally, included quite nominal allowances in their materials estimates for waste: off-cuts, loss, theft, damage, misuse – the list of sources of wast is extensive. However, the BRE has demonstrated on several occasions (Skoyles 1974, 1976, 1978, 1981) that waste of building materials on site is greatly in excess of estimators' allowances. Skoyles (1981) found that '. . . the overall loss of principal materials is about 100 per cent more than is usually allowed for in estimating. . . . This figure is, of course, highly variable and is much lower on some sites. . . .'

Due to increasing awareness of the actual material waste incurred, the allowances included by estimators have tended to increase. It is interesting to postulate the possible consequences of an estimate including only one-half of the requisite materials wastage allowance, especially during a period of slump, when small profit margins prevail.

If it is assumed that the total materials content cost is one-third of the project cost according to the estimate, waste allowance being an average of 6 per cent, actual waste is thus 12 per cent and profit addition on cost is 2 per cent. Thus,

$$\frac{\text{Project cost}}{3} = 1.06 \times \text{materials basic estimate } (m)$$

$$\frac{100\%}{3} = 1.06m$$

therefore,

$$m = \frac{100\%}{3.18} = 31.45\%$$

But actual waste of materials is 12% × m; thus, the 'excess' waste, not included in project estimate (and, hence, excluded from the project price) is

$$6\% \times m = 1.89\%$$

Contract sum (project price) is

$$100\% + 2\% \times 100\% = 102\%$$

i.e. anticipated profit margin is 2 per cent. But cost increase due to 'excess' materials waste is 1.89 per cent. Therefore, achieved profit margin is

$$2\% - 1.89\% = 0.11\%$$

The anticipated profit is almost completely eroded due to insufficient allowance in the estimate for waste of materials.

Subcontractors

Subcontractors have traditionally been used in building to carry out specialist operations but, particularly during the post-1945 period, the use of subcontractors has increased, notably in the basic building trades which were traditionally the province of contractors' directly employed operatives. The growth of subcontracting may be attributed to several major causes:

- successive governments' use of the construction industry as an economic regulator;
- higher costs of labour, including 'employers' contributions';
- greater employee protection and the trend away from casual labour;
- higher earnings of operatives in subcontracting organizations;
- ability of main contractors to pass on responsibilities to subcontractors (defective work, delays, etc.);
- greater flexibility for main contractors.

Today, some sites are run with a total absence of main contractors' directly employed labour, others with only a 'token' of a few directly employed labourers. Under management contracting systems, the complete absence of any management contractors' operatives is usual and expected but the situation is quite commonplace across the spectrum of contract forms.

While it may be seen as being cheaper for a main contractor to sub-let work as his responsibilities for defects may be passed on to the subcontractor – e.g. he does not have to organize the details of work execution, he does not have to bear the costs of non-productive time (unless due to default by the main contractor), he does not have to keep expensive operatives (craft and specialist) in employment when he has no work for them in order to ensure their availability for future projects, and so on – there are certain cost-increasing disadvantages caused by subcontracting: the contractor has less control in terms of standard of workmanship, output and performance generally; co-ordination is more complex and so more highly skilled (and, hence, more expensive) management will be required;

the reputation of the contractor is, to some degree, in the hands of the subcontractors and the subcontractors themselves aim to make a profit.

Thus, for several reasons, subcontracting may be advantageous: it promotes division of labour and specialization which should lead to greater productivity; it helps the retention of specialists who, under a subcontracting system, may do work for a variety of main contractors and so keep their skills available in the industry (it is rather rare for an operative who has left the construction industry to return to it); and it allows main contractors to concentrate upon their own specialisms of organization and project administration.

Clients' representatives often view subcontracting with a good degree of scepticism. This is probably because the chain of communication and control is longer and more complex, thus making it more difficult for them to protect their clients' interests. However, it is apparent that with the process of nomination, such subcontractors have much closer contact with and exhibit greater allegiance to the clients' representatives than the contractor although their contract for work is with the latter. This demonstrates that firms show allegiance with the party they perceive as being the true source of their sales.

Thus, subcontracting is often viewed by main contractors as a cost-saving exercise which also permits greater flexibility than using directly employed labour. The flexibility occurs in the main contractors' ability to call subcontractors on to the site only when work is available for them and to require them to comply with periods for their work in accordance with the construction programme. Delays and variations frequently produce programme changes, and while in slump periods a main contractor may be in a strong position relative to the subcontractors, during a boom the positions are often reversed and the subcontractors will require continuous site working or will charge extras for leaving and returning to site and for delays, disruptions, etc. It is also notoriously difficult to persuade subcontractors to return to site to complete work when their skills are in great demand. Some less scrupulous subcontractors are also very reluctant to return to a completed project to remedy defects.

It may be concluded, therefore, that subcontracting is not necessarily a cost-reducing process but, if current industrial trends have a sound basis, there are strong indications that this is the case at present.

Plant

Construction plant is usually hired by the contractor but may be owned by him. In the case of a large contractor it is usual for a plant hire subsidiary to own all the plant and to hire it out to the construction divisions. Apart from the advantages to the company of having its own equipment specialists, it also permits the company to benefit from discounts on cross-hiring from other plant companies when very specialist plant, not owned by the contractor's organization, is required.

The hire of large, driven plant usually includes a driver; the hire charge covers normal plant usage costs, driver's wages, fuel, etc., but not such items as breakdowns or damage attributable to the main contractor (e.g. a puncture

179

caused by rubbish being left on an untidy site). Major plant will also have 'on' and 'off' charges as lump sums for bringing the plant to the site and taking it away. The normal hire charge will be a certain amount per hour or per week.

Although the contractor must pay a greater amount for the use of plant if it is hired rather than owned by him, it must be remembered that the contractor also saves by hiring plant as he does not have to bear the cost of plant being idle between projects or of obsolescence, major servicing, etc., which, for owned plant, are usually included as overhead (although there will, of course, be an inclusion in the hire charges for these aspects). Perhaps the most significant aspect, however, is that hiring is a revenue charge only, but if plant is owned, a capital investment is required for the purchase. Thus, hiring plant allows the contractor to operate upon a smaller capital base which, other things being equal, should produce a greater return on the capital employed.

One significant costing problem in connection with hired plant occurs where plant is not required on site for a continuous period. In such a situation the decision whether to keep the plant on site for the entire period or to off-hire it when it is programmed to be idle should be based upon an examination of the hire charges for the programmed idle period against the additional on–off charges. It is obviously good programming practice to require plant to be on site for one period only and to be fully utilized within that period. (This analysis is similar to that for subcontracted work.)

Small tools are usually owned by the contractor. Costing systems vary between firms, from those who do not cost small tools to a particular site (their cost being part of overheads) to those who operate a complex system of cost to the site and credits for returns (such a system creates problems of second-hand valuations). A common system is to charge small tools to a site at their new price (even if second-hand) and give no credits for returns (but to require the physical return of still useful items).

It is apparent that the amount of plant used on a project increases as the size of the project increases. This trend is likely to continue and, indeed, will probably be enhanced by the tendency for construction to become an on-site assembly process and a more mechanized process. Thus, plant costs are likely to increase as a proportion of total project costs.

Line management

Line management includes all those who supervise the production work but do not actually execute the work themselves. In the context of a construction contractor the line management will comprise walking gangers, forepersons, site agents, and contracts managers (the titles allocated to those functions vary between firms).

Walking gangers are employed to supervise the work of several gangs, often the labouring gangs, on a site. Their conditions of employment are governed by the rules appertaining to operatives, and so this type of management may be considered to be a variable cost.

Forepersons are often employed on a more permanent basis and are now usually salaried. As they are frequently tradesmen who have been promoted to a supervisory role, one foreperson will generally oversee the working of one (or several related) trade on a site. This intermediary level of management is a semi-variable cost to the firm.

Site agents, including sub-agents, are salaried staff and, in most instances, are fixed costs, but in smaller organizations, and in more traditional firms, all staff who are site-based are wage-earning and so, due to the different conditions of employment applicable, they may be regarded as forming part of the semivariable costs. There is an increasing trend for site management to be salaried and have conditions of employment similar to head office staff. Thus the trend is away from semi-variable towards fixed costs.

Hillebrandt (1974) considers that as site management may be hired and fired with ease and with little expense, it is a variable cost. The argument also hinges on the assertion that site management costs increase in a directly proportional way to the output of the organization. Such a situation may occur due to either more site management being employed to cope with an increase in the contractor's workload or better quality (more able), and hence more expensive, site management being employed, or some combination of these two.

Hillebrandt (1974) also considers that there is a lack of highly skilled construction managers, that their recruitment is more expensive, and that firms will wish to retain their services, indicating that they are a fixed cost. This argument is probably most applicable to the contracts management who are usually salaried and employed as head office based staff. It is probably due to the lack of skilled managers, at all levels, in construction that the trend has been towards employing such personnel on a salaried, permanent basis.

The total cost of line management is small in relation to a contract sum or a contractor's annual turnover. The importance of management lies in its influence over the site production activities through its organizational abilities and so, despite its being itself of quite minor cost significance, is of major importance to the profitability of the firm.

Overheads

Overheads are generally considered to be those costs which must be borne even if there is no output from the firm. They are thus fixed costs. In a contracting firm, overheads will comprise such costs as head office rent, estimating, accounts. It would be exceedingly time-consuming and expensive to record accurately, and then cost, the overheads to each project undertaken by the firm.

Overheads are, therefore, *apportioned* among the firm's activities and are *absorbed* by each activity in its costing system.

Head office services to site.   Although the personnel involved work largely on site, they are normally employed, and costed, as head office staff. The discussion under 'line management' in respect of their supply, expertise, cost significance, etc., also applies to these personnel.

181

Supplementary departments. These head office staff constitute fixed costs, although, as with any staff, the more junior personnel constitute semi-variable costs. These departments are charged to projects as part of general overheads.

It is noteworthy that the estimating department (and in some ways marketing) is unusual as most of the work undertaken produces no return for the costs incurred – i.e., the majority of tenders submitted do not result in the firm being awarded the contract. Thus if, on average, the firm is successful in one of every six tenders submitted, the one-sixth of successful tenders must bear the cost of the five-sixths of unsuccessful tenders. Hence, if estimating costs can be reduced, while maintaining the level of accuracy of estimating, the firm's profitability will be enhanced or, if the savings are reflected in slightly lower tender prices, the firm will win more contracts (other things remaining constant).

A pilot investigation into tendering costs carried out at Brunel University by Harding (1980) indicated that the costs of submitting a tender for a 'typical' building project of £1 million to £3 million contract sum is approximately 0.8 per cent of the contract sum, but with quite wide variation about this figure.

Sir Maurice Laing stated in 1978 that '. . . Tendering throughout the industry costs one quarter of one per cent or less of all work. . . .' However, the Economist Intelligence Unit (EIU 1978) stated that '. . . it appears likely that average estimating costs for building projects fall below 1 per cent of turnover'.

It appears therefore, that the larger firms undertaking high-value, large projects enjoy economies of scale in tendering. It must be noted that success rates have a major influence over tendering costs in the context of cost as a proportion of turnover.

Equipment. Equipment such as office machinery, computers, cars, etc., may be purchased outright by a firm and so constitute a capital lock-up in a similar manner to plant purchase. Increasingly popular alternatives to outright purchase are hire purchase, leasing or renting the equipment (cars are usually either purchased outright or leased). Hire purchase is the only one of these three options under which the firm eventually owns the equipment; when leasing or renting the equipment, ownership remains with the leasing company (lessor).

Under hire-purchase arrangements, the company may offset the capital allowance in respect of the equipment against taxable profits. The ownership of the equipment eventually passes from the hire-purchase company to the trading firm.

If equipment is leased, the lessor always owns the equipment. The lessee (trading firm) agrees to make payments to have the use of the equipment for a prescribed period (usually in terms of years) and to take out a maintenance contract on the equipment.

Equipment may also be rented. Under such an arrangement the trading firm pays only for the period for which the equipment is required (and rented) and does not bear the cost of repairs (these forming part of the rental charge). Renting is thus the most flexible option.

Renting is possible usually on quite minor equipment only. For major items of equipment, purchasing or leasing are often the only alternatives. Leasing has advantages for cash flow by not tying up considerable amounts of capital and leasing arrangements often permit the lease period to be extended (a popular option during a recession).

Head office and other premises. These are fixed costs and are charged to projects as part of overheads. The costs of premises contain two major elements: the initial capital purchase of the lease or freehold, and the annual expenses associated with the premises. Some of the annual expenses associated with premises are postponable (e.g. maintenance), while others are, to a certain degree, variable in that they are dependent upon the occupancy and use of the premises (e.g. heating, lighting).

For some time construction economists have been concerned with costs-in-use in attempting to predict the life-cycle costs of buildings. In these evaluations much attention has often been paid to the time intervals between works of maintenance, due not only to the maintenance costs but also the costs of disruption occasioned by the work. However, it would now appear that such attention is of less significance and more attention must be devoted to running cost economies, particularly related to heating costs. A study into life cycle costing of buildings is currently being carried out by the Department of Construction Management at Reading University.

Capital provision. The costs of capital have been discussed in Chapter 8. It is important that the capital itself is not added to the other costs of the firm's operations as this would be double counting (the capital being physical items used in the production processes). The costs of the capital provision, however, are part of the total costs of the firm's operations and must be included in the costing processes. The inclusion could be effected by calculating and adding the cost of working capital provision together with the interest on longer term debt (as parts of overheads) and return to the owners (as the profit addition).

9.1.2 Cost patterns

Cost patterns are useful to indicate how costs vary over different levels of output. Figure 9.1 shows a simple long-period cost pattern where variable cost increases linearly with output but the fixed cost increases are staged.

However, the various categories of fixed cost will have stages of cost increase of different size, occurring at different times, thereby tending to change the pattern of fixed costs to one which is a stepped upward slope, as shown in Fig. 9.2.

It is probable that certain staged fixed cost increases, such as the purchase of an additional office, will be of such a size as to exert a major influence over the cost pattern. It is likely that these major stages of size alteration will be possible over a range of outputs and will comprise not just one major fixed cost increase but a number of associated increases – e.g. a firm's workload increases and thus

183

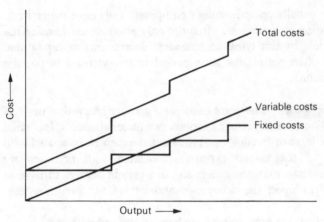

Fig. 9.1 Simple long-period cost pattern

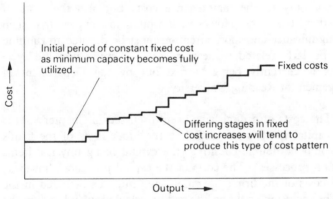

Fig. 9.2 Changes in fixed costs with output

requires more office staff, then merits larger office premises and, again, further staff. Such a situation is illustrated in Fig. 9.3 and shows the levels of activity at which changes in scale occur.

Figure 9.4 shows the influence of the changes in variable costs due to changes in efficiencies of operation (economies of bulk purchasing, inefficiencies of crowded workplaces, etc.). These are particularly notable as the firm grows from zero output and over each range of output where changes in the scale of production may occur.

9.1.3 Systems of costing

The system of costing used depends primarily upon the nature of the production system, but the aim of any costing system is cost control which is achieved by recording the costs actually incurred, comparing those costs with a pre-

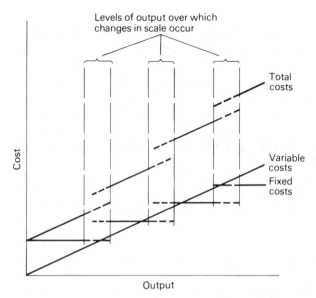

Fig. 9.3 Stages during which changes in fixed costs may occur

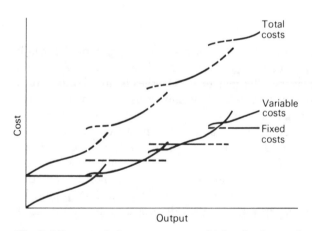

Fig. 9.4 Long-period cost pattern, combining fixed costs change stages with variable costs

determined standard, and taking any necessary corrective action. The construction industry largely produces major, one-off products, each of which contains many common and repetitive operations that are usually executed under slightly varying conditions. Also, the price of the product is almost invariably a greed prior to its actual production (speculative housing being a notable exception).

For a typical construction project the price is based upon a cost prediction and is agreed between the client and contractor prior to the work being commenced.

185

Overall historic costing

This is the simplest costing system whereby the overall cost of a completed project is compared with the revenue generated to determine whether the project achieved the required level of profit. The results of such an analysis may be used to predict the cost of proposed projects, after making adjustments for such variables as general cost escalation (fluctuations), specification changes (quality), quantity charges, cost effects of different locations, technological changes, etc.

A great deal of data are required for accuracy in this exercise. Such data are provided from several sources, the primary source being the Building Cost Information Service (BCIS) of the RICS.

Several techniques exist (which are fully described in other texts) to enable private quantity surveyors to predict the cost of proposed projects. It is by such techniques that clients are made aware of the cost of proposed buildings.

Periodic historic costing

This is a similar process to the overall historic costing described above, but is carried out for each project at predetermined intervals (often monthly). This enables the contractor to determine if the project is operating within its budgeted cost and to take action, when necessary, to get the project back 'on course' (see also 9.5.1).

Job and unit costing

This system is most suited to production in which a unit of output may be readily identified throughout the production process so that all costs attributable to the production of that unit may be allocated to it. Overheads are allocated on a predetermined basis; in construction this will usually be as a percentage of cost.

The system should be designed to facilitate the comparison of the estimated cost with the actual cost achieved on site, and such comparison should provide useful feedback to the estimating department. Potential problems arise under this costing system in respect of overhead allocation and miscellaneous non-productive times (due, for example, to bad weather, delays in normal activities, etc.). Overheads are thus best treated as a separate allocation. Non-productive times should also be recorded separately to provide programming information.

Standard costing

This is the costing system most extensively used in the construction industry. It is a system whereby costs are predetermined and subsequently compared with actual costs achieved to facilitate control. The predetermined costs are standard costs and are obtained through the application of work study and extensive cost recording. In the construction industry the labour constants used in estimating are of the nature of standard costs (note also production bonus target times).

Comparison of the cost of actual production with the standard cost gives the variance. Variances will usually be calculated for each cost centre of labour, plant, materials, and overheads for each operation or set of operations.

Naturally, due to the variety of products produced by the construction industry, the application of standard costing is rather complex. The more extensive use of computers in connection with cost recording (particularly for bonus calculations) and with estimating (to determine labour constants) has led to this system of costing being used more widely.

It is usual for cost variances to be determined on a weekly basis as costing is usually carried out in conjunction with the system of bonus payments – the measure for labour production bonus calculation being used to determine the cost of the direct labour expended upon the project. Difficulties arise when comparing the bonus measure with the BQ measure (the basis of valuation, and hence, revenue) as the measurement methods are not always the same. However, these difficulties may be overcome, enabling this system to be used for rapid response project cost control.

The measure for production bonus purposes is of an operational nature whereas the measure for valuations is usually based upon a prescribed standard method of measurement (e.g. SMM6), which is more geared to quantity surveying than production requirements. Attempts have been made to bridge this gap, such as the operational bills developed and promoted by BRE some years ago, but, as yet, no universally satisfactory solution has been found.

9.2 Profit

Profit, in its basic forms of normal and super-normal profit, has been defined in Chapter 8. It is also useful to consider the accountant's concepts of profit: gross profit is total sales revenue minus production and sales expenses; net profit is gross profit minus depreciation and interest on loans; profit after tax is net profit minus tax payable upon that profit and thus represents the earnings available as a surplus, which may be used as a source of capital or may be distributed among the owners of the firm.

Neo-classical economics regards profit as the return rightly accruing to the entrepreneur for enterprise and use of funds. Marxist economics, however, regards profit as a surplus earned by the labour employed and appropriated by the entrepreneur, asserting that the single source of profits is the labour element of production in converting raw materials into consumables. A basic belief is that everyone is entitled to share equally in the resources available. Therefore, quirks of birth, ability, inheritance, etc., should be ignored and the fruits of human labour, in various forms and in various activities, should be shared equally by society.

In a capitalist society, profitability dictates which organizations survive and prosper and which do not; need is subordinate to effective demand. Thus most economies are mixed, to ensure the supply of essential goods and services which a free market economy would either ignore or supply inadequately to fulfill the needs of society.

9.3 Financial policy

The basic assumption of economic theory, that a firm operates in such a way as to maximize its profits, has come under considerable scrutiny in recent times. It has been acknowledged that firms have other operating criteria which render the profit-maximizing assumption inadequate. Although the objectives of each individual firm are peculiar to that organization, a generally applicable spectrum of objectives would include profitability, growth, continuity of existence, market share, turnover, size, image, and influence.

Further parameters may be brought to bear on a firm's operations. Lack of managerial ability may preclude a firm's growth beyond a certain size. The size of a firm may be restricted by the owner wishing to retain control or to retain the type of organization. The firm, or industry, may be regarded as a 'way of life' and so a firm will remain in business despite earning very low profits (notable among small, personally controlled construction firms). Many more parameters exist.

Firms, therefore, operate under somewhat conflicting objectives (increased turnover, for example, is by no means necessarily synonymous with increased profits although this is a quite widely held belief among construction managers). In such a situation the operational pattern is one of compromise; acceptable in respect of each individual criterion, but suboptimal. This behaviour was described by H. A. Simon (1960) as 'satisficing'. A firm will, thus, require a given profit level in the long period but this is unlikely to be the maximum achievable, being mitigated by the firm's other objectives. (This concept is, perhaps, especially relevant to the consideration of dividends.)

It is likely to be the objective of the firm's continuing existence which predominates during slump periods. In such times interest rates and unemployment tend to be high, work scarce and, hence, profits low. During these periods some construction firms 'buy' work (that is, they bid for work at a price which is less than the direct costs of carrying out the work plus overhead costs, etc., and normal profit; in fact, in extreme cases the price may be less than the costs of executing the work). Buying work may be justified for several reasons, such as: it keeps resources employed and therefore avoids redundancies; it keeps the name of the firm at the attention of potential clients and consultants; and it ensures the continued existence of the firm in readiness for an improvement in the market.

Theoretically, as long as the firm covers its variable costs as a minimum, it should continue in business in the short-period, because any revenue earned in excess of the variable costs is a contribution to fixed costs which the firm must pay whether it produces or not. Buying work is a short-term expedient only. There are considerable dangers in even a short-term policy of this nature as it can very rapidly lead to a downward spiral, ending in bankruptcy. A firm losing money on one project may be tempted to finance that project from one which is profitable; it may then be forced to take on more projects at an overall loss (due to the economic situation in a recession and the necessity that the firm must obtain more work) but with the pricing so manipulated that the operations executed early in the projects are profitable at the expense of subsequent, loss-making operations. This situation is quite obviously rapidly progressive, is very difficult to reverse, and is a common cause of construction liquidations.

Although buying work may be seen as occasionally essential to survival, it is important that the pitfalls are recognized and that progress is monitored vigorously. Buying work is also occasionally employed in more buoyant periods as a policy in exceptional circumstances, the most common of which are: to obtain a small project for an influential client (usually a client who requires a large amount of construction work); or to obtain a particular project of great prestige.

Particularly in the period since 1945, the construction industry has been used as a regulator for the UK economy. Parry-Lewis (1965) found that, throughout modern times, construction had been subject to sizeable cyclical fluctuations in workload. The increasing influence of government action has perhaps tended to make the workload of the industry less predictable and has, therefore, acted to deter investment, mechanization, R & D, training, employment; in fact, most of the requirements for a modern and efficient industry.

Government appears to regard construction as a homogeneous entity when, in reality, this is far from the case. Civil engineering contractors, for example, cannot and do not switch from major motorway construction to building advance factories. There is a set of distinct sub-industries within the construction industry. Nor is there a pool of good construction labour of all categories available at the end of a recession. Once a person leaves the construction industry it is unlikely that that individual will return, despite higher wages brought about by labour shortages at an upturn (other working conditions are also very relevant!). Thus, the labour shortage in construction is a very common feature at the start of an industrial recovery, for not only has much labour permanently left the industry during the recession but there have been few new entrants and little training has been done.

Likewise, fluctuations in demand for construction output promote conservatism in the industry. New, untried, and unproven techniques, plant, etc., are ignored and investment is minimized. Research and development and education and training are all too frequently the first budgets to be cut by firms when a recession begins.

Firms do respond to fluctuations in workload and shifts in demand. Larger firms tend to diversify their activities horizontally and vertically: horizontally to give a greater spectrum of activities at about the same stage of production (e.g. a contractor setting up a rehabilitation division), and vertically to diversify activities over the stages of production (e.g. by a contractor setting up a brick production division or a property development division). Such diversification, which occurs during boom periods, permits the firm to divert resources more easily to the profitable areas of activity in the event of changes in the pattern of demand and provides a broader base for continuing existence since, although all sectors of the industry may be subject to recession, some sectors will be more adversely affected than others.

Small firms are often more adaptable and can switch from speculative 'new-build' to extensions to renovation work with only minor difficulties. In fact, small firms often prosper (relatively) in recessions because there is an expansion in small renovation and extension work; firms and householders tend to 'stay put' and 'make do', and will renovate or extend existing premises in preference to moving to new premises. In recessions preventative maintenance is usually regarded as a postponable cost.

During recessionary periods the need for good credit control is paramount. Interest rates are high, credit periods are reduced, and finance is expensive and in short supply. It is thus vital that debtors pay promptly and that the periods of credit allowed *by* the firm do not exceed those allowed *to* the firm. Inadequate credit control can easily turn a potential profit into a loss.

Thus, although effective cost monitoring and control should be employed by any firm, the importance of this action is greatly magnified during recessions. It is essential that firms formulate policies for their operations, but it is also vital that the limitations and implication of those policies are fully appreciated and taken into account in budgeting.

9.4 Revenues

Under a budgeting system the complement of cost prediction and control is revenue prediction and control. In the construction industry revenue predictions are vital to enable a contractor to match expenditure and income. However, although several techniques are available, no prediction method or formula is universally applicable.

Generally, revenue prediction may be divided into two subsections: pre-contract and post-contract. In the pre-contract situation, the prediction is likely to be of a less detailed nature, while in the post-contract setting the prediction will be based upon information appertaining to each particular project.

Most revenue prediction techniques, due to the methods normally used to price construction projects, are based upon cost predictions. The cost control techniques already discussed in this chapter are usually applied to projects on a micro (or operation) level, whereas the predictions used for revenue purposes are usually applied on a macro (or project) level.

9.4.1 Predictions of revenue and cost

Pre-contract predictions are frequently of a universal nature, based upon a typical project model, whereas post-contract predictions are related to each individual project. As such, pre-contract predictions tend to provide a guide to revenue and cost expectation without necessarily making allowances for the peculiarities of the particular project in question. The situation is justifiable as there is no certainty that the firm will carry out the project, and therefore a mere indication of the costs and revenues which the project will generate is sufficient.

Some predictive techniques, discussed above in the context of costs, may be applied to revenue predictions but these also tend to be of a general nature.

A method that has been developed and found to be useful in practice is the S-curve analysis. The technique is fully described by Cooke and Jepson (1979), and, in application to health service projects, in Hudson (1978). Cooke and Jepson (1979) utilize the typical building project model in which the pattern of value accrual is based upon the cost accrual over the project duration (pre-contract costs are recovered as part of overheads).

In the typical project, the cost accrual assumes the following pattern:

(a) During the first third of project duration, the cost accumulates in a parabolic pattern to achieve one-quarter of costs incurred at one-third project duration.
(b) During the second third of the project duration, the cost accumulates in a linear fashion such that at two-thirds project duration, the accumulated costs total three-quarters of project total costs.
(c) During the final third of project duration, the cost accumulation is a mirror image of the first third duration, to achieve 100 per cent cost at physical completion.

The value of the project also accumulates in the same pattern but, naturally, exceeds the cost accumulation by the applied mark-up. Obviously, it is equally possible to construct the cost pattern from the value pattern as it is to construct the value pattern from the cost pattern. In its simplest form, only the value (or cost), mark-up, and duration are required to carry out this projection.

It is quite simple task to program a computer to output cumulative project costs and values based upon this pattern of accumulation. Using the typical parabola equations, the S-curve is given by:

$$y = \frac{9x^2}{4}; \qquad 0 \leqslant x \leqslant \frac{1}{3}$$

$$y = \frac{3x}{2} - \frac{1}{4}; \qquad \frac{1}{3} \leqslant x \leqslant \frac{2}{3}$$

$$y = \frac{9x}{2} - \frac{9x^2}{4} - \frac{5}{4}; \qquad \frac{2}{3} \leqslant x \leqslant 1$$

where x is the cumulative proportion of project duration ($0 \leqslant x \leqslant 1$) and y is the cumulative proportion of project budget cost or value ($0 \leqslant y \leqslant 1$). (The equation developed by DHSS, in Hudson (1978), is slightly at variance with the above but was devised specifically for DHSS projects.)

The predictions may also be executed manually, either by using the equations given above or by purely graphical means, the middle section ($\frac{1}{3}$ time, $\frac{1}{4}$ cost to $\frac{2}{3}$ time, $\frac{3}{4}$ cost) being a straight line and the parabolic 'lead-in' and 'lead-out' sections being drawn freehand. From the basic cost S-curve, the value S-curve and the actual (delayed and stepped) receipts graph may be constructed. A further sophistication is to apply a delay factor to the payments made (usually weighted average) such that the resultant graphs and tables give quite an accurate cash flow forecast.

The information so obtained may be further utilized to produce a breakdown of the finance requirements for the project, both long-term finance and short-term finance. Such information is of value to a company in deciding whether to tender for a project and to control its capital both for individual projects and in aggregate.

The analysis described above is for a typical project. Each type of project and each firm will have its own individual peculiarities and organizations may develop prediction techniques, on the S-curve basis, that are adapted to suit their project

Table 9.2 Cash flow calculations

(A) Month No.	(B) Cum proportion time elapsed (%)	(C) Cum proportion project completed (%)	(D) Cum cost (£)	(E) Cost per period (£)	(F) Cash outflow per period (£)	(G) Cum value (£)	(H) Cum retention (£)	(I) Cum net value (£)
½	4.2	0.4	440	440				
1	8.3	1.6	1,760	1,320		1,848	92	1,756
1½	12.5	3.5	3,850	2,090	440			
2	16.7	6.3	6,930	3,080	1,320	7,277	364	6,913
2½	20.8	9.7	10,670	3,740	2,090			
3	25.0	14.1	15,510	4,840	3,080	16,286	814	15,472
3½	29.2	19.2	21,120	5,610	3,740			
4	33.3	25.0	27,500	6,380	4,840	28,875	1,444	27,431
4½	37.5	31.25	34,375	6,875	5,610			
5	41.7	37.5	41,250	6,875	6,380	43,313	2,166	41,147
5½	45.8	43.75	48,125	6,875	6,875			
6	50	50.0	55,000	6,875	6,875	57,750	2,888	54,862
6½	54.2	56.25	61,875	6,875	6,875			
7	58.3	62.5	68,750	6,875	6,875	72,187	3,609	68,578
7½	62.5	68.75	75,625	6,875	6,875			
8	66.7	75.0	82,500	6,875	6,875	86,625	4,331	82,294
8½	70.8	80.8	88,880	6,380	6,875			
9	75.0	85.9	94,490	5,610	6,875	99,214	4,961	94,253
9½	79.2	90.3	99,330	4,840	6,380			
10	83.3	93.7	103,070	3,740	5,610	108,223	5,411	102,812
10½	87.5	96.5	106,150	3,080	4,840			
11	91.7	98.4	108,240	2,090	3,740	113,652	5,683	107,969
11½	95.8	99.6	109,560	1,320	3,080			
12	100	100	110,000	440	2,090	115,500	2,887	112,613
12½					1,320			
13					440			
18								115,500
18½								

Notes: Column B is calculated on a straight line basis. Column C is calculated from the typical S-curve equations for cost on value accrual. Column F is as column E but with a delay (derived from weighted average payments delay) applied.

types, methods of working, and organization. Although the S-curve prediction is reasonably accurate, it is still perhaps best suited for use as a preliminary predictor at a relatively early stage.

A somewhat more refined, and hopefully more accurate approach, is to cost and price the project programme on the basis of large cost centres at tender stage and more precisely, perhaps by operations, at the construction stage (as different levels of accuracy are required at these two stages). These exercises require more information and are more time-consuming than S-curve predictions, but have the advantage of being based upon the individual project data. Most quantity surveyors currently carry out this form of analysis to recover the preliminaries of a project.

(J) Net value per month (£)	(K) Cash inflow per month (£)	(L) Cum cash outflow (£)	(M) Cum cash inflow (£)	(N) Net cash flow (£)	(P) Max cash flow (£)	(R) Net cash flow (£)	(S) Max cash flow (£)
				−440	−440		
1,756				−1,760	−1,760		
	1,756	440	1,756	−2,090	−3,850	+1,316	−440
5,157		1,760					
	5,157	3,850	6,913	−3,757	−8,914	+3,063	−2,094
8,559		6,930					
	8,559	10,670	15,472	−5,648	−14,207	+4,802	−3,757
11,959		15,510					
	11,959	21,120	27,431	−6,944	−18,903	+6,293	−5,648
13,716		27,500					
	13,716	34,375	41,147	−6,978	−20,694	+6,772	−6,944
13,715		41,250					
	13,715	48,125	54,862	−7,013	−20,728	+6,737	−6,978
13,716		55,000					
	13,716	61,875	68,578	−7,047	−20,763	+6,703	−7,013
13,716		68,750					
	13,716	75,625	82,294	−6,586	−20,302	+6,669	−7,047
11,959		82,500					
	11,959	88,880	94,253	−5,077	−17,036	+5,373	−6,586
8,559		94,490					
	8,559	99,330	102,812	−3,338	−11,897	+3,482	−5,077
5,157		103,070					
	5,157	106,150	107,969	−1,591	−6,748	+1,819	−3,338
4,644		108,240			−7,188		
	4,644	109,560	112,613	+2,613	+2,613	+3,053	−1,591
		110,000				+2,613	+2,613
2,887							
	2,887		115,500	+5,500	+5,500	+5,500	+5,500

Column K is as column J but with the delay on receipts of cash applied. Column N (no payments delay) is column M minus column D. Column P (no payments delay) is column M for the previous month minus column D for the current month. It shows the maximum capital required immediately prior to cash inflows being received.   Columns R and S (with payments delay) correspond to columns N and P, above, but are calculated using column L in place of column D.

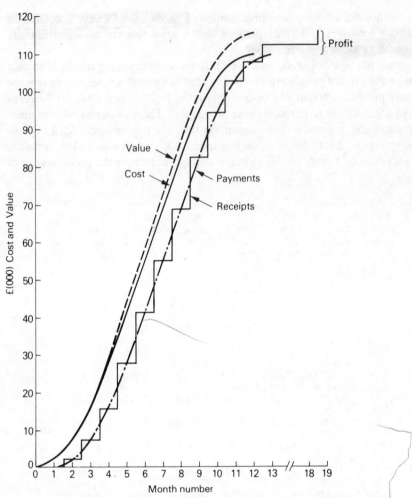

Fig. 9.5 S-curve analyses. (*Note*: the payments curve may be constructed with a lead-in
delay accumulation from the origin. It is shown here as a simple delay on the cost
curve throughout its length.)

S-curve example

S-curve analysis may use either cost or value as its basis. In this example, cost
is used. (*Note:* If the value is, say, cost + 10%, then cost is $\frac{10}{11} \times$ value, *not*
90% × value.)

Estimate for a fixed price project of one year's duration = £100,000
Overheads = 10% × estimate
Profit   = 5% × cost
Certificates are monthly (*always* calendar months)
Income is received two weeks after certification
Weighted average payments delay by contractor = 1 month (see Table 9.3)

Retention = 5%; half released at practical completion, half released at end
  of defects liability period
Defects liability period (DLP) = 6 months
Assume: 1 month = 4 weeks; no holidays
Cost of project = £100,000 × 1.1 = £110,000
Value of project = £110,000 × 1.05 = £115,500

The budgets produced from S-curve and programme analyses provide the
overall framework within which the firm can monitor and control its activities.
The monitoring and controlling functions are reliant upon information from the
site as both cost and value data.

The cost data are usually provided via the accounts department for materials,
wages, and salaries; via the cost surveyors as costs of operations; and via the
quantity surveyors in relation to subcontractors. Overheads are treated as a
separate cost, usually as a percentage addition to the direct costs.

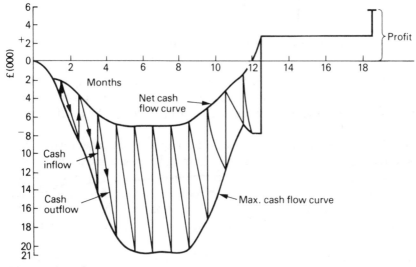

Fig. 9.6 Cash flow curves.
Notes to Figs. 9.6 and 9.7
1. Net and maximum cash flows may be determined directly from the relevant S-curves.
2. The area between the abscissa and the net cash flow curve, whilst the latter is below the
   abscissa, shows the long-term finance required for project.
3. The area between the max. cash flow curve, whilst below the abscissa, and the lower of
   the abscissa and the net cash flow curve shows the short-term finance required for the
   project.
4. The project is self financing (entirely) only when both net and max. cash flow curves are
   above the abscissa.
5. In the example quoted, payments delay (of one month weighted average) by the
   contractor obviates the requirement for long-term capital for the project.
6. In neither instance shown in the example does the project become entirely self financing
   until the payment (inflow) following practical completion is received (month $12\frac{1}{2}$).
7. The payments delay by the contractor also greatly reduces the project's short-term
   finance requirements.

195

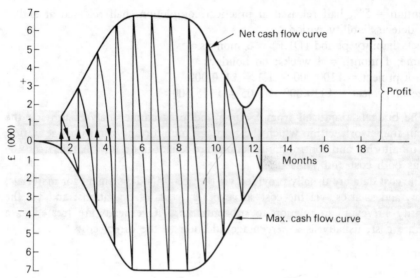

Fig. 9.7 Cash flow curves with payments delay applied (*See also Notes below Fig. 9.6*)

Value data are usually obtained from the firm's quantity surveyors. As this information is normally prepared on a monthly basis for valuation and certification purposes, the costs and values are also normally reviewed by the firm at the same time intervals.

Firms differ in the ways in which costs and values are kept under review. This may be carried out in detail every month or in outline each month but with a detailed review at longer intervals, e.g. every three months. The time intervals should be selected to suit the firm's requirements and are governed by such considerations as the value of the project, the rate of physical progress, the project value as a proportion of the firm's turnover, and familiarity with the methods of working.

As short-term finance is cheaper than long-term finance, a firm should keep its long-term finance to the minimum. At any time, the maximum cash flows required by projects (in aggregate) minus the funding available on a short-term basis (including any overdraft facility not taken up) indicates the long-term finance required by the firm. (Naturally, however, some overdraft facility will usually be maintained as a contingency.)

9.5 Monitoring and control

9.5.1 Cost value reconciliations

While cost control systems, such as standard costs and variance analyses, are extensively used at site level for cost control of the individual project (often on a weekly basis), cost/value reconciliation is the form of budgeting control most commonly used by upper (usually head office) management. Cost/value reconciliations are usually prepared by the firm's quantity surveyors and are statements of the total costs and values in respect of each project, usually at the date on which the monthly valuation was carried out.

The value section comprises the gross valuation (as agreed and checked against the associated certificate) plus statements of the retention held, the amounts any claims should actually yield, the value of materials on site, the amount of fluctuations, the value of variations included in the valuation, and the amounts certified for nominated subcontractors.

The cost section comprises materials and wages paid plus any necessary accruals for items delivered but for which payment has not been made, and for time worked for which wages have not been paid. The materials cost should be net of discounts and the wages bill should be the cost to the firm of using that labour. Hired plant, owned plant, and small tools can be costed from plant returns and invoices with any necessary accruals. Subcontractors may be costed from their total paid account to the relevant date and adjusted for discounts, claims, and contracharges. Normally, nominated subcontractors (and often nominated suppliers) are listed in detail, separately, as particular contractual conditions appertain to their accounts.

Overheads are usually added as a prescribed percentage of cost and the profit or loss, both to date and for the month, are clearly indicated.

It is of obvious importance that all relevant costs and values are included, making accruals and estimates where necessary. As this document is a management control tool its accuracy is of the essence. Top management should inform the relevant people of the profit pattern the project should produce, as this may easily have been manipulated by project pricing techniques.

The cost/value reconciliations will be used to monitor profitability performance against some predetermined expectation (S-curve analysis, priced programme, etc.). For such monitoring to be meaningful, management requires notification of the accuracy of the information and techniques being employed. Thus, a knowledge of any error inherent in estimating, programming, overhead allocations, and so on, as well as any error in the budgeting, costing, and valuing systems is required. Any distortion of the information – such as not declaring early profits – may lead to unrequired and incorrect actions being instigated.

It would be useful if, for profit monitoring, a technique were employed similar to the statistical technique used for quality control. The expected profit level should be plotted for the duration of the project, with the calculated error limits plotted on each side. Upper and lower control limits would then also be established and the achieved profits would be superimposed as they occurred. This system shows the profits expected together with possible inherent variances and the actual achievements. Trends can easily be identified and corrective action taken at an early stage. The system will also show whether the variance is due to error in the prediction system employed or to performance requiring corrective action.

9.5.2 Variances

Whatever system of cost prediction is used it is highly probable that actual costs incurred in the production process will differ from those predicted, i.e. cost variances will occur. As there are very many causes of variances, it is desirable to implement a monitoring system which permits the causes of variances to be detected at an early stage in order that corrective measures can be implemented.

In the construction industry, the cost/value reconciliations will show if a contractor is performing as predicted by regularly examining costs, value, and profit which may then be compared with a prediction. If a variance occurs which cannot be adequately explained (e.g. claims outstanding), more detailed investigation will be necessary to establish the cause(s) of the variance. On site, the production data, often used for bonus calculations, are commonly compared with the *costed* BQ to detect labour variances. Materials and plant cost control may be executed in a similar manner. (*Note*: Variances arising due to price increases must be examined in the context of the fluctuations recovery provisions of the contract.)

(a) Labour variances

The predicted cost of labour for an operation (or set of operations, if more convenient to aggregate) may be obtained from the estimators' data – the estimate for that particular project. The cost will have been calculated by multiplying an estimated time for the execution of the work (the labour 'constant', adjusted as necessary to suit the particular project to produce the *standard hours*) by the applicable wage rate (*standard wage rate*). The site will then obtain data of the time taken to perform the operation(s) and the labour cost of that work (*actual hours* × *actual wage rate* = labour cost). These data permit the source(s) of any variance to be established. It is clear (see Fig. 9.8.) that labour cost variance arises due to actual hours differing from standard hours or/and actual wage rate differing from standard wage rate. The wage rates are functions of labour and management negotiations which occur at national level and may be modified at local level. The time to execute work is a function of innumerable

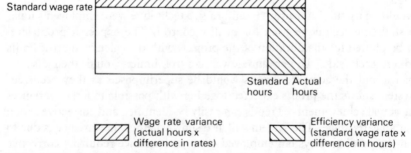

Fig. 9.8 Labour variances (Source: Bierman, H. Jr, 1963)

variables, such as weather, managerial abilities, health, and payments and incentives. . . .

In examining an efficiency variance it is unlikely that the true causes will be established absolutely and evaluated accurately, but it is necessary to determine if the variance is due to an incorrect allocation of standard hours or the actual performance (work study should be used for this purpose). If the actual performance has caused the variance, it should be investigated to establish if it is attributable to managerial organization or operative performance. The results of all investigations should be fed back into the firm's data banks for future use by estimators, work study engineers, and managers.

(b) Materials variances

Materials price variances may be largely eliminated by efficient purchasing. The estimators should obtain quotations for the supply of the requisite materials for the project (at least the major materials supplies) on the same fluctuations recovery terms as those applicable to the main contract. (This should also apply to the quotations obtained from subcontractors.) The quotations should remain open for acceptance for a sufficient period to allow them to form the basis of an order should the main contractor be awarded the contract. (*Note*: If a fixed price quotation and order are used upon a fluctuations contract, this will probably result in a material price variance for the main contractor.)

Materials usage variances arise for many reasons and should be investigated in a manner analogous to that employed for the investigation of labour efficiency variances. For instance, if the material usage variance on timber joists is high, is it due to pilferage, damage, or larger off-cuts due to incorrect sizes having been purchased or due to management inadequacies where joists are used in the wrong location? Again, feedback is essential for avoidance of similar problems in the future.

(c) Plant variances

These are governed by somewhat different factors depending upon whether the plant is owned or hired. In the latter case, minimum hire periods are relevant.

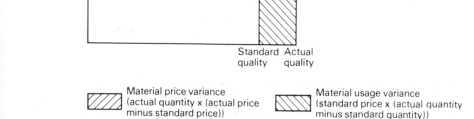

Fig. 9.9 Material variances (Source: Beirman, H. Jr, 1963)

The variance may be split into price and usage (or efficiency) components. In any situation the operation of the plant is governed by two factors: the plant and the operator. Thus, any efficiency variance analysis must consider the choice of plant for the operation and the abilities of the operator.

(d) Overhead variances
Overhead variances may be usefully considered as variable overhead variances and fixed overhead variances. In the construction industry overheads are calculated as a budget for the period and are allocated to projects on the basis of expected total project value for the period or expected total direct labour cost for the period.

Variable overhead variances occur in similar ways to labour variances and may be analysed as:

- Budget variance = (Actual variable overhead) − [(Actual hours) × (Variable overhead rate)];
- Efficiency variance = (Variable overhead rate) × [(Actual hours) − (Standard hours)].

Fixed overhead variances may be analysed into three components:

- Budget variance = (Actual fixed overhead costs) − (Budgeted fixed overhead costs);
- Idle capacity variance = (Fixed overhead rate) × [(Budgeted hours) − (Actual hours)];
- Efficiency variance = (Fixed overhead rate) × [(Actual hours) − (Standard hours)].

The idle capacity variance highlights the problem of excess capacity and is caused by the actual time worked being different from the budgeted hours. Graphical representations of variable and fixed overhead variances are illustrated in Fig. 9.10.

It is unusual for overheads to be allocated in an exact manner to the individual projects that a contractor undertakes (consultants usually allocate overheads in a similar way to contractors). Thus, a firm will examine overhead allocations, absorptions, and variances periodically (often annually) and on an aggregate basis (i.e. for the whole firm). It is on the basis of such investigations that adjustments to future budgets are made to take account of variances.

9.5.3. Pricing manipulations

It is usual to assume that any construction project is priced in such a way that the price of each item comprises the cost of that item plus the relevant share of overheads and profit (and any other) additions. This is not always the case. It has been shown earlier (see S-curve) that a typical building project does not become

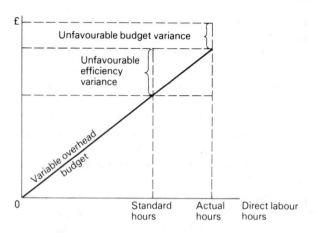

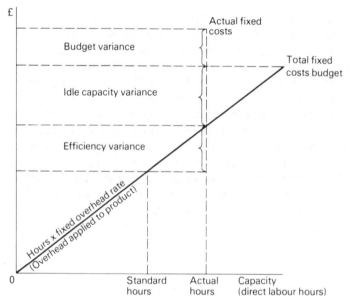

Fig. 9.10 Overhead variances (Source: Beirman, H. Jr, 1963)

self-financing until it is near completion and, in addition, requires the contractor to provide considerable amounts of capital as both working capital and long-term capital. As a cost is associated with the provision of captial (see Ch. 8), contractors often seek to use less of their own capital in the execution of a project and to make the project self-financing at an earlier stage.

Thus, the capital requirements of the contractor may be reduced by a site set-up payment (as often happens in international contracting), by a reduced retention deduction and earlier retention releases, by more frequent payments to the contractor, by subcontracting more work, and so on. It is also possible for the contractor to manipulate the item prices in a project to achieve these ends. The

201

technique is called front–end loading and occurs where items of work which the contractor expects to be executed early in the project have prices which contain a disproportionately large content of overheads and profit, and items of work to be executed in the later stages of the project have their prices reduced accordingly. The situation is of further benefit to the contractor due to the time value of money.

Front–end loading manipulations are limited in the extent to which they may be carried out by the role of the private quantity surveyor (PQS) in checking priced BQs prior to the contracts for the works being awarded.

As variations are an expected occurrence on any building project (for extent and value prediction techniques see Bromilow 1970, 1971, 1974), contractors are occasionally tempted to price low those items which they anticipate will be omitted or reduced in extent and to price high those items they expect to be increased. Again the checking role of the PQS acts as a restriction upon such manipulations.

It is arguable whether the contractor should be required to provide much capital for the execution of a construction project or whether the capital should be provided by the client. Construction is considered to be a high-risk industry and so returns on investments in construction should be higher than returns on comparable investments elsewhere. Just over half the UK construction work is executed for the public sector, a low-risk sector of the economy. Most private sector clients of contractors will be engaged in activities which are less risky than construction; therefore, clients should enjoy a lower cost of capital than contractors. Thus, if clients provided the capital for construction projects (given sufficient safeguards which really already exist), the prices charged for construction should be reduced. The alternative is, of course, that if such a system of financing construction projects were implemented, it would result not in price reductions through savings being passed back to client organizations, but in contractors maintaining price levels and thereby earning greater profits.

9.5.4 Inflation

Inflation, in application to the prices of construction projects, is covered by the inclusion of a fluctuations recovery provision. (In respect of the JCT '80 contract, see Fellows 1981 for a discussion of the provisions.) Fluctuations may be non-recoverable or recoverable in whole or in part. If full recovery of fluctuations is permitted, adherence to the prescribed system is necessary to ensure recovery. Full fluctuations are recovered in most cases either by application of the NEDO formulae or by application of a manual system.

The manual system permits recovery in respect of all but minor items. The normal partial fluctuations system permits recovery of tax and similar government imposed fluctuations only, and a fixed price contract permits no fluctuation recovery at all.

It is evident, therefore, that the price the contractor submits for the project should include an adequate allowance for fluctuations which will be incurred by

Table 9.3 Weighted average payments delay

Cost Centre	Payment interval	Average delay (weeks)	Project cost proportion (%)	Weighted average delay (weeks)
Direct labour*	Weekly	$\frac{5}{6}$	10	0.08
Salaried labour, etc.	Monthly	2	5	0.11
Domestic suppliers	As JCT nom.	$6\frac{1}{2}$	20	1.30
Nominated suppliers	As JCT	$6\frac{1}{2}$†	15	0.98
LO subcontractors	Weekly	$\frac{1}{2}$	10	0.05
Domestic subcontractors	Monthly	2	14	0.30
Nominated subcontractors	As JCT	$4\frac{3}{4}$‡	20	0.95
Plant hire	Monthly	2	5	0.11
				3.88

3.88 weeks weighted average payments delay = 0.9 months.
* Direct labour:
   Assume that a production bonus scheme is in operation and that pay =
   $\frac{2}{3}$ basic plus $\frac{1}{3}$ bonus; bonus payments lagging behind basic by one week.
   Basic pay = $\frac{1}{2}$ week delay $\times \frac{2}{3} = \frac{2}{6}$ ⎱
   Bonus = $\frac{3}{2}$ week delay $\times \frac{1}{3} = \frac{3}{6}$ ⎰ $\frac{5}{6}$

   Salaried labour, etc.
   Assume this includes other overhead payments
† $\frac{1}{2}$ month + 30 days = $6\frac{1}{2}$ weeks
‡ $\frac{1}{2}$ month plus 17 days = $4\frac{3}{4}$ weeks

the contractor and which the contract states to be non-recoverable. This non-recoverable element must, therefore, be predicted for inclusion in the tender sum. Several methods of prediction exist. One useful method analyses cost increases to date and then extrapolates from them three predications: an average, a high prediction, and a low prediction. It is for the contractor to assess the most likely prediction of cost increases in each individual case, whether on an overall project basis for each tender, or trade by trade for each tender. The tender programme will be of value in this analysis to indicate the timing of operations. A slight variation might be to apply escalation indices of building costs to the S-curve cost prediction and thence the derived price curve, etc.

Failure to make sufficient allowance for non-recoverable fluctuations will lead to a reduction in project profit. Inclusion of an excessive allowance for non-recoverable fluctuations may mean that a project is awarded to a competitor.

9.5.5 Periods of credit

Periods of credit are of importance in determining capital requirements. It has already been shown that a prudent firm will attempt to give shorter periods of credit to its debtors than it enjoys from its creditors.

The period of credit a contracting firm must give to the client is usually prescribed in the contract. Under JCT '80, the *1980 JCT Standard Form of Building Contract* 1980 edition, certification is monthly and payment to the contractor must be made within two weeks of the certificate date. Thus, the contractor receives the first payment one month and two weeks after starting work on the site, and at monthly intervals thereafter.

Assuming the value of each month's work is spread evenly throughout the month, the period of credit given by the contractor for the sums paid monthly is one half of one month plus two weeks. (The average value of the month's work occurs half way through the month.) The retention provision means that the contractor gives credit in respect of the sums involved; this should be the subject of a credit assessment and should be combined with the analysis of the monthly payments for evaluation.

Various credit periods are enjoyed by the contractor. Table 9.3 indicates the usual periods, the proportion of total cost of each cost centre and the resultant weighted average payments delay (which can be incorporated into an S-curve and other budgets). Retention on subcontractors may also be evaluated although they have been ignored in Table 9.3 and are usually of minor significance.

Once the credit facilities offered and enjoyed have been assessed, the relevant sums of money should be applied to them to ensure that the credit offered is, at minimum, no less than the credit enjoyed.

9.6 Clients

Clients, especially industrial or commerical organizations, will use budgeting techniques in respect of their own activities which, although often similar in their underlying principles to those used in the construction industry, will be adapted to the clients' requirements. Thus, for their financial forecasting and control purposes clients are usually reliant upon information supplied by the design team. (Large industrial, commercial, and governmental employers who undertake a good deal of construction work will often have 'in house' design teams.)

The information required is dependent upon the stage which the project has reached. During the initial stages (see RIBA 1973 and Fig. 9.11) – inception and feasibility – the employer will be primarily concerned with the overall cost of the project (the timing of cash outflows is also receiving greater attention, even at the early stages of a project, due to the prevailing high interest rates and increasing use of investment appraisals which employ discounting).

Once the decision to proceed with the project has been taken, the amount of detailed cost information required by the client will increase as the design progresses and the construction period approaches. The PQS, or cost consultant, will prepare a cost plan for the project which will become more refined and precise as the design evolves. The cost planning activities are an integral part of the design process. The cost plan will be used to provide the employer with quite detailed cost information regarding the cost consequences of design requirements and a pattern of anticipated cash outflows during the construction and completion stages. Only after tenders have been obtained, scrutinized, and the contract awarded can the cost plan be adjusted to reflect the actual contract sum and its distribution within the work sections. The requirement of JCT '80 (normally) –

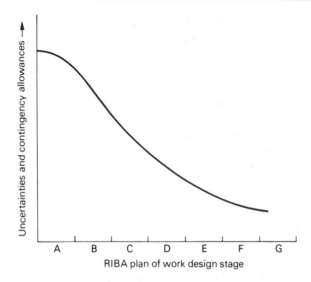

Stages: A inception; B feasibility; C outline proposals; D scheme design;
E detail design; F production information; G bills of quantities.

Fig. 9.11 Reduction of necessary contingency allowances as design progresses

that the contractor should provide a master programme for the project (a requirement which reflects previous good practice) – will also considerably aid accurate cash flow forecasting for clients.

As a project progresses through the construction stage, numerous alterations will be made to the cost plan to keep it up to date. The alterations necessary will be caused by such occurrences as changes in client's requirements, design amendments, other variations, fluctuations, and delays. The client must be informed of the changes to the cash flow projection. A useful system to ensure the client is aware of cost developments during a contract is to provide him with a statement at monthly intervals (i.e. a statement will accompany each interim certificate) detailing the expected payments for each of the following three months, the expected total of the payments for the three months following those, and the anticipated final account sum. Such a statement will keep the client aware of his total commitment to the project and of the liquidity requirements of that commitment. (The liquidity aspect is important, not merely to ensure that payments can be made when due but also to permit the employer to maximize his earnings from his available capital as liquid investments attract a lower return than illiquid investments – see Ch. 8.)

9.7 Consultants

Consultants – the architect, PQS, structural engineers, and services engineers – are usually employed under standard contracts with the client and charge a fee for their services, often on a scale prescribed by the appropriate professional institution. Their activities are primarily design oriented and highly labour intensive (although the situation is changing with increased use of computers). Thus, their budgeting activities are mainly concerned with keeping their costs within a predetermined limit – a limit often out of their control – with sufficient profit margin. Their budgeting, therefore, is frequently of the form of time allocations to personnel for the performance of prescribed tasks.

It may be argued that although the fees charged by consultants are a reasonably small proportion of a construction project's total cost (about 10 per cent on large building projects), the significance of the consultants lies in their influence over the construction cost element and the costs of using the completed building. Good design can significantly reduce both construction and building-user costs.

Cost planning plays its most vital role in the achievement of good design. It will initially establish the overall cost of the proposed building and, once the cost has been agreed by the client, will progress to consider all cost aspects of the design, as it evolves, in increasing levels of detail. Cost planning permits the cost consequences of each design decision to be fully evaluated to ensure that a good solution to the client's requirements (contained in the project brief) is obtained by the provision of a building in which the costs are correctly balanced.

Naturally, at the early stages when a comparative exercise is commonly carried out to establish the project cost, several contingency sums should be included. These should be reduced or may even be completely eliminated as the design evolves and construction progresses. Perhaps one important aspect, which to a certain extent is psychological, is that the client will invariably remember, and base everything upon, the initial project cost projection; and, therefore, reasonable savings will be welcomed, but even small cost escalations will be viewed with abhorrence. It is, therefore, important that each change in the project cost is recorded and justified.

9.8 Investment appraisal

Investment appraisal is most widely considered in the context of the decision of whether to purchase, or acquire by some other means, capital equipment, often in the form of plant or buildings. In the context of construction, investment appraisal is used by clients (or consultants) in their evaluation of proposed construction works whether as new work or rehabilitation. Contractors use investment appraisal techniques to assess their own capital investments (plant, equipment, buildings, etc.) and in their assessments of potential projects – i.e. it is part of the bidding process. In the context of bidding (by competitive tender or an alternative method) investment appraisal is used to evaluate the envisaged capital requirements of the projects.

In an investment appraisal only the incremental expenditures and receipts directly attributable to the project under scrutiny should be included; sunk costs (i.e. those which have already been incurred) should be ignored as they are irrelevant to decisions about the future.

9.8.1 Payback method

The payback method is very simple. It calculates the period required for the incremental net cash inflows generated by the investment to amount, in total, to the initial incremental capital outlay. It is thus not a discounting method but is nonetheless popular, probably due to its simplicity.

As it is not a discounting method, its applicability is limited to short-duration investments, due to the resultant inadequacies in ignoring the time-value of money. The period over which this method may be considered reasonable decreases with each rise in the interest rate. The method also fails to take account of any cash inflows which the project generates beyond the break-even point (after the payback period). Nor does it take into account the pattern of the payments stream prior to the break-even point.

Its value lies in its simplicity and the ease of its use as an initial filter for investment proposals.

9.8.2 Discounted cash flow (DCF) methods

Discounting is a technique which takes the time-value of money into account and may be considered to operate as a reversal (or, perhaps more accurately a reciprocal) of compound interest. It thus facilitates comparisons of projects with different investment requirements and with varying cash flow patterns. It is also possible to compare projects with different life spans but additional care is required to select the most appropriate method to employ.

One major problem with any DCF method is the determination of the rate of interest to use in the evaluation. The full selection method is too extensive for this text, but several selection guides are:

- commercial bank base rates and trends therein
- interest rates on government securities
- stock market indicators
- interest rates prevailing in the commercial sector for similar ventures.

Basic calculation formulae

1. *Amount of £1* (compound interest): The amount received at the end of a period in which £1 is invested at a given rate of compound interest.
   $A = (1 + i)^n$ where A is the amount of £1, i is the rate of interest, and n is the number of years. For example, £1 invested for 3 years at 10% gives:

   Year 1 $A_1 = 1.00 + 0.10 = 1.10$

   Year 2 $A_2 = 1.10 + 0.11 = 1.21$

   Year 3 $A_3 = 1.21 + 0.12 = \mathbf{1.33}$

   Now, using $A = (1 + i)^n$, the answer for year 3 above is:
   $A_3 = (1 + 0.10)^3 = \mathbf{1.33}$

2. *Present value* (PV) *of £1* (reciprocal of compound interest): The present value of receiving £1 at the end of a given number of years with a certain rate of compound interest prevailing.

It has been shown above that if an investment made today for a period is subject to compound interest, the investor will, at the end of the period, receive a sum greater than the original sum invested. Thus, considering the PV, the sum received by that investor at the end of the period is worth £1 to him today. Thus,

$$PV = \frac{1}{A} = \frac{1}{(1 + i)^n}$$

3. *Amount of £1 per annum* (APA): The amount of £1 per annum is the amount which will accumulate if £1 is invested each year of a period at a prescribed rate of interest (investments carried out at the end of each year); e.g. endowment policies.

$$APA = \frac{A - 1}{i} = \frac{(1 + i)^n - 1}{i}$$

4. *Annual sinking fund* (ASF) (reciprocal of amount of £1 per annum): The amount which must be invested annually to produce £1 at the end of a given period, where the amount invested is subject to compound interest at a given rate (again, end of year investments are considered).

$$SF = \frac{i}{A - 1} = \frac{i}{(1 + i)^n - 1}$$

5. *Present value of £1 per annum or years' purchase* (YP) (reciprocal of rate of compound interest): The capital value of an investment; the present value of receiving an annual amount of £1 for a given number of years at a given rate of interest – usually applied to the income from rental property.

$$YP = \frac{1}{i}(\text{for long periods})$$

For example, an investor will purchase a freehold costing £10,000 only if it will yield him at least 10% p.a.; i.e. £10,000 × $\frac{10}{100}$ = £1,000.

Consider the situation in reverse:

A freehold yields net income of £1,000 p.a. If an investor requires 10 per cent return on any investment, how much should he pay for the freehold?

$$£1,000 \times \frac{100}{10} = £10,000; \qquad \frac{100}{10} = 10 \text{ YP.}$$

However, if the property were leasehold, the capital invested to purchase the lease must also be considered as this may be regarded as a 'wasting asset' and so should be redeemed at the expiry of the lease. The SF is used to provide the capital redemption:

$$YP = \frac{1}{i + SF}$$

where i is expressed as a decimal and SF is the figure derived from the table for the period at the given rate.

Thus, YP calculates the capital value; the SF being to provide for the redemption of the original capital outlay at the expiry of the lease.

Interest and SF rates will often be different, interest usually being the greater.

Note: As YP is PV of £1 p.a., then

$$YP = APA \times PV = \frac{A - 1}{i} \times \frac{1}{A}$$

$$= \frac{(1 + i)^n - 1}{i} \times \frac{1}{(1 + i)^n}$$

$$= \frac{(1 + i)^n - 1}{i(1 + i)^n} = \frac{1}{i}\left[1 - \frac{1}{(1 + i)^n}\right]$$

which, for long periods, approximates to:

$$YP = \frac{1}{i}$$

6. *Effects of tax:* The rate of tax (RT) will affect the calculation of all the above. This is accounted for by a modification to the rate of interest (RI) applied to obtain the effective rate of interest (ERI). Thus:

$$ERI = \frac{£1 - RT}{£1} \times RI$$

For example, if RI = 5% and tax is 40%, then

$$ERI = \frac{100 - 40}{100} \times \frac{5}{100} = \frac{300}{100} = 3\%$$

The sinking fund is different. The net SF is significant, i.e. matured fund at the end of the period is paid to the investor free of tax as the tax authorities regard the SF deposits as capital deposits and, as such, are made after payment of tax. This means the SF is taxed *before* it is paid; for example,

Investor's income	£1,000 p.a. (net before tax)
Tax at 50%	500
Income net of tax	500 p.a.
SF to redeem capital = (say)	100 p.a.

209

Thus:

Net of tax income to provide SF payment = £100 p.a.

Gross of tax income required for SF = £100 × 2 = £200 p.a.

Thus, SF (net) to obtain gross of tax, SF payments must be multiplied by

$$\frac{£1}{£1 - RT}$$

Thus, YP (dual rate), with allowance for tax on the SF, is

$$YP = \frac{1}{i + SF \dfrac{100}{100 - T}}$$

where T = % tax.

Net present value (NPV) *method*

The NPV method is a discounting method in which a predetermined rate of interest is used to discount the incremental net cash flows generated by an investment throughout its entire life to (usually) the present-day value. The evaluation includes inflows and outflows, the capital expended on the investment and any inflow from selling the investment (scrap value for plant, etc.).

For a single project analysis, the investment should be undertaken if the NPV is positive. Where a spectrum of investment projects are assessed, those with a positive NPV should be undertaken or, if the capital available for investment is limited, those projects with the highest positive NPV should be undertaken in descending order until the capital available is fully expended.

Thus an NPV calculation assumes the form:

NPV = (NPV of incremental net cash inflows)
　　　－ (NPV of incremental net cash outflows)
　　　＋ (NPV of terminal cash inflow)
　　　－ (Initial incremental capital investment)

Internal rate of return (IRR) *method*

The internal rate of return is that rate of interest which, when applied to discounting the net incremental cash flows of an investment, produces a net present value equal to the capital sum expended on the investment. Thus, the NPV so determined minus the original investment equals zero. In an IRR calculation, the cash flows are predicted (these are usually net of tax although, for greater accuracy, tax payments may be incorporated as they are envisaged to occur, and discounted separately–this separate tax treatment is not worthwhile unless large sums are involved, and predictions may be carried out with precision) and the rate of interest is the determinant of the project's viability.

Provided that the IRR is at least as great as the rate of interest the firm must pay on the capital to be invested in the project, the project is a reasonable investment. Where a spectrum of possible projects is under examination, that (or those) with the largest positive differential between the IRR and interest to be paid on the capital should be selected.

The actual calculation commonly employs trial and error an interpolation to find the IRR. A reasonable rate of interest is selected, discounting calculations are made, and the original capital sum is then deducted. If the result is a positive sum, the rate of interest selected was too low, and vice versa. Discounting tables have rates of interest in stages, often of one or one-half per cent; thus to determine the exact IRR, interpolation between a close high result and a close low result is employed, normally assuming a straight-line, proportional relationship to exist.

Annual equivalent (AE) *method*

The annual equivalent method is derived from the NPV method. Its value lies in its usefulness for comparison of investments with different life periods and the readiness with which it is comprehended by management.

This method considers the sum of equivalent *annual* expenditures and receipts appertaining to a project over its life: the initial, annual, and periodic cash flows. To obtain annual equivalents, the capital sum is multiplied by the rate of interest expressed as a decimal; annual sums require no amendment as they are already annual; and periodic sums are discounted to NPV and then multiplied by the rate of interest expressed as a decimal. If a sinking fund is required for capital maintenance (as with the purchase of a lease), the sinking fund factor (calculated or from tables) is multiplied by the relevant capital sum.

Annual equivalents are used to evaluate such proposals as whether to purchase or lease a building in which the capital sums, cash flows, and lengths of the investment periods will be vastly different. The NPV method pays no attention to the life of the investment; thus, for comparison of investments of different lives it makes no acknowledgement of a shorter life investment releasing capital earlier for new investment projects.

9.8.3 Return on capital employed

The capital employed is the capital used in the business but excludes current liabilities except bank loans and overdrafts. The capital employed in relation to a particular project should be the capital required for that project, the incremental capital.

Provided that the return generated by the project exceeds the required return on the capital employed, the project is viable. It should be noted that discounting is commonly not used in this analysis.

9.8.4 Break-even analysis

Break-even analysis is a sensitivity analysis technique to aid decision-making where a spectrum of investments is being considered. The investment appraisal methods described above may be supplemented by break-even analysis.

211

Graphical presentation is useful as management can then easily appreciate the information shown. The two analyses most commonly employed consider the rate(s) of interest at which two (or more) projects have zero NPV (i.e. the IRRs of the projects). The alternative, which is of particular value for the consideration of running costs of buildings, considers the NPV of each investment at the end of each selected period (usually each year or five years) of its life, the rate of interest being prescribed. This alternative is of great use in the evaluation, both total and as comparisons, of various heating systems for buildings (these systems constituting an increasingly large proportion of a building's running costs due to fuel cost increases). It is common for a system with a low capital outlay to have a high running cost and vice versa. Break-even analysis will indicate which system is cheapest for a given time period as it is likely that the system with low installation but high running costs will become the most expensive after some time in use.

9.8.5 Sensitivity analysis

Sensitivity analysis is a final stage in investment appraisal. It examines the effects of changes in the variables. As it is usually quite easy to determine which variables are of greatest influence over the outcome of the appraisal, only those major variables need be considered. Each of these variables is in turn slightly altered and the effects on the appraisals are noted. Only if two investments present quite close outcomes in the orignial analysis is there likely to be a significant change in the results.

If the results of the original appraisals are well distinguished (in value, etc.) and if each variable is only of limited significance to the outcome of the analysis, then sensitivity analysis may not be worthwhile. If the original results are close and/or if a few variables exert major influences over the results, sensitivity analysis should be employed.

Although sensitivity analysis is usually applied to investment decisions, it could be of considerable use in tendering where, for instance, the effect on the tender sum of a change in the bonus payments to direct labour could be evaluated (via the effects on hourly rates of pay, and the labour content of the estimate).

9.8.6 Developer's budget

At the initial stages of a development proposal a developer will often be faced with the problem of how much to pay for a site. The relevant sum is usually determined by a residual method which utilizes the planning parameters, projected construction cost, fees, finance costs, and the estimated value of the completed development. This technique is of merit as it implicitly recognizes the effects on the value of land due to developments carried out or to be carried out (the development potential, or hope value) upon it. The following simple example illustrates the technique.

A vacant plot, frontage 40 m and depth 30 m, has planning permission for an office building with the parameters: may cover up to two-thirds of the site, with the building plot ratio = 3. A valuer considers that the proposed building should produce a gross income of £110.00 per m² usable floor area. Landlord's outgoings will be £20,000 per annum. Construction costs for the building will be £400 per m² and site works will cost £90,000. Circulation space is 15 per cent of gross floor area. Construction period is two years.

Floor area of building:
Assume road to front of site of overall width 10 m.
Site area = 40 × 30 = 1,200 m².
Area for planning purposes includes $\frac{1}{2}$ × road width = 40 × 35 = 1,400 m².

Planning area	1,400
Plot ratio	×3
	4,200 m²

Usable floor area to generate income = 4,200 × 85% = 3,570 m².

Value:	(£)	(£)
Annual rental income (3,570 × £110)		392,700
Less: Landlord's expenses		20,000
		372,700
Years purchase in perpetuity for offices, say 7%		×14.3
Gross development value (GDV)		5,329,610

Deduct costs:		
Cost of building 4,200 × £400	1,680,000	
Cost of site works	90,000	
	1,770,000	
Professional fees at 10%	177,000	
	1,947,000	
Finance for construction, compounded at 15% p.a. (1,947,000/2 at 15% p.a.)	313,954	
Legal, agents', etc., fees at $2\frac{1}{2}$%	133,240	
Developer's profit at 20% × GDV	799,442	3,193,636
Value of site plus site finance		2,135,974
Cost of site finance, compounded at 15% p.a. for two years = 2,135,974 × (0.3225/1.3225)		520,871
Site value		£1,615,103

The developer should pay to £1,615,103 (usually this would be rounded to £1,615,000) for the site.

Costs:	(£)
Construction, etc.	1,947,000
Finance for construction , etc.	313,954
Legal, etc.	133,240
Site	1,615,103
Finance for site	520,871
GDV *minus* developer's profit	£4,530,168

A net return of £372,700 p.a. on £4,530,168 = 8.2%.

This return should be compared with the prevailing returns on similar investments, on alternative investments, and examined in the context of the developer's requirements to determine the viability of the project.

The developer's profit included in the above calculation is the profit the developer requires for his role in undertaking the project as the developer. The building contractor's profit on the construction work will constitute part of the construction and site works costs to the developer.

Summary

Survival is probably the primary objective of any business enterprise. Particularly during periods of economic recession, construction firms are exceedingly conscious of the problems of survival and seek to predict, monitor, and control costs and revenues with diligence far surpassing that employed during more buoyant times.

Predicted costs are the normal basis for price calculation and may be classified in several ways, but whatever classification is used the cost elements remain, each being worthy of separate attention. Patterns of cost may be determined and employed for predictions. Costs should be monitored by a suitable system, tuned to the requirements of the firm or individual project.

Profit is often seen as being the primary objective of economic activity. This view is open to question and again 'satisficing' may be used to evaluate the profit goal in the context of all the objectives of a firm. Indeed, profit may be regarded as an unjustified appropriation of the returns due to the factor of production labour. Some firms may dispense with profit altogether in the short period to facilitate their survival for a profitable future, but such a policy is fraught with problems.

Revenues are calculated on the basis of the predicted cost of the work plus a profit mark-up. It is possible to predict both revenues and costs for a project at an early stage and, subsequently, to monitor the performance. Naturally, predictions should be updated to take the latest available information into account.

Both costs and revenues must be monitored and controlled. This may be achieved by analysis of variances so that the required corrective action is instigated. Pricing manipulations may distort expected cost and revenue patterns, and inflation may erode profits. Credit control is of great importance. The period of credit offered to customers should be no greater than that enjoyed by the firm.

Clients also require cost information regarding construction projects. Total and periodic costs are both important, the former indicating their total commitment and the latter, the cash flow requirements of the project.

Consultants usually operate on a fee system prescribed by the appropriate professional institution. Thus, while the revenue is predetermined, cost control is essential to ensure adequate profit.

Investment appraisal is used to determine whether a proposed project is worthwhile or to select the most suitable project from several options. Many techniques are available, the more suitable of which for long-life investments include the time-value of money in the evaluation. Should several projects produce close results, sensitivity analyses should be employed to determine the responses to changes in the basic data, thereby providing more information upon which a decision may be based.

Questions

1. Discuss the various costs incurred by a building contractor in the context of the firm's ability to survive during a recession.
2. Why is subcontracting of major importance in the building industry?
3. What systems of costing are appropriate for firms engaged in the building industry? Outline the main features of the systems.
4. 'If a firm acts rationally, it will endeavour to maximize its profits.' Discuss.
5. Why is it important for a client to receive a budget for a building project at an early stage of the design process? Discuss an appropriate budgeting technique and any necessary modifications as the project progresses to completion.
6. Why is it usually necessary for a contractor to monitor the profitability of each project as it progresses? How may such monitoring be *effectively* achieved?
7. Discuss the importance of credit control in the building industry.
8. What factors are considered to determine the most appropriate investment appraisal technique to use? Why is the use of discounted cash flow techniques fraught with problems?

References and bibliography

Bierman, H. Jr (1963) *Financial and Managerial Accounting – An Introduction*, Macmillan
Bromilow, F. J. (1970) The nature and extent of variations to building contracts, *The Building Economist* **9**, 93–104

Bromilow, F. J. (1971) Building contract cost performance, *The Building Economist* **9**, 126–38

Bromilow, F. J. (1974) Measurement and scheduling of construction time and cost performance in the building industry, *Chartered Builder*, **10**, 57–65

Cooke, B. and Jepson, W. B. (1979) *Cost and Financial Control for Construction Firms*, Macmillan

Economist Intelligence Unit (1978) *Public Ownership in the Construction Industries*, Economist Intelligence Unit

Fellows, R. F. (1981) *1980 JCT Standard Form of Building Contract – A Commentary for Students and Practitioners*, Macmillan

Freedman, R. (1961) *Marx on Economics*, Penguin

Harding, J. (1980) 'Tendering in the Construction Industry.' Final Year Project, Department of Building Technology, Brunel University

Hillebrandt, P. M. (1974) *Economic Theory and the Construction Industry*, Macmillan

Hudson, K. W. (1978) DHSS expenditure forecasting model, *Quantity Surveying Quarterly*, **5**, No. 2 (Spring)

Laing, Sir Maurice (1978) Cool response to public ownership, *Building*, 24 Mar.

Parry-Lewis J. (1965) *Building Cycles and Britain's Growth*, Macmillan

RIBA (1973) *Plan of Work*, Royal Institute of British Architects

RICS (1975) *Definition of Prime Cost of Daywork Carried Out under a Building Contract*, Royal Institute of Chartered Surveyors and National Federation of Building Trade Employers

Seeley, I. H. (1972) *Building Economics*, Macmillan

Simon, H. A. (1960) *Administrative Behaviour*, 2nd edn Macmillan

Skoyles, E. R. (1974) Wastage of building materials on site, *BRE CP 44/74*, HMSO

Skoyles, E. R. (1976) Materials wastage – a misuse of resources, *BRE CP 67/76*, HMSO

Skoyles, E. R. (1978) Site accounting for waste of materials, *BRE CP 5/78*, HMSO

Skoyles, E. R. (1981) Waste of building materials, *BRE Digest No. 247*, HMSO

Turin, D. A. (ed.) (1975) *Aspects of the Economics of Construction*, Godwin

Chapter 10

Financial performance

Performance is concerned with the achievement of objectives. The objects of a company are contained within the Memorandum of Association (see Ch. 8) and concern such aspects as the activities of the company and its sphere of operation. Other types of organization will have objects of a similar nature. However, any firm will also have unwritten objectives, objectives which must be determined from examination of the firm's performance and discussion with those involved – the owners and the managers.

The unspecified objectives will include profitability, growth, continuity of existence, market share, turnover, size, image, and influence. The achievement of these objectives is affected by a vast number of both endogenous and exogenous variables.

To permit a firm to work towards the achievement of its objectives, decisions must be made. The decisions prescribe what the firm will do and the method of execution. Decisions are made in a great variety of ways from pure intuition to quasi-scientific anaylsis.

The outcomes of the decisions taken by a firm invariably have financial consequences either directly or indirectly. Direct consequences may be monitored as the action progresses, but not so with indirect consequences. The indirect financial consequences are often separated from the decision(s) by a time-lag. Thus, these effects may be evaluated only in a global fashion by examination of the firm's performance as detailed in the accounts.

The accounts contain a wealth of information about the firm but their interpretation is not always straightforward. Comparisons with competitors and analysis of trends are as important as the information contained within each set of accounts.

10.1 Decisions

Decisions are necessary due to the dynamism of the economy and society. A decision is a judgement. As such it is concerned with imperfect information. If all the requisite information were available the result, or course of action, would be obvious (in fact, a decision would not be required) but this is rarely, if ever, the case, especially in connection with the construction industry where time periods are usually long and variables are numerous.

A decision is the human element in the determination of a course of action and will therefore be governed not only by the information available and techniques used but also by the outlook of the individual.

10.1.1 Risk and uncertainty

Decisions are concerned with variables which are normally classified as risks or uncertainties. Risks are unknowns, the probability of the occurrence of which *can* be assessed by statistical means (risks are usually insurable). Uncertainties are unknowns, the probability of the occurrence of which *cannot* be assessed (uncertainties are uninsurable). It is possible, however, for a decision-maker to assign a subjective probability to an uncertainty. As knowledge increases, in conjunction with the amount and detail of statistical data, areas of uncertainty are progressively converted to areas of risk (the evolution of weather data is a good example).

10.1.2 Optimism and pessimism

Optimism and pessimism are concerned with describing how a decision-maker evaluates the range of possible outcomes from the decision. Schofield (1975) considers that optimists and pessimists put very similar values upon positive outcomes, the difference in their evaluations lying in the values placed upon negative outcomes.

Thus an optimist may regard a possible loss of, say £1,000 resulting from an investment decision as of little consequence, whereas a pessimist would regard such a loss possibility as a very serious problem, possibly of sufficient magnitude to exclude that investment despite other possible outcomes yielding large profits.

10.1.3 Competition

The type of competitive environment in which the firm operates will have considerable influence in the decision-making processes. Within the construction industry almost every type of competition may be found in operation. The range is from monopolistic competition (competition amongst the many, often considered as the 'real world's' equivalent to the theoretical concept of perfect competition) to near monopoly. Thus, the spectrum of the various forms of imperfect competition prevails within which oligopoly (competition among the few, sometimes in the form of imperfect oligopoly where there is a dominant firm – a price leader) is of prime importance in major contracting.

On the demand side, there is an equally wide range of competition prevailing from near perfect to monopsony (a single buyer, the demand side equivalent to monopoly). The situation of monopsony is applicable to specific types of construction projects (e.g. motorways, nuclear power stations) as government bodies constitutes the only customers for these types of project in the domestic market.

Under monopolistic competition the firm is a 'price taker', there is a market price for each job and, other things being equal, the firm should obtain a proportion of the work for which it bids governed by the number of firms submitting bids. In a monopolistic situation, the price the monopolist puts on the work is limited by the source of the monopoly power but, perhaps more importantly, also by the existence of legislation to abolish monopolies which act against the public interest. Under monopsony, which exists for much public sector work, various forms of cost limits are imposed by government bodies (e.g. university halls of residence).

For a large proportion of construction projects, a situation of oligopoly exists. This situation may be caused by the method of letting projects (single-stage selective tendering), by locational effects, or by sectoral effects (work type). The actions of firms operating under oligopoly can often be explained in terms of the hypothesis of qualified joint profit maximization. This hypothesis acknowledges the existence of two sets of economic forces operating concurrently: one set inducing the firms to operate in such a way as to maximize the joint profits of all the firms, the other set inducing firms to act so as to maximize the profits of the individual firm. This hypothesis may be usefully employed to explain the actions of firms, often clearly evidenced by the way in which work is allocated in a localized market wherein the local firms tactitly agree the type of project to be undertaken by each. Firms will not 'poach' each other's work and joint action is usually pursued to exclude a firm from elsewhere gaining a foothold in that market. (The reader is referred to texts on economic theory, such as those listed at the end of the chapter, for a detailed discussion of this hypothesis.)

Oligopoly is by no means limited to localized building markets. Many features of this form of competition are exhibited by national building and civil engineering contractors.

Thus, the competition of the market-place provides the context in which there are spatial (as outlined, above), sectoral, and time effects also, most especially when the pattern of demand is subject to major and rapid change.

Nor can the competitive elements be excluded by the increasingly popular method of obtaining contracts by negotiation rather than by competitive tender. As Hillebrandt (1974) discusses, if the contractor's price escalates too much during negotiations, the client always has the option of shelving the project or engaging another contractor; however, the more advanced the negotiations, the greater the commitment of the client and so the greater the potential for price increasing by the contractor.

Traditionally, competition is viewed as the major limiting force upon the pricing level. However, competition may also act to increase prices. The costs of submitting tenders has already been discussed in outline (see Ch. 9) and what might be considered as the ultimate situation of competition, open tendering, has received a good deal of condemnation due, *inter alia*, to its cost implications. It is generally acknowledged that the right price is not necessarily the lowest tender:

219

the expansion of negotiated systems of letting contracts is industrial evidence of this, where the contractors obtain work on the basis of expertise, quality, performance, etc. Elements of competition other than price are becoming increasingly significant.

10.1.4 Probability and distributions

By its very nature a decision will have at least two possible outcomes. More usually, there will be a range of possible outcomes between quite well defined extremes. A decision-maker will, of course, be concerned with the determination of the possible outcomes but will also wish to qualify the possibilities by an assessment of how likely (or unlikely) the outcomes are. Where the possible outcomes are in the form of a continuum between extreme cases, the extremes and several intermediate outcomes will be examined.

Provided the extreme outcomes have been correctly assessed, it is certain that the actual outcome will lie within that range. However, it is not likely that the probability of the occurrence of each possible outcome is everywhere equal within the range, some outcomes will be more probable than others. The probabilities may be represented as a graph of probability against possible outcome, a probability density function. The normal distribution curve is the commonest example of this type of function.

The shape of the probability density functions relating to the possible outcomes of a decision are of importance, particularly when considering the views of an optimist and a pessimist. In this context the tails of the distributions will be of significance as well as the clustering of the distribution about the modal value. The greater the spread of the tails, the greater is the doubt about the outcome (it will occur within a wider range). Further, the distribution may not be symmetrical, it may be skewed towards a high or a low value or might be bi-modal.

10.1.5 Probable profit contribution

Probable profit contribution (PPC) is a concept similar to that of mathematical expectation. PPC is obtained by multiplying the anticipated profit by the probability of realizing that profit. Thus, in a situation where, for example, a contractor submits bids for work, it could be used to indicate the optimum level of mark-up, or bid.

This technique is reliant upon bids for a large number of contracts being submitted; this would apply to each individual submarket as well as the overall situation for the firm. Previously submitted bids and successes, together with information about competitors' bids, are the data upon which this technique is based.

A simplified graph of the situation appertaining to a contract may be plotted, as in Fig. 10.1. The distribution shown in Fig. 10.1 may then be used to obtain the graph of PPC, as in Fig. 10.2.

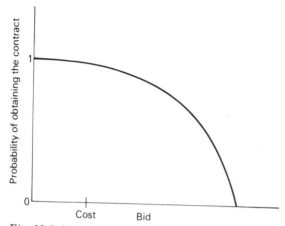

Fig. 10.1 Assessment of a bid's chance of success

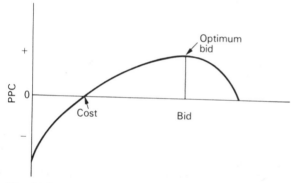

Fig. 10.2 Determination of the optimum bid

While a firm operates and submits bids in a fairly constant environment, each individual project for which a bid is submitted may be analysed, as shown in Table 10.1 (see also Fig. 10.3). It should be noted that if, in the long period, the firm cannot achieve an adequate return on capital at the optimum bid level (for many projects), it will eventually go out of business.

Table 10.1 may also be represented graphically, as shown in Fig. 10.4. If it is assumed that Fig. 10.4 represents the situation where plant is owned by the contractor, it is possible to contrast the situation if the plant required for the project execution were hired, as illustrated in Fig. 10.5.

The hiring of plant, instead of owning it, will have several effects, often dependent upon the degree of utilization of plant if owned. However, if the assumption is made that the utilization of plant is of a similar level, whether it is owned by the contractor or by a plant hire company (this is reasonable, if viewed on the basis of a contractor having a plant hire subsidiary and the contractor's overall position is being examined; however, many firms do not have

Table 10.1 Determination of the optimum bid

% Return on capital	Cost	Bid	Profit	Probability of success	PPC
−20	10	9	−1	1.0	−1
0	10	10	0	0.9	0
20	10	11	1	0.7	0.7
40	10	12	2	0.5	1.0
60	10	13	3	0.2	0.6
80	10	14	4	0.05	0.2
100	10	15	5	0.01	0.05

The optimum bid is 12; the bid which yields the greater PPC.

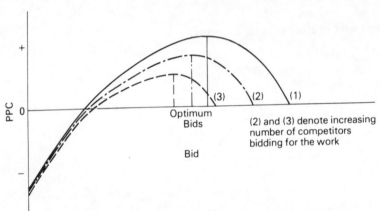

Fig. 10.3 The effects of increasing the number of competitors. (*Note:* cost increases with increased number of competitors as fewer projects for which bids are submitted are obtained, thereby increasing overheads on successful bids)

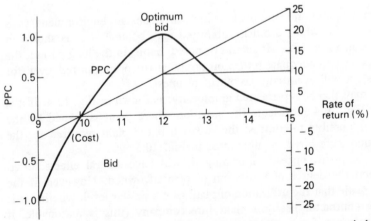

Fig. 10.4 Determination of the optimum bid and the return on capital it would yield (plant owned by the contractor)

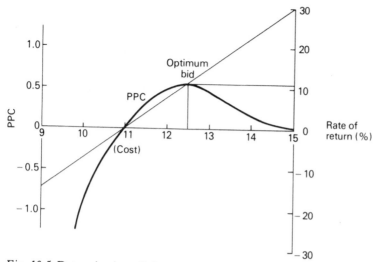

Fig. 10.5 Determination of the optimum bid and the return on capital it would yield (plant hired by the contractor)

a plant hire subsidiary and so are unable to fully utilize any owned plant) the main effects of hiring plant (instead of owning it) will be:

(a) the cost of the project will increase (the plant hire firm must earn a profit in its own right);
(b) the PPC curve will tend to flatten in shape and the cost and optimum bid will move to the right;
(c) the rate of return on capital at the optimum bid will be raised due to the decreased capital used by the contractor for the project execution.

In any situation requiring a decision where subjective probabilities are an integral part (e.g. bidding), it is useful to consider a three-point probability analysis. This analysis considers an optimistic, a pessimistic, and a most likely probability for the particular outcome and determines the mean probability by application of formula (based on the β distribution, but note the analogy with the prismoidal rule in land surveying):

$$\text{Mean} = \frac{O + 4M + P}{6}$$

where   O is the optimistic probability, M the most likely probability, and P the pessimistic probability.

Investment-decision example
An investment is available which involves a capital expenditure of £10,000. The investment has a two-year life such that at the end of year one it may produce an income of £10,000, £5,000, or £0 and at the end of year two it may produce a

223

Table 10.2 Calculation of monetary expectation

Path	PV of cash flows on path (£)	Probability of path	Monetary expectation (ME) (£)
A	+ 23,884	0.12	+ 2,886
B	+ 4,876	0.18	+ 878
C	− 4,215	0.30	− 1,265
D	+ 20,248	0.04	+ 810
E	+ 331	0.06	+ 20
F	− 8,760	0.10	− 876
G	+ 14,793	0.04	+ 592
H	− 4,215	0.06	− 253
I	− 13,316	0.10	− 1,331
Expected NPV			+ £1,441

further income of £30,000, £7,000, or −£4,000 (a loss). The prevailing rate of interest is 10 per cent.

Figure 10.6 (see also Table 10.2) shows the possibilities of the investment's cash flows over its life together with the probabilities of their occurrence. The expected NPV is of considerable significance as it expresses the probable outcome over the spectrum of possibilities.

Having executed a monetary analysis of the problem, it is possible to proceed to evaluate the utility of each outcome. The assessment of utility is, in itself,

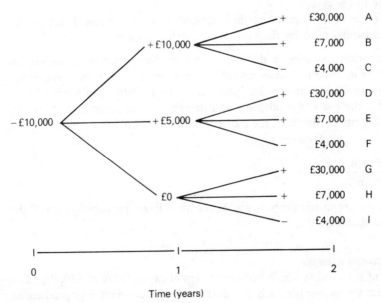

Fig. 10.6 Possible money outcomes

difficult as utility is a subjective concept and can be measured only on a relative scale. By careful analysis and questioning of the decision-maker(s) it is possible to construct a scale of utility, the units of which are termed 'utiles'. A utility scale for use in this example is shown for an optimist and another for a pessimist; a graphical representation of the utilities is illustrated in Fig. 10.7 (see also Table 10.3).

The outcomes shown by Table 10.4 indicate that, for the optimist, 2.50 represents a monetary expectation of £700 and for the pessimist, 0.07 represents a monetary expectation of £300, indicating that both the optimist and the pessimist would decide to take up the investment.

This type of analysis may be of value to developers in evaluating possible investments. In such a situation, the time periods would be considerably longer and the probabilities allocated to cash flows would not necessarily be independent. The technique could easily accommodate evaluation of possible construction cost escalation due to both fluctuations and variations as well as the evaluation of income flows from the completed building and/or its selling price.

The analysis is of use to a contractor for evaluation of a project's cash flow and profitability, being an extension of the evaluation techniques discussed in Chapter 9. It could also be used on a macro level for the firm to evaluate policy options – for instance, whether or not to maintain the level of the firm's resources during a period of reduced workload.

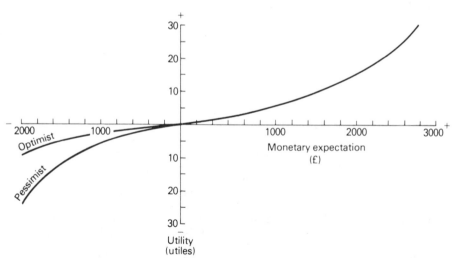

Fig. 10.7 Evaluation of monetary expectations (*Note*: this represents only one of several possible analyses of optimism and pessimism. An alternative view is identical for the optimist by the pessimist's curve is displaced downwards (kinked at the point where it becomes negative) throughout the negative portion of its length. It is likely that both positive and negative values will adhere (eventually) to the law of diminishing returns – decreasing marginal utility/disutility – and hence both positive and negative portions of the graph will assume an 'S' shape accordingly.)

Table 10.3 Utilities of monetary expectations

Monetary expectation	Utility of expectation	
(£)	Optimist	Pessimist
− 2,000	− 8.75	− 23.20
− 1,500	− 4.55	− 11.40
− 1,331	− 3.65	− 9.00
− 1,265	− 3.05	− 8.30
− 1,000	− 2.20	− 5.55
− 876	− 1.70	− 4.50
− 500	− 0.65	− 2.10
− 253	− 0.20	− 0.95
0	0	0
+ 20	0.03	
+ 500	1.50	
+ 592	1.95	
+ 810	3.20	
+ 878	3.55	
+ 1,000	4.40	
+ 1,441	7.55	
+ 1,500	8.10	
+ 2,000	12.80	
+ 2,500	19.00	
+ 2,866	26.00	
+ 3,000	30.00	

Table 10.4 Evaluation of monetary expectations

Monetary expectation	Probability of path	Optimist		Pessimist	
		Utility of outcome	Expectation of utility	Utility of outcome	Expectation of utility
+ £2,866	0.12	26.00	3.12	26.00	3.12
+ £878	0.18	3.55	0.64	3.55	0.64
− £1,265	0.30	− 3.05	− 0.92	− 8.30	− 2.49
+ £810	0.04	3.20	0.13	3.20	0.13
+ £20	0.06	0.03	0.00	0.03	0.00
− £876	0.10	− 1.70	− 0.17	− 4.50	0.45
+ £592	0.04	1.95	0.08	1.95	0.08
+ £253	0.06	− 0.02	− 0.01	− 0.95	− 0.06
− £1,331	0.10	− 3.65	− 0.37	− 9.00	− 0.90
			2.50		0.07

Where problems are quite complex, it may be difficult to adapt the technique described above to cope adequately. The more comprehensive aid to decision-making, called decision analysis, is now considered.

10.1.6 Decision analysis

Decision analysis is a methodology for problem-solving in that it plots all the possible decision paths and outcomes and then enables and objective evaluation of each to be made. It is a relatively new approach, being developed primarily by Robert Schlaifer and Howard Raifa at the Harvard Business School during the 1960s.

The application of decision analysis does not itself solve a problem but, on the basis of the criteria judged to be of importance, does evaluate the possible outcomes. It is therefore of use in introducing a measure of objectivity into an otherwise subjective area of management. It is vital that all possible courses of action are identified and evaluated, including the 'do nothing' option.

Any aid to decision-making which presents a ranking of possibilities, especially if evaluated on some form of monetary basis, may be perceived by decision-makers as purporting to make the decision itself. This is not the case. The decision must still be made but in the light of additional, more objective evaluation of alternatives.

The application of decision analysis has six distinct stages which are outlined below in the order in which they are normally executed.

1. Analysis of the problem. Here the objective is to split the problem down into simple components such that each component may be easily managed by the decision-maker. In most cases the problem will be complex and so a decision tree will be constructed, a type of flow chart, showing all the stages involved in the solution of the problem and all possible outcomes. It is important that each decision stage is coherent – i.e. fit together, in a meaningful way, with all other associated decision stages.

2. Description of the outcomes. It is essential that the objectives are clear. A complete description of each possible outcome is given at the right-hand end of each path through the decision tree.

3. Assess the value of the outcomes. This assessment is based upon utility. The relative desirability (utility) of each possible outcome is assessed. In the case of more complex problems, where several criteria are to be considered relative to each outcome, this will involve the use of multi-attribute utility analysis. The criteria are listed and their relative importance is evaluated. Each outcome is assessed against each criterion. Each outcome is then evaluated by summing its utility score against each criterion weighted by the relative importance of each criterion.

4. Assessment of probabilities. The alternative outcomes of each decision stage are allocated a probability of the likelihood of their occurrence. These are rather subjective assessments but past data may be used to lend objectivity. A mix of data and intuition is usual for most probability assessments.

5. 'Fold back' the decision tree. This may be done physically but is more often the process of working from right to left (i.e. commencing with the final outcomes), calculating the expected (weighted average) utility at each *event* node. Where several activity paths enter an activity event node from the right, the path with the highest utility is selected and the others are eliminated. The 'best' path through the decision tree is thereby determined.

6. Sensitivity analyses (see also Ch. 9) Sensitivity analyses are employed to identify the crucial elements of the decision. Special care is required where two or more paths are of nearly equal utilities.

Example. A simple example illustrates not only how decision analysis may be formally applied to problem-solving but also how there is a certain logic in decisions apparently made by intuition. Even if the analysis is not formally applied, the technique is of value in focusing thought upon the items of major importance in the decision.

A contractor receives a set of tender documents for a project of a type with which he is familiar. The firm has a reasonable current workload and the potential client and consultants are reputable organizations. There are no peculiarities or pressures relating to the tender. The contract is to be JCT '80, private, with quantities, and the code of procedure for single-stage selective tendering applies.

The contractor has to decide what to do: first, whether to return the documents or to submit a tender and if to submit a tender, how to do so. It is assumed that a tender may be submitted in one of three ways:

(a) by obtaining a 'cover price', or
(b) by preparing a tender based on an accurate estimate, or
(c) by preparing a tender based on an approximate estimate.

The approximate method is quicker and uses less resources. Figure 10.8 shows the decision tree derived from the above information.

The 'do nothing' option is considered inapplicable due to the role of normal commerical practice and the potential harm such a course of action would cause the contractor.

Having determined the possible courses of action open to the firm, the next stage is to evaluate them. In order to carry out the evaluation, the criteria applicable to the outcome must be established and themselves evaluated. This is done by the technique of multi-attribute utility analysis, as illustrated in Fig. 10.9.

There is sufficient time for (see path leading to outcome E) an accurate estimate to be prepared, should the approximate method produce an unacceptable result, but obviously such a situation is costly to the firm. Alternatively (path

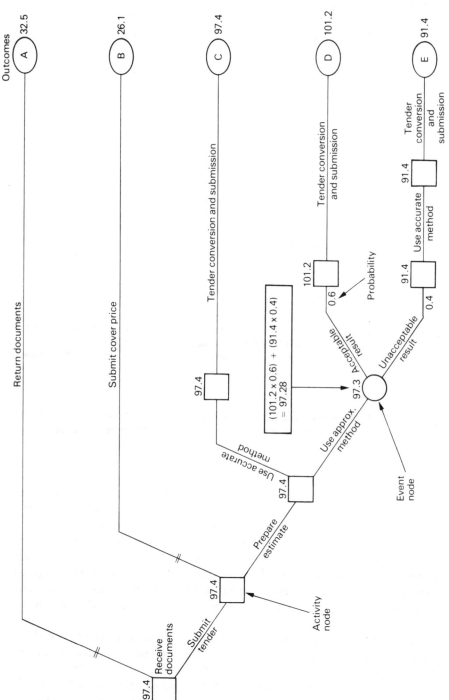

Fig. 10.8 Decision tree

229

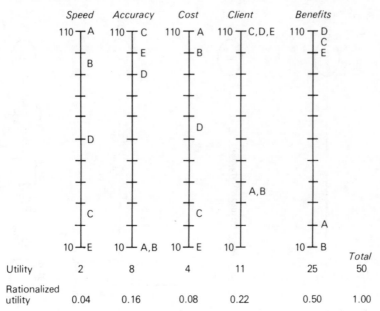

	Speed	Accuracy	Cost	Client	Benefits	
Utility	2	8	4	11	25	Total 50
Rationalized utility	0.04	0.16	0.08	0.22	0.50	1.00

Fig. 10.9 Multi-attribute utility analysis. Key – *Speed*: speed of obtaining a solution/ tender. *Accuracy*: accuracy of the solution. *Cost*: cost of solution. *Client*: client and consultants – attitudes, risks, etc. *Benefits*: benefits potential to the contractor – profitability, resource employment, work type, work continuity, etc.

to outcome A), returning the tender documents may be perceived by the firm as unsatisfactory because it might mean exclusion from future tender lists (strictly, this should not be the case according to the code of procedure).

Thus, every argument, appertaining to each outcome will be considered and objectively evaluated (as far as possible) against each criterion. A scale of utility of 10 to 110 has been used for each criterion to avoid conceptual problems of outcomes with zero utility against certain criteria which could occur if a scale of, say, 0 to 100 were used. It must be remembered that, when evaluating the outcomes against each of the criteria, each criterion must be considered individually and the outcomes are assessed relative to each other against each criterion. (The numbers on the scale are for the purposes of subsequent calculation but are of value in ensuring that the relative positions of the outcomes on the scale are correct; e.g. cost criterion – A is very cheap, E is expensive, C is almost four times as expensive as D.)

Table 10.5, the outcome evaluation, is obtained from Fig. 10.9 by considering each criterion in turn and calculating the utility of each outcome against each criterion by multiplying the measure on the criterion scale by the rationalized utility of the criterion. The values obtained for each outcome are then summed to obtain the total utility of each outcome, the values then being recorded against each outcome on the decision tree (as Fig. 10.8).

Table 10.5 Outcome evaluation

Criterion Outcome	Speed	Accuracy	Cost	Client	Benefits	Total
A	4.4	1.6	8.8	7.7	10.0	32.5
B	3.8	1.6	8.0	7.7	5.0	26.1
C	1.1	17.6	2.0	24.2	52.5	97.4
D	2.4	14.4	5.2	24.2	55.0	101.2
E	0.4	16.0	0.8	24.2	50.0	91.4

Where an event node occurs, the paths leading outwards from it to the right represent alternatives and so probabilities must be allocated to each path (the sum of the probabilities of the paths from an event node must, of course, equal unity).

The decision tree is then 'folded back'. Working from right to left the utilities at the nodes are calculated, as shown. At an activity node, where more than one paths enters that node from the right, a decision must be made; logically the path with the higher (or highest) utility is selected and the utility value allocated to the node. All other paths entering the node from the right are ignored and blanking off lines are drawn across them.

Thus, the logical path for the decision is obtained (path C in Fig. 10.8), being that path with the greatest utility.

It is possible that other paths will have only slightly lower utilities and so sensitivity analyses should be employed to evaluate the effects of changes in the variables – positions on the utility scales, probabilities, rationalized utilities of the criteria and, perhaps, even the criteria themselves. If, in the example, the probability of the approximate method producing an acceptable result is increased to only 0.62 (from 0.6), that course becomes the logical one to follow.

Note: The technique of multi-attribute utility analysis may be used in the evaluation of buildings, either constructed or proposed. Such evaluation introduces a significant measure of objectivity and is of great value in requiring the criteria for judgement and their relative importance to be determined.

Such an assessment has been used to evaluate housing provision such that various types of housing unit of different standards may be compared. It is also possible by use of this technique, which considers notional units of housing, to calculate total housing requirements, etc. (For a more detailed account see Hillebrandt 1974.)

10.2 Financial reporting

Financial reporting is the process of recording and communicating the financial performance of a firm. The best-known financial reports are those which appear in sets of published accounts: the profit and loss account and the balance sheet. These two reports are closely linked but of quite different natures: the profit and loss account being a statement of the firm's income and expenditure over a period (usually a year) and the resultant profit (or loss); the balance sheet being a statement of the firm's assets and liabilities at a particular instant (usually the year end).

Although a good deal of information is contained within a set of accounts and their accompanying notes, the information is frequently not in the most useful form thereby necessitating a degree of gleaning of meaningful figures and of interpretation. Such activities cannot be carried out in isolation from the accounting principles and conventions which have considerable influence, not only on the way the accounts are presented but also upon the figures appearing within the accounts.

Analysis of financial reports and statements, useful though these may be, are also subject to quite severe time limitations for validity. Essentially, such analyses are valid only in the relatively short period; in the long period, the success of a firm is governed by such fundamentals as technology, economic conditions, tastes, and fashions — items for which there is no financial measure.

Accurate financial reporting and interpretation constitutes a useful information input to management for the decision-making function. In this context it is important not only to consider current performance but also to analyse trends in order that a time dimension may be introduced.

Figure 10.10 illustrates the operational framework of a firm and the information required for and influences upon the profit and loss account and the balance sheet. Figure 10.11 depicts a profit and loss account for a building contractor and Fig. 10.12 depicts a balance sheet.

10.2.1 Profit and loss account

The profit and loss account (see Fig. 10.11) (or, for some organizations, the income and expenditure account) is a statement of the incomes and expenditures of the firm which occurred during the accounting period (usually a year) and the resultant profit or loss. A considerable variety of formats are used for profit and loss accounts, but each account should indicate, as appropriate:

(a) gross profit from trading;
(b) supplementary costs and expenses;
(c) operating profit;
(d) investment income and expenses, if any;
(e) profit before taxation;
(f) taxation;
(g) profit after tax.

It is also essential for the account (or a separate profit and loss appropriation account) to provide information regarding the disposal of the profit between distribution to the owners and the balance retained within the firm. Any amount retained within the firm is added to the owners' investment in the firm. Retained

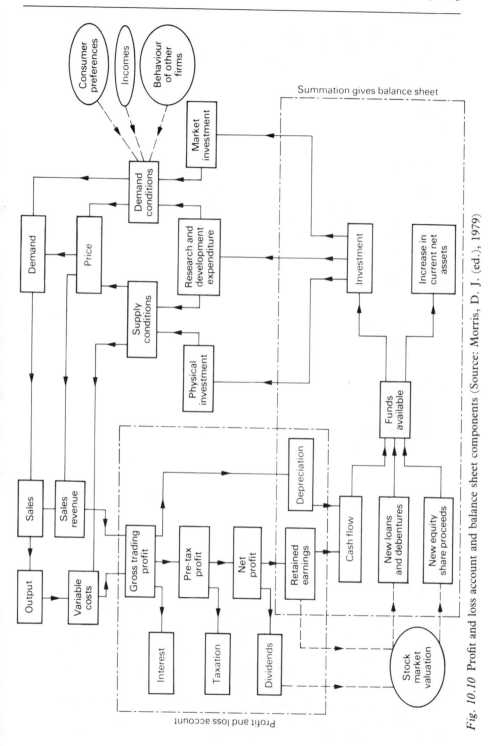

Fig. 10.10 Profit and loss account and balance sheet components (Source: Morris, D. J. (ed.), 1979)

Figure 10.11 Profit and loss account
D.M.O'Lition (Contractors) Ltd
Profit and loss account for the year ended 1 April 1981

	(£000)	(£000)
Turnover		1,071
Cost of production:		
Wages	207	
Materials	332	
Plant hire	41	
Small tools	16	
Sub-contractors	340	
Site overhead expenses	19	955
Profit on production:		116
Head office salaries and overheads	54	
Directors' emoluments	47	101
Profit on trading		15
Investment income		5
		20
Depreciation		2
Net profit		18
Debenture interest (10%)		4
		14
Corporation tax at 50%		7
Profit after tax		7
Dividends	2	
Transfer to general reserve	4	6
Balance carried forward		1

profits are a major source of capital for the financing of future activities and for growth.

Thus, the profit and loss account is a statement of the firm's performance over the period and provides a measure of how successful that performance has been.

10.2.2 Balance sheet

The balance sheet (see Fig. 10.12) is a statement of the financial position of a firm as at a particular instant (usually the end of the accounting period of the firm, its year end). In economic terms, it may be regarded as a statement of the wealth of the firm at a particular time, whereas the profit and loss account is a statement of the change in the wealth of the firm over the stipulated period. Hence the 'snapshot' concept of the balance sheet.

A balance sheet comprises two distinct sections, one detailing the assets of the firm and the other detailing the liabilities, including owners' investment. Traditionally, the liabilities (capital from owners, reserves, creditors, etc.)

Figure 10.12 Balance sheet
D.M.O'Lition (Contractors) Ltd
Balance sheet as at 1 April 1981

	(£000)	1981 (£000)	1980 (£000)
Assets employed:			
Current assets:			
Cash at bank and in hand	9		4
Debtors	26		29
Net work in progress	49		46
Stocks	7	91	5
Current liabilities:			
Bank loans	5		5
Creditors	24		21
Debenture interest	4		4
Current taxation	7		8
Dividend	2	42	4
Net current assets		49	42
Trade investments		7	7
Investment properties		46	46
Plant and equipment		13	15
Buildings		83	83
Goodwill		10	10
		208	203
Sources of capital:			
Authorized capital:			
200,000 ordinary shares of £1 each		200	200
Issued capital:			
100,000 ordinary shares of £1 each fully paid		100	100
Debentures 40,000 10% debentures at £1 each		40	40
Reserves:			
General		34	30
Profit and loss account		14	13
Capital		20	20
		208	203

comprise the left-hand side of the balance sheet and the assets (cash, investments, buildings, etc.) comprise the right-hand side. The more modern layout is for the liabilities to be detailed beneath the assets. Moreover, the assets details now usually include a statement of current assets less current liabilities to give the net current assets or the net working capital, the 'liabilities' part of the balance sheet comprising details of the owners' investment in the firm and of the firm's long-term liabilities.

Whatever format of presentation is adopted, *the two parts of the balance sheet must balance*.

The assets of a firm comprise fixed assets, current assets, investments and intangible assets. The fixed assets include such items as buildings, land, plant, machinery, equipment, fixtures and fittings, lorries and cars; items which an economist would regard as components of fixed costs. These assets should be considered subject to depreciation and/or periodic revaluation, dependent upon the circumstances (land and buildings tend to be periodically revalued; plant, machinery, cars etc., should be depreciated over their useful lives).

Current assets are liquid assets often of short duration, such as cash, debtors, stocks, and work in progress. The current assets are those used in the operating cycle of the firm.

Intangible assets, such as goodwill and patents, are assets of no physical substance (except the paper of patents). Their inclusion in the assets of a firm may be justified on the basis that their existence enhances the value of the firm. However, the valuation of intangible assets is a difficult exercise and it is probable that the sums included in accounts for such items are, in reality, only educated guesses.

The liabilities of a firm include both long-term and current (short-term) liabilities. The long-term liabilities comprise debentures, long-term loans and future taxation provisions. The current liabilities, those associated with the firm's day-to-day operations, include creditors, current taxation and proposed dividends to shareholders, are subtracted from the firm's total current assets to determine the net working capital. It is the inability of construction firms to meet their current liabilities which is the most common cause of bankruptcies and liquidations within the industry; thus both solvency and liquidity are vital considerations.

The owners' investment comprises the subscribed share capital, both preference and ordinary shares, and the reserves which act to increase the owners' investment in the firm. (Unpaid dividends are also attributable to the owners but are part of current liabilities.)

10.2.3 Other financial statements

Although the profit and loss account and balance sheet are the best known financial statements, many more statements are available. An income and expenditure statement takes the place of a profit and loss account for certain types of organization, e.g. professional institutions.

The other financial statements which are prepared periodically within a firm are dependent upon the type and activities of the firm. Most construction firms will prepare trading accounts, cash flow statements, and profit and loss appropriation accounts.

A trading account is a statement of the sales of the firm for the period (excluding capital items which are treated separately elsewhere) and the costs of those sales. The resultant figure is the gross trading profit (or loss), which is transferred to the profit and loss account. As this account is concerned with the trading operations of the firm, not only direct production costs but also distribution, marketing, research and development, administrative, etc., costs are also considered in the calculation of the trading profit.

A profit and loss appropriation account is a statement of the deployment of the net profit after tax – the profit available for distribution to the owners. The account provides details of the distribution to the owners of the firm and the amount (if any) retained within the firm as reserves.

Cash flows have been examined in Chapter 9 and are of use for evaluation of individual projects as well as for considerations of the firms's overall position and prospects. A cash flow statement for a firm for a given period should distinguish internal and external sources of cash flow. Internal sources comprise such items as profit before tax, depreciation, and investment income while external sources comprise cash flow from outside the firm such as loans to the firm. The statement should also distinguish sources and applications of cash flow arising from the sale or acquisition of fixed assets (capital items) from those arising from changes in the firm's working captial (revenue items). Statements of this type commonly appear in sets of accounts as statements of 'sources and applications of funds' and denote the changes in balance sheet items which have occurred during the accounting period.

10.2.4 Accounting terminology

Certain words and phrases have particular meanings in an accounting context. The following is a glossary of some common accountancy terms:

Accruals (usually expenses) – items which have been utilized by the firm prior to payment therefore, but the appropriate cost or value is included in the firm's accounts.

Asset – an item, owned by an individual or a firm, which has a monetary value.

Capital – the goods which are used in the production and have themselves been produced; the investment in the business by the owners.

Capital Employed – the capital in use in a business; net assets.

Capital Reserve – a reserve created to provide for future capital gains tax liabilities, etc. (Capital gains tax is payable *on the sale* of an asset which has appreciated in value, e.g. a building.)

Credit – a bookkeeping entry denoting an increase in a liability account or a decrease in an asset account.

Creditor – someone (or another firm) to whom the firm owes money.

Debit – a bookkeeping entry denoting an increase in an asset account or a decrease in a liability account.

Debtor – someone (or another firm) who owes money to the firm.

Depreciation – the process of reducing the value of an asset (as shown in the firm's accounts) for its wearing out and obsolescence. The annual reduction in value of the asset is also a cost to the firm and appears as such in the profit and loss account. This does not mean that cash is set aside for future replacements but depreciation is an important source of capital (see Ch. 8).

Dividend – the residual profits distributed to the shareholders.

External Liabilities – the debenture loans, other loans, and creditors of a firm.

General Reserve – the residual profits retained within the firm for reinvestment. This represents an increased stake in the firm by the owners.

Goodwill – an intangible asset, the amount by which the value of a business exceeds the value of its physical assets. This arises through the reputation of the firm and its potential future earnings.

Liquidation – the winding-up of a company; its termination.

Liquidity – the ease with which an asset may be exchanged for (turned into) cash; the ability to meet short-period requirements for cash.

Net Assets – net current assets plus fixed assets.

Net Worth – the total assets of a firm minus the external liabilities.

Over-Trading – the situation where current creditors cannot be paid fully out of the receipts from current sales.

Profit – *gross profit* is the total sales revenue minus costs incurred directly in the operations of the firm; *net profit* is the gross profit minus interest on loans and depreciation.

Revenue – income.

Revenue Expenditure – expenditure on items other than fixed assets; current expenditure.

Solvency – the ability to raise cash to meet debts; the ability of a firm to meet its current liabilities by realizing its current assets.

Turnover – the total revenue from sales of a business (excludes capital items).

10.2.5 Accounting concepts and conventions

Accountancy is based upon the application of a common set of rules for the preparation of all acounts. This is essential in order that comparisons may be made and, more importantly, to facilitate understanding and interpretation and to avoid frauds. Many of the concepts and conventions of accountancy in the UK are embodied within statutes, particularly the Companies Acts, but others are applied due to accountants adopting standard procedures in the practice of their profession. An appreciation of the main accounting concepts and conventions is vital for the understanding and the correct interpretation of accounts.

Accruals – costs and revenues are accrued (taken into account) as they are incurred or earned.

Business Entity – each business is treated as a distinct and separate entity in its own right.

Conservatism (or prudence) – provision is made in the accounts for liabilities (costs, expenses) as soon as they become apparent whereas profits usually are not included in the accounts until they are realized.

238

Consistency – identical or very similar items must be treated in the same way in different accounting periods and in different sets of account.

Cost Concept – assets are initially recorded in the accounts of the business at their cost and thereafter depreciated on that basis. Revaluations may occur periodically for fixed assets so that more realistic values are shown.

Current Cost Accounting – assets and liabilities are included in the accounts at their current value or current cost.

First In First Out (FIFO) – the convention of considering that the oldest stocks of materials, etc., are used first in production.

Going Concern – a business is regarded as an entity which has a continuing life of infinite length.

Historical Cost Accounting – assets are included in the accounts on the basis of their original cost. (Fixed assets may be subject to occasional revaluation.) Liabilities are treated in the same way. This convention is used for taxation purposes.

Last In First Out (LIFO) – the convention of considering that the newest stocks of materials, etc., are used first in production.

Monetary Measurement – accounts record monetary effects upon the business; events, the effects of which cannot be measured in monetary terms, are therefore excluded from the accounts. This concept implies a stable monetary unit to facilitate direct comparisons and so leads to problems during inflationary periods.

10.2.6 Recording transactions

Each transaction in which a firm is involved will be recorded. The recording will occur in the various books of account of the firm and will be executed by the process of double-entry bookkeeping. The double-entry aspect is fundamental, as every transaction will constitute an increase in one account of the firm and a decrease in another; the purchase of 1,000 bricks by the contractor for a cash sum of £50 will be recorded in the contractor's books as an increase in the stock of bricks of £50 and a decrease in the firm's cash of £50.

It is useful to consider the accounting aspects of transaction by the use of 'T-accounts' (so named due to their format). Note that the left-hand side of a T-account is *always* the debit side and the right-hand side *always* the credit side. Thus, the example given above would be recorded in T-account format as:

Stock – bricks		*Cash*	
(Dr)	(Cr)	(Dr)	(Cr)
50			50

As all transactions may be recorded by the use of T-accounts, the following example illustrates the establishment and first year of trading of a new contracting company (taxation is ignored).

1. The owners invest £15,000.
2. The company purchases £4,500 materials on account; the account is subsequently paid.
3. The company purchases £500 small tools for cash.
4. The company purchases a yard and office building for £21,000 for which it pays cash of £7,000 and issues a debenture of £14,000 which bears interest at 10 per cent per annum.
5. During the trading period, the company executes work which costs in wages £5,000, salaries £1,000, materials £4,000, and plant hire £1,000 and for which it receives £15,000.
6. At the end of the period, an incomplete contract has cost £400 materials, £100 salaries and £200 wages, is 50 per cent completed and the contract sum is £2,000; no payments have been received for this work.
7. Depreciation is charged on a straight-line basis at 10 per cent per annum, except for buildings, etc., which are depreciated at 2 per cent per annum.
8. Dividends of £1,000 are paid.

Shareholders

	15,000 (1)

Materials

(2) 4,500	4,000 (5, P&L)
	400 (6, P&L)
	100 Bal. c/d
4,500	4,500
Bal. b/d 100	

Small tools

(3) 500	50 (7)
	450 Bal. c/d
500	500
Bal. b/d 450	

Buildings

(4) 21,000	420 (7)
	20,580 Bal. c/d
21,000	21,000
Bal. b/d 20,580	

Wages

(5) 5,000	5,200 (P&L)
(6) 200	
5,200	5,200

Cash

(1) 15,000	4,500 (2')
(4) 14,000	500 (3)
(5) 15,000	7,000 (4)
	14,000 (4)
	5,000 (5)
	1,000 (5)
	1,000 (5)
	100 (6)
	200 (6)
	1,000 (8)
	9,700 Bal. c/d
44,000	44,000
Bal. b/d 9,700	

Creditors	
(2') 4,500	4,500 (2)

Debentures	
	14,000 (4')

Salaries	
(5) 1,000	1,100 (P&L)
(6) 100	
1,100	1,100

Plant hire	
(5) 1,000	1,000 (P&L)

Work in progress	
1,000	1,000 Bal. c/d
Bal. b/d 1,000	

Debenture interest	
(4") 1,400	1,400 (P&L) Bal. c/d
Bal. b/d 1,400	

Retained earnings	
Bal. b/d 1,430	1,430 (P&L)

Sales	
(P&L) 16,000	15,000 (5)
	1,000 (6)
16,000	16,000

Depreciation	
(7) 50	
(7) 420	470 (P&L)
470	470

Dividends	
(8) 1,000	1,000 (P&L)

Profit and loss account

Materials	4,400	16,000	Sales
Wages	5,200		
Salaries	1,100		
Plant hire	1,000		
Depreciation	470		
Interest	1,400		
Dividends	1,000		
Retained earnings	1,430		
	16,000	16,000	

Balance sheet

Assets employed:	(£)	(£)
Current assets:		
Cash	9,700	
Materials stock	100	
Work in progress	1,000	10,800
Current liabilities:		
Debenture interest:		1,400
Net current assets		9,400
Small tools		450
Buildings		20,580
		£30,430

Sources of capital:	(£)
Authorized and issued ordinary shares	15,000
Debenture	14,000
Reserves:	
Retained earnings	1,430
	£30,430

Because a firm undertakes many transactions during any single accounting period, T-accounts are not suitable for recording purposes; instead, various books of account are employed. The book in which transactions are initially recorded is the *journal*, the book of original entry. This book may take various forms but traditionally is a bound volume with the pages of columnar layout, as illustrated in Fig. 10.13. Journal entries are subsequently posted (transferred) to the ledger accounts, the ledger folio column being for cross referencing.

The ledger is the main book of account. It is traditionally in the form of a bound volume in which each page is devoted to recording transactions affecting one individual account. The traditional format has given way to loose-leaf and card systems which have themselves been superseded by electronic data storage systems. Figure 10.14 shows the ledger accounts appertaining to the transaction recorded in the journal as Fig. 10.13.

Both these books of account record all the transactions of the firm but in rather different ways. Each firm will develop individualities in the recording procedures and processes but the principles of accounting will be followed in every instance.

The posting of the journal records to the ledger accounts will occur at intervals determined by the number and frequency of transactions. Often this will be done on a daily or weekly basis. Prior to the posting of entries, it is sound practice to check the arithmetic accuracy of the entries; this is conveniently done by totalling the debit column and the credit column to ensure that they balance (the totals are equal). This process is called 'proving'. It does not substantiate the theory of the entries as recorded but arithmetic errors are easily detected and may be corrected

Figure 10.13   Traditional journal format

Date	Account	Ledger folio	Debit		Credit	
1980						
Sept. 3	Materials	12	731	52		
	Y-bar Steels Ltd	71			731	52
Sept. 29	Y-bar Steels Ltd	71	731	52		
	Cash	5			731	52

Records the credit purchase of reinforcement form Y-bar Steels Ltd and the subsequent cash payment.

Figure 10.14   Ledger accounts

Cash   Folio 5

Date	Description	Ref.	Dr		Date	Description	Ref.	Credit	
1980					1980				
Sept. 1	Balance b/d	√	3,062	05	Sept. 29	Purchase reinf. bars	J23	731	52

Materials   Folio 12

Date	Description	Ref.	Dr		Date	Description	Ref.	Credit
1980					1980			
Sept. 1	Balance b/d	√	2,710	17				
3	Pur. reinf. bars	J23	731	52				

Y-bar Steels Ltd   Folio 71

Date	Description	Ref.	Dr		Date	Description	Ref.	Credit	
1980					1980				
Sept. 29	Sept. 3 a/c paid	J23	731	52	Sept. 1	Balance b/d	√	92	01
					3	Reinf. bars	J23	731	52

with a minimum of difficulty (if errors are not found until a much later stage, the correcting process is considerably more problematic).

At the end of each accounting period the ledger accounts are balanced and closed (for that period), the balances being carried down to the next period (thus becoming the opening balances of the next period). These closing ledger balances are also abstracted to a separate list, called the unadjusted trial balance, on the basis of which the statements of account of the firm are prepared. The expenses and revenues of the period just ended will be abstracted to an expense and revenue summary from which the profit and loss account is obtained.

Several ledger accounts are used frequently – the cash account, the materials purchases account, and the sales account. For convenience, these accounts are commonly kept separate from the general ledger, each in its own book – the cash book (usualy with a subsidiary book for petty cash items), the purchases day-book, and the sales day-book. The cash book is somewhat different from the day-books in that it is the entire cash account, both debits and credits, whereas the day-books record only the debits of the purchases and sales accounts (the credit entries being recorded in the ledger against the suppliers' and customers' personal accounts) and are totalled and posted to the ledger sales and purchases accounts annually.

10.3 Financial management

Successful financial management is founded upon an appreciation of accounts, capital provision and the ability to apply that expertise.

It therefore remains to consider the financial effects of some operating mechanisms and how interpretation of financial statements may be aided (notably by the use of ratios).

Given a knowledge of capital provision, financial reports, and their interpretation and the operations and objectives of the firm, successful management is the ability to make decisions which lead the firm towards the realization of its objectives.

It is perhaps interesting to consider the paradox in which contracting firms operate; each contractor wishes to continue in business, to be profitable, and (usually) to grow – objectives which are achieved by successfully managing each individual contract out of business!

10.3.1 Net working capital

Net working capital is calculated by subtracting current liabilities from current assets; it is, thus, that portion of current assets which is financed from long-term funds. The flow of working capital in a business is of a cyclical nature, as illustrated in Fig. 10.15. Due to the nature of construction, stocks and work in progress form a relatively large proportion of a building firm's working capital.

The cycle, as shown in Fig. 10.15, may be modified to allow for the payment provisions under the typical system of contracting. Completed items of work, not just complete buildings, are paid for by the client in his honouring of the monthly, interim certificates. Stocks of materials on site, and sometimes off site, are also included in the payments together with sums for fluctuations and variations. It is apparent that the cycle, as shown, applies for each individual work item but that there is also a direct route from materials to sales when materials on and off site are included in interim certificates. One further amendment occurs at the sales point where retention is withdrawn from the cycle

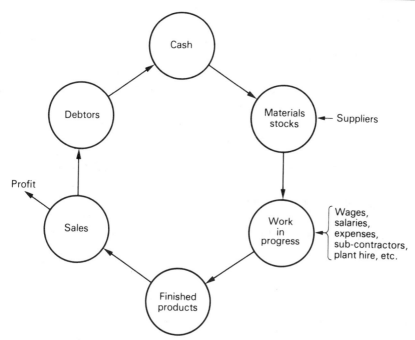

Fig. 10.15 The working capital cycle

to constitute a subsequent two-stage cash injection at practical completion (first moiety released) and at final certificate (second moiety released).

However, medium and long-term capital is more expensive than short-term capital and so profitability may be enhanced by:

(a) maintaining the proportion of short-term to long-term liabilities at as high a level as possible commensurate with the working capital ratios required;
(b) keeping net working capital to a minimum (net working capital is financed from long-term funds);
(c) ensuring that the working capital cycle is as short as possible.

10.3.2 Cash

Cash is an element of working capital but is of major importance in its own right. Cash is not wanted for its own sake (as money is merely the medium of exchange) but to 'oil the wheels' of business. No firm wishes to hold more than the minimum amount of cash as this an asset which earns nothing. It is important to a firm's profitability, therefore, that it manages its cash efficiently to minimize the cash held. Deposit accounts offer a useful form of investment for short-term cash surpluses.

Successful cash management is dependent upon the ability to manage the elements of the business cycle of the firm. The more rapidly the cash cycle revolves, the less is the firm's requirement for working capital.

10.3.3 Debtors

Clearly, debtors represent a delay to the cash inflow of the firm. Their existence constitutes a lengthening of both the cash and working capital cycles. However, in construction, as in most industries, the offering of a period of credit to customers is a normal and accepted business practice. Most construction contracts (main, subcontracts, supply contracts, etc.) stipulate the period of credit to be applicable, sometimes also specifying discounts to be offered for payment within the period of credit allowed (e.g. NSC/4).

It is possible to speed up the debtors' section of the cycle by the process of factoring the debts. In factoring a debt, the creditor sells the debt to a bank or other financial institution (some specialize in this activity) at a discount (dependent upon the period prior to payment becoming due and the credit worthiness of the debtor). The creditor thus receives a reduced amount of cash but at an earlier time. After the debt has been factored, the risks and collection responsibilities lie with the factoring agent.

Debt factoring is, perhaps rather surprisingly, not very common in construction.

10.3.4 Work in progress

Work in progress is included in the accounts of most business at a valuation which accords with the principle of 'cost or market value, whichever is the lower', and is included to reflected fairly the value of the goods which are actually within the production process. Clearly, this is reasonable for manufacturing and similar industries, but construction represents an exception.

Building contractors produce finished articles in which there are very many components, and although the finished article (the building) requires a long time to produce, individual components (such as those identified as separate items in BQs) are completed over much shorter time periods. Further, with all but small contracts, the client makes periodic (usually monthly) progress payments to the contractor in respect of the work completed.

As, in effect, the building is sold prior to its construction and the construction period is long, contractors' work in progress is included in the accounts at cost plus profit less allowances for contingencies such as patent and latent defects. Such procedure enables the accounts to reflect the true profit earned and the financial position of the contractor at the end of the accounting period. The balance sheet will thus include work in progress as the total value of work executed to date on uncompleted contracts less payments received to date in respect of those contracts.

10.3.5 Depreciation

Depreciation, the process of reducing the value of a fixed asset (writing off) for obsolescence and wear and tear (the proportion of depreciation due directly to the utilization of the asset in the production process), appears as a cost in the profit and loss account. It is included in the balance sheet by its effect of reducing the value of the assets. Thus, the values of fixed assets to which depreciation has been applied, as shown in a balance sheet (their written down values), are the proportions of the costs of those assets which remain available to the firm.

It is a fallacy to consider depreciation to be a fund set aside for the replacement of fixed assets which wear out and become obsolete. The appearance of depreciation as a cost in the profit and loss account is a key to its true purpose – to ensure that the costs of capital use and ownership by the firm are included in the accounts (and thus the profit shown) and that the capital of the firm is not consumed. An example of capital consumption would be where an excavator, which cost £100,000, had a life of ten years and no depreciation had been included in the accounts of the firm over that period. If all profits were distributed, the owners would have received £10,000 per year extra dividend (assuming a straightline basis for depreciation) but at the end of the ten years when the excavator was scrapped there would be an imbalance in the accounts of £100,000. The balance sheet would show the firm's assets to be £100,000 less than the liabilities and owners' investment, the remedy to redress the balance being to reduce the owners' investment by £100,000.

10.3.6 Reserves

Reserves, as has already been noted, may be established against a specific future liability (e.g. a capital reserve for the future payment of capital gains tax on the sale of a building, the value of which is appreciating), or may be of a general nature. In either case reserves represent increases in the owners' investment in the firm.

Firms grow via increased investment and this is most easily obtained by retaining profits. Thus, reserves tend to grow quite rapidly. As the funds (undistributed net profits, after tax), from which the reserves have been created, have been spent by the firm in purchasing fixed assets, etc., the reserves do not represent stocks of money that are available for distribution to the owners. Hence, public companies periodically have scrip issues of shares; the shareholder's investment (as per the accounts) is increased by the value of the issue and the reserves are reduced by a corresponding amount. Such a process alters the capital structures of the companies and maintains a proportionality between issued shares and reserves.

10.3.7 Accounting ratios

Figure 10.16 shows the interrelationships of the main accounting ratios. Accounting ratios are used to aid the analysis of sets of accounts which, themselves, are often rather complex. It is important that not too much reliance for drawing conclusions is placed upon any individual ratio but that several ratios are considered together to produce a meaningful analysis.

Ratios can be broadly classified under three headings: working capital ratios, operating and profitability ratios, and supplementary ratios.

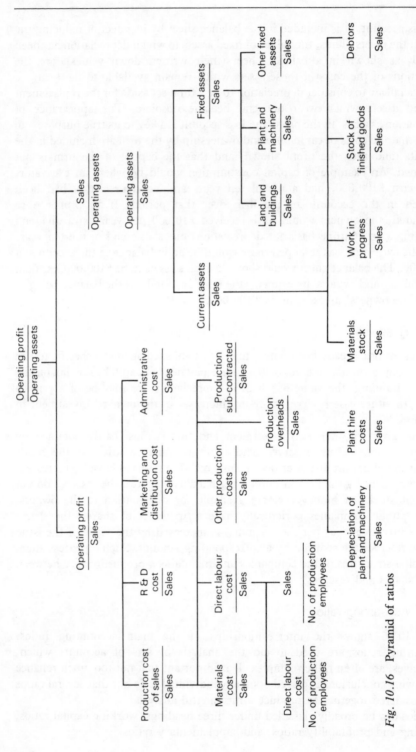

Fig. 10.16 Pyramid of ratios

Working capital ratios

(a) Current ratio

$$\text{Current ratio} = \frac{\text{Current assets}}{\text{Current liabilities}}$$

This ratio, given normal operating, indicates the ability of the firm to meet its short-term liabilities. This ratio should approximately be from 1.5:1 to 2:1.

(b) Quick ratio (or acid test)

$$\text{Quick ratio} = \frac{\text{Very liquid assets (cash plus debtors)}}{\text{Current liabilities}}$$

This ratio indicates the ability of the firm to meet its (short-term) immediate liabilities in the worst circumstances. Thus, this ratio should be 1:1 or possibly slightly greater. If the ratio is much greater than 1:1, funds which could be gainfully employed are idle; if it is much less than 1:1, the firm may find it difficult to pay bills and so may be forced to wind-up its operations.

(c) Working capital ratio

$$\text{Working capital ratio} = \frac{(\text{Current assets}) - (\text{Current liabilities})}{\text{Turnover}}$$

This ratio should be established for each firm (together with permissible variability) and should be maintained. This control will ensure that sufficient working capital is maintained to allow the firm to operate smoothly. The ratio will vary between firms (and between periods) due to the nature of the items which working capital comprises.

Operating ratios (usually expressed as percentages)

(a) $\dfrac{\text{Total costs, expenses, and taxes}}{\text{Total income}}$

This is the main operating ratio.

(b) $\dfrac{\text{Net profit before tax}}{\text{Turnover}}$

Investment income should be excluded from this analysis as it is not included in turnover and would produce a false result if included in the net profit before tax.

(c) $\dfrac{\text{Net profit before tax}}{\text{Capital employed}}$

It is useful to compare the ratio obtained when investment income is included in the net profit before tax with that obtained when investment income is excluded. Such an analysis will assist a decision of whether to sell the investment, to maintain the investment, or to acquire further investments.

(d) $\dfrac{\text{Turnover}}{\text{Capital employed}}$

In this case, also, the effect of including any investment income should be examined. A low ratio indicates that the firm is capital intensive in its operations. A firm which owns its own plant, for instance, will have a lower ratio than a similar sized firm which hires plant.

There are many more operating ratios which are used to examine the detailed performance of firms. Sizer (1979) provides a full discussion of such ratios.

Supplementary ratios

(a) *Periods of credit*

(1) $\dfrac{\text{Debtors}}{\text{Turnover}} \times 12$

gives the period, in months, for which credit is offered by the firm.

(2) $\dfrac{\text{Creditors}}{\text{Purchases}} \times 12$

gives the period of credit, in months, which the firm enjoys.

Both these ratios are only quick, approximate indicators. As the sums involved for debtors and creditors may fluctuate significantly, the periods obtained may not be very meaningful. It is preferable to calculate the periods of credit offered and enjoyed on a weighted average basis, as discussed in Chapter 9.

(b) *Productivity*
Productivity is a measure of the output obtained from given amounts of input. The two factors of production whose productivity is most frequently considered are labour and capital. In the construction industry, it is usual to consider, primarily, labour productivity as construction is a labour-intensive industry.

(1) $\dfrac{\text{Turnover}}{\text{No. of employees}}$ (2) $\dfrac{\text{Turnover}}{\text{Direct wages}}$ (3) $\dfrac{\text{Turnover}}{\text{Direct wages and salaries}}$;

(4) $\dfrac{\text{Turnover}}{\text{Wages, salaries, and directors' emoluments}}$;

(5) $\dfrac{\text{Turnover}}{\text{Direct plant and equipment}}$;   (6) $\dfrac{\text{Turnover}}{\text{Total plant and equipment}}$;

(7) $\dfrac{\text{Direct plant and equipment}}{\text{No. of employees}}$;   (8) $\dfrac{\text{Direct plant and equipment}}{\text{Direct wages}}$

Many ratios may be constructed to render monitoring information. It is useful to consider ratios which evaluate the performance at the workplace (site) with those which evaluate the overall performance of the firm. Such analyses will indicate, over a period, the sources of productivity changes; i.e. whether they are due to on-site performance or managerial performance, etc.

(c) Returns to investors

(1) $\dfrac{\text{Net profit}}{\text{Capital employed}}$

(Net profit is profit before interest payments and taxation.) This ratio indicates the overall return the firm has earned on its total capital employed, and thus the efficiency of the operations.

(2) Return on shares $= \dfrac{\text{Net profit after tax}}{\text{Shareholders' investments}}$

The net profit after tax is the residue attributable to the shareholders. The shareholders' investments comprise the capital subscribed by the shareholders plus the reserves attributable to the shareholders.

(3) Return on equity $= \dfrac{\text{Net profit attributable to equity holders}}{\text{Equity holders' investment}}$

Ratios (1), (2), and (3) reflect the capital structure of a firm and are subject to considerable influence from the gearing of the organization and the system of taxing firms' earnings.

Numerous ratios may be used in the analysis of published accounts but many firms, usually the smaller firms in an industry, are not required to publish such information (see Ch. 8). Also, as much more internal information is available for the analysis of performance, ratio analysis forms an integral part of a firm's internal system of control. Construction firms, for instance, often use ratio analysis to monitor productivity on each site as well as for the firm as a whole.

10.3.8 Interpretation of financial statements

Interpretation of financial statements usually revolves around the profit and loss account and the balance sheet. Internally, firms have more information and details to use for decision-making. It is, of course, useful to study several periods so that 'trends' may be detected rather than to view each set of accounts in isolation.

The profit and loss account will provide information about bank charges, interest on loans and bad debts which the firm has incurred during the period. These items provide an insight into the firm's financial management capabilities and its credit control, including assessments of customers' credit worthiness.

Ratios may then be extracted and examined – income form each source to turnover; profit (gross, net, net of tax) to turnover; etc. Ratio analysis is particularly valuable in determining whether the firm is benefiting as it should from an increase in turnover, and if not, why not. Here it is essential that several consecutive sets of accounts are examined in the context of prevailing economic conditions and the policies and objectives of the firm.

As the balance sheet is a picture of the firm's assets and liabilities at a particular instant, the importance of comparisons with previous accounts is enhanced. Ratios are again used for the analyses. The working capital ratios indicate the solvency of the firm, the quick ratio indicating the firm's liquidity. The ratios of debtors : turnover and creditors : turnover indicate the credit control of the firm. The return on capital employed (profit expressed as a percentage of net assets) provides the answer to the primary question, 'Is it worthwhile remaining in business or could the capital earn a better return if invested elsewhere?' In a recession a contractor's return on capital employed may be very low but over a long period (which will hopefully include some buoyant times) should be significantly higher, sufficient to keep the firm in business.

A firm must consider, monitor, and control its performance in both the long and the short periods as inadequacies in either (or both) instance may cause the firm to be wound up. In the short period, solvency and liquidity requirements dominate; in the long period it is profitability, in particular the returns available to the owners for their investment when compared with alternative investments (the opportunity cost of the investment). Trends provide vital warnings of impending failure; the earlier unfavourable trends are detected, the easier is their correction. All firms prepare accounts annually and many prepare interim accounts at mid-year; building contractors monitor performance on their projects at one- or three-month intervals – a sound and essential policy in an industry where economic fluctuations occur rapidly and often unpredictably and tend to be of great amplitude.

As with the monitoring techniques discussed in Chapter 9, the more frequent and sophisticated the monitoring system, the more expensive it is (itself adding to overheads and thereby reducing profit). Again a cost-benefit evaluation should be carried out to determine the optimum frequency and detail of the system. Failure of an individual project to earn the required profit is serious but failure of the firm to earn adequate long-period profits or, more particularly in building, the inability of a firm to meet its short-term demands for cash (a liquidity failure) is untenable.

Summary

A prime function of management is decision-making. Many decisions will be made in connection with the financing of the firm and its activities. Such decisions must be based upon sound data and act towards the realization of defined objectives. There is much subjectivity in decision-making but it is possible to introduce a measure of objectivity by the application of decision-making techniques such as decision analysis. The personality of the decision-maker cannot be ignored but the application of scientific decision-making techniques do promote consistency, thoroughness, and objectivity, even in the evaluation of unknowns.

The data upon which financial decisions are made are obtained from financial reports and statements. To interpret such information it is necessary to appreciate the system under which the information is produced. The accounting system in the UK has its own terminology, concepts, and conventions which are used to record the transactions entered into by firms and ultimately to produce financial statements, the best known of which are the profit and loss account and the balance sheet.

Thus, financial management is the ability to understand and interpret financial statements and reports and to make reasoned and objective decisions in controlling the operations of the firm. This will inevitably involve the successful management of working capital and all its components. Ratio analyses are very useful in interpreting accounts, particularly for comparisons with standards, competitors, and to identify trends. The ability to correctly interpret financial statements is a first, but significant, step towards successful financial management.

Questions

1. (a) 'Building is a risky business.' Discuss.
   (b) Why are builders more likely to be optimists than pessimists?
2. How may a contractor assess the best mark-up to apply in bidding competitively for a project?
3. Describe and discuss a technique by which a developer may select the most appropriate method of letting a new building project.
4. What is depreciation and why is it necessary? How may depreciation be applied to (a) plant and (b) buildings? Discuss the effects of depreciation provisions on the profit and loss account and the balance sheet.
5. In what ways are accounting conventions, when applied to building contractors, at variance with their usual application?
6. What is working capital and why is it considered to be of major importance to building firms?
7. Record the necessary accounting entries and produce a profit and loss account and a balance sheet for the following transactions which occurred in the first year of trading of A. Bodger Ltd.

   (a) Jan. Cash sale of 6,000 shares of £1 each (total authorized share capital).
   (b) 3 Jan. Purchase of builder's yard on 3 months' credit for £5,000, cash deposit of 20 per cent paid.
   (c) 21 Jan. Issue of debenture – 10 years, 15 per cent, £3,000.

(d) 28 Jan. Purchase of mortar mixer and sundry small items of plant for £1,500, cash deposit 10 per cent, credit for balance of 1 month.

(e) 4 Feb. Cash purchase of equipment and small tools, £500.

(f) 28 Feb. Purchase materials £700 on 1 month credit.

(g) 30 April. Cash receipt £2,200.

(h) 21 May. Purchase materials £900 on 1 month credit.

(i) 1 July. Cash receipt £3,200.

(j) 1 July. A. Bodger – half-year salary £2,000.

(k) 8 July. Purchase materials £650 for cash.

(l) 10 Aug. Cash receipt £3,000.

(m) 1 Sept. Cash receipt £2,100.

(n) 3 Nov. Purchase materials £1,000 on 1 month credit.

(o) 1 Dec. Cash receipt £2,000.

From 1 Mar. Wages paid at £500 per month.
At 31 Dec. a contract of value £4,600 is 50 per cent complete, £2,000 having been received as the single-stage payment; stocks of materials is £400. Depreciation charged on plant and equipment at 25 per cent per annum.

8. Draft a report for A. Bodger Ltd on its first year of trading and its position at 31 Dec. (information given in Question 7).

References and bibliography

Bierman, H. Jr (1963) *Financial and Managerial Accounting – An Introduction*, Macmillan

Fellows, R. F. and Langford, D. A. (1980) Decision theory and tendering, *Building Technology and Management*, Oct.

Hanson, J. L. (1970) *A Textbook of Economics*, Macdonald and Evans

Hillebrandt, P. M. (1974) *Economic Theory and the Construction Industry*, Macmillan

Kaufman, G. M. and Thomas, H. (eds) (1977) *Modern Decision Analysis*, Penguin

Lipsey, R. G. (1979) *An Introduction to Positive Economics* (5th edn), Weidenfeld and Nicolson

Moore, P. G. and Thomas, H. (1976) *The Anatomy of Decisions*, Penguin

Morris, D. J. (ed.) (1979) 'The behaviour of firms', *The Economic System in the UK* (2nd edn), Oxford U.P.

Scholfield, C. D. A. (1975) What is the cost of capital? *The Quantity Surveyor*, April

Sizer, J. (1979) *An Insight into Management Accounting* (2nd edn), Penguin

Chapter 11

Quantitative methods

Many management problems are described in numerical terms and call for numerical answers. We use numbers to measure our resources – human, financial, and material – and to judge our success. Every construction project involves monetary calculations and examples of these are to be found in this and earlier chapters, but mathematical techniques can also be brought to bear on problems that were previously tackled intuitively or by trial-and-error. These include such diverse matters as the determination of company strategy, the distribution of resources to competing activities, and the allocation of responsibilities to staff. The success of such developments has encouraged researchers to use numerical indices in dealing with problems of management that imply subjective judgement such as landscape quality. Furthermore, the advent of the computer and pocket calculator has stimulated the use of numerical analysis by removing much of the arithmetical tedium.

The general approach is to set up a 'model' – that is, some representation, usually on paper, that possesses certain properties of the object, system or organization in which we are interested. The model might be a graph, a network, a table of values, a mathematical formula, or a computer program. By investigating the behaviour of the model we can predict to some extent what will happen in practice, and this can help us in making decisions. However, no model can reproduce every feature of the original and the results obtained from models must be interpreted in the light of the data from which they are built and the approximations inherent in their construction.

In most instances the manager is dealing with future activities and a measure of uncertainty is inevitable. For this reason it is often necessary to apply probability theory and statistical techniques, and to regard the results of the analysis as 'average' or 'expected' values.

11.1 Cost models

Examples of cost modelling are to be found throughout this book. In Chapter 9, for instance, it is shown that the graph representing the accumulation of expenditure throughout the life of a construction project takes the form of an S-curve (Fig. 9.5). On the other hand, the relationships between current and future costs used in *discounted cash flow or present worth* analysis are more conveniently represented by mathematical formulae and tables of values (Ch. 9).

The construction and use of such models are best illustrated by numerical examples and the following problems are typical.

Problem 11.1. A contractor is considering the purchase of a van that is expected to cover 20,000 miles per annum. He examines the running costs of two vans in his existing fleet that perform similar duties but are of different types. He finds that in the last year van A covered 15,000 miles at a total cost of £6,120, the corresponding figures for B being 25,000 and £7,700. Can a decision be made on the basis of this information as to which of these types is likely to prove the cheaper?

In a more detailed analysis he divides the costs into two groups. The 'fixed' annual charges such as tax, insurance, depreciation and the replacement of components that wear out with age rather than mileage are estimated to be £3,120 for A and £4,200 for B. The remaining costs arise from those items – such as fuel, routine servicing, and tyre replacements – that are related to the distance covered. Which type of van is likely to prove the cheaper for the expected annual mileage of 20,000?

Solution: It is not possible to forecast which van will be cheaper for an annual mileage of 20,000 from the data given in the first paragraph. The gross annual cost for A (£6,120) is less than B (£7,700) but the average cost per mile is smaller for B (£7,700/25,000 = 30.8p as against 40.8p for A). We are not justified in applying these average values to other mileages because part of the total cost is attributed to tax, insurance, and other items that are independent of distances covered.

The second paragraph of the question suggests that the cost may be divided into two groups, the 'fixed' or 'standing' charges that are independent of how much the vehicles are used and those costs that are related to the distances covered. Assuming that the mileage-related costs are directly proportional to distance, a simple and familiar model is obtained. If a is the annual standing charge and b is the additional cost per mile, the total cost C for a year in which x miles are covered is given by

$$C = a + bx \tag{11.1}$$

Working in £ and using the figures for van A, $a = 3,120$ and $b = (6,120 - 3,120)/15,000 = 0.2$. For this van, therefore,

$$C = 3,120 + 0.2x$$

The corresponding result for van B is

$$C = 4,200 + 0.14x$$

Figure 11.1 presents these results in graphical form. They give straight lines which intersect at a point corresponding to 18,000 miles. For smaller annual

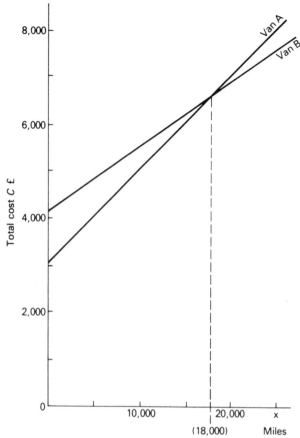

Fig. 11.1

mileages van A has the lower total cost but above this figure van B is the cheaper. With the assumptions made in this analysis and the data given in the question, van B has the lower cost if the annual mileage is 20,000. The limitations of this analysis should be borne in mind, however. The cost information for the vehicles relates to a single mileage in each case and the assumptions made in establishing the model should be assessed carefully. We shall return to these matters in 11.4.

It is instructive to consider the variation in average cost per mile. From equation [11.1] the average cost is seen to be

$$\frac{C}{x} = \frac{a}{x} + b \tag{11.2}$$

and Fig. 11.2 shows the variations for the two types of van. Each graph is a curve that approaches a limiting value or *asymptote* as the mileage increases. These two graphs also intersect at the point where $x = 18,000$.

The cost model represented by equations [11.1] and [11.2] has wide applications. In the case of industrial production, the quantity a represents the

257

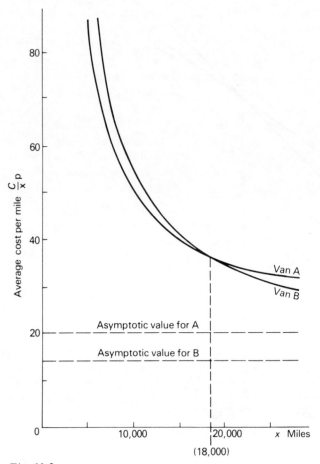

Fig. 11.2

overheads or fixed costs and *b* is the marginal cost for each unit produced. The total cost of producing *x* units is given by equation [11.1] and the average cost per unit by [11.2]. As before, the average unit cost decreases as *x* increases, an effect known as the *economy of scale*. However, there is a limit set by the asymptotic value *b*, the marginal cost, and no increase in the number of units can bring the average cost below this figure.

The same cost model applies to electricity, gas, and telephone charges. These are normally based on a standing charge per quarter to which is added a sum for each unit used.

Problem 11.2. In reviewing the operation of plant on a construction site it was found that, in one quarter, £2,000 was spent on preventive maintenance, and the total cost of breakdowns, including repairs and consequential losses, was £12,000. Advise on the scale of the maintenance programme, basing your decision on the assumption that the costs under these two heads are inversely proportional to one another.

Solution: There are many activities in which an increase in expenditure under one heading can lead to a cost reduction elsewhere. One example – health and safety – is analysed in Chapter 5, and another – stock control – is examined later in this chapter (11.5).

The exact relationship between the costs under the two heads is likely to vary from one case to another and the assumption suggested in the question is only one of many possibilities. It leads to a very simple model in which an increase in preventive cost by a given factor is accompanied by a reduction in breakdown cost by the same factor. Tabulating values and totalling costs, we have:

Factor	1	2	3	4	5	6
Preventive cost (£)	2,000	4,000	6,000	8,000	10,000	12,000
Breakdown cost (£)	12,000	6,000	4,000	3,000	2,400	2,000
Total cost (£)	14,000	10,000	10,000	11,000	12,000	14,000

If these results are plotted on a suitable base (e.g. the factor) it will be found that the minimum total cost is a little less than £10,000. It corresponds to a point at which the separate preventive and breakdown costs are equal – a result which can be shown by calculus to be universally true for this particular cost model. Furthermore, the product of the two separate costs is the same in all cases (24×10^6) and, at this minimum point, each is equal to the square root of this value. Thus, for minimum total cost:

$$\text{Preventive cost} = \sqrt{24 \times 10^6}$$
$$= £4,900$$

On the basis of the assumption suggested, the maintenance programme should be expanded from its present level of £2,000 per quarter to £4,900. Two points are worth noting. The minimum total cost is £9,800 but the variation in this figure is small (only 2 per cent) for all values of preventive cost in the range £4,000–£6,000. The incentive to achieve the minimum total cost will be greater if one person is responsible for expenditure under both headings.

Problem 11.3. What is the annual mortgage repayment on a building society loan of £22,000 at 12 per cent over 20 years under the usual reducing sum agreement if interest is added annually? How long will it take to discharge the mortgage if the interest rate is increased to (a) 13 per cent and (b) 14 per cent, the annual repayments being unaltered?

Solution: This is an example of *present worth* (or *value*) introduced in Chapter 9. From Table C.4 in Appendix C the present worth factor for unit sum per annum over 20 years at 12 per cent ($i = 0.12$) is found to be 7.469. Hence, for the loan of £22,000 we have:

$$\text{Annual repayment} = \frac{22,000}{7.469} = £2,946$$

The total repayments during the life of the mortgage are $20 \times 2,946 = £58,920$, a considerable increase on the sum initially borrowed. However, the rise in property values has outstripped such increases in recent decades to the benefit of the borrower. It should be noted that many building societies add interest half-yearly or quarterly and their figures will differ from those calculated with the factors given in Table C.4.

If the interest rate changes but the repayments are unaltered we look for the same present worth factor, 7.469, in a different column. For case (a), 13 per cent, interpolation of the table gives a repayment period of approximately 29 years. For case (b), 14 per cent, it is not possible to achieve a factor as high as 7.469 and the mortgage is never discharged. The interest added in the first year, 14 per cent of $£22,000 = £3,080$, is greater than the repayment and the debt grows, rather than diminishes, year by year.

Problem 11.4. An item of earth-moving equipment has a capital cost of £50,000 and the following table shows the estimated maintenance costs and depreciation for the first eight years of its life:

Year	1	2	3	4	5	6	7	8
Maintenance cost (£)	1,500	2,000	3,000	4,000	5,000	8,000	11,000	15,000
Depreciation (£)	8,000	8,000	7,000	6,000	6,000	5,000	4,000	3,000

If there is expected to be a permanent need for this item and the cost of capital is 15 per cent per annum, when should it be replaced?

Solution: In this example present worth techniques are used to effect a comparison between the costs for various life periods. It is convenient to set out the calculations in a table, as shown in Table 11.1, (where PW = present worth and all cash values are in £).

The present worth factors for single payments, shown in column ②, are taken from Appendix C, Table C.2. Column ③ lists the initial capital expenditure and maintenance costs for each year. The present worth of these items, obtained as the product of columns ② and ③, is shown in column ④. Column ⑤ gives the cumulative total of the present worth of the outgoings obtained by summing the values in column ④ up to the required year in each case.

The resale values shown in column ⑥ are obtained by deducting the depreciation amounts from the initial capital cost and their present worth

Table 11.1

① Year	② PW factor for single payment $i = 0.15$	③ Cash payments	④ PW of cash payments ② × ③	⑤ Cumulative total of PW of payments	⑥ Resale value	⑦ PW of resale value ② × ⑥	⑧ Net PW of life costs ⑤ − ⑦
0	1.0000	50,000	50,000	50,000	50,000	50,000	—
1	0.8696	1,500	1,304	51,304	42,000	36,523	14,781
2	0.7561	2,000	1,512	52,816	34,000	25,707	27,109
3	0.6575	3,000	1,973	54,789	27,000	17,753	37,036
4	0.5718	4,000	2,287	57,076	21,000	12,008	45,068
5	0.4972	5,000	2,486	59,562	15,000	7,458	52,104
6	0.4323	8,000	3,458	63,020	10,000	4,323	58,697
7	0.3759	11,000	4,135	67,155	6,000	2,255	64,900
8	0.3269	15,000	4,904	72,059	3,000	981	71,078

Table 11.2

⑨ Year	⑩ PW factor for equal annual payments	⑪ Net PW of life costs	⑫ Annual sum required in perpetuity ⑪ ÷ ⑩
0	—	—	—
1	0.870	14,781	16,990
2	1.626	27,109	16,672
3	2.283	37,036	16,223
4	2.855	45,068	15,786
5	3.352	52,104	15,544
6	3.784	58,697	15,511
7	4.160	64,900	15,601
8	4.487	71,078	15,841

amounts are shown in column ⑦ as the products of the corresponding figures in columns ② and ⑥. Finally in Table 11.1 the present worth of the net life costs for the various periods are shown in column ⑧, being the differences between the values in columns ⑤ and ⑦.

The figures in column ⑧ are not directly comparable because they apply to different life periods. For example it is not obvious whether the expenditure of £37,036 every three years is preferable to, say, the expenditure of £64,900 every seven. However, if we calculate the equal annual payments that would produce these amounts, we have the annual sums that would cover the costs in perpetuity. The calculations are shown in Table 11.2.

The values in column ⑩ are taken from the table on pages 332 – 3 and those in column ⑪ are reproduced from column ⑧. Finally, in column ⑫ we have the annual sums required to cover the costs of this item for the various life periods.

The minimum value corresponds to replacement after six years, but the figure for five years is only slightly higher. The item should therefore be replaced every five or six years.

11.2 Probability

Many of the problems facing management are fraught with uncertainties. Success cannot be guaranteed and may well depend upon matters outside our control such as the weather, the state of the economy, and the decisions taken by our competitors. In these circumstances we have to speak of probabilities rather than certainties.

Mathematicians denote probability by p and measure it on a scale of 0 to 1, the higher values representing the greater probabilities. Thus, $p = 1$ represents absolute certainty and $p = 0$ corresponds to impossibility. Where two or more different outcomes are possible the probability of each may be regarded as the proportion of the occasions on which it occurs *in the long run*. Thus, the probability of a tossed coin coming down heads is $p = 0.5$ and the probability of drawing the ace of diamonds from a pack of cards is $p = \frac{1}{52} = 0.0192$.

We often need to combine the probability values of two or more outcomes and we do this with the aid of two rules. If A and B are alternative outcomes in a given case, the probability of one or the other occurring is the sum of their separate probabilities. This is known as the *addition rule* and may be stated thus:

If A and B are mutually exclusive,

$$p(A \text{ or } B) = p(A) + p(B)$$

A particular application of this rule is that the sum of the probabilities of all the possible outcomes in a given case is 1.

The other rule concerns different cases or events. The probability of outcome A in one case and outcome B in another both occurring is the product of their separate probabilities. This is known as the *multiplication rule* and may be stated thus:

If A and B are independent,

$$p(A \text{ and } B) = p(A) \times p(B)$$

Returning to the example of the pack of cards, the probability of drawing either the ace of diamonds or the queen of hearts is obtained by the addition rule since each excludes the other. The result is

$$p = \frac{1}{52} + \frac{1}{52} = \frac{1}{26} = 0.0385$$

Suppose, however, we have two packs. The probability of drawing the ace of diamonds from the first and the queen of hearts from the second is given by the multiplication rule since the two events are independent. The result is

$$p = \tfrac{1}{52} \times \tfrac{1}{52} = 0.000370$$

Some examples involving the concept of probability are to be found in Chapter 10; other applications are illustrated by the following problems.

Problem 11.5. Observations over 100 days on the use of dumper trucks on a construction site gave the following pattern of demand:

Number of dumper trucks required	0	1	2	3
Number of days	23	36	27	14

It is expected that this pattern of demand will continue. What is the average cost if the trucks are hired by the day when required at an all-in cost of £25 per day? The trucks are also available on long-term leasing at a basic charge of £5 per day with an additional cost of £10 for each day on which they are used. Will it pay to use long-term leasing to meet part of the demand and, if so, how many trucks should be leased?

Solution: From the table given in the question the probability of requiring none, one, two, or three trucks on a particular day are $p = 0.23, 0.36, 0.27$, and 0.14, respectively, and these four values add up to 1. Combining these values with the corresponding costs, we have:
Average daily cost = $0.23 \times £0 + 0.36 \times £25 + 0.27 \times £50 + 0.14 \times £75 = £33.00$
If one truck is leased the costs on days when no trucks, one, two, and three trucks are required are, respectively, £5, £15, £40, and £65. The calculation becomes:
Average daily cost = $0.23 \times £5 + 0.36 \times £15 + 0.27 \times £40 + 0.14 \times £65 = £26.45$
It will be found that with two trucks leased the result is £25.30 and with three it becomes £28.20. Leasing therefore pays, and two trucks should be leased.

Problem 11.6. A company is preparing its strategy for the next five years. It is estimated that there is a 0.3 probability of high growth in the construction market during this period, a 0.5 probability of low growth, and a 0.2 probability of zero growth. Three courses of action are considered:

(a) Expansion now. By recruiting staff immediately and developing regional offices the company would be in a strong position if growth were high but this policy would reduce profitability in the event of zero growth.
(b) No expansion. This would put the company at a disadvantage should the market grow but would enable it to operate economically if the size of the market were static.
(c) Reappraisal after two years. Under conditions of high growth this policy would lead to lower profits than (a) but it would enable the company to keep its options open and to choose an appropriate level of expansion for the remaining years.

The estimated outcomes, in terms of percentage profitability, are as follows:

	High growth	Low growth	Zero growth
Expansion now	20	13	0
No expansion	10	9	8
Reappraisal after two years	16	14	8

Analyse the problem and recommend a course of action.

Solution: A convenient model for this problem is the 'decision tree' introduced in the previous chapter. Figure 11.3 gives the details, with decision points indicated by $\boxed{A}$, $\boxed{B}$, $\boxed{C}$, and $\boxed{D}$, and chance points by circles. At each of the decision points $\boxed{B}$, $\boxed{C}$, and $\boxed{D}$ there is a choice of no expansion or an expansion appropriate to the state of the market.

In the case of zero growth $\boxed{D}$, the reappraisal merely confirms the policy of no expansion, but at $\boxed{B}$ and $\boxed{C}$ the expansion choices are preferred. With these choices the decision tree is reduced to the form of Fig. 11.4.

The 'average' profitability corresponding to initial decision (a) is:

$$0.3 \times 20 + 0.5 \times 13 + 0.2 \times 0 = 12.5\%$$

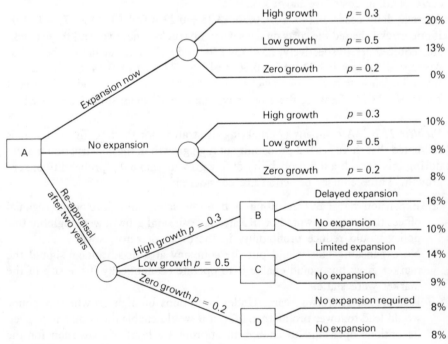

Fig. 11.3

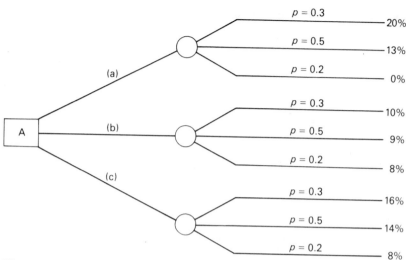

Fig. 11.4

The corresponding results for (b) and (c) are 9.1 and 13.4 per cent, respectively. The highest of the three values is given by (c) and the initial decision should therefore be to re-appraise the policy after two years.

In this problem the probability figures have been used to arrive at an average profitability even though this particular set of circumstances will be faced only once. The result is called the 'expected' value but this is, in one sense, a misnomer; with the information given in the question it is a value that will certainly not occur.

Problem 11.7.   A safety protection system comprises three units – detector, microprocessor, and shutdown valve – linked in series as shown in Fig. 11.5. The system will only operate correctly if all three units are working satisfactorily. In a given period the probabilities of failure of these units are 0.08, 0.06, and 0.10, respectively. What is the probability that the system will fail during this period?
    The reliability is to be improved by duplicating the detector with an equally reliable unit. What will the probability of system failure now become?

Solution: If success and failure are denoted by s and f, respectively, then, for each of the units or the complete system,

$$p(s) + p(f) = 1$$

Fig. 11.5

265

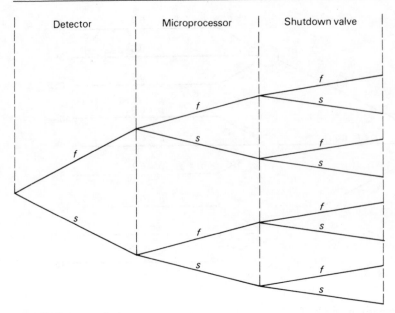

Fig. 11.6

Using this result, the success probabilities of the individual units are $p(s) = 0.92$, 0.94, and 0.90. A tree diagram for the system, Fig. 11.6, shows that there are eight possible outcomes. Seven of these contain one or more failures and only one, shown at the bottom, constitutes success of the system. The multiplication rule can be applied to this path and thus, for the system,

$$p(s) = 0.92 \times 0.94 \times 0.90 = 0.778$$

Hence

$$p(f) = 1 - 0.778 = 0.222$$

Figure 11.7 shows the modified system with the detector duplicated. Failure at the detector stage will only occur if both units fail. Hence, by the use of the multiplication rule, probability of failure of both detector units is

$$p(f) = 0.08 \times 0.08 = 0.0064$$

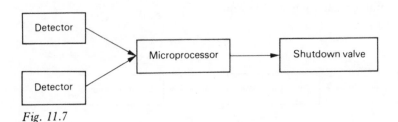

Fig. 11.7

266

and the probability of success of at least one detector unit is

$p(s) = 1 - 0.0064 = 0.9936$

Probability of success of whole system is now

$p(s) = 0.9936 \times 0.94 \times 0.90 = 0.841$

and the corresponding probability of overall failure is

$p(f) = 1 - 0.841 = 0.159$

This represents a marked improvement in reliability.

11.3 Some statistical ideas

Problem 11.5 gave the results of 100 observations on the number of dumper trucks required on a construction site. Figure 11.8 presents a convenient way of displaying this information and a diagram of this kind is called a *histogram*. The number of days on which a given number of trucks was required is called the *frequency* and is represented by the height of the corresponding column. If the widths of the columns are equal, these frequencies are proportional to the areas of the columns.

In this example there are only four possibilities for the number of trucks required on a given day and there are distinct 'steps' in the histogram. If there were many it might approximate to a continuous curve of the type shown in Fig. 11.9. It is called *frequency distribution* curve. The height of this curve at a given point represents the relative frequency at which the corresponding of x (plotted horizontally) occurs.

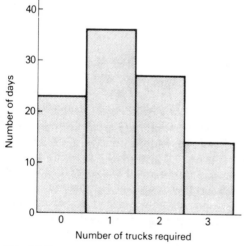

Fig. 11.8

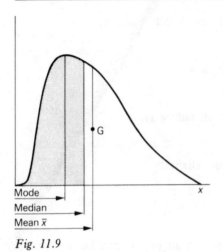

Fig. 11.9

For many purposes it is convenient to have some central value of x as a point of reference but the value we obtain depends, in general, upon the definition used. Three possibilities are illustrated in Fig. 11.9.

The *mode* or *modal value* is the value of x that occurs most frequently and it corresponds to the highest point on the curve. The *median* is the value that would come exactly half way if all the observations were listed in order of size. Thus, half of the observations are of values greater than the median. Since the area under the graph represents the frequency of the observations, the median occurs at that value of x whose ordinate divides the area in half.

The *mean*, denoted by $\bar{x}$, is the average of all the observed values of x, i.e. the sum of all the observations divided by the number of observations n. In mathematical notation $\bar{x} = \Sigma x/n$. Strictly speaking it should be called the *arithmetic* mean to distinguish it from the *geometric* and *harmonic* means. Its ordinate passes through the point G, which corresponds to the centre of gravity of a uniform sheet cut to the shape of the curve.

The curve of Fig. 11.9 is unsymmetrical and is described as a *skew* distribution. If the distribution is symmetrical the mode, median, and mean coincide. Two symmetrical distributions are shown in Fig. 11.10. There are similarities of shape between these two curves but they differ in position and 'proportions', A being more slender. Comparisons between such curves are more easily made if they are shifted horizontally so that they are located on the same axis of symmetry. This is achieved by plotting them $x - \bar{x}$ instead of x as shown in Fig. 11.11. The vertical axis through the origin is now the axis of symmetry for both distributions. The shapes indicate that A has more observations that are close to the mean than B, and it is useful to have numerical measure of this dispersion. The most important such measure is called the *standard deviation* denoted by s or σ (sigma), and in mathematical terminology it is the *root-mean-square deviation*. This means that the $x - \bar{x}$ values are squared, their squares are averaged, and

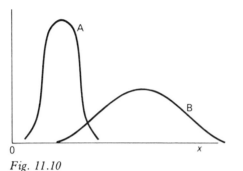

Fig. 11.10

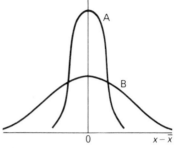

Fig. 11.11

the square root of this average is taken. In symbols,

$$s = \sqrt{\frac{\Sigma(x - \bar{x})^2}{n}}$$

Where n is the number of observations.

It is shown in textbooks on statistics that this formula underestimates the standard deviation if it is applied to a small sample and that a better estimate is obtained by using the expression

$$\sqrt{\frac{\Sigma(x - \bar{x})^2}{n - 1}}$$

For our purposes the difference between the results produced by these formulae will be negligible. Pocket calculators with statistical functions are able to compute directly the mean $\bar{x}$ and standard deviation s of a set of values and, in the examples that follow, the details of the calculations will be omitted.

It would be very time-consuming to treat each distribution in isolation and we have already seen how the two curves of Fig. 11.10 can be brought to the same axis of symmetry (Fig. 11.11) by changing the variable x to $x - \bar{x}$. In order to relate distributions having different amounts of dispersion or scatter we can express the difference between an observed value x and the mean $\bar{x}$ as a proportion of the standard deviation s. This leads to a new variable z, defined as

$$z = \frac{x - \bar{x}}{s}$$

The distribution curves obtained by applying this result to different sets of observations will not necessarily coincide, but there is a particular curve that is found to be a good approximation in many cases. It is known as the *normal* or *Gaussian distribution* and is defined by a mathematical formula involving the exponential function. Its general shape is indicated by Fig. 11.12 and it should be noted that the curve continues indefinitely in both directions.

The equation for this curve is such that the total area under it, from $-\infty$ to $+\infty$, is equal to 1. Furthermore, it is equivalent to a histogram for a quantity which is

269

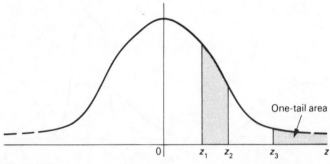

Fig. 11.12

varying continuously instead of in steps. As a consequence, the area under the curve between two values such as z_1 and z_2 represents the frequency with which values of z fall within this range. Since the total area is 1, the area between z_1 and z_2 is the proportion of all the observations that fall within this range. It therefore gives the *probability* of an observation being between z_1 and z_2.

A quantity of considerable importance is the one-tail area. This is the area under the curve between a value such as z_3 and infinity. It equals the probability that an observed value is greater than z_3. A table of one-tail areas for the normal curve is given in Appendix D. It will be seen that the one-tail areas of $z = 1$ and $z = 2$ are 0.1587 and 0.02275, respectively. This means that for a normally distributed set of values, just under 16 per cent are more than one standard deviation above the mean. For two standard deviations it is just over 2 per cent.

Problem 11.8. The lighting in a company's new office block requires 500 fluorescent tubes. These have an average life of 3,000 hours with a standard deviation of 220 hours. The tubes are switched on for 40 hours per week. Assuming that tube life is normally distributed, how soon should the company expect to start replacing tubes? Within what period are the first 50 replacements likely? How many tubes are likely to require replacement within 80 weeks?

Solution: Since the normal curve extends to infinity in both directions it would appear to indicate that any tube life is possible, including negative values! However, a life of zero hours would correspond to a value about 14 standard deviations below the mean, and an examination of the table in Appendix D will show that this theoretical objection to the use of the normal distribution is of no consequence in the present case.

The first failure in a set of 500 tubes corresponds to a probability of $p = 1/500 = 0.002$. From the table of one-tail areas (or by statistical calculator) this corresponds to a z-value of 2.878. Thus,

$$\frac{x - \bar{x}}{s} = 2.878$$

and $\quad x - \bar{x} = 2.878 \times 220 = 633$ hours

Since the normal curve is symmetrical, this result applies above and below the mean. Hence, the tube life at which the first failure is expected to occur is 633 hours below the mean, i.e. 2,367 hours, and this corresponds to $2,367/40 = 59$ weeks approximately.

For 50 failures the corresponding one-tail area is $50/500 = 0.1$, and this leads to z-value of 1.282. The corresponding period is

$$3,000 - 1.282 \times 220 = 2,718 \text{ hours or } 68 \text{ weeks}$$

A period of 80 weeks or 3,200 hours is above the mean tube life of 3,000 hours and

$$z = \frac{x - \bar{x}}{s} = \frac{3,200 - 3,000}{220} = 0.909$$

From Appendix D, the corresponding one-tail area is 0.1817, and this is the probability of a tube having a life above the stated value. Hence, the number of tubes that are expected to exceed this life are $0.1817 \times 500 = 91$ and the number expected to fail within this period is $500 - 91 = 409$.

11.4 Linear regression

The importance of the straight-line graph as a model of costs was explained in 11.2, and equation [11.1] showed the corresponding relationship between cost C and number of units x in algebraic terms. The constants a and b in this equation define the graph completely, a being the intercept on the vertical axis and b the slope or gradient of the line. Establishing the values of a and b is therefore the key step in setting up a model of this kind.

Suppose a set of such values for C and x are plotted as in Fig. 11.13. A straight line can be drawn 'by eye' to fit the data and the values of the constants a and b determined by measurement of the graph. A statistical method for finding the straight line that best fits the set of points is known as *linear regression*. Details can be found in the standard textbooks of statistics but pocket calculators with statistical functions are programmed to determined the intercept and slope values directly from the data.

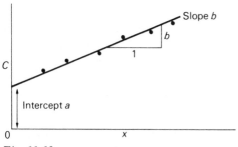

Fig. 11.13

271

Problem 11.9. A transport manager keeps records over a one-year period for a fleet of six vans of a particular type. He finds that the total cost and distance covered for the vans are as follows:

Van	1	2	3	4	5	6
Total cost (£) C	5,680	6,120	5,390	7,070	7,250	6,500
Distance covered (miles) x	13,400	15,000	10,900	19,500	21,100	16,400

Determine the annual 'fixed' or 'standing' charge and marginal cost per mile to be expected for this type of van and calculate the expected total cost for an annual mileage of 25,000.

Solution: The reader is advised, as a first step, to plot the values (C vertically and x horizontally), draw a straight-line graph by eye, and find the intercept and slope by measurement. Using the linear regression key on a pocket calculator with statistical functions the intercept and slope are found to be 3,212 and 0.195, respectively. Hence, the expected annual fixed or standing charge is £3,212 and the marginal cost per mile is £0.195 or 19.5 pence. The cost equation becomes

$$C = 3,212 + 0.195x$$

and this can be used to estimate the costs for other mileages. In particular, the expected total annual cost for 25,000 miles will be

$$C = 3,212 + 0.195 \times 25,000$$
$$= £8,087$$

This analysis should be compared with that used in the solution to Problem 11.1. Note that the last part of the present example requires the application of the cost equation to a value of x outside the range of the set of observed values. This is an example of *extrapolation*, a process that should be regarded with caution. *Interpolation*, the estimating of the results within the original range of values, may be carried out with more confidence.

11.5 Stock control

Every organization needs to maintain stocks of materials if it is to operate without interruption, and the principles of stock control are equally applicable to the hundreds of components needed on a construction site, the stationery supplies used in an office, and the food stored in a larder. Stocks may be classified under three headings, as follows:

active – the stock required to meet the expected demand for a given item;
buffer – the additional stock needed to cope with fluctuations in demand;
strategic – those stocks that are held in anticipation of shortages or price rises.

The time interval between taking a decision to place an order and having the goods available for use is known as *lead time*. It includes the time taken to prepare the order, delays in despatch, and the time for delivery, and the checking of goods on arrival. If the lead time is underestimated, or the buffer stocks prove inadequate, an item may become out-of-stock, a condition usually referred to as *stockout*. Stock control is usually organized in one of two ways. Under the *fixed order quantity* system the size of the order is always the same but the interval between successive orders is varied to meet demand. The alternative is the *fixed interval* system under which orders are placed at regular intervals but the size varies according to demand.

An important parameter in stock control analysis is the *batch size* or *order quantity*. If this is very large, there will be heavy costs associated with storage, insurance, and the interest on capital. On the other hand, small batches mean frequent orders and this can lead to high costs in the buying department. The batch size that minimizes the total cost is known as the *economic batch size* or *economic order quantity*.

A simple theory can be developed from the following assumptions:

(a) the demand is uniform;
(b) the supplier is completely reliable;
(c) the unit cost of the item is constant (i.e. no discounts for specified quantities);
(d) there is sufficient storage capacity;
(e) there is sufficient ordering capacity.

The first assumption leads to a variation in stock level of the kind shown in Fig. 11.14. The level falls steadily until stocks are exhausted. A new batch is then received from the supplier and the process is repeated.

Let x = batch size;
Q = quantity used per annum (or month or week);
p = unit price of the item;
i = the cost per annum (month or week) of holding the stock including warehousing, insurance, and interest on capital as a proportion of the average value of the stocks held;
S = cost of placing each order.

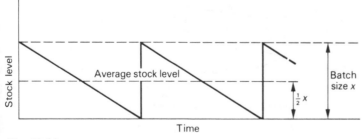

Fig. 11.14

273

From the graph it can be seen that the average stock level is $\frac{1}{2}x$ and the cost of holding stock is therefore $\frac{1}{2}xpi$ per annum (month or week). The number of orders placed during the period is Q/x and the corresponding cost is QS/x. The total cost (holding plus ordering) is therefore given by:

$$C = \tfrac{1}{2}xpi + \frac{QS}{x} \qquad [11.3]$$

Differentiating to find the minimum total cost, we have

$$\frac{dC}{dx} = \tfrac{1}{2}pi - \frac{QS}{x^2} = 0$$

from which

$$x = \sqrt{\frac{2QS}{pi}} \qquad [11.4]$$

The positive root corresponds to a minimum and this value of x gives the economic batch size. There is a close similarity between equation [11.3] and the cost model arising in Problem 11.2. The two terms of equation [11.3] are inversely proportional to one another and the minimum value of total cost C occurs when they are equal; this leads again to the result arrived at in equation [11.4]. The variation of the separate and total costs with batch size is shown in Fig. 11.15

The following problems illustrate the principles discussed in this section.

Problem 11.10. A stationery store supplies an office in which there is a steady demand for paper at the rate of 20 reams per week. It is estimated that the cost of processing each order is £4.80 and the cost of holding the paper in stock is 3 pence

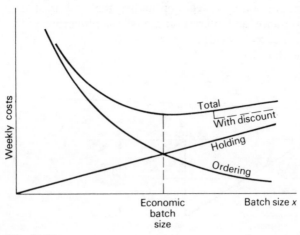

Fig. 11.15

per ream per week. What is the economic batch size for orders and the minimum weekly cost of stocking this item? What would the results be if four such offices were served by the same store?

Solution: Table 11.3 covers a range of intervals between orders and shows the corresponding average weekly cost for each. Note that the average ordering cost decreases as the interval increases since fewer orders are required.

Table 11.3

Order interval (weeks)	Batch size (reams)	Average stock level (reams)	Average weekly costs (£)		
			holding	ordering	total
1	20	10	0.30	4.80	5.10
2	40	20	0.60	2.40	3.00
3	60	30	0.90	1.60	2.50
4	80	40	1.20	1.20	2.40
5	100	50	1.50	0.96	2.46
6	120	60	1.80	0.80	2.60

It is seen that the economic batch size is 80 and the minimum weekly cost is £2.40. The same result can be obtained from equations [11.3] and [11.4], by noting that the product pi is given by the figure £0.03 per week.

The second part of the problem can be solved by a revised tabulation. However, as equation [11.4] shows, the economic batch size is proportional to the square root of the quantity used, Q. Hence with a fourfold increase in Q the economic batch size x is increased by the factor $\sqrt{4}$, i.e. 2. Hence, the economic batch size is now 160, the corresponding interval between orders is two weeks, and the average weekly stock cost is £4.80.

On this basis it therefore pays to combine smaller stores into bigger ones.

Problem 11.11. Suppose, in the first part of the previous problem the supplier offers discounts of 1 per cent on orders of 200 reams and 5 per cent on orders of 400 reams on the basic price of £4 per ream. What should be the ordering policy?

Solution: As the batch size increases beyond the economic quantity there is a rise in the stockholding cost as indicated by the upper curve of Fig. 11.15. If a discount is offered at some larger batch size, this should be deducted from the stockholding cost as shown by the broken curve of the diagram.

In the present case the weekly cost of the paper used (20 reams) is $20 \times £4 = £80$. Discounts of 1 per cent and 5 per cent therefore represent weekly savings of £0.80 and £4.00, respectively. By extending Table 11.3 we have the results shown in Table 11.4.

These results show that there is no advantage in changing the batch size to 200 but a small saving results with a batch size of 400.

Table 11.4

Order interval (weeks)	Batch size (reams)	Average stock level (reams)	Average weekly cost (£)			
			holding	ordering	discount	total
4	80	40	1.20	1.20	–	2.40
10	200	100	3.00	0.48	0.80	2.68
20	400	200	6.00	0.24	4.00	2.24

Problem 11.12. On a construction site the number of 50 kg bags of cement used per week is recorded over a period of 50 weeks and the following results obtained:

Weekly demand	53	54	55	56	57	58	59	60	61	62	63	64	65
Number of occurrences	1	2	3	5	6	8	7	6	5	3	2	1	1

Determine the mean demand and, assuming weekly deliveries and a normal distribution of demand, the necessary buffer stocks if the stockout risk is not to exceed 1 in 100.

Solution: Using the results of 11.3, the mean demand is

$$\bar{x} = \frac{\Sigma x}{n} = \frac{2{,}931}{50} = 58.6$$

and the standard deviation is:

$$s = \sqrt{\frac{\Sigma(x - \bar{x})^2}{n - 1}} = 2.67$$

The stockout risk of 1 in 100 represents a stockout probability of $p = 1/100 = 0.01$ and, from the table of one-tail areas in Appendix D, the corresponding values of z is 2.326. Hence, the buffer stock $(x - \bar{x})$ is given by $x - \bar{x} = zs = 2.326 \times 2.67 = 6.21$ (say 7)

Adding the buffer stock result to the mean demand suggests that the stock level should be set at $58.6 + 6.2 = 65$ bags at the time of each delivery.

Problem 11.13. In a joinery shop a particular type of window frame is made in batches. The annual demand for this item is 600 at a unit cost of £30 and the cost of changeover is £135 per batch. The cost of holding stock is 24 per cent per annum of the average value of the stocks held.

  Calculate the economic manufacturing batch size and the corresponding total annual cost of changeover and stockholding if the production rate is (a) very large compared with the rate of demand, and (b) three times the rate of demand.

Solution: If each batch is produced very rapidly the stock level variation is similar to that shown in Fig. 11.14. As a consequence, the batch size that minimizes

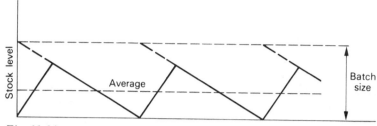

Fig. 11.16

cost can be found by the methods used in Problem 11.11. The ordering cost is replaced by the changeover cost associated with the interruption and rearrangement of jigs that arise each time a new batch is made. In the notation of equation [11.4], and working in £, $S = 135$, $p = 30$, $Q = 600$, and $i = 0.24$. The economic batch size is therefore

$$x = \sqrt{\frac{2QS}{pi}} = \sqrt{\frac{2 \times 600 \times 135}{30 \times 0.24}} = 150$$

This corresponds to four batches a year and an average stock level of 75. Hence,

Annual cost $= 4 \times £135 + 75 \times £30 \times 0.24$
$= £1,080$

In case (b) the stock level variation is modified as shown in Fig. 11.16. The peak level of stock is now lower than the batch size because part of the batch is sold during the production period. In the present example this level, and hence the associated holding costs, are two-thirds of the values corresponding to very rapid production. The required result can therefore be obtained by reducing the denominator of the fraction in the equation [11.4] in the same proportion. Hence, the economic batch size is

$$x = \sqrt{\frac{2 \times 600 \times 135}{30 \times 0.24 \times (2/3)}} = 184$$

This does not lead to a whole number of batches per year but, on average, there will be $600/184 = 3.26$. The peak stock level will be $\frac{2}{3} \times 184 = 122$ and the average stock level 61. Using these figures,

Annual cost $= 3.26 \times £135 + 61 \times £30 \times 0.24$
$= £880$

Summary

This chapter has surveyed a number of models and numerical techniques that are used in the analysis of management problems – notably those associated with costs. It must be remembered that each model is an idealization and the results it

277

produces are, at best, approximations. However detailed the analysis and however powerful the computing techniques, it is impossible to compensate for imperfections in the data. Furthermore, the results in some cases are but average or 'expected' values.

Three cost models are of particular importance. The first of these applies to systems or operations in which the total cost may be divided into two parts, one of which is fixed and the other is proportional to the number of units produced or received. Under these conditions the average cost per unit decreases as the number of units increases.

In the second type, part of the cost is proportional to the number of units and the rest is inversely proportional to that number. For the model the minimum total cost corresponds to the number of units for which the two parts of the cost are equal. Stock control and batch production provide examples of this particular model.

The third model is concerned with the present equivalent of future expenditure or income, taking interest payments into account. This technique of present worth or discounted cash flow is used in making decisions on the choice of competing systems and the replacement of plant.

Questions (and answers)

1. A transport manager estimates that the cost of running a particular lorry owned by his company is £3,000 per annum plus 30p per mile. He is offered a similar lorry on contract hire at £8,000 per annum, which includes maintenance, replacements, tax, and insurance, the only additional cost being diesel fuel at 9p per mile.

   What are the total annual costs for annual mileages of (a) 20,000, (b) 30,000 in the two cases? For what circumstances is the hired vehicle cheaper?
   Answer: (a) £9,000 and £9,800 and (b) £12,000 and £10,700. Hiring is cheaper for mileages above about 23,800.

2. A manufacturer of architectural ironmongery finds that the sales per week s of a particular item varies with the selling price £p as shown in the following table:

p	4	6	8	10	12	14	16	18
s	115	95	79	63	50	37	25	15

   Draw a graph of weekly revenue, plotted vertically, against sales. Estimate the maximum weekly revenue and the level at which the price should be set to achieve it.

   If the production cost is £3 per item, plus a fixed overhead charge of £300 per week, for what range of sales is the operation profitable? What is the maximum profit achievable under these conditions and what are the corresponding sales per week?
   Answer: £640 approximately; 9. From 22 to 93. £153 approximately; 54.

3. Use the tables in Appendix C to find the present worth of £80,000 in 10 years' time if interest is added

   (a) annually at 16 per cent
   (b) half-yearly at 8 per cent
   (c) quarterly at 4 per cent.

   Answer: (a) £18,136 (b) £17,160 (c) £16,664

4. What is the annual repayment on a 20-year building society mortgage of £24,000 if interest, added annually, is at 14 per cent? Assuming no change in the interest rate, what is the outstanding debt after (a) 10 years, (b) 15 years? If, at the outset, the interest rate is increased to 15 per cent and the repayments are unchanged, how long will it take to discharge the debt?
   Answer: £3,624. (a) £18,900; (b) £12,440. Approximately 36 years.

5. Two types of boiler are under consideration for a factory heating installation. The system is likely to be replaced in eight years' time. Type A has a capital cost of £25,000 and an estimated fuel cost of £1,000 per annum. For B the figures are £22,000 and £1,100, respectively.
   Depreciation for both types is 25 per cent per annum of the value at the beginning of the year. The maintenance costs for A and B in the first year are estimated to be £600 and £800, respectively, both figures rising at the rate of 10 per cent per annum thereafter. (Assume that the annual maintenance charge is payable at the end of each year.)
   Using this information and the present worth (or value) criterion, which type should be selected? Take interest at 15 per cent per annum.
   Answer: Type B.

6. A contractor runs a fleet of lorries costing £40,000 each when new. His records show that the annual depreciation on each vehicle amounts to 25 per cent of its value at the beginning of the year. He also observes that repairs and maintenance amount to £1,250 in the first year of its life, increasing annually by 40 per cent thereafter. The cost of capital is 15 per cent. At what intervals should the lorries be replaced if a permanent need is envisaged for vehicles of this type. Consider periods up to 10 years.
   Answer: 7 years.

7. A civil engineering contractor is reviewing the next five years of his activities and needs to make a decision about earthmoving equipment. He considers three possible courses of action:

   (a) purchasing a large fleet at a capital cost of £800,000;
   (b) purchasing a small fleet at a cost of £250,000;
   (c) relying on hired equipment.

   He estimates that there is a 0.6 probability of obtaining enough work to fully use the large fleet. This level of activity would show an annual return of £400,000 if he possessed the large fleet but, because of hire charges, the net return would be reduced to £200,000 if he possessed the small fleet, and £80,000 if he relied entirely on hired equipment.

On the other hand, there is a 0.4 probability that the level of work will be sufficient only for a small fleet and that this would produce an annual return of £120,000 if he possessed the equipment but only £50,000 if he had to hire. He could sell excess equipment after two years at 60 per cent of its initial cost.

The scrap value of equipment after five years is 20 per cent of the initial cost. Take the cost of capital as 15 per cent annum . On the basis of these data, what should his decision be?

Answer: Purchase small fleet.

8. (a) A builders' merchant finds that there is a steady demand at the rate of 5,000 per annum for a certain item which costs £0.80. The cost of each order is £4 and the stockholding cost is 20 per cent per annum of the value of the stocks held.

Calculate the economic ordering batch size and the corresponding annual cost of stocking this item.

(b) For another item, the demand is variable with a mean demand of 250 per week. It is found that, on average, the weekly demand is between 220 and 280 for four weeks out of five. Assuming that the demand is normally distributed and the stock is replenished weekly, find the buffer stock required to give stockout risk of 0.02, i.e. once in 50 deliveries.

Answer: (a) 500, £80; (b) 48.

9. On a housing development the demand for bricks (in thousands) was recorded over a period of 100 weeks and the following results being obtained:

Weekly demand	40–50	50–60	60–70	70–80	80–90	90–100	100–110	110–120
Number of weeks	2	8	15	23	27	14	6	5

Determine the average weekly demand and the necessary buffer stocks if the stockout risk is not to exceed 1 in 100. Assume weekly deliveries, zero lead time, and a normally distributed demand.

Answer: 80,600; 37,000.

Bibliography

Battersby, A (1970) *A Guide to Stock Control*, Pitman
Levin, R. I. (1987) *Statistics for Management* (4th edn) Prentice-Hall
Mole, R. H. (1985) *Basic Investment Appraisal*, Butterworth
Moroney, M. J. (1953) *Facts from Figures*, Pelican
Pilcher, R. (1973) *Appraisal and Control of Project Costs*, McGraw-Hill

Chapter 12

Operational research

Operational research has its origins in World War II when the methods of science and mathematics were applied to problems of organization and management associated with military operations. The subject has since developed rapidly and is now concerned with a wide range of problems facing managers in industry, business, and government. In particular it deals with resources – manpower, machines, materials, and money – and how they can be used to best effect. As stated in the definition adopted by the Operational Research Society (UK):

> The distinctive approach is to develop a scientific model of the system incorporating measurements of factors, such as chance and risk, with which to predict and compare the outcomes of alternative strategies or controls.

There are a number of characteristics common to many operational research problems:

(a) they are described and analysed in numerical terms;
(b) there are constraints such as limitations of resources;
(c) the objectives are expressed as optimisations;
(d) they involve uncertainties.

A solution that satisfies the constraints is termed *feasible* and there may be several or many feasible solutions to a particular problem. The aim is to determine the one that is 'best' by whatever criterion is adopted: it can be maximum production, or earliest completion, or least cost, or the optimum value of some other measure.

From its inception operational research has made use of existing mathematical techniques, particularly from the field of statistics, and the topics covered in the previous chapter might be classified as parts of the subject. On the other hand, some of the problems encountered over the years by operational researchers could not be solved by existing techniques and new methods of analysis, such as *linear programming*, have been developed as a result. This process has gained such momentum that the theory of the subject has grown quickly and become highly mathematical. However, the present chapter is an introduction to operational research and concentrates on some of its applications using elementary mathematics only.

12.1 Network analysis

In most construction contracts time is important and delays can be costly. It is essential, therefore, to achieve the earliest possible completion and various models are used to plan and control the progress of complex projects. The best-known of these is the *bar chart* (Fig. 12.1) whose base is a time-scale of days or weeks; alternatively, it can be labelled in calender form. Each job that contributes to the total project is shown as a horizontal bar whose length is proportional to its estimated duration and whose position indicates the period within which it is due to take place. What is less obvious from this diagram is the sequence in which jobs follow one another, but this shortcoming can be overcome by the use of a *network* or *arrow diagram* (Fig. 12.2), in which each job, or *activity* as it is called, is represented by an arrow whose direction shows how it leads to subsequent activities. A junction or node where activities begin or end is called an *event* and is usually represented by a circle. In the form shown here, the length and slope of each line are unimportant, and the one rule for constructing diagrams of this kind is that all activities approaching an event must be completed before any activity leaving it can commence. There can be only one starting event and one finishing event, and no other loose ends.

Three possible sequences of four activities are shown in Fig. 12.3. At (a) there are two separate relationships; activity A must be completed before B can commence, and C must be completed before D can commence. The logic illustrated by (b) is that neither B nor D can commence until A and C are both completed. There are other possibilities: suppose B depends on the completion of A only but D requires the completion of A and C. This is achieved in (c) by the introduction of an extra activity called a *dummy*. This arrangement satisfies the requirements because B can start when A is finished, whereas D depends upon the completion of C and the dummy, and the dummy in turn depends upon the completion of A. The dummy is assigned zero duration.

Once the network is constructed and the estimated duration of each activity established, the minimum time for completing the project is easily calculated. As can be seen in Fig. 12.2, there will be a number of routes through the network from the starting to finishing events. The total time for each route is the sum of the durations of the activities along it and the greatest of these totals is the minimum time for completion. The route having the longest duration is called the *critical path* and the activities along it are called *critical activities*. Any delay in one of these will affect the time of completion. Other activities have time to spare, and this spare time is called *float*. There is more than one type of float and the distinctions between them are given later.

The details of constructing and analysing such networks are explained in the numerical problems that follow. A thorough treatment of the subject with much useful advice on its application to construction projects is to be found in the paper by Nuttall and Jeanes (1963). Among other matters it indicates how a time-scale can be applied to a network, thus retaining one of the advantages of the

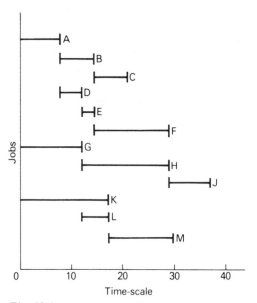

Fig. 12.1

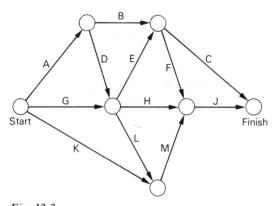

Fig. 12.2

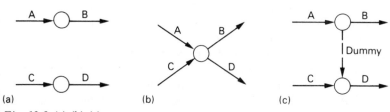

(a)

(b)

(c)

Fig. 12.3 (a) (b) (c)

bar chart. A number of computer programs are available for the analysis of these networks, one of the best known being PERT (Programme Evaluation and Review Technique). It uses a duration for each activity based on the weighted mean of the optimistic, most likely, and pessimistic time estimates, the weightings being $\frac{1}{6}$, $\frac{4}{6}$, and $\frac{1}{6}$ respectively. The basis of this approach is the same as that referred to in Chapter 10 for obtaining a mean probability when determining a bid strategy. The application of probability theory to network analysis is described in the paper by Mitchell and Willis (1973).

Problem 12.1. Suppose the durations (in weeks) of the activities in the network of Fig. 12.2. are: A,7; B,1; C,10; D,3; E,2; F,3; G,12; H,13; J,8; K,17; L,4, and M,12. Find:

(a) the minimum project time;
(b) the earliest and latest times for each event;
(c) the critical path; and
(d) the total float, free float, interfering float and independent float on each non-critical activity.

Solution: (a) The minimum project time can be found, albeit laboriously, by considering every possible route from start to finish that follows the directions of the arrows. There are eleven altogether, and they have the following sequences of activities (see Fig. 12.2): ABC, ABFJ, ADEC, ADEFJ, ADHJ, ADLMJ, GEC, GEFJ, GHJ, GLMJ, and KMJ. Their durations are, respectively, 18, 19, 22, 23, 31, 34, 24, 25, 33, 36, and 37. Since every activity is essential to the project, it is the greatest of these, 37 weeks, that corresponds to the minimum project time.

  (b) The more usual method of analysing networks is shown in Fig. 12.4. Each event circle is divided by a horizontal diameter and the upper half carries a reference number for that event. The nodes at the tail and head of an activity arrow are called the *preceding* and *succeeding* event, respectively; in computer programs they are usually denoted by i and j. It is convenient to refer to activities by their i and j numbers. In the present network, for example, activity D is (2, 5) and E is (5, 3).

  The lower half of each event circle is divided into two quadrants and the left-hand one shows the earliest time at which all the activities approaching the event can be completed. Starting at time 0, event ② can be reached after 7 weeks, the duration of activity A (1, 2). Event ⑤ is approached by two activities D and G and these have arrival times of $7 + 3 = 10$ and $0 + 12 = 12$ weeks, respectively. The greater value, 12, is recorded and the procedure repeated at events ③ and ⑦ which have earliest times of 14 and 17 weeks, respectively. Note that event ⑥ is approached by three activities, F, H, and M, giving earliest arrival times of 17, 25, and 29 weeks, respectively. Again the greatest value, 29, is recorded and the process is repeated for event ④ giving an earliest completion time of 37 weeks – a result that tallies with the value found in (a).

  The right-hand quadrant shows, in each case, the latest time by which all activities approaching the event must be completed. If, as is usually the case, this

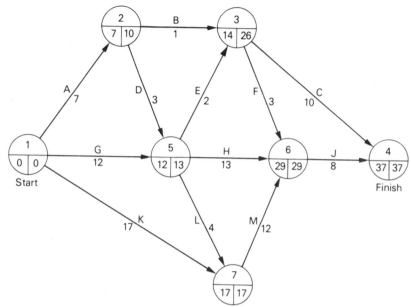

Fig. 12.4

project is to be completed in the minimum time, the figure 37 is recorded in the right-hand quadrant at event ④. Working backwards, the corresponding value at event ⑥ is 37 − 8 = 29 and for event ⑦ it is 29 − 12 = 17. At event ③, two routes must be considered: along activity C the result is 37 − 10 = 27 and along F it is 29 − 3 = 26. The lower value is recorded and the process is repeated for events ⑤, ②, and ①. (The reader is invited to check all the results shown in Fig. 12.4.)

(c) A critical activity is one for which the two *i*-values coincide, the two *j*-values coincide, and the difference between the *i*- and *j*-values equals the duration. In the present case the critical activities are K, M, and J (bearing out the result found in (a)) and, in terms of event numbers, the critical path is ① − ⑦ − ⑥ − ④.

(d) *Total float* is defined as the amount by which the maximum time available for an activity exceeds the time needed to perform it. For example, activity B could start after 7 weeks (if A were finished at the earliest time) and finish as late as 26 weeks. Thus, 19 weeks are available and, since only 1 week is required, the total float is 18 weeks.

Free float is the spare time available assuming that the activity can start at the earliest time but must finish by the earliest time of the succeeding event. In the case of activity B, therefore, the free float is (14 − 7) − 1 = 6 weeks.

Interfering float is the difference between the total float and the free float. For activity B it is 18 − 6 = 12 weeks. This result can also be obtained as the difference between the earliest and latest times of the succeeding event.

Table 12.1

Activity	*i*	*j*	Duration	Total float	Free float	Interfering float	Independent float
A	1	2	7	3	0	3	0
B	2	3	1	18	6	12	2
C	3	4	10	13	13	0	1
D	2	5	3	3	2	1	-1
E	5	3	2	12	0	12	-1
F	3	6	3	12	12	0	0
G	1	5	12	1	0	1	0
H	5	6	13	4	4	0	3
J	6	4	8	critical			
K	1	7	17	critical			
L	5	7	4	1	1	0	0
M	7	6	12	critical			

Independent float may be regarded as the spare time available for a given activity without affecting the float of activities that come earlier or later. On this basis activity B could start after 10 weeks and finish at 14 weeks, giving an independent float of $(14 - 10) - 1 = 3$ weeks.

Table 12.1 shows the collected results for the whole network, with times measured in weeks.

Problem 12.2 School laboratories for biology, physics, and chemistry are to be built in that order using an industrialized building system. Three teams are to be employed in the construction, working in the following order on each building: erectors, plumbers, electricians. No team can commence work on a given building until the previous team has finished. Table 12.2 gives the estimated durations of the various activities in weeks.

Determine the minimum project time and the critical path. State the weeks during which the teams can take holidays without delaying the completion.

Table 12.2

Building	A *(biology)*	B *(physics)*	C *(chemistry)*
Erection	2	4	3
Plumbing	3	2	3
Electrical installation	2	5	2

Solution: In the previous problem the network was presented in the question but in the practical application of critical path analysis it is usually necessary, as in the present case, to construct the network diagram. To do this we must first establish the order in which the various activities follow one another and a convenient way of doing this is shown in Table 12.3.

Table 12.3

Activity reference	Activity name	Preceding activities	Duration (weeks)
1	Erection A	—	2
2	Erection B	1	4
3	Erection C	2	3
4	Plumbing A	1	3
5	Plumbing B	2, 4	2
6	Plumbing C	3, 5	3
7	Electrical A	4	2
8	Electrical B	5, 7	5
9	Electrical C	6, 8	2

It will be seen that each activity (other than the first) requires the completion of one or two earlier activities. For instance, the plumbing of the second building cannot begin until its erection is completed and the team of plumbers has finished its work in the first building. This table contains all the information needed for completing the analysis and there are 'network generator' computer programs that can handle the data in this form. For a manual analysis, however, a network diagram is needed, and Fig. 12.5 shows one of several possible configurations.

Note that two dummies are needed to relate the activity 'plumbing B' to its predecessors and achieve the correct sequences at events ③ and ④. The earliest and latest event time are shown on the network.

The minimum project time is 15 weeks and, in terms of events, the critical path is

①-②-③-⑤-⑥-⑧-⑨-⑩

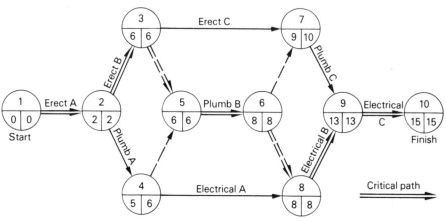

Fig. 12.5

287

The corresponding activities, in order, are erection A, erection B, plumbing B, electrical B, and electrical C, together with two dummies.

The reader is advised to gather all the results in a table similar to that given in the previous solution and to draw a bar chart to scale. From the latter it will be seen that if each activity were to begin at the earliest possible time the erectors could be on holiday from the beginning of week 10. They could take one week's holiday (free float) in the period weeks 7–9 without affecting other teams and two weeks' holiday (total float) in period weeks 7–10 but the latter would restrict the possibilities for other teams.

Again, if all activities were completed at the earliest possible times, the plumbers could be on holiday in weeks 1, 2, 6, 9, and 13–15 and the electrical installers in weeks 1–5 and 8.

12.2 Linear programming

The manager is frequently faced with the task of allocating resources to various activities and many problems of this type are examples of linear programming. The word 'programming' is now closely associated with the use of computers and, although computers are frequently used to solve linear programming problems, it has a different meaning in the present context. 'Planning' might be a better word for describing the allocation of resouces. 'Linear' refers to the form of the equations and graphs that arise in the analysis.

Linear programming problems fall into two categories: *transport* and *mixture*. Transport problems are concerned with the scheduling of goods and vehicles from various starting points (or *sources* as they are called) to a number of destinations. The method of solution can also be used to allocate staff to various roles so as to make the best use of their abilities.

Problems of the mixture kind arise when resources have to be shared among two or more products or activities. No special formulae are required at this stage and the methods are best illustrated by numerical examples.

Problem 12.3. A contractor is organizing the supply of ready-mixed concrete to four sites. He estimates that the total daily requirement amounts to twenty-four lorry loads and he finds three suppliers who are able to meet this demand between them. The separate amounts available from the suppliers are (in lorry loads):

A, 4; B, 8; C, 12

and the quantities needed at the four sites are:

K, 5; L, 2; M, 10; N, 7

Show, on a suitable matrix, an allocation schedule that matches these amounts.

In the price negotiation it is agreed that the transport costs will be charged to the contractor in proportion to the mileage incurred. The distances involved are:

	K	L	M	N
A	6	12	2	5
B	18	21	13	12
C	11	16	5	6

Calculate the total one-way daily distance for the allocations made and obtain the schedule that gives the minimum total distance.

Solution: It is convenient to show the allocations on a matrix such as Fig. 12.6 (a) in which the sources are listed on the left and the destinations at the top. Each element or cell then represents one of the routes, there being twelve in the present problem. The number of lorry-loads available at each source is shown to the right of the corresponding row and the number required at each destination is given at the foot of the appropriate column.

A feasible solution is one in which the numbers in the rows and columns add up to these values. Also, by the nature of this problem, fractional and negative numbers are excluded. Some routes are unused and the corresponding cells in the matrix are left empty. It is easy to find a feasible solution by trial-and-error and two of the many possibilities are shown by Fig. 12.6 (a) and (b). Indeed, with the data of the present problem, there are nearly two thousand feasible solutions.

If the numbers in the matrix of Fig. 12.6 (a) are combined with the appropriate mileages, the total distance is

$$1 \times 12 + 2 \times 2 + 1 \times 5 + 3 \times 18 + 5 \times 12 + 2 \times 11$$
$$+ 1 \times 16 + 8 \times 5 + 1 \times 6 = 219 \text{ miles}$$

and the corresponding total for (b) is 229 miles. Although these solutions are both feasible, (a) is to be preferred in that it involves the lower total mileage.

It might be possible to obtain a more economical solution with a 'common-sense' approach of avoiding long routes and making as much use as possible of

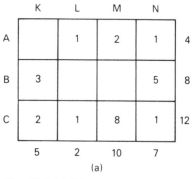

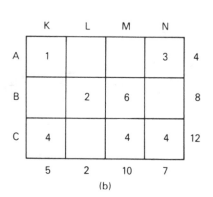

Fig. 12.6 (a) (b)

short ones. However, with such a large number of feasible solutions, this process could take a long time and there would be no way of knowing when the optimum was reached.

A more systematic way of tackling the problem is to modify the initial solution step by step in order to reduce the total mileage while retaining feasibility – a process known as *iteration*. When it is found that no further improvement is possible, the optimum arrangement has been achieved. To facilitate this process the matrix is displayed with the route distances in the corners of the cells, as shown in Fig. 12.7.

In seeking an initial solution we first note that if there are m rows and n columns a feasible solution can be found with not more than $m + n - 1$ routes in use. These are called *occupied* elements, the others being *free* elements. The value $m + n - 1$ is called the *critical number* and in the present case, with $m = 3$ and $n = 4$, a feasible solution can be found with not more than six occupied elements. A solution satisfying this rule, and known as the 'north-west corner' solution, is found as follows.

The largest possible number is entered in the top left-hand cell (Fig. 12.7). It must be 4, the row total, and the remaining cells in this row remain empty (free elements). In the first cell of the second row the largest possible number is 1 since this completes the requirements of the first column. In the second cell of this row the maximum number is 2 (the column total) and in the third it is 5, thus completing the row total. In the bottom row 5 lorry-loads are needed in the third cell to complete the requirements at destination M and the remaining cell or element has the value 7. This procedure satisfies the critical number rule and is an efficient way of finding an initial solution. At this stage the total distance is

$$4 \times 6 + 1 \times 18 + 2 \times 21 + 5 \times 13 + 5 \times 5 + 7 \times 6 = 216 \text{ miles}$$

The unused routes in this solution are now investigated one by one to see if improvements can be obtained by incorporating them. Consider, for instance, the effect of allocating one lorry-load to route AL; this is indicated by placing a $\oplus$ sign in the AL cell as shown in Fig. 12.7. This move would upset the totals of the

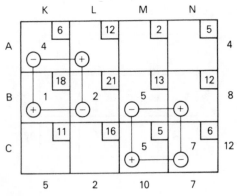

Fig. 12.7

first row and second column, and to preserve the feasibility of the solution corresponding reductions of one lorry-load each are made in the cells AK and BL, indicated by $\ominus$ signs. Finally a lorry-load would have to be added to the BK route, as shown by the $\oplus$ sign in its cell. Together these four changes would lead to a different, but still feasible, solution. The effect on mileage would be

$$+ 12 - 6 + 18 - 21 = +3$$

The use of route AL at this stage would therefore increase the mileage. On the other hand, the allocation of one lorry-load to route BN with corresponding adjustments to other routes, as shown in the bottom right-hand corner of Fig. 12.7, causes a change in total mileage of

$$+ 12 - 13 + 5 - 6 = -2$$

and this represents an improvement. The change in the allocation to each of the routes involved need not be limited to a single lorry-load, but for each one added to BN there is a reduction of one on each of the routes BM and CN. At present BM has 5 and CN has 7, so that the proposed rearrangement can be made for a maximum of 5 lorry-loads. The reduction in miles is therefore 10, the new total being 206 and the modified allocations are shown in Fig. 12.8. The process, usually called the 'stepping-stone' method, is now repeated. An empty cell is selected and linked with three occupied cells by horizontal and vertical steps – 'rook' moves in chess parlance. If the allocation of one lorry-load to the empty cell, and the corresponding adjustments to the others, lead to a reduction in total mileage the change is made for as great a quantity as possible, the limit being reached when one of the occupied cells becomes empty.

The four cells involved do not necessarily form a square. The addition of one lorry-load to CK for example cannot be offset in the bottom row by subtracting one from CL because this route is empty already. Instead, CK is linked with CN, BN, and BK as shown in Fig. 12.8. The change in mileage is

$$+ 11 - 6 + 12 - 18 = -1$$

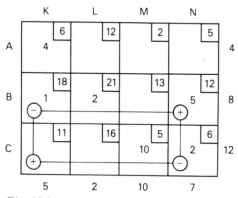

Fig. 12.8

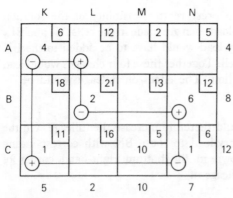

Fig. 12.9

but the improvement can only be made for one lorry-load because BK is then empty. The total mileage is reduced to 205 and the new allocations are shown in Fig. 12.9.

If all the empty routes are tested at this stage it will be found that no further improvement is possible. AL presents a special problem because it cannot be linked with three occupied routes in a square or rectangle. The links form a more complicated path, as shown in Fig. 12.9, but the solution remains feasible because each row and column involved contains one $\oplus$ and one $\ominus$ sign. The change in mileage is

$+ 12 - 6 + 11 - 6 + 12 - 21 = + 2$

The minimum total mileage is 205 and the allocations are

A to K, 4; B to L, 2; B to N, 6;
C to K, 1; C to M, 10, and C to N, 1

Of all the feasible solutions this is the optimum: the one with the minimum total mileage. It is noteworthy in that it does not involve the shortest route, AM, at all and it makes the greatest possible use of the longest route, BL. Site L requires only two lorry-loads and they are both coming from supplier B. Furthermore, site N receives all but one of its loads on the longest of the three routes approaching it, BN. These allocations may seem surprising and it might have taken a considerable time to find this optimum solution using a 'commonsense' approach.

Problem 12.4.   Suppose, in the previous problem, the quantities available from the sources, in lorry-loads, are increased to the following amounts:

A, 6; B, 12; C, 14

the quantities required at the destinations being unaltered.

Determine the new minimum total distance for a feasible solution and list the allocations that achieve it.

Solution: The total of lorry-loads is now thirty-two, eight more than are required at the destinations. This imbalance is allowed for by introducing an extra destination called a *dummy* to receive the excess loads. It is represented by an additional column in the matrix, Fig. 12.10 (a), and the dummy is taken to be at zero distance from each of the sources. The optimum arrangement can be found by the methods of the previous solution and loads scheduled to the dummy destination remain, in practice, at the sources.

The north-west corner solution for this extended matrix is shown in Fig. 12.10 (a). It gives a total mileage of 241 and contains the critical number of occupied elements, seven. The eight free elements are now tested to see if an improvement can be made by incorporating one of them in the allocation arrangement. Instead of testing each free element separately (as in the previous solution) they can all be tested simultaneously by a technique known as the method of *shadow costs*.

For this a new matrix is drawn up, Fig. 12.10 (b). First the lengths of the occupied routes are noted, the circled numbers in the diagram. Next, numbers known as u- and v-values are assigned to the rows and columns such that $u + v$ for an occupied element equals the corresponding distance. The first of these numbers is chosen arbitrarily, the others being derived from it. In the present case, for example, the u-value for the first row was chosen as 6 and the v-values for the first and second columns become 0 and 6, respectively, to satisfy the values of the AK and AL routes. The u-value for the second row can now be deduced from the distance of the BL route. The process is continued until all the u- and v-values are determined. Note that these may be negative. For each of the free elements the appropriate value of $u + v$ is substracted from the route distance. The results, shown in Fig. 12.10 (b), are called the shadow costs and each represents the effect on total mileage of allocating one load or vehicle to the route and making the necessary adjustments to the related occupied routes. Thus, the effect of putting unit load on route BK is to increase the total mileage by 3, whereas the allocation of unit load to B/Dummy would reduce the mileage by 6.

At this stage the greatest reduction can be achieved by the use of CM, with corresponding adjustments to CN, BN, and BM. The saving is two miles for each load and a maximum of six can be reallocated, thus reducing the total mileage to 229. The revised allocations are shown in Fig. 12.11 (a) and the corresponding

	K	L	M	N	Dummy	
A	[6] 5	[12] 1	[2]	[5]	[0]	6
3	[18]	[21] 1	[13] 10	[12] 1	[0]	12
C	[11]	[16]	[5]	[6] 6	[0] 8	14
	5	2	10	7	8	

(a)

u \ v	0	6	−2	−3	−9
6	(6)	(12)	−2	2	3
15	3	(21)	(13)	(12)	−6
9	2	1	−2	(6)	(0)

(b)

Fig. 12.10 (a) (b)

	K	L	M	N	Dummy
A	6 / 5	12 / 1	2	5	0
B	18	21 / 1	13 / 4	12 / 7	0
C	11	16	5 / 6	6	0 / 8

(a)

u \ v	0	6	-2	-3	-7
6	(6)	(12)	-2	2	1
15	3	(21)	(13)	(12)	-8
7	4	3	(5)	2	(0)

(b)

Fig. 12.11 (a) (b)

shadow costs appear in Fig. 12.11 (b). The results were obtained by, again, choosing 6 as the u-value for the first row but other initial choices lead to the same shadow costs. The use of route B/dummy with adjustments to BM, CM, and C/dummy saves eight miles per load and with a maximum of four loads, the total mileage is reduced to 197.

The next stage is shown in Fig. 12.12, the details being left to the reader. The shadow cost for CN is now -6, and by allocating four loads to this route the total mileage is reduced to 173. The new solution and corresponding shadow costs are given in Fig. 12.13 (a) and (b). There are no negative shadow costs at this stage and no further reduction in total mileage is possible. However, the shadow cost for AM is zero and this means that one or more other solutions can be found having the same total mileage. The relevant changes are indicated by the $\oplus$ and $\ominus$ signs of Fig. 12.13 (a) and it can be seen that six elements are involved. In the

	K	L	M	N	Dummy
A	5	1			
B		1		7	4
C			10		4

(a)

(6)	(12)	6	2	9
3	(21)	8	(12)	(0)
-4	-5	(5)	-6	(0)

(b)

Fig. 12.12 (a) (b)

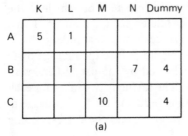

(a)

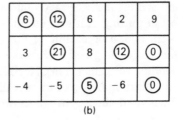

(b)

Fig. 12.13 (a) (b)

294

present example these changes can only be made in respect of one load because this will cause AL to become an empty route. The two optimal solutions, therefore, are

A to K, 5; A to L, 1; B to L, 1; B to N, 3; C to M, 10; C to N, 4

as shown in Fig. 12.12 (a) and

A to K, 5; A to M, l; B to L, 2; B to N, 2; C to M, 9; C to N, 5

obtained by an alteration of one lorry-load in each of the cells containing $\oplus$ or $\ominus$.

The total mileage is 173 in both cases, the quantities available from sources A and C are fully utilized, but eight of the twelve loads available from supplier B are scheduled to go to the dummy destination and therefore remain at B.

Problem 12.5. Five managers (A, B, C, D, and E), who differ in ability and experience, are to be placed in charge of five projects which are different in type and value. The suitability of each manager for each project is assessed on a numerical scale with a maximum of 20 points, the results being shown in Fig. 12.14. To which project should each manager be assigned in order to obtain the highest total points score?

Solution: Questions of this type are related to linear programming problems of the kind dealt with in the last two examples. The matrix of points values (Fig. 12.14) is equivalent to the cost or distance tables of those examples except that we are here seeking the maximum total value. The problem is converted to one of minimization by subtracting each element from the maximum value, 20. The results are shown in Fig. 12.15.

It is a property of the cost matrix that the optimum solution is unchanged if all the elements in any row or column are increased or decreased by the same amount. This result follows from a consideration of the stepping-stone method in which each row and column involved in a rearrangement contains one $\oplus$ and one $\ominus$ sign so that the shadow costs are unaffected by such increases or decreases. However, the total cost or distance must be determined from the original values.

Projects

Managers	1	2	3	4	5
A	18	16	11	19	5
B	14	10	15	8	6
C	9	13	8	8	6
D	15	14	10	12	10
E	11	11	14	10	8

2	4	9	1	15
6	10	5	12	14
11	7	12	12	14
5	6	10	8	10
9	9	6	10	12

Fig. 12.14   *Fig. 12.15*

The linking of each manager to a project corresponds to a 'route' in the transport problem. In the present example there will be five routes in use, a smaller figure than the critical number which is $5 + 5 - 1 = 9$. A problem of this kind in which the numbers of sources and destinations are equal, and only one unit is available at each source or required at each destination, is called an *assignment* problem. It can be solved by an algorithm known as the *Hungarian method* and consisting of the following steps:

(a) *The smallest element in each row is subtracted from every element in that row.* In Fig. 12.15 the smallest row elements are 1, 5, 7, 5, and 6 so that this step leads to the matrix of Fig. 12.16.

(b) *The smallest element in each column is subtracted from every element in that column.* In the matrix of Fig. 12.16 four of the columns already contain zeros and it is only the fifth that requires modification. The result is shown in Fig. 12.17.

(c) *The zeros in the matrix are covered by the minimum number of horizontal and vertical lines.* In Fig. 12.17 at least four such lines are necessary (more than one configuration being possible). If this number equals the number of columns (or rows) an assignment can now be made as explained in step (e) below. If not, as in the present case, the matrix is modified in the following way.

(d) *The smallest element not covered is selected. It is subtracted from the elements which are not covered and added to those which are covered twice. The elements which are covered once are unaltered.* In the case of Fig. 12.17 the smallest uncovered element is 1 and the modifications lead to the matrix shown in Fig. 12.18. If the assignment test of step (c) is now applied it will be found that at least five lines are needed to cover all the zeros and an assignment can therefore be made. (If this were not the case, step (d) would have to be repeated.)

(e) *An element of zero value is selected for each assignment.* In some lines there is only one zero and this one must be used. In others a choice presents itself.

Fig. 12.16

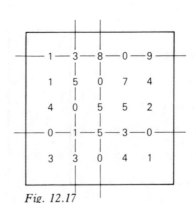

Fig. 12.17

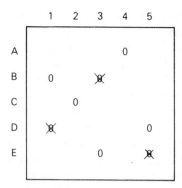

Fig. 12.18   Fig. 12.19

For example, the zeros in the present case (Fig. 12.19) are so distributed that C must be assigned to project 2 and A to project 4. Each remaining line contains two zeros and the next choice is arbitrary. Suppose B1 is selected. This eliminates D1 and D must be assigned to project 5. It follows that E5 is crossed out and E is assigned to project 3.

The corresponding points total must be calculated from the original values of Fig. 12.14. Thus:

Manager	Project	Points
A	4	19
B	1	14
C	2	13
D	5	10
E	3	14
	Total	70

Problem 12.6. An estate developer is planning the development of a 25 hectare site with a mixture of bungalows and two-storey houses. The capital available to him is £3,750,000, and the estimated construction cost is £30,000 per house and £25,000 per bungalow.

Planning permission allows for a maximum of six houses or four bungalows per hectare, but there are two additional stipulations:
(a) at least twenty bungalows must be included in the scheme;
(b) at least one-third of the units must be houses.

Determine the number of houses and bungalows to be built to achieve each of the following:

1. the maximum number of houses;
2. the maximum number of bungalows;
3. the maximum total profit (assuming that all units can be sold) if the profit per house is 10 per cent higher than per bungalow.

Solution: This problem, like the three preceding ones, is concerned with the allocation of resources and it is a further example of linear programming. However, a graphical analysis (Fig. 12.20) is now more effective than the matrix techniques used in the earlier solutions. If the axes represent houses and bungalows, each combination of units can be shown by a point whose co-ordinates are the numbers of each type involved. By the nature of the problem, negative and fractional values are excluded.

The capital available, £3,750,000, is sufficient to build 125 houses at £30,000 each or 150 bungalows at £25,000 each. There are other possibilities involving mixtures such as 25 houses and 120 bungalows, or 100 houses and 30 bungalows and the points representing the possible combinations lie on the straight line shown as the *financial constraint*. Points on or below this line represent combinations of houses and bungalows for which there is sufficient capital; points above it lead to schedules for which there is insufficient money.

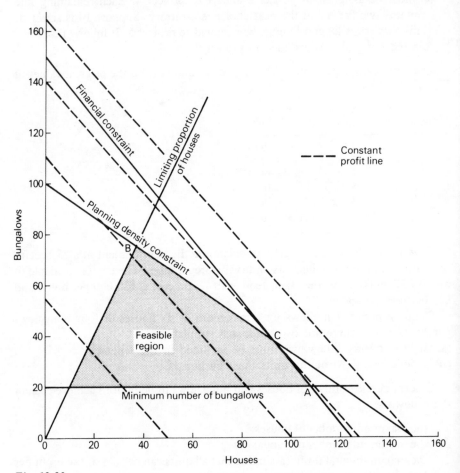

Fig. 12.20

By similar reasoning the planning densities permit a maximum of 150 houses (and no bungalows), or 100 bungalows (and no houses) or proportions of each that total 1. The straight line marked *planning density constraint* includes the points representing all such combinations. At this stage the diagram can be used to test proposed combinations of houses and bungalows in terms of the capital available and the permitted density of building. A point that is above both lines represents a combination of houses and bungalows that requires more capital than is available and exceeds the planning density. A point below both lines corresponds to a schedule that satisfies both constraints. Points within the triangular regions between these two constraint lines give schedules that satisfy one of the constraints but not the other.

Two other constraints are specified in the question. It is stipulated that there must be at least twenty bungalows and this requirement is represented by a horizontal line through the '20' mark on the vertical axis. Since this is a minimum requirement, acceptable combinations of houses and bungalows are represented by points on or above this line.

The limitation imposed by the specified proportion of houses, one-third of the total number of units, is represented by a sloping straight line through the origin. With forty bungalows there must be at least twenty houses, with eighty bungalows a minimum of forty, and so on. Hence the required line has a slope of 2, and acceptable solutions are represented by points on or to the right of it.

The four constraints delineate a *feasible region* on the diagram and all feasible solutions lie within it or on its perimeter. The specific solutions required in the question are as follows:

1. The maximum number of houses corresponds to point A and by measurement of the diagram (Fig. 12.20), or by calculation, the schedule is 108 houses and 20 bungalows. This combination uses all the capital available (within the limits set by practical considerations) but requires only 23 hectares at the stipulated densities.
2. The maximum number of bungalows is given by point B, the 'exact' result being 37.5 houses and 75 bungalows. Of the nearest whole-number answers, the solution 37 houses and 75 bungalows does not satisfy the requirement for the minimum proportion of houses. On the other hand 38 houses and 74 bungalows meets this constraint and is just within the stipulated planning density.
3. If each house produces 10 per cent more profit than a bungalow, 50 houses will produce the same profit as 55 bungalows, 100 houses the same as 110 bungalows, and so on. Lines of constant profit will link these pairs of points on the co-ordinate axes and it can be seen from the diagram that they are parallel. The highest one of the set to touch the feasible region does so at C, and the required result is therefore 94 houses and 37 bungalows.

The graphical method used in this solution is only suitable when there are two 'products' – houses and bungalows in the present case. However, there is an

299

algorithm known as the *Simplex method* which can deal with any number of products. See for example the book by Krekó (1968).

12.3 Queueing

Queueing is a familiar feature of everyday life. We queue at the bus stop, in the post office, and in self-service restaurants. These examples all involve people shuffling forward to a service point but the 'customers' can be lorries waiting to load or unload, letters in an in-tray waiting to be answered, or telephone calls jamming a switchboard.

Queues may be classified by the number of channels, the number of service points, and the queue 'discipline' – the rules by which it operates. For many queues the rule is 'first-come, first-served' but there are other possibilities and the in-tray may work on the basis of 'last-in, first-answered'.

A *simple queue* is defined by the following properties:

1. Single channel, single service point.
2. First-come, first-served.
3. Customers are individuals.
4. No simultaneous arrivals.
5. No limit to the number of potential customers.
6. Variable service times and variable times between successive arrivals.
7. The variability of the number of arrivals and of the number of customers being served in given time intervals conform to the statistical distribution known as the Poisson distribution.

In the examples that follow it will be assumed that these conditions are satisfied. The key parameter in queueing theory is *traffic density* or *intensity*. It is denoted by ρ (rho) and is defined as

$$\text{Traffic density } \rho = \frac{\text{Mean rate of arrival}}{\text{Mean rate of service}} \qquad [12.1]$$

For the statistical distribution referred to above it can be shown that the mean rate of service is the reciprocal of the mean service time, and that the mean rate of arrival is the reciprocal of the mean time between successive arrivals. From equation [12.1], therefore, we have

$$\rho = \frac{\text{Mean service time}}{\text{Mean time between arrivals}} \qquad [12.2]$$

If, for example, customers arrived at the rate of four per minute and could be served at the rate of five per minute, the traffic density, by the first definition, would be $\rho = \frac{4}{5} = 0.8$. The corresponding mean service time would be 12 s and

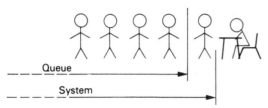

_____Queue_____►

_____System_____►

Fig. 12.21

the mean time between arrivals 15 s. Thus, using [12.2],

$$\rho = \frac{12}{15} = 0.8$$

Although there will be instances of the service time being greater than the time between successive arrivals, the mean values must be such that ρ is less than 1. Otherwise the queue will grow indefinitely.

In analysing the simple queue it is necessary to distinguish between the queue and the *system*, the latter including the customer being served (see Fig. 12.21). Suppose $p_0, p_1, p_2, \ldots$, are the probabilities of there being 0, 1, 2, $\ldots$, customers, respectively, in the system. These probabilities can also be regarded as the proportions of the total time for which the corresponding numbers of customers are to be found in the system. Table 12.4 shows how the numbers of customers in the queue and the system are related.

Since the sum of the probabilities of all the possibilities is 1, we have

$$p_0 + p_1 + p_2 + p_3 + \cdots = 1 \qquad [12.3]$$

and the series is infinite since we assume no limit to the number of potential customers. It might be expected that each term in the series will be smaller than its predecessor because, on average, customers can be served more rapidly than they arrive. A full analysis (see, for example, Bunday 1986) shows that each of the probability values is ρ times its predecessor.

Thus $p_1 = \rho p_0$

$p_2 = \rho p_1 = \rho^2 p_0$, etc. $\qquad [12.4]$

Table 12.4

Number of customers in system	Number of customers in queue	Probability
0	0	p_0
1	0	p_1
2	1	p_2
3	2	p_3

and, substituting in equation [12.3], we have

$$p_0 + \rho p_0 + \rho^2 p_0 + \rho^3 p_0 + \cdots = 1$$

This is a *geometric series* or *progression* having a first term $a = p_0$ and common ratio $r = \rho$. If, as in the present case, the common ratio is less than 1, the series converges and the sum to infinity is given by $a/(1 - r)$. Therefore,

$$\frac{p_0}{1 - \rho} = 1$$

and $p_0 = 1 - \rho$ [12.5]

Thus, the probability of there being no-one in the system, and hence the probability of a customer not having to wait, is $1 - \rho$. It follows that the probability of having to wait is ρ since the two values must total 1.

It is useful to have an expression for the average number of customers in the system and this can be determined by noting that there is no-one in the system for p_0 of the time, one person in the system for p_1 of the time, and so on. Thus:

$$\text{Average number of customers in system} = \frac{0 \times p_0 + 1 \times p_1 + 2 \times p_2 + \cdots}{p_0 + p_1 + p_2 + \cdots}$$

The denominator is identical to the series in [12.3] and equals 1. The first term of the numerator is zero and the remaining terms form a series which, with the relationship of [12.4], can be written as

$$S = \rho p_0 + 2\rho^2 p_0 + 3\rho^3 p_0 + 4\rho^4 p_0 + \cdots$$

This is not a geometric series, but multiplying through by ρ we have

$$\rho S = \rho^2 p_0 + 2\rho^3 p_0 + 3\rho^4 p_0 + \cdots$$

and, by subtraction,

$$S - \rho S = \rho p_0 + \rho^2 p_0 + \rho^3 p_0 + \rho^4 p_0 + \cdots$$

This is another geometric progression and, summing to infinity,

$$S(1 - \rho) = p_0 \left(\frac{\rho}{1 - \rho} \right)$$

Finally, substituting for p_0 from [12.5], we have:

$$\text{Average number of customers in system} = \frac{\rho}{1 - \rho} \qquad [12.6]$$

By similar methods expressions can be found for the average number of customers in the queue and for the average times spent by customers in the queue and in the system. The main results are collected below and it will be seen that they all involve traffic density ρ.

Probability of a customer having to wait $= \rho$

Average number of customers in the system $= \dfrac{\rho}{1 - \rho}$

Average number of customers in the queue when there is a queue $= \dfrac{1}{1 - \rho}$

Average number of customers in the queue including times when there is no queue $= \dfrac{\rho^2}{1 - \rho}$

Average time a customer is in the queue $= \dfrac{\rho}{1 - \rho} \times \left(\begin{array}{c} \text{Mean service} \\ \text{time} \end{array} \right)$

Average time a customer is in the system $= \dfrac{1}{1 - \rho} \times \left(\begin{array}{c} \text{Mean service} \\ \text{time} \end{array} \right)$

Problem 12.7. In a study of the operation of an unloading bay it was observed that 117 lorries and vans made deliveries during a 40-hour week. With two men employed on unloading, the average time to unload each vehicle was found to be 15 min. Treating the operation as simple queueing, determine:

(a) the probability of a vehicle not having to wait;
(b) the average number of vehicles in the system;
(c) the average time a vehicle is waiting to be unloaded;
(d) the average time a vehicle is in the system.

For a trial period the number of unloaders was increased. It was found that with 3, 4, and 5 persons involved the average unloading times were 12, 10, and 9 min, respectively. If the all-in-rate for each unloader is £6 per hour and the cost of waiting for a van and driver is £20 per hour, how many unloaders should be employed to minimize the total cost?

Solution: With 117 arrivals in 40 hr, we have:

$$\text{Mean rate of arrival} = \frac{117}{40} = 2.925 \text{ per hr}$$

Also,

$$\text{Mean rate of service} = \frac{60}{15} = 4 \text{ per hr}$$

Hence,

$$\text{Traffic density } \rho = \frac{2.925}{4} = 0.731$$

(a) The probability of a vehicle having to wait is ρ. Hence, probability of vehicle not having to wait is

$1 - \rho = 1 - 0.731$

$\qquad = 0.269$

(b) The average number of vehicles in the system is

$$\frac{\rho}{1 - \rho} = \frac{0.731}{1 - 0.731}$$

$$= 2.72$$

(c) The average time a vehicle is in the queue is

$$\frac{\rho}{1 - \rho} \times \text{(Average service time)} = 2.72 \times 15$$

$$= 40.8 \text{ min}$$

(d) The average time a vehicle is in the system is

$$\text{(Average time in queue)} + \text{(Average service time)} = 40.8 + 15$$

$$= 55.8 \text{ min}$$

Alternatively, by use of the appropriate formula,

$$\text{Average time in system} = \frac{1}{1 - \rho} \times \text{(Average service time)}$$

$$= \frac{1}{1 - 0.731} \times 15 \text{ min}$$

$$= 55.8 \text{ min}$$

Using this result:

$$\text{Total waiting time per week} = \frac{55.8}{60} \times 117$$

$$= 108.8 \text{ hr}$$

Hence,
Weekly waiting cost $= 108.8 \times £20.00$

$\qquad\qquad\qquad\quad = £2177$

Also,
Weekly unloading cost $= 2 \times 40 \times £6.00$

$\qquad\qquad\qquad\qquad = £480$

When more unloaders are employed the first of these costs is reduced but the second is increased. If the two costs are borne by the same organization, there is an incentive to minimize their sum and, by repeating the calculations for the

Table 12.5

① No. of unloaders	② Service time (min)	③ ρ	④ $\dfrac{1}{1-\rho}$	⑤ = ② × ④ Average time in system (min)	⑥ Weekly costs (£)		
					waiting	unloading	total
2	15	0.731	3.72	55.8	2,177	480	2,657
3	12	0.585	2.41	28.9	1,127	720	1,847
4	10	0.488	1.95	19.5	761	960	1,721
5	9	0.439	1.78	16.0	624	1,200	1,824

given numbers, the results shown in Table 12.5 are obtained. The figures in the final column show that the minimum total cost is obtained when four unloaders are employed.

Summary

Operational research is largely concerned with the allocation of resources and therefore has many applications in construction management.

Critical path (or network) analysis is used to plan and control the progress of complex projects by considering the sequence in which the contributions of different people take place. It identifies those activities which must be finished on time if the completion of the project is not to be delayed and pinpoints those activities which have time to spare.

Linear programming problems of the transport kind are concerned with the allocation of resources when these are available from several sources and are required at various destinations. The methods of solution can be adapted to assignment problems in which staff or plant are allocated to a number of projects. In mixture problems resources have to be divided between different products or services subject to overall constraints.

In the construction industry there are many examples of queueing associated with the delivery of materials and the availability of plant. Estimates of queue length and waiting time are based upon probability concepts and the results can be used to predict the most economical way of providing the particular service required.

Operational research does not reduce the manager's responsibility but it aims to present him with the information on which decisions can be based, particularly the returns that can be expected from alternative strategies. It must be borne in mind, however, that operational research models are always approximations and the results they give cannot be more accurate or reliable than the data on which they are based.

In some cases the analysis will confirm the 'commonsense' view, but in others, such as Problem 12.3, the results may be unexpected. Experience is a valuable asset when dealing with familiar processes but the role of operational research is likely to grow in importance as projects increase in size and complexity.

Questions (and answers)

1. The figures on the lines of the network given in Fig. 12.22 represent the durations of the various activities in convenient units. How many paths are there through the network and what is the total duration of each? Determine the minimum time for completing the project and locate the critical path. Calculate the total float for each of the non-critical activities.

   Answer: 11 paths with durations of 24, 25, 26, 27, 28 (4 times), 29 (twice), and 30 units. Minimum time is 30 units and the critical path is:

   ①-②-⑤-⑥-③-④. Total floats:
   ①-⑤, 1; ①-⑦, 2; ⑦-⑤, 2;
   ⑦-⑧, 2; ⑥-⑧, 1; ②-③, 2;
   ⑥-④, 4; ⑧-④, 1.

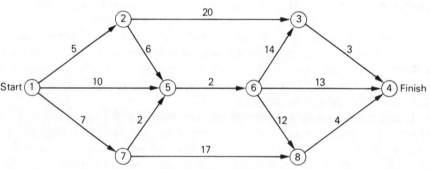

Fig. 12.22

2. The following table gives the preceding and succeeding event numbers (*i* and *j*) and durations (*t*) for a project with fourteen activities. Draw a network, determine the minimum project time, locate the critical path, and calculate the total and free floats for each non-critical activity.

i	*j*	*t*		*i*	*j*	*t*
0	1	7		2	5	3
0	2	5		3	5	0
0	4	12		4	5	2
1	3	11		4	6	2
1	2	2		3	7	22
2	3	4		5	7	12
2	4	11		6	7	10

Answer: 40 units; critical path is ⓪-①-③-⑦. Floats are:

i	j	Total float	Free float		i	j	Total float	Free float
0	2	9	4		3	5	10	4
0	4	14	8		4	5	6	0
1	2	5	0		4	6	8	0
2	3	5	5		5	7	6	6
2	4	6	0		6	7	8	8
2	5	16	10					

3. Figure 12.23 relates to a factory redevelopment scheme, the present and proposed use of the four areas being as follows:

(a) A is wasteland, ready for building on;
(b) B and C contain scattered workshops that are to be replaced by new buildings on A at twice the present density;
(c) D is occupied by an office block that is to be replaced by a new one on B;
(d) C and D will be used for a car park and landscaped area.

The building programme for A is to be divided into two parts (for the relocation of the units on B and C, respectively), each half requiring a ten months' construction period. The new office block will take eighteen months to build.
Building can only take place on one area at a time; the demolition on areas B, C, and D will require two months each, only one area being dealt with at a time. The contract for the car park and landscaping will require seven months.
Draw a network diagram for these activities, allowing one month for each of the three moves to the new buildings. Determine the minimum time for the completion of the project, list the critical activities in sequence, and state the total float on each of the others.

Answer: Ten activities can be identified (three building, three demolition, three moves and the car park/landscaping contract). There is more than one possible sequence; for example, the office block could be built before or after the second half of A. Assuming the latter, the minimum time for completion is forty-eight months. The critical activities are: build A part 1; build A part 2; build office block; move D; demolish D; car park/landscaping. The total floats on the other activities in months are: demolish B, 7; demolish C, 16; move B, 7; move C, 16.

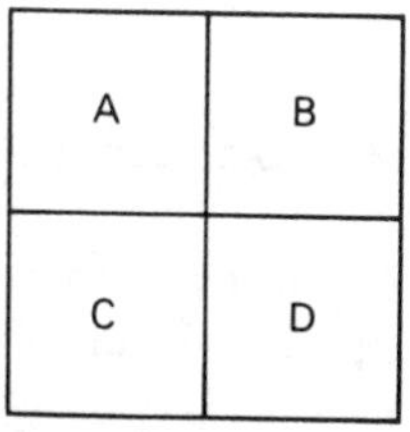

Fig. 12.23

4. A demolition contractor is working on five sites that are expected to yield the following quantities of hardcore, measured in lorry-loads:

A, 1; B, 6; C, 4; D, 3; E, 5

He undertakes to supply the same material to three building sites in the following numbers of lorry-loads:

K, 2; L, 7; M, 10

Show, on a suitable matrix, a schedule that satisfies these numbers.

		To		
		K	L	M
From	A	3	10	19
	B	6	7	22
	C	21	5	4
	D	9	11	13
	E	20	23	26

The table above shows the distances between the sites in miles. Calculate the total of lorry-miles for the schedule you have drawn up, find the feasible solution having the smallest total and state the lorry-miles involved.

Answer: Optimum solution is: A to K, 1; B to L, 6; C to M, 4; D to M, 3; E to K, 1; E to L, 1; E to M, 3. Total distance, 221 lorry-miles.

5. In a joinery shop five teams are to be assigned to five jobs, one to each. An analysis of the skills, experience and resources of each team, and the complexity of each job leads to the following estimates, in hours, of the times required by the teams to complete the jobs:

		Job				
		1	2	3	4	5
Team	A	50	52	48	53	52
	B	46	27	50	63	60
	C	39	48	40	62	50
	D	31	42	58	48	51
	E	41	49	46	68	58

Determine the allocations of teams to jobs as to minimize the total team-hours. What is the total time involved in this arrangement?

Answer: A to 4, B to 2, C to 5, D to 1, and E to 3. 207 team-hours.

6. Find an alternative optimum solution to Problem 12.5 (pp. 295–7) and show that it leads to the same total points score.

Answer: A to 4, B to 3, C to 2, D to 1, E to 5.

7. In the planning of a new town a site of 400 hectares has been selected for a mixture of housing and industry. The development is subject to the following constraints:

(a) the supply of water and drainage capacity is sufficient for a maximum of 320 hectares of industry alone or 480 hectares of housing alone, or combinations in proportions that total 1;
(b) at least 120 hectares must be used for housing;
(c) in order to provide enough employment locally, the land allocated to industry must be least one-quarter as much as for housing;
(d) at the other extreme the land for industry must not exceed that for housing.

Determine the respective allocations of land to housing and industry that will produce:

1. the greatest amount of housing;
2. the greatest amount of industry;
3. the greatest rateable value if the value per hectare is 40 per cent higher for industry than for housing.

Answer: In hectares: (1) housing 320, industry 80; (2) housing 192, industry 192; (3) housing 240, industry 160.

8. A contractor distributes materials to one of his sites by his own lorries where they are unloaded by two men and a mobile crane. A lorry is despatched every 20 min. and, on average, it requires 15 min. to unload each one. Treating the system as a simple queue, calculate the average time a lorry has to wait before it is unloaded.

The labour costs for unloading amount to £5 per hour for each man employed and the cost of a lorry (with driver) is £15 per hour for waiting and unloading time. Assuming that the speed at which a lorry can be unloaded is proportional to the number of men employed, should the number be changed from two and, if so, to what figure?

Answer: 45 min. The total hourly cost of unloading and waiting has a minimum of £29 when four men are employed on unloading.

References and bibliography

Battersby, A. (1967) *Network Analysis*, Macmillan
Bunday, B. D. (1984) *Basic Linear Programming*, Arnold
Bunday, B. D. (1986) *Basic Queueing Theory*, Arnold
Makower, M. S. and Williamson, E. (1985) *Operational Research*, (4th edn) English Universities Press
Mitchell, G. and Willis, M. J. (1973) The determination of realistic probability levels for project completion dates, *Aeronautical Journal* (Dec.)
Nuttall, J. F. and Jeanes, R. E. (1963) The critical path method, *The Builder* (14 and 21 June)
Pilcher, R. (1966) *Principles of Construction Management*, McGraw-Hill
Singh, Jagjit (1971) *Operations Research*, Pelican

Regulations attached to the Health and Safety at Work etc. Act 1974: Safety Representatives and Safety Committee Regulations

Safety representatives

Attached to the Health and Safety at Work etc. Act 1974 are a series of regulations and, for construction, the Safety Representatives and Safety Committee Regulations introduced in 1978 have considerable bearing. These allied regulations require employers to consult with the employees' legally appointed safety representatives. Employees are entitled to appoint safety representatives by two methods:

(a) by election from among the employees on a site;
(b) by appointment by a recognized trade union.

A recognized trade union is one where the union is free of domination by the employer and is free to negotiate with the employer. The NJC have attempted to advise the industry by issuing guidelines, whereby an employees' safety representative should be employed by the main contractor, should represent all unionized employees at work whether they are employed by the main contractor or subcontractors, and, finally, where the subcontractor is outside the scope of the NJC, a safety representative may be appointed by the subcontractor. The number of safety representatives will depend upon the total number of personnel employed on a site, along with the variety of occupations and trade unions represented on the site, with an assessment of the type of work and its inherent dangers. The safety representative may not be a shop steward, but in practice many trade unions will only have safety representatives drawn from accredited shop stewards.

The regulations suggest that, as far as practicable, the safety representative should have two years' service with a company, but again the NJC have recognized that this is an impractical requirement in an industry such as construction with its high labour turnover and have, therefore, shortened the qualification period to one year. The duties of safety representatives are comprehensive in scope and can be catalogued as follows:

(a) to investigate hazards and examine the cause of accidents;
(b) to investigate employee complaints on health, welfare, and safety;

(c) to represent to management items arising out of (a) and (b).
(d) to carry out inspections;
(e) to discuss matters with the Health and Safety Executive;
(f) to receive information from inspectors;
(g) to attend meetings of the safety committee.

Item (d) in the above list of duties is one which is likely to create the most difficulties. Safety representatives can legally carry out formal inspections on site every three months, but the employer must be notified in writing before inspections are carried out. Normally the employer must provide the representative with any requested information, but this may be withheld if such information endangers national security or the trading success of the company. Further, if the inspection relates to an individual, the individual concerned must give prior consent to an inspection. Finally, if legal proceedings are pending, the employer may legitimately refuse to provide the information requested.

On large sites it may be necessary to provide special facilities for safety representatives. Such facilities could include an office, access to a telephone, a notice board, a camera, noise level meter and a rudimentary library, as well as allowing the safety representative to attend courses which the TUC run for elected representatives.

Safety committees

If two safety representatives feel that a safety committee is required, they are legally empowered to ask that one be set up. The employers should construct the constitution of the committee as well as establish its membership and functions. The normal procedure is that the committee should have equal numbers of employee and employer representatives, with a chairman who shall usually be the site manager. It is important that the management representatives should have sufficient authority to act upon the committee's decisions. The functions of safety committees will vary from site to site, but they may include the following points:

(a) the monitoring of health and safety;
(b) the development of site safety rules, systems, and methods;
(c) the study of accident trends;
(d) the investigation of accidents;
(e) the examination of safety problems.

Construction (Health and Welfare) Regulations 1966

The Construction (Health and Welfare) Regulations 1966 insist upon the provision of a first-aid box on every site of over five operatives; and where the site is large, enough first-aid boxes must be provided to ensure that a first-aid box is available in all areas of the site.

311

When a site has over fifty operatives, then the person in charge of the first-aid box must be a State Registered or State Enrolled nurse, or hold a current first-aid certificate. However, if a contractor has made every effort to obtain a qualified first-aid person but has been unsuccessful, then the contractor is exempt from this requirement.

If the contractor employs more than twenty-five operatives on site, he must inform the local ambulance authority of the location of the site and the expected completion date and provide a suitable stretcher. On larger sites of over a total of 250 operatives, a contractor employing more than forty men must provide a first-aid room which is to be supervised by a qualified first-aid person. The room shall be properly fitted out for the administration of first-aid. Where appropriate, these facilities can be shared by contractors operating on the same site.

Welfare

On every site a contractor must provide a shelter for protection against bad weather and for the taking of meals, with facilities for the boiling of water. On sites with more than five workers, this accommodation should be heated and have arrangements for drying clothes. Where a site has ten or more operatives, there must be facilities for heating food unless a canteen is provided on site. Drinking water, washing facilities, and toilets should also be available. Toilet provision should be one WC for every twenty-five operatives up to 100, and one for every thirty-five operatives over 100 (i.e. 100 workers, four WCs; 135 workers, five WCs).

Construction (General Provisions) Regulations 1966

These regulations apply to all building operations and works of engineering construction and lay down regulations concerning a wide range of hazards frequently encountered within the industry. The primary responsibility is for a contractor to appoint a suitably qualified safety supervisor. This person need not be employed full time in this capacity, but the person appointed to this position must recognize that the control of safety is his primary responsibility. Among the other regulations are:

(a) safety within excavations with minimum standards established for the materials to be used in shoring; inspections and examinations of every excavation at the beginning of each shift is also required;
(b) the ventilation of excavations;
(c) the prevention of dangerous fumes derived from grinding, cleaning, spraying, etc.;
(d) the control of construction plant operators (i.e. they must be at least 18 years old, and riding on machines that have not been properly adapted to this purpose is prohibited);

(e) the control of demolition in terms of the competence of supervision and the integrity of structures being demolished. There is also a miscellaneous section which incorporates the fencing of machinery, the need for protection against falling material, the lighting of working places, knocking back nails, the lifting of excessive weights, etc.

Construction (Lifting Operations) Regulations 1961

These regulations give specific requirements for the operatives of cranes, lifting gear, and hoists. With respect to cranes, the regulations demand that all working parts be constructed of sound materials and erected under the supervision of a competent and experienced person. Particular emphasis is placed upon the stability of cranes; the siting of cranes on sloping ground or on soft and uneven surfaces is to be avoided. Ballast and anchorages for cranes should be secure.

All cranes should have a test certificate and it must be retested by a competent person after any structural alteration. The jibs to cranes must be marked along their length, with safe working loads at specific radii and alarm bells being triggered if this safe working load is exceeded.

The driver's cab must be protected against the weather and control levers must have locking devices which prevent their being accidentally displaced. All cranes should also have adequate brakes. Where cranes are rail-mounted the rails should be braced together and each end of the track should be provided with stops or buffers so that there can be no risk of derailment of the crane.

The lifting equipment attached to cranes also comes under the aegis of these regulations. Hooks should be fitted with safety catches, and where a crane driver does not have a clear view of the load, a banksman must be present to give clear and distinctive signals. This banksman must be at least 18 years old unless under training.

Hoists should always be enclosed in a substantial gauge wire mesh, with gates at least two metres high at opening points. These gates must always be closed unless loading or unloading is taking place. Hoists should only be operable from one position and the whole of the hoist should be visible from this station. The hoist platform should not be allowed to travel beyond the highest point within the hoist, and safety devices must be fitted which enable the platform to support itself should the hoist gear or ropes fail. The safe working load, and a notice prohibiting passengers, must be displayed on the cage.

Where hoists are designed to carry passengers extra precautions are demanded, particularly with regard to the gates. The hoist should only operate when all gates are locked, and locking devices should be attached to the gates to prevent their opening until the platform is at the required level. The maximum number of passengers must be displayed within the cage, and this limit adhered to. Any person using a passenger hoist has a statutory duty to close the landing gates immediately he has used it. The employer should see that this regulation is obeyed.

313

If loaded trucks or barrows are to be used, their wheels must be secured to prevent movement and the load so stacked that falls of materials are eliminated. Wherever possible, the barrows or trucks must be placed on the platform so that the person offloading the equipment does not need to enter the cage.

Finally, drivers of all lifting appliances must be at least 18 years old and trained to operate the appliance.

Construction (Working places) Regulations 1966

These regulations specifically deal with working practices on scaffolding and roofs and the provision of a safe means of access to workplaces. The regulations allocate responsibility for their compliance, with employers being held responsible for any breaches committed by their own employees; subcontractors are responsible for those they employ. Employees have a duty to comply with the regulations and to report defects to the employer, foreman, or safety supervisor.

When an accident occurs, the contractor must record the details of the event in an accident book kept on site. If the accident causes the person involved to be absent from work for three or more consecutives days, then the matter should be reported directly to the Health and Safety Inspectorate. Failure to report an accident is an offence.

Other regulations pertinent to construction are:

1. Woodworking Machinery Regulations 1974.
2. Asbestos Regulations 1969.
3. Offices at Building Operations, etc. (First Aid) Regulations 1964.
4. Protection of Eyes Regulations 1974.

Noise on construction sites

As previously mentioned, the aim of the Health and Safety at Work Act is to protect people from hazards arising from activities created by people at work. In connection with construction, noise is a pertinent area and is covered by the Control of Pollution Act 1974. This piece of legislation places with the local authority the control of noise emanating from construction sites. Such control means that the permissible level of noise will vary according to the nature and location of the works. In the main, local authorities have tended to allow all construction operations to proceed unless they are beset by an organized and consistent complaint from local residents or workers in nearby businesses. Where complaints are received, the local authority may issue to the contractor a 'consent' notice, which establishes the permissible noise levels emitting from a construction site. Alternatively, a contractor may take the initiative and ask the local authority to make its requirements known; and from this application the local authority must reply within twenty-eight days with a 'consent' certificate stating the local authority's requirements with regard to noise levels for that particular site. It should be noted that it is not mandatory for the contractor to apply for a 'consent' certificate, but it may often be in the interest of the contractor to apply for consent in order to reduce the risk of a local authority serving notice after work has started. Much time, money, and goodwill can be saved if it is known that the nature of operations and plant used are likely to create a noise problem.

The Control of Pollution Act 1974 is supported by a code of practice on reducing the exposure of employed persons to noise. The primary aim of this code of practice is not only to reduce exposure to noise, but to ensure, where possible, that noise does not exceed acceptable levels. The code suggests that if noise exposure is continuous for eight hours a day, the sound level should not exceed 90 dB(A) but at no time should a steady noise level of 135 dB(A) or an impact noise of 150 dB(A) be exceeded.

Particular problems arise out of plant use and most plant manufacturers have noise-reduced versions of standard equipment. The impetus for the production of such machines can be found in Europe, where noise restrictions are more stringent than in the UK. With the harmonizing of manufacturers' specifications for EEC marketing, the industry can expect to see a reduction in the noise generated by construction plant.

Other relevant regulations and codes of practice are:

1. The Control of Noise (Code of Practice for Construction Sites) Order 1975.
2. The Control of Noise (Appeals) Rules 1975.
3. The Control of Noise (Measurement and Registers) Regulations 1976.
4. *Noise Control on Construction and Demolition Sites*, BS 5228, 1975.

A brief summary of relevant employment legislation

These notes are not intended to be comprehensive, but are merely guidelines to the main points within the law. Case law has not been included but will be influential in determining how the courts have interpreted the law. Obviously, Parliament may repeal or amend the Acts at any time. Fuller information can be obtained from *Rights at Work* by J McMullen, published by Pluto Press, 1978.

Employment Protection (Consolidation) Act 1978

Every employee has a contract of employment, even though there may be nothing written or signed at the outset of employment, although most firms feel that it is advisable to prepare a written contract. In the construction industry many of the written terms will be taken from the NWRA drawn up by the NJCBI, or the civil engineering agreement from the CECCB. Unwritten terms of contract can be implied from the customs and practices of the industry.

Within thirteen weeks of starting employment, the employer must provide the employee with a statement which sets out the following:-

1. The name of the employer (e.g. the company name) and the employee.
2. The date employment began.
3. Job title (not a job description).
4. The rate of pay and overtime rates.
5. Whether the pay is weekly or monthly and whether the employee works a week or a month in advance of payment.
6. Hours of work and normal working hours.
7. Holiday entitlements and holiday pay.
8. Sickness and injury benefit.
9. Pension rights.
10. The amount of notice to be given by employer and employee.
11. Disciplinary and grievance procedures.
12. The name or description of the person to whom the employee should apply if dissatisfied with any disciplinary decision, or should the employee wish to register a grievance.

13. If the contract is for a fixed period, the date the contract expires.
14. Whether or not a contracting-out certificate under the Social Security Pensions Act is in force.

Employers often find it beneficial to refer employees to a document which can be read at work, rather than spell out all the conditions above.

Race Relations Act 1976

The first Race Relations Act was introduced in 1965 but has been strengthened by legislation passed in 1968 and 1976. The 1976 Act is the one currently in force. The law forbids discrimination in employment (and other matters) if it is based upon race, colour, nationality, ethnic, or national origins. There are four kinds of discrimination: direct discrimination; indirect discrimination; victimization; and segregation. In each case the comparison to be made is between cases whose 'relevant circumstances are the same, not materially different'.

Direct discrimination

This occurs on the grounds of race, e.g. if an employer treats a black worker 'less favourably than he treats or would treat other persons'. Thus, favouring a white worker to a black worker in recruitment or promotion, when both have the same qualifications, is unlawful if the favouritism is based upon race.

Indirect discrimination

Indirect discrimination can occur when an employer stipulates a requirement which applies equally to all people but

(a) is such that the proportion of possible applicants within a particular racial group is considerably smaller than the proportion of possible applicants outside that racial group (e.g. advertising for a site engineer who must have blue eyes);
(b) is unjustifiably in favour of special characteristics (i.e. why should a site engineer have blue eyes?);
(c) is to the detriment of a particular race of people because they cannot comply with the requirements.

Victimization

The employer cannot lawfully victimize a person on the grounds that that person

(a) brought proceedings against the firm for any alleged discrimination;
(b) gave evidence to, or helped, the Commission for Racial Equality;
(c) made allegations of discrimination (unless they were false and not made in good faith).

317

Segregation

Segregation of people for racial reasons amounts to discrimination.

The Act specifies the stages in the employment chain where discrimination is most likely to occur. Discrimination at recruitment, in terms and conditions, in transfers or promotions, in training opportunities and dismissal are all illegal.

Allied to the Race Relations Act 1976 is the Commission for Racial Equality (CRE) which is empowered to promote equality between racial groups and undertake research and education work. The CRE can investigate particular industries, and firms are required to disclose information to investigators.

Sex Discrimination Act 1975

This particular piece of legislation follows the principles laid down in the Race Relations Act and the procedures are almost identical. It is illegal to discriminate against women in employment, although it is permissible to discriminate if there is a genuine occupational qualification for a particular job. Spurious qualifications such as 'must be six feet tall' and 'must be prepared to strip to the waist during summer months' constitute indirect discrimination against women.

The agency which monitors the Act – the Equal Opportunities Commission – has exactly the same rights as the CRE.

Equal Pay Act 1970

This Act says that in 'certain circumstances' men and women are entitled to be paid the same and receive the same terms and conditions in their contracts and pay structure. Equal pay must be given if

(a) men and women do the same work;
(b) men and women do work of a broadly similar nature and differences are not of practical importance in relation to terms and conditions;
(c) the work being carried out by a woman is rated as equivalent with men in the same employment (i.e. carpenters and bricklayers are both rated as skilled trades).

The Equal Pay Act 1970 deals with matters of contract and every contract of employment is deemed to incorporate 'equality clauses'. Everyone has a contractual right to equal treatment.

Redundancy Payments (part of Employment Protection (Consolidation) Act 1978 Part II)

Redundancy can be said to take place if

(a) the employer ceases to trade;
(b) the employer closes down the place in which the employee is contracted to work;

(c) the requirements of the employer for a particular trade have ceased or diminished.

If items (b) or (c) occur, the employer can offer alternative employment. Offers of alternative employment must be made before the employee's notice expires and the new job must start within four weeks of the old job. If the employee's contract is renewed without changes, it will usually be unreasonable for the employee to refuse it. However, if the work or conditions of a new job are different, the employee forfeits redundancy pay if the new job is suitable and he or she unreasonably refuses it (i.e. a site agent refuses to be transferred to the planning department). Less pay, lower status, and more travelling are, however, factors which will need to be considered by both sides. Finally, the employee is entitled to a four-week trial period in any new job.

Redundancy payments are due to employees if they have lost their job and have at least two years' service with the company. (There are exceptions to this: workers under 20 are not eligible, nor are male workers over 65. Employees working eight to sixteen hours a week require five years' service.) The amount of redundancy pay due varies with the length of service and the formula for calculating redundancy payments is set out below:

Age		Number of weeks pay for each year's service
18		0
Over 18	but less than 22	0.5
Over 22	but less than 41	1
Over 41	but less than 65	1.5

It should be noted that, for a woman aged between 59 and 60 and a man aged between 64 and 65, the cash amount due is reduced by one-twelfth for every complete month by which the age exceeds 59 or 64, respectively. For example, a man aged 64 years 5 months with 20 years' service will be due:

$20 \times 1\frac{1}{2}$ week's pay = Basic redundancy

less: $5 \times 1/12$ of basic redundancy.

A week's pay is defined in Appendix D of the DoE booklet *The Redundancy Payments Scheme.*

It should be noted that these figures are the statutory minimum and that many companies make additional payments. The redundancy pay is tax free and any additional payment up to £25,000 is also free of tax.

An employer is entitled to claim a rebate from a State fund to which all employers contribute. The rebate is 41 per cent of the statutory amount paid to the employee. Payments made in addition to the statutory minimum are not reclaimable. Should a firm be bankrupt, the whole of the statutory payment is guaranteed by the State fund.

Employment Protection (Consolidation) Act 1978

This is the most comprehensive statute concerning employment law. It covers a wide range of issues including dismissal, maternity rights, discipline at work, lay-offs and short-time working, and compensation payments.

Dismissal

An employee is considered to be dismissed if

(a) the employer sacks the employee (with or without notice);
(b) the employer forces the employee to resign;
(c) the employee walks out because the employer's behaviour entitles the employee to do so (see 'constructive dismissal' below);
(d) the employee is made redundant;
(e) the employee was on a fixed-term contract which has expired.

Constructive dismissal can arise if the employee walks out because of a serious breach of contract by the employer (e.g. insisting that overtime be worked, overtime without pay, accusation of theft without investigation, sexual harrassment, forcing a cut in pay or status).

Dismissals may be 'fair' for five reasons:

(a) lack of ability to do the job;
(b) misconduct (e.g. theft, insolence, bad time-keeping);
(c) redundancy (see Redundancy Payments);
(d) illegality (if it is illegal for the employer to continue employment);
(e) other substantial reason (e.g. if the employer feels that it is in the best interests of the firm that the employee be dismissed).

The ACAS code of practice on disciplinary practice and procedures recommends that any dismissal should be prefaced by a verbal and two written warnings which point out to the employee the reason for the warning. However, summary dismissal may be fair in cases of serious misconduct.

Maternity rights

All pregnant women have the right to be paid for absences from work for ante-natal care. Women who have two years and eleven weeks' service at the time of giving birth are eligible for maternity pay, which is nine-tenths of normal pay for each week that the employee is absent from work before the birth, up to a maximum of six weeks. Women having given birth have the right to return to work at any time before the end of twenty-nine weeks after the birth of the baby (also see Employment Act 1980).

Discipline

Employees cannot be disciplined for belonging to a trade union or participating in its activities at an appropriate time. Union officers have the right to carry out trade union duties during their normal working hours.

Lay-offs and short-time working

The Act gives all employees the right to a minimum payment if they are laid off in certain circumstances. These circumstances are:

(a) a reduction in the employer's need for the kind of work done;
(b) an 'occurrence' which affects normal working (i.e. flood, fire, bad weather, some industrial dispute, etc.).

Payments are made for 'workless days' and there is a statutory maximum for a 'day's pay'.

Compensation

Employees can claim compensation from an industrial tribunal if they have been unfairly dismissed or have been subjected to racial or sex discrimination.

Information for bargaining purposes

The Employment Protection Act 1975 imposes a duty on employers to provide recognized unions with information for bargaining. ACAS has published a code of practice giving guidelines on what should and should not be disclosed. The code lists the following data that should be given:

1. Pay and benefits: pay structure, job evaluation schemes, total pay bill, fringe benefits, earnings, and hours worked.
2. Conditions of service: policies on recruitment, redundancy, training, promotion, health and safety.
3. Manpower: numbers employed and in which departments, labour turnover, absenteeism, overtime, changes in work methods, equipment used, organization structure.
4. Performance: productivity data, savings from increased productivity, return on capital, sales and order book.
5. Financial: cost structure, gross and net profits, sources of earnings, assets, liabilities, government financial aid, loans, etc.

Employment Protection (Consolidation) Act 1978

This Act has extended trade union rights at the collective level and reinforces existing law on unfair dismissal for the individual.

Unfair dismissal

There are five situations where unfair dismissal may occur:

(a) if a person is victimized because of trade union membership or activities;
(b) if the established custom and practice for dealing with redundancies (e.g. last in – first out) has been breached without special reason;
(c) if any redundancy is announced in an unreasonable manner;

(d) if the employer fails to consider the possibility of alternative work;

(e) if alternative work is offered but the employee is not given enough information to enable a realistic decision to be made.

Points (c)–(e) are case law.

Trade union bargaining

Issues eligible for collective bargaining will include:

(a) terms and conditions of employment, physical conditions at work;

(b) engagement, termination, or suspension of employees;

(c) allocation of work to employees;

(d) discipline;

(e) trade union membership;

(f) facilities for trade union officials;

(g) machinery for negotiation or consultation.

If employers and employees come to agreement on any of these matters it is termed a 'collective agreement'. An agreement is not legally binding. It is immaterial whether the agreement is made at national, regional, local, or site level, but generally a local or site agreement has precedence over national bargains.

Union Membership Agreement (UMA) (a closed shop) can be negotiated under the Trade Union and Labour Relations Act 1974 and a UMA has the practical effect of requiring employees to be members of one of the trade unions which is party to the UMA. Exemption is available for those persons who object to trade unions on the grounds of 'conscience or other deeply held personal conviction'. The legal consequences of the UMA are:

(a) new and existing employees must join the union;

(b) dismissal for not joining the trade union is 'unfair' (Employment Act 1980);

(c) there is no obligation to participate in a union's activities.

Strikes and picketing

The Employment Protection (Consolidation) Act 1978 does not forbid an employer from dismissing *all* workers on strike as such dismissals are fair; but if an employer dismisses only *some* of those on strike, then such actions are construed as unfair dismissals.

Trade unions have a legal right to picket for the purposes of peacefully obtaining or communicating information, or peacefully persuading any person to work or to abstain from working.

Employment Act 1980

This piece of legislation amended some of the procedures for unfair dismissal and maternity rights at the individual level and the law on picketing, union recognition, and the closed shop in collective cases as such it merely amended the Employment Protection (Consolidation) Act 1978 in the following areas.

Unfair dismissal

The Act established the principle that industrial tribunals take into account the size and administrative resources of the employer in deciding if a dismissal was reasonable. Also, if a firm has under twenty employees, then a person cannot claim unfair dismissal if he/she has not worked at the firm for two years (the normal right is one year). Also, the burden of proving that any dismissal was 'fair' no longer rests with the employer.

Maternity rights

The employee must request a return to work in writing not earlier than forty-nine days after the beginning of the expected week of confinement. Also, the employee must give written notice of her return at least twenty-one days before the proposed date of return (previously seven days was sufficient).

If the employer cannot offer the woman the same job on return and the woman refuses suitable alternative work, then this is deemed to be a fair dismissal. Also, if the employer has less than six employees and it is not practicable for the woman to return to her original job, she need not be re-employed at all.

Closed shops, picketing, union recognition, and strikes

The Employment Act 1980 put forward new rules for the signing of UMAs. New agreements must have the support of 80 per cent of those to be covered by the agreement. The vote is to be conducted by secret ballot.

Picketing is covered by a new code of practice on picketing, and while the Act has not substantially amended the provisions of the Trade Union and Labour Relations Act 1978, the code of practice suggests that six workers is a sufficient number of pickets, although the police have discretion in this matter.

The statutory procedure for dealing with trade union recognition is abolished and this Act repeals Sections 11–16 of the Employment Protection (Consolidation) Act 1978.

On strikes, lawful industrial action is limited to action against an employer or a supplier or customer. All other 'sympathy' strikes are unlawful.

The Employment Act 1982

This piece of legislation primarily concerned trade union immunities and dismissal of employees in relation to trade union membership.

Trade union immunities

The main points are as follows:

(a) Trade unions are no longer immune from tortious actions. As such trade unions are liable for damages caused in the event of unlawful industrial action or if unlawful acts are done on their behalf.
(b) Injunctions may be issued against trade unions as well as individuals.
(c) The Act defines the parties within the union who may authorize a strike – generally it has to be endorsed by senior officials or committees of the union.
(d) Any damages payable to the employer are limited by the size of the union. Damages of £10,000 are payable if the union has less than 5,000 members and £250,000 if it has over 100,000 members.

Union membership and commercial contracts

Here commercial contracts which seek to impose industrial relations conditions upon a contractor are unlawful. For instance, a contract between a local authority and a contractor cannot specify that a closed shop has to be agreed as part of the contract. Equally, a main contractor cannot enforce a subcontractor into an industrial relations policy against the subcontractor's will. Such contracts are illegal. It is also illegal for workers to undertake industrial action with the object of securing such clauses in a commercial contract. If contracts are terminated because a contractor will not abide by an industrial relations stipulation in a contract then the contractor may claim damages.

Union membership, closed shops and dismissals

There are two frameworks for considering the law here. Firstly, within closed shops and secondly, outside of closed shops.

1. Within closed shops
(a) A worker is deemed to be unfairly dismissed if he/she has been unreasonably excluded from the union.
(b) From November 1984 a dismissal for not being a union member in a closed shop firm will be unfair if the closed shop has not been endorsed by ballot within the previous five years. Endorsement requires 80 per cent of those entitled to vote or 85 per cent of those voting.

2. Outside the closed shop
(a) It is unfair to dismiss a person for not being a member of a union.
(b) It is unfair to dismiss a worker for refusing to make payments to a charity *in lieu* of union subscriptions.
Should a person be unfairly dismissed then compensation is available from the employer and the government.

Finally, it is now legal for an employer to selectively dismiss workers participating in a strike. If a section of the workforce returns to work, those remaining on strike may be fairly dismissed.

Definitions of a trade dispute

If a strike is to be lawful then it must comply with the following points:

(a) The strike must be wholly related to industrial matters (i.e. no political strikes).
(b) The strike must be related to a dispute with one's own employer (i.e. no sympathy strikes).
(c) Strikes against a multinational employer are illegal unless workers in the UK are affected by the outcome.

Discounted cash flow

Table C.1 Amount of unit sum invested for *n* periods – compound interest $A = (1 + i)^n$

Compound interest rate i from 0.03 to 0.10 (3% to 10%)

n	Interest rate i								n
	0.03 (3%)	0.04 (4%)	0.05 (5%)	0.06 (6%)	0.07 (7%)	0.08 (8%)	0.09 (9%)	0.10 (10%)	
1	1.0300	1.0400	1.0500	1.0600	1.0700	1.0800	1.0900	1.1000	1
2	1.0609	1.0816	1.1025	1.1236	1.1449	1.1664	1.1881	1.2100	2
3	1.0927	1.1249	1.1576	1.1910	1.2250	1.2597	1.2950	1.3310	3
4	1.1255	1.1699	1.2155	1.2625	1.3108	1.3605	1.4116	1.4641	4
5	1.1593	1.2167	1.2763	1.3382	1.4026	1.4693	1.5386	1.6105	5
6	1.1941	1.2653	1.3404	1.4185	1.5007	1.5869	1.6771	1.7716	6
7	1.2299	1.3159	1.4071	1.5036	1.6058	1.7138	1.8280	1.9487	7
8	1.2668	1.3686	1.4775	1.5938	1.7182	1.8509	1.9926	2.1436	8
9	1.3048	1.4233	1.5513	1.6895	1.8385	1.9990	2.1719	2.3579	9
10	1.3439	1.4802	1.6289	1.7908	1.9672	2.1589	2.3674	2.5937	10
11	1.3842	1.5395	1.7103	1.8983	2.1049	2.3316	2.5804	2.8531	11
12	1.4258	1.6010	1.7959	2.0122	2.2522	2.5182	2.8127	3.1384	12
13	1.4685	1.6651	1.8856	2.1329	2.4098	2.7196	3.0658	3.4523	13
14	1.5126	1.7317	1.9799	2.2609	2.5785	2.9372	3.3417	3.7975	14
15	1.5580	1.8009	2.0789	2.3966	2.7590	3.1722	3.6425	4.1772	15
16	1.6047	1.8730	2.1829	2.5404	2.9522	3.4259	3.9703	4.5950	16
17	1.6528	1.9479	2.2920	2.6928	3.1588	3.7000	4.3276	5.0545	17
18	1.7024	2.0258	2.4066	2.8543	3.3799	3.9960	4.7171	5.5599	18
19	1.7535	2.1068	2.5270	3.0256	3.6165	4.3157	5.1417	6.1159	19
20	1.8061	2.1911	2.6533	3.2071	3.8697	4.6610	5.6044	6.7275	20
22	1.9161	2.3699	2.9253	3.6035	4.4304	5.4365	6.6586	8.1403	22
24	2.0328	2.5633	3.2251	4.0489	5.0724	6.3412	7.9111	9.8497	24
26	2.1566	2.7725	3.5557	4.5494	5.8074	7.3964	9.3992	11.9182	26
28	2.2879	2.9987	3.9201	5.1117	6.6488	8.6271	11.1671	14.4210	28
30	2.4273	3.3436	4.3219	5.7435	7.6123	10.0627	13.2677	17.4494	30
35	2.8139	3.9461	5.5160	7.6861	10.6766	14.7853	20.4140	28.1024	35
40	3.2620	4.8010	7.0400	10.2857	14.9745	21.7245	31.4094	45.2593	40
45	3.7816	5.8412	8.9850	13.7646	21.0025	31.9204	48.3273	72.8905	45
50	4.3839	7.1062	11.4674	18.4202	29.4570	46.9016	74.3575	117.391	50
55	5.0821	8.6464	14.6356	24.6503	41.3150	68.9139	114.408	189.059	55
60	5.8916	10.5196	18.6792	32.9877	57.9464	101.257	176.031	304.482	60
65	6.8300	12.7982	23.8399	44.1450	81.2729	148.780	270.846	490.371	65
70	7.9178	15.5716	30.4264	59.0759	113.989	218.606	416.730	789.747	70
75	9.1789	18.9453	38.8327	75.0569	159.876	321.205	641.191	1,271.90	75
80	10.6409	23.0408	49.5614	105.796	224.234	471.955	986.552	2,048.40	80
85	12.3357	28.0436	63.2544	141.579	314.500	693.457	1,517.93	3,298.97	85
90	14.3005	34.1193	80.7304	189.465	441.103	1,018.92	2,335.53	5,313.02	90
95	16.5782	41.5114	103.035	253.546	618.670	1,497.12	3,593.50	8,556.68	95
100	19.2187	50.5040	131.501	339.302	867.716	2,199.76	5,529.04	13,780.6	100

Table C.1 (cont'd)

Compound interest rate i from 0.11 to 0.20 (11% to 20%)

n	Interest rate i								n
	0.11 (11%)	0.12 (12%)	0.13 (13%)	0.14 (14%)	0.15 (15%)	0.16 (16%)	0.18 (18%)	0.20 (20%)	
1	1.1100	1.1200	1.1300	1.1400	1.1500	1.1600	1.1800	1.2000	1
2	1.2321	1.2544	1.2769	1.2996	1.3225	1.3456	1.3924	1.4400	2
3	1.3676	1.4049	1.4429	1.4815	1.5209	1.5609	1.6430	1.7280	3
4	1.5181	1.5735	1.6305	1.6890	1.7490	1.8106	1.9388	2.0736	4
5	1.6851	1.7623	1.8424	1.9254	2.0114	2.1003	2.2878	2.4883	5
6	1.8704	1.9738	2.0820	2.1950	2.3131	2.4364	2.6996	2.9860	6
7	2.0762	2.2107	2.3526	2.5023	2.6600	2.8262	3.1855	3.5832	7
8	2.3045	2.4760	2.6584	2.8526	3.0590	3.2784	3.7589	4.2998	8
9	2.5580	2.7731	3.0040	3.2519	3.5179	3.8030	4.4355	5.1598	9
10	2.8394	3.1058	3.3946	3.7072	4.0456	4.4114	5.2338	6.1917	10
11	3.1518	3.4785	3.8359	4.2262	4.6524	5.1173	6.1759	7.4301	11
12	3.4985	3.8960	4.3345	4.8179	5.3503	5.9360	7.2876	8.9161	12
13	3.8833	4.3635	4.8980	5.4924	6.1528	6.8858	8.5994	10.6993	13
14	4.3104	4.8871	5.5348	6.2613	7.0757	7.9875	10.1472	12.8392	14
15	4.7846	5.4736	6.2543	7.1379	8.1371	9.2655	11.9737	15.4070	15
16	5.3109	6.1304	7.0673	8.1372	9.3576	10.7480	14.1290	18.4884	16
17	5.8951	6.8660	7.9861	9.2765	10.7613	12.4677	16.6722	22.1861	17
18	6.5436	7.6900	9.0243	10.5752	12.3755	14.4625	19.6733	26.6233	18
19	7.2633	8.6128	10.1974	12.0557	14.2318	16.7765	23.2144	31.9480	19
20	8.0623	9.6463	11.5231	13.7435	16.3665	19.4608	27.3930	38.3376	20
22	9.9336	12.1003	14.7138	17.8610	21.6447	26.1864	38.1421	55.2061	22
24	12.2392	15.1786	18.7881	23.2122	28.6252	35.2364	53.1090	79.4968	24
26	15.0799	19.0401	23.9905	30.1666	37.8568	47.4141	73.9490	114.476	26
28	18.5799	23.8839	30.6335	39.2045	50.0656	63.8004	102.967	164.845	28
30	22.8923	29.9599	39.1159	50.9502	66.2118	85.8499	143.371	237.376	30
35	38.5749	52.7996	72.0685	98.1002	133.176	180.314	327.997	590.668	35
40	65.0009	93.0510	132.782	188.884	267.864	378.721	750.378	1,469.77	40
45	109.530	163.988	244.641	363.679	538.769	795.444	1,716.68	3,657.26	45
50	184.565	289.002	450.736	700.233	1,083.66	1,670.70	3,927.36	9,100.44	50
55	311.003	509.321	830.452	1,348.24	2,179.62	3,509.05	8,984.84	22,644.8	55
60	524.057	897.597	1,530.05	2,595.92	4,384.00	7,370.20	20,555.1	56,347.5	60
65	883.067	1,581.87	2,819.02	4,998.22	8,817.79	15,479.9	47,025.2	140,211	65
70	1,488.02	2,787.80	5,193.87	9,623.65	17,735.7	32,513.2	107,582	348,889	70
75	2,507.40	4,913.06	9,569.37	18,529.5	35,672.9	68,288.8	246,122	868,147	75
80	4,225.11	8,658.48	17,630.9	35,677.0	71,750.9	143,430	563,068	2,160,228	80

Table C.2 Present worth (PW) of unit sum spent after n periods $PW = \dfrac{1}{(1 + i)^n}$

Compound interest rate i from 0.03 to 0.10 (3% to 10%)

n	Interest rate i								n
	0.03 (3%)	0.04 (4%)	0.05 (5%)	0.06 (6%)	0.07 (7%)	0.08 (8%)	0.09 (9%)	0.10 (10%)	
1	0.9709	0.9615	0.9524	0.9434	0.9346	0.9259	0.9174	0.9091	1
2	0.9426	0.9246	0.9070	0.8900	0.8734	0.8573	0.8417	0.8264	2
3	0.9151	0.8890	0.8638	0.8396	0.8163	0.7938	0.7722	0.7513	3
4	0.8885	0.8548	0.8227	0.7921	0.7629	0.7350	0.7084	0.6830	4
5	0.8626	0.8219	0.7835	0.7473	0.7130	0.6806	0.6499	0.6209	5
6	0.8375	0.7903	0.7462	0.7050	0.6663	0.6302	0.5963	0.5645	6
7	0.8131	0.7599	0.7107	0.6651	0.6227	0.5835	0.5470	0.5132	7
8	0.7894	0.7307	0.6768	0.6274	0.5820	0.5403	0.5019	0.4665	8
9	0.7664	0.7026	0.6446	0.5919	0.5439	0.5002	0.4604	0.4241	9
10	0.7441	0.6756	0.6139	0.5584	0.5083	0.4632	0.4224	0.3855	10
11	0.7224	0.6496	0.5847	0.5268	0.4751	0.4289	0.3875	0.3505	11
12	0.7014	0.6246	0.5568	0.4970	0.4440	0.3971	0.3555	0.3186	12
13	0.6810	0.6006	0.5303	0.4688	0.4150	0.3677	0.3262	0.2897	13
14	0.6611	0.5775	0.5051	0.4423	0.3878	0.3405	0.2992	0.2633	14
15	0.6419	0.5553	0.4810	0.4173	0.3624	0.3152	0.2745	0.2394	15
16	0.6232	0.5339	0.4581	0.3936	0.3387	0.2919	0.2519	0.2176	16
17	0.6050	0.5134	0.4363	0.3714	0.3166	0.2703	0.2311	0.1978	17
18	0.5874	0.4936	0.4155	0.3503	0.2959	0.2502	0.2120	0.1799	18
19	0.5703	0.4746	0.3957	0.3305	0.2765	0.2317	0.1945	0.1635	19
20	0.5537	0.4564	0.3769	0.3118	0.2584	0.2145	0.1784	0.1486	20
22	0.5219	0.4220	0.3418	0.2775	0.2257	0.1839	0.1502	0.1228	22
24	0.4919	0.3901	0.3101	0.2470	0.1971	0.1577	0.1264	0.1015	24
26	0.4637	0.3607	0.2812	0.2198	0.1722	0.1352	0.1064	0.0839	26
28	0.4371	0.3335	0.2551	0.1956	0.1504	0.1159	0.0895	0.0693	28
30	0.4120	0.3083	0.2314	0.1741	0.1314	0.0994	0.0754	0.0573	30
35	0.3554	0.2534	0.1813	0.1301	0.0937	0.0676	0.0490	0.0356	35
40	0.3066	0.2083	0.1420	0.0972	0.0668	0.0460	0.0318	0.0221	40
45	0.2644	0.1712	0.1113	0.0727	0.0476	0.0313	0.0207	0.0137	45
50	0.2281	0.1407	0.0872	0.0543	0.0339	0.0213	0.0134	0.00852	50
55	0.1968	0.1157	0.0683	0.0406	0.0242	0.0145	0.00874	0.00529	55
60	0.1697	0.0951	0.0535	0.0303	0.0173	0.00988	0.00568	0.00328	60
65	0.1464	0.0781	0.0419	0.0227	0.0123	0.00672	0.00369	0.00204	65
70	0.1263	0.0642	0.0329	0.0169	0.00877	0.00457	0.00240	0.00127	70
75	0.1089	0.0528	0.0258	0.0126	0.00625	0.00311	0.00156	0.00079	75
80	0.0940	0.0434	0.0202	0.00945	0.00446	0.00212	0.00101	0.00049	80
85	0.0811	0.0357	0.0158	0.00706	0.00318	0.00144	0.00066	0.00030	85
90	0.0699	0.0293	0.0124	0.00528	0.00227	0.00098	0.00043	0.00019	90
95	0.0603	0.0241	0.00971	0.00394	0.00162	0.00067	0.00028	0.00012	95
100	0.0520	0.0198	0.00760	0.00295	0.00115	0.00045	0.00018	0.00007	100

Table C.2 (cont'd)

Compound interest rate i from 0.11 to 0.20 (11% to 20%)

n	0.11 (11%)	0.12 (12%)	0.13 (13%)	0.14 (14%)	0.15 (15%)	0.16 (16%)	0.18 (18%)	0.20 (20%)	n
1	0.9009	0.8929	0.8850	0.8772	0.8696	0.8621	0.8475	0.8333	1
2	0.8116	0.7972	0.7831	0.7695	0.7561	0.7432	0.7182	0.6944	2
3	0.7312	0.7118	0.6931	0.6750	0.6575	0.6407	0.6086	0.5787	3
4	0.6587	0.6355	0.6133	0.5921	0.5718	0.5523	0.5158	0.4823	4
5	0.5935	0.5674	0.5428	0.5194	0.4972	0.4761	0.4371	0.4019	5
6	0.5346	0.5066	0.4803	0.4556	0.4323	0.4104	0.3704	0.3349	6
7	0.4817	0.4523	0.4251	0.3996	0.3759	0.3538	0.3139	0.2791	7
8	0.4339	0.4039	0.3762	0.3506	0.3269	0.3050	0.2660	0.2326	8
9	0.3909	0.3606	0.3329	0.3075	0.2843	0.2630	0.2255	0.1938	9
10	0.3522	0.3220	0.2946	0.2697	0.2472	0.2267	0.1911	0.1615	10
11	0.3173	0.2875	0.2607	0.2366	0.2149	0.1954	0.1619	0.1346	11
12	0.2858	0.2567	0.2307	0.2076	0.1869	0.1685	0.1372	0.1122	12
13	0.2575	0.2292	0.2042	0.1821	0.1625	0.1452	0.1163	0.0935	13
14	0.2320	0.2046	0.1807	0.1597	0.1413	0.1252	0.0985	0.0779	14
15	0.2090	0.1827	0.1599	0.1401	0.1229	0.1079	0.0835	0.0649	15
16	0.1883	0.1631	0.1415	0.1229	0.1069	0.0930	0.0708	0.0541	16
17	0.1696	0.1456	0.1252	0.1078	0.0929	0.0802	0.0600	0.0451	17
18	0.1528	0.1300	0.1108	0.0946	0.0808	0.0691	0.0508	0.0376	18
19	0.1377	0.1161	0.0981	0.0829	0.0703	0.0596	0.0431	0.0313	19
20	0.1240	0.1037	0.0868	0.0728	0.0611	0.0514	0.0365	0.0261	20
22	0.1007	0.0826	0.0680	0.0560	0.0462	0.0382	0.0262	0.0181	22
24	0.0817	0.0659	0.0532	0.0431	0.0349	0.0284	0.0188	0.0126	24
26	0.0663	0.0525	0.0417	0.0331	0.0264	0.0211	0.0135	0.00874	26
28	0.0538	0.0419	0.0326	0.0255	0.0200	0.0157	0.00971	0.00607	28
30	0.0437	0.0334	0.0256	0.0196	0.0151	0.0116	0.00697	0.00421	30
35	0.0259	0.0189	0.0139	0.0102	0.00751	0.00555	0.00305	0.00169	35
40	0.0154	0.0107	0.00753	0.00529	0.00373	0.00264	0.00133	0.00068	40
45	0.00913	0.00610	0.00409	0.00275	0.00186	0.00126	0.00058	0.00027	45
50	0.00542	0.00346	0.00222	0.00143	0.00092	0.00060	0.00025	0.00011	50
55	0.00322	0.00196	0.00120	0.00074	0.00046	0.00028	0.00011		55
60	0.00191	0.00111	0.00065	0.00039	0.00023	0.00014			60
65	0.00113	0.00063	0.00035	0.00020	0.00011				65
70	0.00067	0.00036	0.00019	0.00010					70
75	0.00040	0.00020	0.00010						75
	0.00024	0.00012							

Less than 0.0001

329

Table C.3 Amount of unit sum invested each period for n periods $A = \dfrac{(1 + i)^n - 1}{i}$

Compound interest rate i from 0.03 to 0.10 (3% to 10%)

n	Interest rate i								n
	0.03 (3%)	0.04 (4%)	0.05 (5%)	0.06 (6%)	0.07 (7%)	0.08 (8%)	0.09 (9%)	0.10 (10%)	
1	1.0000	1.0000	1.0000	1.0000	1.0000	1.0000	1.0000	1.0000	1
2	2.0300	2.0400	2.0500	2.0600	2.0700	2.0800	2.0900	2.1000	2
3	3.0909	3.1216	3.1525	3.1836	3.2149	3.2464	3.2781	3.3100	3
4	4.1836	4.2465	4.3101	4.3746	4.4388	4.5061	4.5731	4.6410	4
5	5.3091	5.4163	5.5256	5.6371	5.7507	5.8666	5.9847	6.1051	5
6	6.4684	6.6330	6.8019	6.9753	7.1533	7.3359	7.5233	7.7156	6
7	7.6625	7.8983	8.1420	8.3938	8.6540	8.9228	9.2004	9.4872	7
8	8.8923	9.2142	9.5491	9.8975	10.2598	10.6366	11.0285	11.4359	8
9	10.1591	10.5828	11.0266	11.4913	11.9780	12.4876	13.0210	13.5795	9
10	11.4639	12.0061	12.5779	13.1808	13.8164	14.4866	15.1929	15.9374	10
11	12.8078	13.4864	14.2068	14.9716	15.7836	16.6455	17.5603	18.5312	11
12	14.1920	15.0258	15.9171	16.8699	17.8885	18.9771	20.1407	21.3843	12
13	15.1678	16.6268	17.7130	18.8821	20.1406	21.4953	22.9534	24.5227	13
14	17.0863	18.2919	19.5986	21.0151	22.5504	24.2149	26.0192	27.9750	14
15	18.5989	20.0236	21.5786	23.2760	25.1290	27.1521	29.3609	31.7725	15
16	20.1569	21.8245	23.6575	25.6725	27.8881	30.3243	33.0034	35.9497	16
17	21.7616	23.6975	24.8404	28.2129	30.8402	33.7502	36.9737	40.5447	17
18	23.4144	25.6454	28.1324	30.9057	33.9990	37.4503	41.3013	45.5992	18
19	25.1169	27.6712	30.5390	33.7600	37.3790	41.4463	46.0185	51.1591	19
20	26.8704	29.7781	33.0660	36.7860	40.9955	45.7620	51.1601	57.2750	20
22	30.5368	34.2480	38.5052	43.3923	49.0057	55.4568	62.8733	71.4028	22
24	34.4265	39.0826	44.5020	50.8156	58.1767	66.7648	76.7898	88.4973	24
26	38.5530	44.3117	51.1135	59.1564	68.6767	79.9544	93.3240	109.182	26
28	42.9309	49.9676	58.4026	68.5281	80.6977	95.3388	112.968	123.210	28
30	47.5754	56.0849	66.4388	79.0582	94.4608	113.283	136.308	164.494	30
35	60.4621	73.6522	90.3203	111.435	138.237	172.317	215.711	271.024	35
40	75.4013	95.0255	120.800	154.762	199.635	259.057	337.882	442.593	40
45	92.7199	121.029	159.700	212.744	285.749	386.506	525.859	718.905	45
50	112.797	152.667	209.348	290.336	406.529	573.770	815.084	1,163.91	50
55	136.072	191.159	272.712	394.172	575.929	848.923	1,260.09	1,880.59	55
60	163.053	237.991	353.584	533.128	813.520	1,253.21	1,944.79	3,034.82	60
65	194.333	294.968	456.798	719.083	1,146.76	1,847.25	2,998.29	4,893.71	65
70	230.594	364.290	588.529	967.932	1,614.13	2,270.08	4,619.22	7,887.47	70
75	272.631	448.631	756.654	1,300.95	2,269.66	4,002.56	7,113.23	12,709.0	75
80	321.363	551.245	971.229	1,746.60	3,189.06	5,886.94	10,950.6	20,474.0	80
85	377.857	676.090	1,245.09	2,342.98	4,478.58	8,655.71	16,854.8	32,979.7	85
90	443.349	827.983	1,594.61	3,141.08	6,287.19	12,723.9	25,939.2	53,120.2	90
95	519.272	1,012.78	2,040.69	4,209.10	8,823.85	18,701.5	39,916.6	85,556.8	95
100	607.288	1,237.62	2,610.03	5,638.37	12,381.7	27,484.5	61,422.7	137,796	100

Table C.3 (cont'd)

Compound interest rate *i* from *0.11* to *0.20* (11% to 20%)

n	Interest rate i								n
	0.11 *(11%)*	*0.12* *(12%)*	*0.13* *(13%)*	*0.14* *(14%)*	*0.15* *(15%)*	*0.16* *(16%)*	*0.18* *(18%)*	*0.20* *(20%)*	
1	1.0000	1.0000	1.0000	1.0000	1.0000	1.0000	1.0000	1.0000	1
2	2.1100	2.1200	2.1300	2.1400	2.1500	2.1600	2.1800	2.2000	2
3	3.3421	3.3744	3.4069	3.4396	3.4725	3.5056	3.5724	3.6400	3
4	4.7097	4.7793	4.8498	4.9211	4.9934	5.0665	5.2154	5.3680	4
5	6.2278	6.3528	6.4803	6.6101	6.7424	6.8771	7.1542	7.4416	5
6	7.9129	8.1152	8.3227	8.5355	8.7537	8.9775	9.4420	9.9299	6
7	9.7833	10.0890	10.4047	10.7305	11.0668	11.4139	12.1415	12.9159	7
8	11.8594	12.2997	12.7523	13.2328	13.7268	14.2401	15.3270	16.4991	8
9	14.1640	14.7757	15.4157	16.0853	16.7858	17.5185	19.0859	20.7989	9
10	16.7220	17.5487	18.4197	19.3373	20.3037	21.3215	23.5213	25.9587	10
11	19.5614	20.6546	21.8143	23.0445	24.3493	25.7329	28.7551	32.1504	11
12	22.7132	24.1331	25.6502	27.2707	29.0017	30.8502	34.9311	39.5805	12
13	26.2116	28.0291	29.9847	32.0887	34.3519	36.7862	42.2187	48.4966	13
14	30.0949	32.3926	34.8827	37.5811	40.5047	43.6720	50.8180	59.1959	14
15	34.4054	37.2797	40.4175	43.8424	47.5804	51.6595	60.9653	72.0351	15
16	39.1899	42.7533	46.6717	50.9804	55.7175	60.9250	72.9390	87.4421	16
17	44.5008	48.8837	53.7381	59.1176	65.0751	71.6730	87.0680	105.931	17
18	50.3959	55.7497	61.7251	68.3941	75.8364	84.1407	103.740	128.117	18
19	56.9395	63.4397	70.7494	78.9692	88.2118	98.6032	123.414	154.740	19
20	64.2028	72.0524	80.9468	91.0249	102.444	115.380	146.628	186.688	20
22	81.2143	92.5026	105.491	120.436	137.632	157.415	206.345	271.031	22
24	102.174	118.155	136.831	158.659	184.168	213.978	289.494	342.484	24
26	127.999	150.334	176.850	208.333	245.712	290.088	405.272	567.377	26
28	159.817	190.699	227.950	272.889	327.104	392.503	566.481	819.223	28
30	199.021	241.333	293.199	356.787	434.745	530.312	790.948	1,181.88	30
35	341.590	431.663	546.681	693.573	881.170	1,120.71	1,816.65	2,948.34	35
40	581.826	767.091	1,013.70	1,342,03	1,779.09	2,360.76	4,163.21	7,343.86	40
45	986.639	1,358.23	1,874.16	2,590.56	3,585.13	4,965.27	9,531.58	18,281.3	45
50	1,668.77	2,400.02	3,459.51	4,994.52	7,217.72	10,435.6	21,813.1	45,497.2	50
55	2,818.20	4,236.01	6,380.40	9,623.13	14,524.1	21,925.3	49,910.2	113,219	55
60	4,755.07	7,471.64	11,761.9	18,535.1	29,220.0	46,057.5	114,190	281,733	60
65	8,018.79	13,173.9	21,677.1	35,694.4	58,778.6	96,743.5	261,245	701,048	65
70	13,518.4	23,223.3	39,945.2	68,733.2	118,231	203,201	597,673	1,744,440	70
75	22,785.4	40,933.8	73,602.8	132,346	237,812	426,798	1,367,339	4,340,732	75
80	38,401.0	72,145.7	135,615	254,828	478,332	896,429	3,128,148	10,801,138	80

Table C.4 Present worth of unit sum per period for n periods $PW = \frac{1}{i}\left(1 - \frac{1}{(1 + i)^n}\right)$

Compound interest rate i from 0.03 to 0.10 (3% to 10%)

n	Interest rate i								n
	0.03 (3%)	0.04 (4%)	0.05 (5%)	0.06 (6%)	0.07 (7%)	0.08 (8%)	0.09 (9%)	0.10 (10%)	
1	0.971	0.962	0.952	0.943	0.935	0.926	0.917	0.909	1
2	1.913	1.886	1.859	1.833	1.808	1.783	1.759	1.736	2
3	2.829	2.775	2.723	2.673	2.624	2.577	2.531	2.487	3
4	3.717	3.630	3.546	3.465	3.387	3.312	3.240	3.170	4
5	4.580	4.452	4.329	4.212	4.100	3.993	3.890	3.791	5
6	5.417	5.242	5.076	4.917	4.767	4.623	4.486	4.355	6
7	6.230	6.002	5.786	5.582	5.389	5.206	5.033	4.868	7
8	7.020	6.733	6.463	6.210	5.971	5.747	5.535	5.335	8
9	7.786	7.435	7.108	6.802	6.515	6.247	5.995	5.759	9
10	8.530	8.111	7.722	7.360	7.024	6.710	6.418	6.145	10
11	9.253	8.760	8.306	7.887	7.499	7.139	6.805	6.495	11
12	9.954	9.385	8.863	8.384	7.943	7.536	7.161	6.814	12
13	10.635	9.986	9.394	8.853	8.358	7.904	7.487	7.103	13
14	11.296	10.563	9.899	9.295	8.745	8.244	7.786	7.367	14
15	11.938	11.118	10.380	9.712	9.108	8.559	8.061	7.606	15
16	12.561	11.652	10.838	10.106	9.447	8.851	8.313	7.824	16
17	13.166	12.166	11.274	10.477	9.763	9.122	8.544	8.022	17
18	13.754	12.659	11.690	10.828	10.059	9.372	8.756	8.201	18
19	14.324	13.134	12.085	11.158	10.336	9.604	8.950	8.365	19
20	14.877	13.590	12.462	11.470	10.594	9.819	9.129	8.514	20
22	15.937	14.451	13.163	12.042	11.061	10.201	9.442	8.772	22
24	16.936	15.247	13.799	12.550	11.469	10.529	9.707	8.985	24
26	17.877	15.983	14.375	13.003	11.826	10.810	9.929	9.161	26
28	18.764	16.663	14.898	13.406	12.137	11.051	10.116	9.307	28
30	19.600	17.292	15.372	13.765	12.409	11.258	10.274	9.427	30
35	21.487	18.665	16.374	14.498	12.948	11.655	10.567	9.644	35
40	23.115	19.793	17.159	15.046	13.332	11.925	10.757	9.779	40
45	24.519	20.720	17.774	15.456	13.606	12.108	10.881	9.863	45
50	25.730	21.482	18.256	15.762	13.801	12.233	10.962	9.915	50
55	26.774	22.109	18.633	15.991	13.940	12.319	11.014	9.947	55
60	27.676	22.623	18.929	16.161	14.039	12.377	11.048	9.967	60
65	28.453	23.047	19.161	16.289	14.110	12.416	11.070	9.980	65
70	29.123	23.395	19.343	16.385	14.160	12.443	11.084	9.987	70
75	29.702	23.680	19.485	16.456	14.196	12.461	11.094	9.992	75
80	30.201	23.915	19.596	16.509	14.222	12.474	11.100	9.995	80
85	30.631	24.109	19.684	16.549	14.240	12.482	11.104	9.997	85
90	31.002	24.267	19.752	16.579	14.253	12.488	11.106	9.998	90
95	31.323	24.398	19.806	16.601	14.263	12.492	11.108	9.999	95
100	31.599	24.505	19.848	16.618	14.269	12.494	11.109	9.999	100
∞	33.333	25.000	20.000	16.667	14.286	12.500	11.111	10.000	∞

Table C.4 (cont'd)

Compound interest rate i from 0.11 to 0.20 (11% to 20%)

n	Interest rate i								n
	0.11 (11%)	0.12 (12%)	0.13 (13%)	0.14 (14%)	0.15 (15%)	0.16 (16%)	0.18 (18%)	0.20 (20%)	
1	0.901	0.893	0.885	0.877	0.870	0.862	0.847	0.833	1
2	1.713	1.690	1.668	1.647	1.626	1.605	1.566	1.528	2
3	2.444	2.402	2.361	2.322	2.283	2.246	2.174	2.106	3
4	3.102	3.037	2.974	2.914	2.855	2.798	2.690	2.589	4
5	3.696	3.605	3.517	3.433	3.352	3.274	3.127	2.991	5
6	4.231	4.111	3.998	3.889	3.784	3.685	3.498	3.326	6
7	4.712	4.564	4.423	4.288	4.160	4.039	3.812	3.605	7
8	5.146	4.968	4.799	4.639	4.487	4.344	4.078	3.837	8
9	5.537	5.328	5.132	4.946	4.772	4.607	4.303	4.031	9
10	5.889	5.650	5.426	5.216	5.019	4.833	4.494	4.192	10
11	6.207	5.938	5.687	5.453	5.234	5.029	4.656	4.327	11
12	6.492	6.194	5.918	5.660	5.421	5.197	4.793	4.439	12
13	6.750	6.424	6.122	5.842	5.583	5.342	4.910	4.533	13
14	6.982	6.628	6.302	6.002	5.724	5.468	5.008	4.611	14
15	7.191	6.811	6.462	6.142	5.847	5.575	5.092	4.675	15
16	7.379	6.974	6.604	6.265	5.954	5.668	5.162	4.730	16
17	7.549	7.120	6.729	6.373	6.047	5.749	5.222	4.775	17
18	7.702	7.250	6.840	6.467	6.128	5.818	5.273	4.812	18
19	7.839	7.366	6.938	6.550	6.198	5.877	5.316	4.843	19
20	7.963	7.469	7.025	6.623	6.259	5.929	5.353	4.870	20
22	8.176	7.645	7.170	6.743	6.359	6.011	5.410	4.909	22
24	8.348	7.784	7.283	6.835	6.434	6.073	5.451	4.937	24
26	8.488	7.896	7.372	6.906	6.491	6.118	5.480	4.956	26
28	8.602	7.984	7.441	6.961	6.534	6.152	5.502	4.970	28
30	8.694	8.055	7.496	7.003	6.566	6.177	5.517	4.979	30
35	8.855	8.176	7.586	7.070	6.617	6.215	5.539	4.992	35
40	8.951	8.244	7.634	7.105	6.642	6.233	5.548	4.997	40
45	9.008	8.283	7.661	7.123	6.654	6.242	5.552	4.999	45
50	9.042	8.304	7.675	7.133	6.661	6.246	5.554	4.999	50
55	9.062	8.317	7.683	7.138	6.664	6.248	5.555	5.000	55
60	9.074	8.324	7.687	7.140	6.665	6.249	5.555	5.000	60
65	9.081	8.328	7.690	7.141	6.666	6.250	5.555		65
70	9.085	8.330	7.691	7.142	6.666	6.250	5.556		70
75	9.087	8.332	7.692	7.142	6.667	6.250	5.556		75
80	9.089	8.332	7.692	7.143	6.667	6.250	5.556		80
∞	9.091	8.333	7.692	7.143	6.667	6.250	5.556	5.000	∞

Table C.5 Annual sinking fund (ASF) amount to be invested each year to accumulate to unit sum at end of period ASF $= \dfrac{i}{(1 + i)^n - 1}$

Compound interest rate i from 0.03 to 0.10 (3% to 10%)

n	Interest rate i								n
	0.03 (3%)	0.04 (4%)	0.05 (5%)	0.06 (6%)	0.07 (7%)	0.08 (8%)	0.09 (9%)	0.10 (10%)	
1	1.0000	1.0000	1.0000	1.0000	1.0000	1.0000	1.0000	1.0000	1
2	0.4926	0.4902	0.4878	0.4854	0.4831	0.4808	0.4785	0.4762	2
3	0.3235	0.3203	0.3172	0.3141	0.3111	0.3080	0.3051	0.3021	3
4	0.2390	0.2355	0.2320	0.2286	0.2252	0.2219	0.2187	0.2155	4
5	0.1884	0.1846	0.1810	0.1774	0.1739	0.1705	0.1671	0.1638	5
6	0.1546	0.1508	0.1470	0.1434	0.1398	0.1363	0.1329	0.1296	6
7	0.1305	0.1266	0.1228	0.1191	0.1156	0.1121	0.1087	0.1054	7
8	0.1125	0.1085	0.1047	0.1010	0.0975	0.0940	0.0963	0.0874	8
9	0.0984	0.0945	0.0907	0.0870	0.0835	0.0801	0.0768	0.0736	9
10	0.0872	0.0833	0.0795	0.0759	0.0724	0.0690	0.0658	0.0627	10
11	0.0781	0.0741	0.0704	0.0668	0.0634	0.0601	0.0569	0.0540	11
12	0.0705	0.0666	0.0628	0.0593	0.0559	0.0527	0.0497	0.0468	12
13	0.0640	0.0601	0.0565	0.0530	0.0497	0.0465	0.0436	0.0408	13
14	0.0585	0.0547	0.0510	0.0476	0.0443	0.0413	0.0384	0.0357	14
15	0.0538	0.0499	0.0463	0.0430	0.0398	0.0368	0.0341	0.0315	15
16	0.0496	0.0458	0.0423	0.0390	0.0359	0.0330	0.0303	0.0278	16
17	0.0460	0.0422	0.0387	0.0354	0.0324	0.0296	0.0270	0.0247	17
18	0.0427	0.0390	0.0355	0.0324	0.0294	0.0267	0.0242	0.0219	18
19	0.0398	0.0361	0.0327	0.0296	0.0268	0.0241	0.0127	0.0195	19
20	0.0372	0.0336	0.0302	0.0272	0.0244	0.0219	0.0195	0.0175	20
22	0.0327	0.0292	0.0260	0.0230	0.0204	0.0180	0.0159	0.0140	22
24	0.0290	0.0256	0.0225	0.0197	0.0172	0.0150	0.0130	0.0113	24
26	0.0259	0.0226	0.0196	0.0169	0.0146	0.0125	0.0107	0.00916	26
28	0.0233	0.0200	0.0171	0.0146	0.0124	0.0105	0.00885	0.00745	28
30	0.0210	0.0178	0.0151	0.0126	0.0106	0.00883	0.00734	0.00608	30
35	0.0165	0.0136	0.0111	0.00879	0.00723	0.00580	0.00464	0.00369	35
40	0.0133	0.0105	0.00828	0.00646	0.00501	0.00386	0.00300	0.00226	40
45	0.0108	0.00826	0.00626	0.00470	0.00350	0.00259	0.00190	0.00139	45
50	0.00865	0.00655	0.00478	0.00344	0.00246	0.00174	0.00123	0.00086	50
55	0.00735	0.00523	0.00367	0.00254	0.00174	0.00118	0.00079	0.00053	55
60	0.00613	0.00420	0.00283	0.00188	0.00123	0.00079	0.00051	0.00033	60
65	0.00515	0.00390	0.00219	0.00139	0.00087	0.00054	0.00033	0.00020	65
70	0.00434	0.00275	0.00170	0.00103	0.00062	0.00036	0.00021	0.00013	70
75	0.00367	0.00223	0.00132	0.00077	0.00044	0.00025	0.00014		75
80	0.00311	0.00181	0.00103	0.00057	0.00031	0.00017			80
85	0.00265	0.00148	0.00080	0.00043	0.00022	0.00011			85
90	0.00226	0.00121	0.00063	0.00032	0.00016				90
95	0.00193	0.00099	0.00049	0.00024	0.00011	Less than 0.0001			95
100	0.00165	0.00081	0.00038	0.00018					100

Table C.5 (cont'd)

Compound interest rate i from 0.11 to 0.20 (11% to 20%)

n	Interest rate i								n
	0.11 (11%)	0.12 (12%)	0.13 (13%)	0.14 (14%)	0.15 (15%)	0.16 (16%)	0.18 (18%)	0.20 (20%)	
1	1.0000	1.0000	1.0000	1.0000	1.0000	1.0000	1.0000	1.0000	1
2	0.4739	0.4717	0.4695	0.4673	0.4651	0.4630	0.4587	0.4545	2
3	0.2992	0.2963	0.2935	0.2907	0.2880	0.2853	0.2799	0.2747	3
4	0.2123	0.2092	0.2062	0.2032	0.2003	0.1974	0.1917	0.1863	4
5	0.1606	0.1574	0.1543	0.1513	0.1483	0.1454	0.1400	0.1344	5
6	0.1264	0.1232	0.1202	0.1172	0.1142	0.1114	0.1059	0.1007	6
7	0.1022	0.0991	0.0961	0.0932	0.0904	0.0876	0.0824	0.0774	7
8	0.0843	0.0813	0.0784	0.0756	0.0729	0.0702	0.0652	0.0606	8
9	0.0706	0.0677	0.0649	0.0622	0.0596	0.0571	0.0524	0.0481	9
10	0.0598	0.0570	0.0543	0.0517	0.0493	0.0469	0.0425	0.0385	10
11	0.0511	0.0484	0.0458	0.0434	0.0411	0.0389	0.0348	0.0311	11
12	0.0440	0.0414	0.0390	0.0367	0.0345	0.0324	0.0286	0.0253	12
13	0.0382	0.0357	0.0334	0.0312	0.0291	0.0272	0.0237	0.0206	13
14	0.0332	0.0309	0.0287	0.0266	0.0247	0.0229	0.0197	0.0169	14
15	0.0291	0.0268	0.0247	0.0228	0.0210	0.0194	0.0164	0.0139	15
16	0.0255	0.0234	0.0214	0.0196	0.0179	0.0164	0.0137	0.0114	16
17	0.0225	0.0205	0.0186	0.0169	0.0154	0.0140	0.0115	0.00944	17
18	0.0198	0.0179	0.0162	0.0146	0.0132	0.0119	0.00964	0.00781	18
19	0.0176	0.0158	0.0141	0.0127	0.0113	0.0101	0.00810	0.00646	19
20	0.0156	0.0139	0.0124	0.0110	0.00976	0.00867	0.00682	0.00536	20
22	0.0123	0.0108	0.00948	0.00830	0.00767	0.00635	0.00485	0.00369	22
24	0.00979	0.00846	0.00731	0.00630	0.00543	0.00467	0.00345	0.00255	24
26	0.00781	0.00665	0.00565	0.00480	0.00407	0.00345	0.00247	0.00176	26
28	0.00626	0.00524	0.00439	0.00366	0.00306	0.00255	0.00177	0.00122	28
30	0.00502	0.00414	0.00341	0.00280	0.00230	0.00189	0.00126	0.00085	30
35	0.00293	0.00232	0.00183	0.00144	0.00113	0.00089	0.00055	0.00034	35
40	0.00172	0.00130	0.00099	0.00075	0.00056	0.00042	0.00024	0.00014	40
45	0.00101	0.00074	0.00053	0.00039	0.00028	0.00020	0.00010		45
50	0.00060	0.00042	0.00029	0.00020	0.00014				50
55	0.00035	0.00024	0.00016	0.00010					55
60	0.00021	0.00013							60
65	0.00012								65
70				Less than 0.0001					70
80									80

Properties of the normal curve

Table D.1 One-tail areas for the normal curve (see Fig. 11.12)

z	0.00	0.01	0.02	0.03	0.04	0.05	0.06	0.07	0.08	0.09
0.0	0.5000	0.4960	0.4920	0.4880	0.4840	0.4801	0.4761	0.4721	0.4681	0.4641
0.1	0.4602	0.4562	0.4522	0.4483	0.4443	0.4404	0.4364	0.4325	0.4286	0.4247
0.2	0.4207	0.4168	0.4129	0.4090	0.4052	0.4013	0.3974	0.3936	0.3897	0.3859
0.3	0.3821	0.3783	0.3745	0.3707	0.3669	0.3632	0.3594	0.3557	0.3520	0.3483
0.4	0.3446	0.3409	0.3372	0.3336	0.3300	0.3264	0.3228	0.3192	0.3156	0.3121
0.5	0.3085	0.3050	0.3015	0.2981	0.2946	0.2912	0.2877	0.2843	0.2810	0.2776
0.6	0.2743	0.2709	0.2676	0.2643	0.2611	0.2578	0.2546	0.2514	0.2483	0.2451
0.7	0.2420	0.2389	0.2358	0.2327	0.2296	0.2266	0.2236	0.2206	0.2177	0.2148
0.8	0.2119	0.2090	0.2061	0.2033	0.2005	0.1977	0.1949	0.1922	0.1894	0.1867
0.9	0.1841	0.1814	0.1788	0.1762	0.1736	0.1711	0.1685	0.1660	0.1635	0.1611
1.0	0.1587	0.1562	0.1539	0.1515	0.1492	0.1469	0.1446	0.1423	0.1401	0.1379
1.1	0.1357	0.1335	0.1314	0.1292	0.1271	0.1251	0.1230	0.1210	0.1190	0.1170
1.2	0.1151	0.1131	0.1112	0.1093	0.1075	0.1056	0.1038	0.1020	0.1003	0.0985
1.3	0.09680	0.09510	0.09342	0.09176	0.09012	0.08851	0.08691	0.08534	0.08379	0.08226
1.4	0.08076	0.07927	0.07780	0.07636	0.07493	0.07353	0.07215	0.07078	0.06944	0.06811
1.5	0.06681	0.06552	0.06426	0.06301	0.06178	0.06057	0.05938	0.05821	0.05705	0.05592
1.6	0.05480	0.05370	0.05262	0.05155	0.05050	0.04947	0.04846	0.04746	0.04648	0.04551
1.7	0.04457	0.04363	0.04272	0.04182	0.04093	0.04006	0.03920	0.03836	0.03754	0.03673
1.8	0.03593	0.03515	0.03438	0.03362	0.03288	0.03216	0.03144	0.03074	0.03005	0.02938
1.9	0.02872	0.02807	0.02743	0.02680	0.02619	0.02559	0.02500	0.02442	0.02385	0.02330
2.0	0.02275	0.02222	0.02169	0.02118	0.02068	0.02018	0.01970	0.01923	0.01876	0.01831
2.1	0.01786	0.01743	0.01700	0.01659	0.01618	0.01578	0.01539	0.01500	0.01463	0.01426
2.2	0.01390	0.01355	0.01321	0.01287	0.01255	0.01222	0.01191	0.01160	0.01130	0.01101
2.3	0.01072	0.01044	0.01017	0.00990	0.00964	0.00939	0.00914	0.00889	0.00866	0.00842
2.4	0.00820	0.00798	0.00776	0.00755	0.00734	0.00714	0.00695	0.00676	0.00657	0.00639
2.5	0.00621	0.00604	0.00587	0.00570	0.00554	0.00539	0.00523	0.00508	0.00494	0.00480
2.6	0.00466	0.00453	0.00440	0.00427	0.00415	0.00402	0.00391	0.00379	0.00368	0.00357
2.7	0.00347	0.00336	0.00326	0.00317	0.00307	0.00298	0.00289	0.00280	0.00272	0.00264
2.8	0.00256	0.00248	0.00240	0.00233	0.00226	0.00219	0.00212	0.00205	0.00199	0.00193
2.9	0.00187	0.00181	0.00175	0.00169	0.00164	0.00159	0.00154	0.00149	0.00144	0.00139
3.0	0.00135	0.00131	0.00126	0.00122	0.00118	0.00114	0.00111	0.00107	0.00104	0.00100

Values of z for selected one-tail areas

Area	z	Area	z	Area	z	Area	z
0.00001	4.265	0.0001	3.719	0.001	3.090	0.01	2.326
0.00002	4.107	0.0002	3.540	0.002	2.878	0.02	2.054
0.00003	4.013	0.0003	3.432	0.003	2.748	0.03	1.881
0.00004	3.944	0.0004	3.353	0.004	2.652	0.04	1.751
0.00005	3.891	0.0005	3.291	0.005	2.576	0.05	1.645
0.00006	3.846	0.0006	3.239	0.006	2.512	0.06	1.555
0.00007	3.808	0.0007	3.195	0.007	2.457	0.07	1.476
0.00008	3.775	0.0008	3.156	0.008	2.409	0.08	1.405
0.00009	3.746	0.0009	3.121	0.009	2.366	0.09	1.341
0.00010	3.719	0.0010	3.090	0.010	2.326	0.10	1.282

Financial provisions for economic regeneration

The decline of several of the UK's major industries in the post-1945 period motivated successive governments to pursue policies of regional economic regeneration. These traditional schemes were initially based on a system of grants paid to firms undertaking investment in the designated development areas. The grant system has been replaced by one of allowances against corporation tax liability, the allowances being determined by the type of investment (e.g. plant, buildings), its purpose (e.g. industrial, commercial) and the designation of the area (investments in the areas in greatest need of regeneration attracting the largest allowances). This form of investment incentive has been much criticized, primarily because the allowances system is indiscriminate between qualifying investments.

The encouraging of firms to move to the development regions was reinforced by planning legislation, notably the use of office development permits (ODPs) and industrial development certificates (IDCs) and by the location of population via the location of employment policies followed in the years 1945–75.

In recent times the UK economy (in common with many other developed countries' economies but to a greater extent than most) has experienced stagnation coupled with inflation (popularly termed 'stagflation'). The recession has been felt most acutely in many urban centres which were traditionally areas of population clustering and employment. Coupled with the trend for most industries to become capital intensive *inter alia*, major problems, particularly unemployment, have resulted.

Two important sets of economic regeneration schemes have emerged. The first set is aimed at encouraging small firms (which are considered to be more adaptable, more labour intensive, more innovative and subject to significant financial disadvantages) by extending their special tax reliefs and by making finance easier for them to obtain (and, hopefully, cheaper). The second set is designed to provide inner city regeneration by development programmes and by financial incentives for private industry.

Small firms

Traditionally small firms (size being determined by measures such as number of employees, annual turnover, annual profit or, perhaps some combination of measures) have received assistance in the form of lower rates of corporaton tax (applicable to companies only). Since the late 1970s, assistance for small firms has been viewed as a vital ingredient for economic regeneration (notably for inner city areas) and so several special schemes have been introduced, commencing with the budget of 1980. The following are some of the provisions.

Small workshops scheme
This was introduced initially for three years. Industrial building allowances of 100 per cent were made available for the construction of small industrial buildings. The allowance applies to qualifying buildings of up to 2500 sq. ft. and is paid as a first year allowance. In the 1982 budget the scope was extended to include buildings used for certain servicing, repairing and warehousing purposes and was extended until March 1985 for very small workshops (up to 1250 sq. ft).

Business start-up scheme
The intention is to encourage outside investors to take up equity in small companies through a system of tax incentive.

Venture capital scheme
To help with the financing of new businesses, this scheme permits losses on equities in certain unquoted companies (which occur after 5 April 1980) to be set off against income tax (instead of against capital gains tax).

Loan guarantee scheme
This scheme applies to loans of up to £75,000 made for a period of 2 to 7 years. The government guarantees 80 per cent of the loan but with a premium of 3 per cent to be paid to the Department of Industry. The loan is advanced usually by a bank at the full commercial rate (a few per cent, commonly $2\frac{1}{2}$, above the bank's base rate). In 1981, the scheme was intended to run for three years with an overall maximum lending of £50 million in each year. It was anticipated that by providing this scheme banks would be encouraged to provide risk capital to industry, particularly small companies.

Considerable further aid for small firms is available via advice centres and specialist schemes. In construction, a significant development has been the relaxation of the taxation rules regulating the issue of tax exemption certificates (714s) so that people do not have to provide a three-year record to obtain an exemption certificate. This should facilitate small, legitimate, sub-contracting firms entering the industry.

Inner cities

Inner city regeneration began in the UK in earnest with the 1977 policy document for the inner cities, followed in 1978 by the Inner Urban Areas Act. Schemes for inner cities (as most small firms schemes) are directed towards capital investments.

Inner Urban Areas Act, 1978

This Act set up three categories of inner city areas qualifying for special assistance depending on the nature and extent of their problems, particularly population loss, housing, unemployment and social deprivation. The Traditional Urban Programme was still available to local authorities not qualifying for partnership or programme assistance which were in an urban area with special social need which entitled them to grand aid for particular projects.

The categories of inner city areas set up under the Act are (in descending order on priority for assistance):

(a) Partnership areas – projects are discussed and approved by a special committee comprising local authority leaders, representatives of central government and health authorities and chaired by a minister from the Department of the Environment. In 1982/3 special resources of £137 million were earmarked for the seven partnership areas.

(b) Programme authorities – draw up investment programmes and submit them to Department of the Environment for approval. In 1982/3 these fifteen authorities could call on £59 million of special funds.

(c) Other designated districts – The fourteen district authorities could call on £8 million of earmarked special funds for industrial and commercial projects. They may also participate in the Traditional Urban Programme.

At the outset, it was intended to designate areas for about three to four years, £1000 million being devoted to the scheme. Both partnership and programme local authorities receive block allocations of the special funds and have increased freedom to promote and assist growth in the designated areas. In particular the funds are used to provide infrastructure to attract firms, to refurbish buildings (about 30 per cent cheaper than demolition and new-build) and to provide housing. It is notable, however, that the majority of funding for such work is still derived from the normal income of local authorities (rates and central government grant). It has been widely argued that, due to the system of financing local government, the special schemes have not provided significant extra funds for those areas, the block allocations being set off against central government grant and, perhaps more particularly, the requirement for economies in local authority expenditure.

Urban Development Corporations (UDCs)

Two UDCs were instigated in 1980 to revitalize the docklands areas of London and Liverpool. They have special powers for land acquisition, reclamation and sale to the private sector and for infrastructure provision as well as being required to encourage the development of existing industry and commerce by creating an attractive environment with both housing and social facilities. In the area of the London Docklands Development Corporation (LDDC) housing for sale has been provided in considerable quantities during the early 1980s.

339

Enterprise zones

Enterprise zones were introduced in the budget of 1980 to encourage industrial and commercial activity by removing tax burdens (Development Land Tax and general rates) and by speeding and easing planning. Seven zones have been designated for 10 years (subject to renewal), of approximately 500 acres in area in which industrial and commercial developments qualify for 100 per cent capital allowances.

Urban Development Grant (UDG)

The UDG is intended to secure significant involvement in inner cities by private organizations by providing the minimum public sector grant contribution to make development projects viable. Based on the USA's Urban Development Action Grants, this scheme was allocated £70 million in 1982. Forty-three local authorities (including partnership authorities etc.) are eligible to bid jointly with a private developer or community group for funds for industrial, social or environmental schemes. The bids are competitive for the funding available, grants awarded being made to the local authority for derelict land clearance or an urban programme project.

Regional Development Grants

Although not strictly part of inner urban special measures, these grants from the Department of Industry for buildings, plant and equipment capital expenditure by the manufacturing sector often accrue to firms in inner cities. In 1982/83 the maximum grants were 22 per cent in Special Development Areas and 15 per cent in Development Areas.

Many more forms of grant and allowance are available (e.g. Derelict Land Clearance, Preservation of Historic Buildings, Conservation Areas, European Regional Development Fund) and, although not paid to contractors but to clients, should provide incentives for development to be carried out and so indicate to the construction industry the location of probable demand.

References

Anon (1982) Finding the Funds, *Building*, Sept., pp. 26–7

Fellows, R. F. (1982) Small Building Firms – some questions of survival, *Building Technology and Management*, May, pp. 21–3

Treasury *Economic Progress Reports*, Treasury, No. 120, Apr. 1980; No. 121, May 1980; No. 126, Oct. 1980; No. 132, Apr. 1981; No. 133, May 1981; No. 142, Feb. 1982; No. 143, Mar. 1982

Use of current cost accounting

Throughout the late 1960s and the 1970s historic cost accounting was increasingly criticised. The high rates of inflation over those years meant that the HCA system produced distorted statements, notably regarding profits and asset values (particularly fixed assets).

Several reports were produced in the late 1970s which discussed various proposals for dealing with inflation in accounts, the primary document being the Sandilands report of 1975 which led to the introduction of CCA via Exposure Draft 18 (ED 18).

The Statement of Standard Accounting Practice 16 (SSAP 16) requires current cost accounts to be produced (for all accounting periods commencing on or after 1 January 1980) by the following companies:

(a) all listed companies, and
(b) all unlisted companies which satisfy two or all of the following criteria:
  (i) annual turnover of £5 million, or more,
  (ii) assets of £2½ million, or more,
  (iii) average number of UK employees 250, or more.

Certain organizations are exempted from the above; these include charities, wholly-owned susidiaries of UK companies, property companies, building societies, investment and unit trusts, pension funds and trade unions.

Current cost accounting, under SSAP 16, relies on two principles:

1. that assets must be shown at their value to the business, and
2. that the profit of a company should be determined after the deduction of sums required to maintain the real value of the business.

Clearly great care is required to ensure the correct figures are presented. Problems may arise in the calculation of profit, which is generally considered to be the amount of total gains arising in the year which, prudently, may be regarded as distributable. The correct provision for depreciation is more complex under CCA.

Naturally, in a period of transition in accounting bases, it is important to maintain comparability between sets of accounts. This is achieved under SSAP 16

341

by preparing accounts either on the HCA basis and providing CCA supplements or *vice versa*, the former method being rather more usual in which the HCA trading profit is subject to three operating adjustments (depreciation, cost of sales, and monetary working capital) to arrive at the current cost operating profit. A gearing adjustment (which allows for the proportion of assets financed by borrowing) is then applied to determine the current cost taxable profit. Generally, the operating adjustments are calculated by the use of index numbers from the annually published book, *Price Index Numbers for Current Cost Accounting*, which is prepared by the Government Statistical Service.

The use of CCA requires frequent revaluations of fixed assets (at least once every five years), and of stocks. The basis of valuation of assets is 'value to the business', i.e. the amount the company would lose if it were deprived of the asset. Such value may be determined from:

(a) the amount which would be realized by the sale of the asset (e.g. sale of a building), or
(b) the cost of purchasing an identical asset (e.g. second hand machine of the same age and condition), or
(c) the sum earned over the remaining life of the asset by holding and using the asset (e.g. a machine), expressed as a NPV.

Usually the value of an asset to the business will be its net replacement cost ((b) in the foregoing), unless this value exceeds both the net realizable value ((a)) and the economic value ((c)) of that asset; in such circumstances, the value to the business will be the greater of the asset's net realizable value and its economic value.

Depreciation provisions are determined from the valuations of assets, described above. An asset's depreciation in year n is its value to the business at the end of year $(n - 1)$ less its value to the business at the end of year n plus the asset's HCA depreciation in year n. Alternatively, an asset's accumulated depreciation is the deduction which must be made from its gross replacement cost to yield its net replacement cost so the depreciation provision for year n is the change in the deduction which must be made between the end of year $(n - 1)$ and the end of year n.

Stocks are valued at the year ends. By use of indices, the impact of price changes of stocks on the cost of sales is calculated (most simply, by averaging the indices – suitable where stock levels are reasonably constant).

Monetary working capital (trade debtors, prepayments, trade bill receivable and any stocks excluded from cost of sales adjustment, e.g. 'land banks' – *less* trade creditors, accruals and trade bills payable) is adjusted by index numbers to allow for changes in the finance required for monetary working capital due to alterations in the prices of goods and services used and financed by the company. The indices applicable are those for the finished goods the company produces.

Further details and discussion of CCA is beyond the scope of this text. The interested reader is referred to the references following.

342

References

Accounting Standards Steering Committee (1976) *Current Cost Accounting*, Exposure Draft 18, Nov.

Accounting Standards Steering Committee (1980) *Current Cost Accounting*, Statement of Standard Accounting Practice 16, Mar.

Gilbert, D. (ed) (1976) *Guidance Manual on Current Cost Accounting*. Tolley

Holmes, G. and Sugden, S. (1982) *Interpreting Company Reports and Accounts* (2nd edn), Woodhead-Faulkner

Sandilands, F. E. P. (Chairperson) (1975) *Inflation Accounting, Report of the Inflation Accounting Committee*, HMSO

Index

345